Grades
3-6

The Complete Book of
Maps & Geography

Thinking Kids®
Carson Dellosa Education
Greensboro, North Carolina

Thinking Kids®
Carson Dellosa Education
PO Box 35665
Greensboro, NC 27425 USA

Printed in the USA • All rights reserved.   ISBN 978-1-4838-2688-2
07-297221151

Table of Contents

Section 4:

North and South America

Section 5:

Section 6:

Global Geography

Name _____

Creating a Floor Plan

Pretend you are looking down at your classroom or a room in your home from the light on the ceiling. Draw how the room looks.

Picture This

This is a photograph that shows part of what is left of the town of Bodie, California. It was a mining town long ago. The photo shows a house, a barn, and an old wagon. It also shows where a fence once was.

Below is a map, or drawing, of the photo. It shows where the things in the photo can be found.

Bodie Map

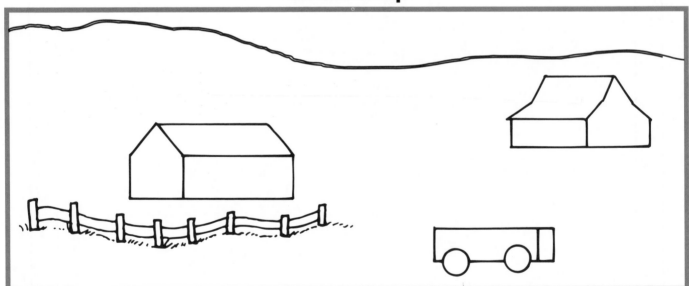

Directions:

1. Color the wagon red.

2. Color the fence brown.

3. Color the house yellow.

4. Color the barn blue.

Name_____

Make a Map

Look closely at this photograph of an old pioneer schoolhouse and playground.

Directions:

In the box, draw a map to show what is in the photograph. Use the shapes to help you draw the pictures on your map that stand for things in the photo.

Pioneer Map

Symbols on Maps

A symbol is a picture that stands for something shown on a map. Symbols used on a map are shown in the Map Key. Look at the symbols. Draw a line from each symbol to what it stands for in the drawing below.

Name _____

Symbols Replace Words

Symbols on a map show where things are located.

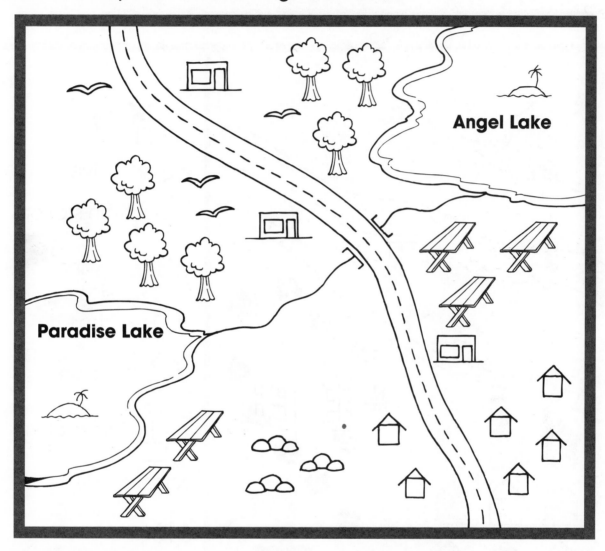

Directions: Use crayons or markers to complete the map.

1. Color the islands brown.

2. Color the trees green.

3. Color the rocks black.

4. Color the houses blue.

5. Color the stores orange.

6. Color the birds purple.

7. Color the picnic tables red.

8. Color the road yellow.

Name _____

The Wild Geese

Twice a day, the wild geese fly from the river to a farm. Use this map with page 21.

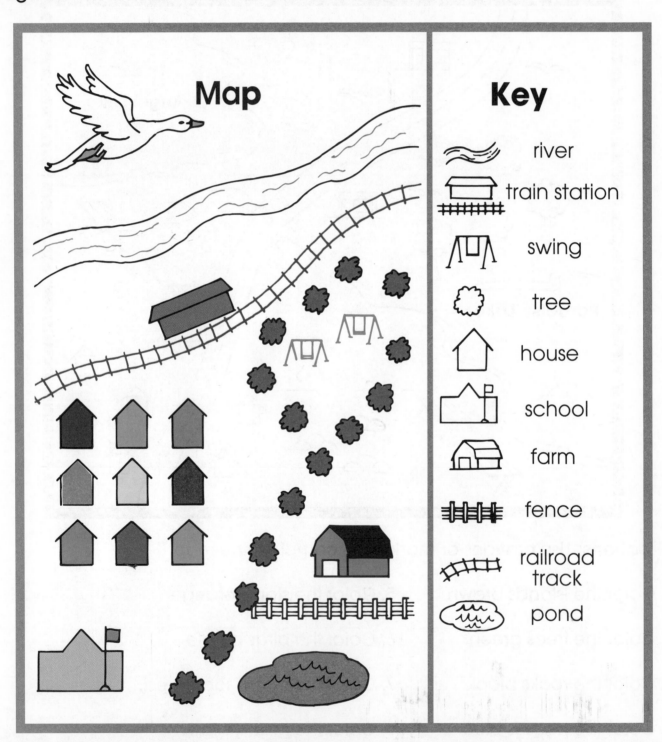

Map

Key

≋ river

train station

swing

tree

house

school

farm

fence

railroad track

pond

Name_____

The Wild Geese

Directions: Write the word on the lines that tells what each symbol from the map key stands for.

1. r i v e r
   $\underset{1}{\ }$

2. S c h o o l
   $\underset{2}{\ }$

3. f a r m
   $\underset{3}{\ }$ $\underset{4}{\ }$

4. h o u s e
   $\underset{5}{\ }$

5. t r e e
   $\underset{6}{\ }$

6. p o n d
   $\underset{7}{\ }$

7. S w i n g
   $\underset{8}{\ }$

8. t r a i n   S t a t i o n
   $\underset{9}{\ }$ $\underset{10}{\ }$

9. f e n c e
   $\underset{11}{\ }$ $\underset{12}{\ }$

10. r a i l r o a d
    $\underset{13}{\ }$ $\underset{14}{\ }$
    t r a c k
    $\underset{15}{\ }$

Use the numbered letters to solve this puzzling question: Why do the geese fly this path twice a day?

a   f a r m e r
$\underset{10}{\ }$ $\underset{3}{\ }$ $\underset{13}{\ }$ $\underset{9}{\ }$ $\underset{4}{\ }$ $\underset{12}{\ }$ $\underset{14}{\ }$

f e e d s   t h e m .
$\underset{11}{\ }$ $\underset{5}{\ }$ $\underset{6}{\ }$ $\underset{7}{\ }$ $\underset{8}{\ }$ $\underset{15}{\ }$ $\underset{2}{\ }$ $\underset{1}{\ }$ $\underset{4}{\ }$

Name_____

"Kool Kids" Mall

Mall Map

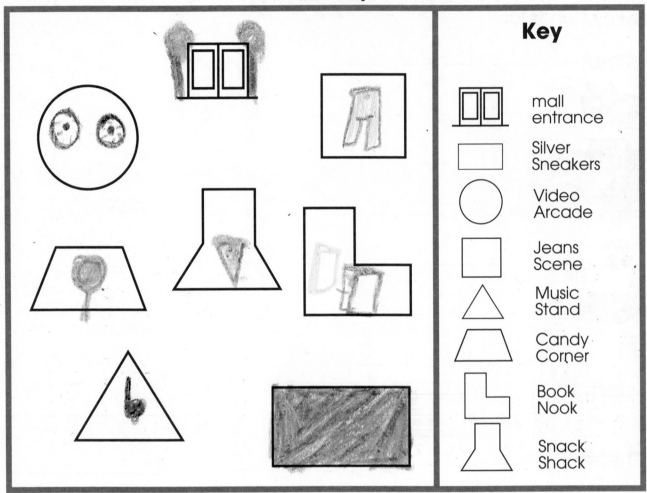

Key

mall entrance

Silver Sneakers

Video Arcade

Jeans Scene

Music Stand

Candy Corner

Book Nook

Snack Shack

Directions: Use the key to locate the stores. Draw the following:

1. a red and blue sneaker in Silver Sneakers
2. a black musical note in the Music Stand
3. a pair of blue jeans in the Jeans Scene
4. a green tree on each side of the mall entrance
5. a red piece of pizza in the Snack Shack
6. a pair of eyes in the Video Arcade
7. a yellow book and a blue book in the Book Nook
8. an orange lollipop in the Candy Corner

Science Sense

This is a floor plan of the Science Sense Museum. Use the floor plan and key to complete this page.

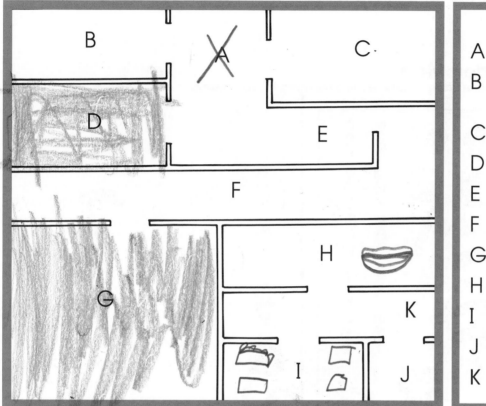

Key	
A	Ticket Gate
B	How Your Body Works
C	Electricity
D	Magnets
E	Solar System
F	Weather
G	Dinosaurs
H	Snack Bar
I	Tables
J	Restrooms
K	Exit Gate

1. In which room would you see dinosaurs? _____G_____
   Color the room brown.

2. In which room would you try using magnets? _____D_____
   Color the room blue.

3. Draw a hot dog in the snack bar.

4. Draw a table in the area in which tables are located.

5. Draw an X where you would buy a ticket to the museum.

6. If you go to room E, what will you learn about? _the solar System_

Name _____

Farmer Fritz

Map symbols can tell how many of something there are. Each symbol can stand for one or any number of that item. This map shows Farmer Fritz's plants. Each crop or tree stands for one plant. Use the map and key to answer the questions.

Garden Map **Key**

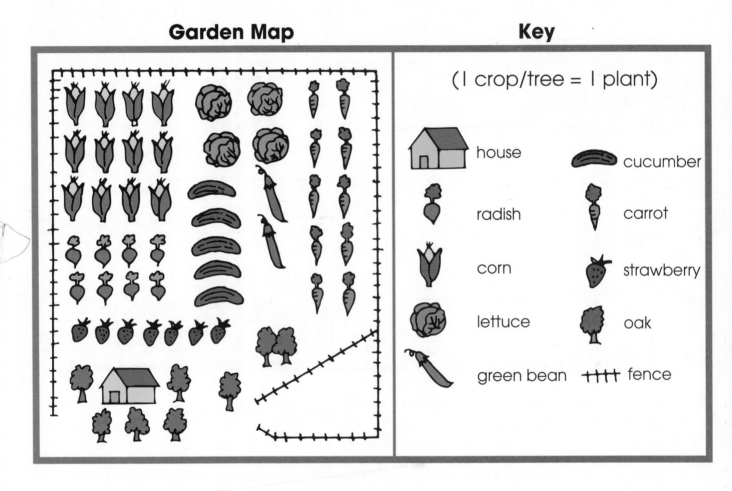

1. How many plants of each crop does Farmer Fritz have?
   radish ___8___   cucumber ___5___   corn ___12___
   carrot ___10___   green bean ___2___   lettuce ___4___

2. What tree did Farmer Fritz plant? _____Oak tree_____
   How many of these plants did he have? _____8_____

3. Farmer Fritz planted the most of which crop? _____corn_____

   My newpus

Name_____

Carmella's Candy

Carmella made a map of her candy store so that her customers could easily find their favorite candy. Use the map and key to answer the questions.

Candy Store Map

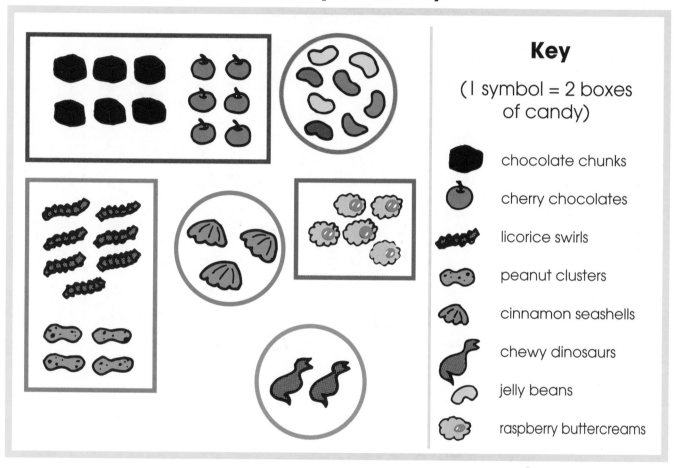

Key

(1 symbol = 2 boxes of candy)

- chocolate chunks
- cherry chocolates
- licorice swirls
- peanut clusters
- cinnamon seashells
- chewy dinosaurs
- jelly beans
- raspberry buttercreams

1. Each symbol equals how many boxes of candy? _____2_____

2. How many boxes of each kind of candy are there?

jelly beans	8	licorice swirls	7
chocolate chunks	6	cherry chocolates	6
peanut clusters	4	chewy dinosaurs	2
raspberry buttercreams	5	cinnamon seashells	3

7F 99
8 44 9
5 69

3. Carmella has the greatest number of boxes of which candy?
____12____

1 11 · 22 33

Name_____

Mixed-Up Mapmaker

Mattie Mapmaker goofed when creating a map of the state of Oopsylvania. Circle her mistakes and put a number by each one. Then, describe each error on the line with the matching number. (Hint: The key shows the correct map symbols.)

Oopsylvania Map

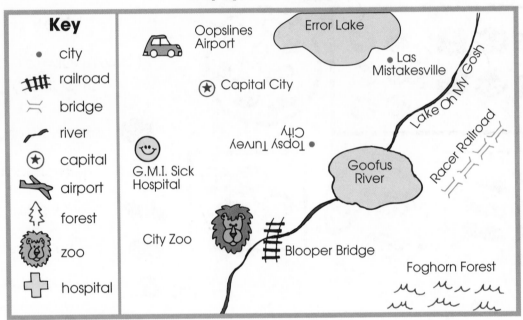

1. _____

2. _____

3. _____

4. _____

5. _____

6. _____

7. _____

8. _____

Time to Go Home

This map shows routes the dinosaur can take to get to its cave. Use the key to find each symbol on the map. Then, follow the directions.

Dinosaur Cave Map

Directions:
1. Write the word **H O M E** on the dinosaur cave.
2. Color the volcano red.
3. Color the trees green.
4. Draw a blue line to show a route the dinosaur can take home that goes past the volcano.
5. Draw a yellow line to show a route the dinosaur can take home. Make it go past the rocks.

Name_____

Seeing the Wildfire

Martin and Norma are excited about visiting the Wildlife Safari. It is different from a zoo. Here they drive slowly along a road to see the animals living freely in large fenced areas. They stop at the gate to buy tickets and to get a map. They will use the map so that they will be sure to see all of the animals.

Safari Map

Key

birds

tigers

zebras

bears

monkeys

lions

Directions: Follow Martin and Norma's route. Write the names of the animals in the order they will see them.

1. _____   4. _____

2. _____   5. _____

3. _____   6. _____

Name_____

Take a Hike

This map shows three hiking trails.

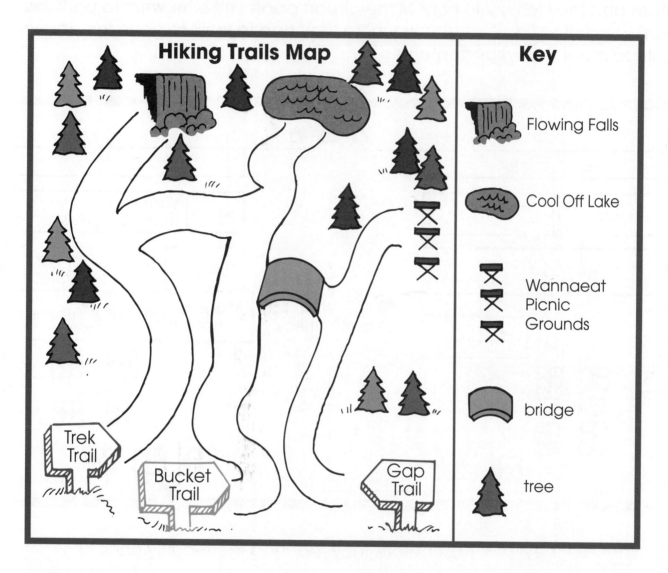

Directions:

1. Draw a red line along the trail that leads to the Wannaeat Picnic Grounds.
2. Draw a yellow line along the trail that leads to Flowing Falls.
3. Draw a green line along the trail that leads to Cool Off Lake.
4. Draw a blue line to show how to go from Trek Trail to Cool Off Lake.
5. Draw an orange line to show how to go from Bucket Trail to the Wannaeat Picnic Grounds.

Name_____

Waiting at the Airport

Jenny and Carl went to the airport to pick up their grandparents. Dad let Mom and the kids out in front of the airport doors while he went to park the van. The dotted line (- - -) shows where they had to walk to go to the correct gate to meet their grandparents.

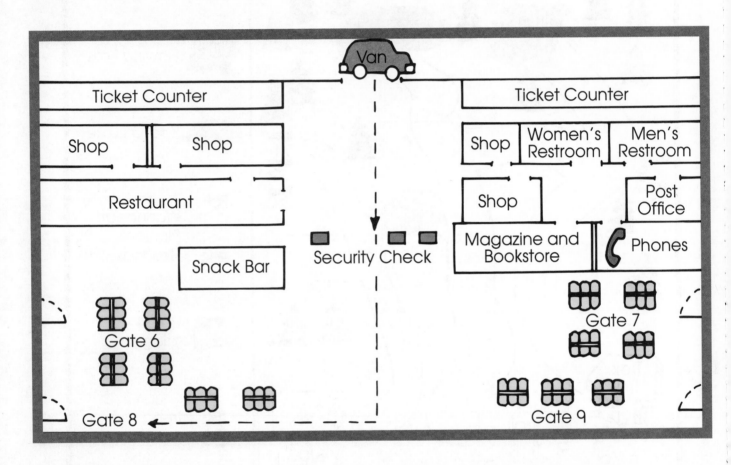

1. What did they walk past before they reached the security check?

   _____

   _____

2. Soon Dad joined them at the gate. Mom remembered she had to make a telephone call. Use an orange crayon to show the route she took to go from the gate to the telephones.

3. At what gate number will Jenny and Carl's grandparents arrive? _____

A Real "Moose-tery"

Horrible Harvey Hunter has disappeared somewhere in the mysterious Moosehead Mansion. Detective Dimwitt is trying to find him. Use the key to identify rooms in the mansion. Then, use a pencil to trace the route Detective Dimwitt took to locate the hapless Harvey.

Moosehead Mansion Map

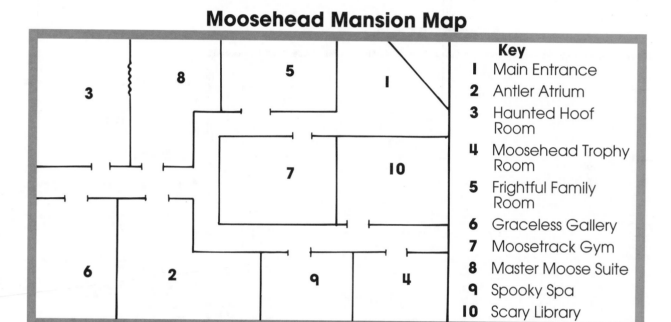

Key

1. Main Entrance
2. Antler Atrium
3. Haunted Hoof Room
4. Moosehead Trophy Room
5. Frightful Family Room
6. Graceless Gallery
7. Moosetrack Gym
8. Master Moose Suite
9. Spooky Spa
10. Scary Library

Detective Dimwitt's Route:

1. He enters the mansion at the Main Entrance.
2. Next, he checks out the Moosetrack Gym.
3. Then, he sneaks down the hall to the Antler Atrium.
4. From there, he checks the Spooky Spa.
5. No luck, so on to the Scary Library he goes.
6. Next, the detective scans the Moosehead Trophy Room.
7. Then, he walks along the hall to look in the Frightful Family Room.
8. No Harvey there, so he moves on to the Graceless Gallery.
9. Could he be in the Master Moose Suite? He checks there.
10. Then, he looks in the Haunted Hoof Room.
11. There, the detective discovers a secret room. Inside he finds Harvey reading a hunting magazine. The search is over!

Name _____

Find it There

To find your way around a town or city, you can use a street map.

Find the bookstore on the key. Now, find it on the map. Look at the name of the street that goes past the bookstore. If you want to go to the bookstore, you will have to go to Smelt Street.

Street Map

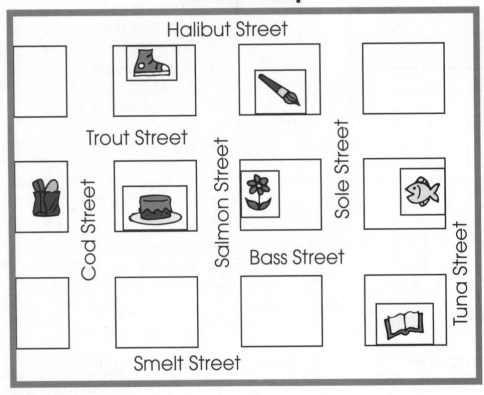

Directions:
Use the street map and map key. Fill in the blanks.

1. You can buy a cake on_____Street.

2. You can buy new shoes on_____Street.

3. You can buy a new fish tank on _____Street.

4. What store is on Salmon Street?_____

Going from Place to Place

Some maps show you where places are located in a town.

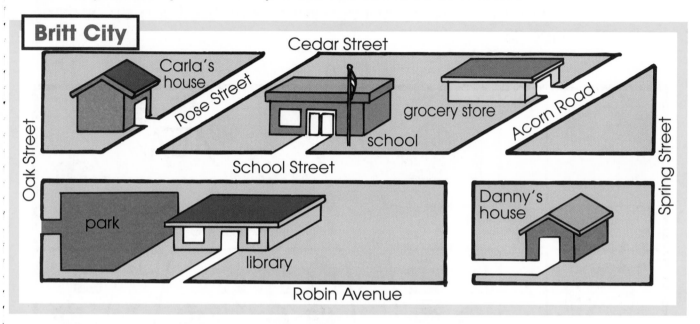

Circle the word that tells which is **closest** to Danny's house.

1. Carla's house   OR   the library
2. Robin Avenue   OR   Oak Street
3. the park   OR   the grocery store
4. Spring Street   OR   Cedar Street

Circle the word that tells which is **farthest** from Carla's house.

1. Spring Street   OR   Rose Street
2. the park   OR   Danny's house
3. the school   OR   the library
4. Oak Street   OR   Acorn Road

Add the following items to the map of Britt City.

1. Draw a flower garden on the corner of Spring Street and Robin Avenue.
2. Draw a swimming pool behind Carla's house.
3. Draw a baseball or football field behind the school.
4. Draw a car in front of Carla's house.
5. Draw a school bus on School Street.
6. Use a red crayon to draw the shortest path from Carla's house to Danny's.

Name _____

Victory Celebration

Betsy, Rachel, and Pat were so happy! They won their first baseball game. To celebrate, they wanted to have pizza and ice cream. Use this map and key to complete page 35.

Map

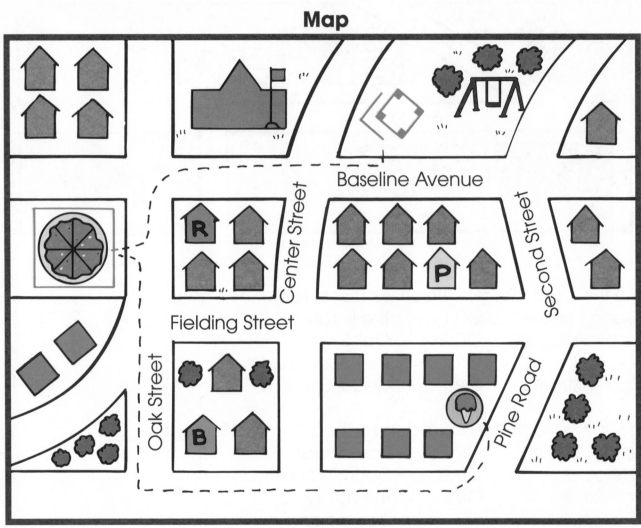

Baseline Avenue

Center Street

Second Street

Fielding Street

Oak Street

Pine Road

Key

- - - - route

school

house

baseball field

store

Rachel's house

park

pizza parlor

Pat's house

ice cream shop

Betsy's house

tree

Name _____

Victory Celebration

1. Use your finger to follow the route the girls took from the baseball field to the pizza parlor. On what street did they walk when they first left the baseball field?

   _____

2. Did they walk past the school? _____

3. Did they walk past a park? _____

4. On what street is the pizza parlor? _____

5. Use your finger to trace their route to the ice cream shop.
   On what street is the ice cream shop?

   _____

6. Then, it was time to go home. Use a blue crayon to mark a route Betsy might have taken home.

7. Use a red crayon to mark a route Rachel might have taken home.

8. Use a purple crayon to mark a route Pat might have taken home.

Name_____

A New Puppy

Mike's dog had puppies. Jason and his parents are going to Mike's house to get one of the puppies. Use the street map and key to help you answer the questions.

Map

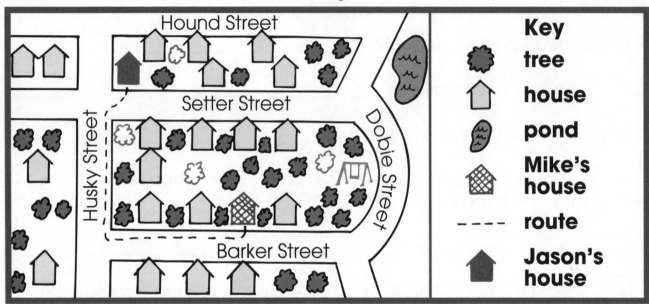

1. Find Jason's house. On what street does he live?

   _____

2. Find Mike's house. On what street does he live?

   _____

3. Use a red crayon to trace the route Mike drew for Jason to follow.

4. Which streets will Jason use to get to Mike's house?

   _____

5. Use a blue crayon to draw a different route Jason could use to get to Mike's house.

Name _____

Places to Go

Mrs. Nelson needs to do many errands this afternoon. She only has a short time in which to do everything. Read Mrs. Nelson's list of things to do. Use the street map and key to answer the questions.

Mrs. Nelson's Street Map

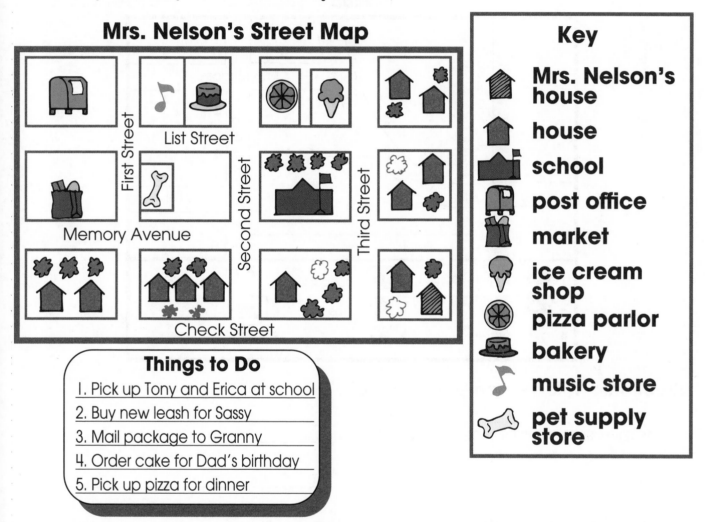

Key
- Mrs. Nelson's house
- house
- school
- post office
- market
- ice cream shop
- pizza parlor
- bakery
- music store
- pet supply store

Things to Do
1. Pick up Tony and Erica at school
2. Buy new leash for Sassy
3. Mail package to Granny
4. Order cake for Dad's birthday
5. Pick up pizza for dinner

1. On the map, find the places Mrs. Nelson needs to go.

2. Mrs. Nelson will go to these places in the same order as her list of things to do. Write the number on each place on the map to show the order in which she will go to these places.

3. Start at Mrs. Nelson's house. Use a red crayon to draw the route Mrs. Nelson will take to do all of her errands.

My Hometown

Complete the map by drawing the symbols from the key by each matching number on the map.

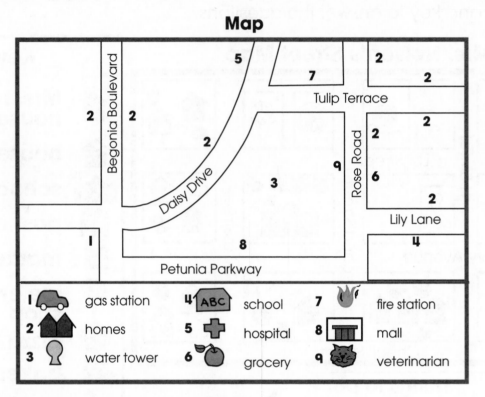

Map

Directions: Write the name of the streets.

1. The gas station is on the corner of _____

   and _____.

2. The veterinarian is on _____.

3. The fire station is on _____.

4. There are no homes on _____.

5. The school is on _____.

6. The grocery store is on _____.

The Compass Rose

This is a compass rose. It tells the directions on a map. There are four arrows. Each arrow points in a different direction. These are called **cardinal** directions.

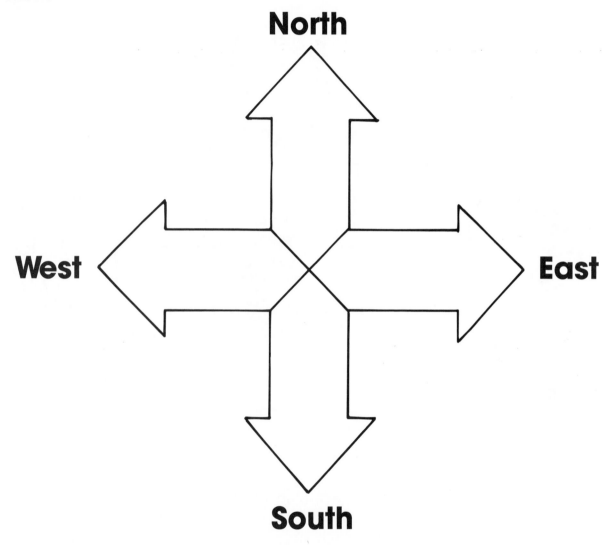

North

West   **East**

South

1. The arrow that points up is **north**. Color it blue.

2. The arrow that points down is **south**. Color it red.

3. The arrow that points to the right is **east**. Color it green.

4. The arrow that points to the left is **west**. Color it brown.

Name

Finding a Snack

The little bear cub is hungry for a snack. Read the clues. In each bear paw print, draw a picture of the snack he will find if he goes in that direction. Use the compass rose to help you.

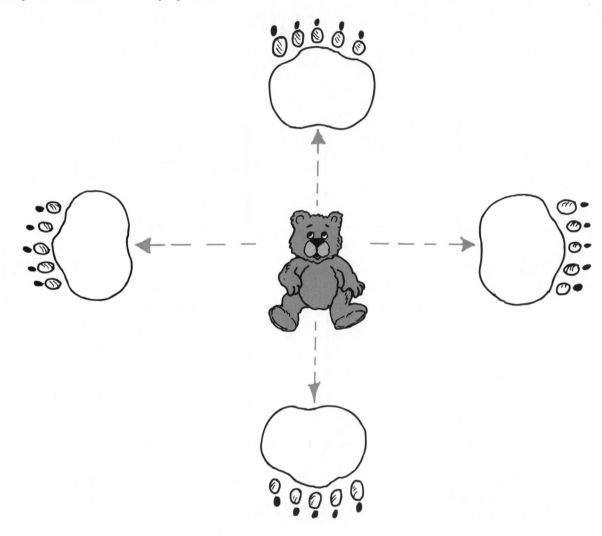

1. He will find  to the **west**.

2. He will find to the **south**.

3. He will find to the **orth**.

4. He will find 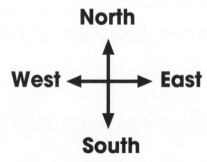 to the **east**.

North

West ◄——► East

South

Name_____

Pirate's Booty

Sedgewick the Pirate must be able to find his buried treasure when he returns to the island. Read the sentences. Write the words **north**, **south**, **east**, and **west** in the blanks to help Sedgewick locate his treasure. Use the compass rose to help you.

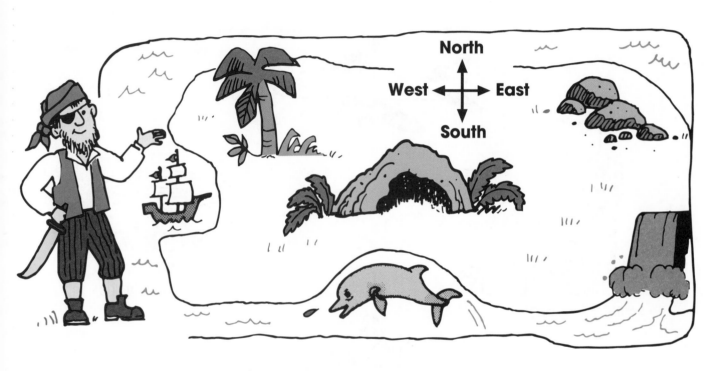

1. Anchor the ship on the_____ side of the island.

2. Walk_____ to the cave.

3. Then, walk_____ to Dolphin Cove.

4. Go _____ to the waterfall.

5. Go_____ to the rocks.

6. Then, go_____ to the palm tree.

7. Draw an X below the palm tree to show where the treasure is buried.

Name_____

Look to the Sky

Mr. McGill took his students on a field trip to the airport. A boy in his class drew this map of things they saw.

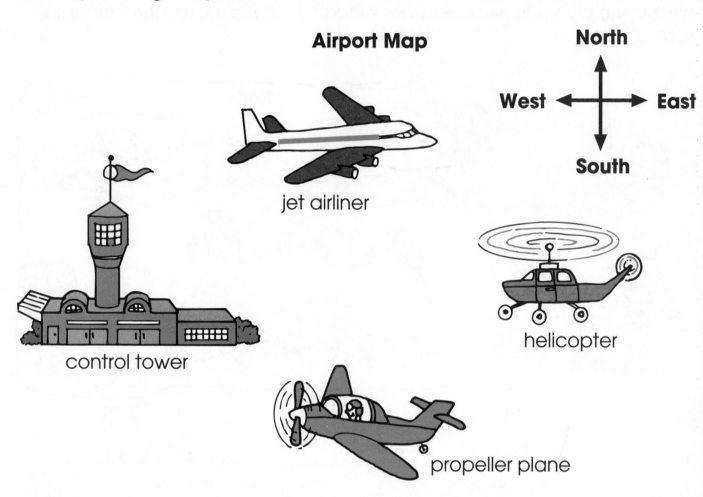

Airport Map

North

West ← → **East**

South

jet airliner

control tower

helicopter

propeller plane

Directions: Write **north**, **south**, **west**, or **east** to complete each sentence.

1. Look _____ to see the jet airliner.

2. Look _____ to see the control tower.

3. Look _____ to see the propeller plane.

4. Look _____ to see the helicopter.

Sign Search

Gina went for a hike. She found a piece of paper. There were strange directions written on it. Then, she looked around and saw pictures drawn on the rocks in the area. Aha! The paper she had found was a route to follow. Read the directions and draw the route on the map.

Map

1. Start at the fish.

2. Go north to the corn.

3. Then, go east to the hunter.

4. Go south to the river.

5. Go west to the buffalo.

6. Go south to the tree.

7. Go east to the arrowhead.

8. Go north to the cave. Draw a picture on the cave to show the treasure chest Gina finds there.

Name_____

What Do Hikers See?

Follow the directions to complete this area map.

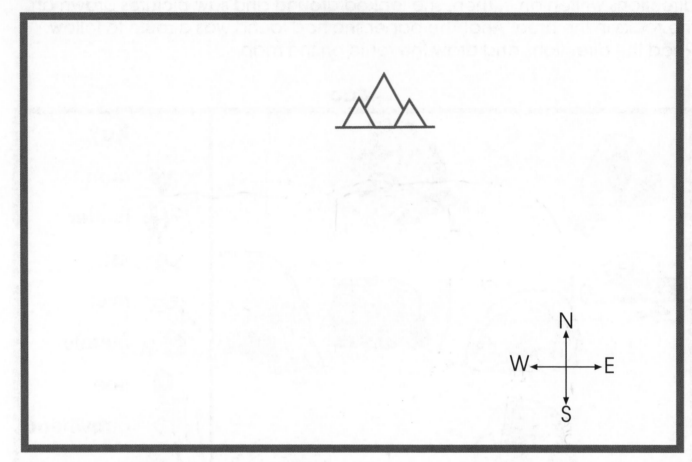

1. Draw a ⬭ west of the △△ .
2. Draw 6 🌲 south of the ⬭ .
3. Draw an 🏝 in the middle of the ⬭ .
4. Draw 10 △ south of the △△ .
5. Draw a 〰 between the △△ and the ⬭ .
6. Draw 2 ⛵ on the east side of the ⬭ .
7. Draw 2 🏠 south of the 6 🌲 .
8. Draw 3 🧍 south of the △ .

You're Invited

Liz sent out invitations to her birthday party. She drew a map to show how to go from school to her house.

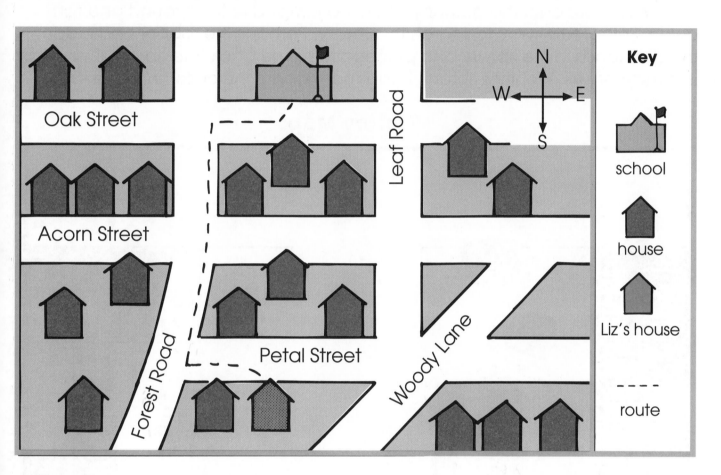

Directions:

Write **north**, **south**, **east**, or **west** and the street name to complete the sentences.

1. Leave the school and go_____ on _____.

2. Turn_____ on _____.

3. Then, turn _____ on _____.

Name_____

Missing Diamonds

Mrs. Wently's diamonds are missing. Seth Sleuth has been hired to find them. He listens to Mrs. Wently's story. She had seen the robber run through the library and out onto the balcony. Then, he jumped to the ground and ran away. Seth Sleuth went to search the library. Perhaps the robber had hidden the diamonds in the library and planned to come back later to get them. This is a map of Mrs. Wently's library. Read more about the case on page 47.

Library Map

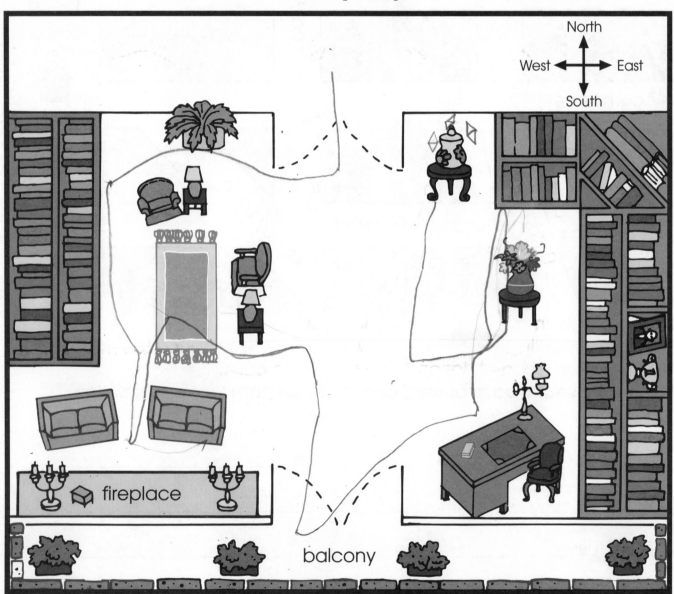

Name_____

Missing Diamonds

Can you find the missing diamonds? Help Seth Sleuth search the library. Read the directions. Use the compass rose to help you. Use a red crayon to draw the route on the library map to show where you search.

1. You walk through the doors at the north end of the library.

2. Walk west to the bookcase and look behind every book.

3. Now, walk south to the fireplace. Look around the things on the mantel.

4. Walk north to the rug. There's a lump! Lift the rug. It is only the cat's toy mouse.

5. Walk east and then south to the balcony doors. Maybe the robber hid the diamonds outside. Look out on the balcony. No diamonds there.

6. Hmmmm. The diamonds must be in the library. Go back inside the balcony doors. Walk east to the desk. No diamonds in sight.

7. Walk north and look behind every book. Look inside the green vase on the small table. Nothing there.

8. Head west and then north to look at the beautiful jar. Lift the lid. Inside are the sparkling diamonds. Draw a ◊ where you found the missing diamonds. Congratulations! You solved the case.

Ice Cream!

Here comes the ice cream truck! On hot summer days, Stan drives his ice cream truck around the neighborhood. He takes the same route every day. This map shows the neighborhood where Stan drives. Follow the directions on page 49.

Ice Cream Truck Route Map

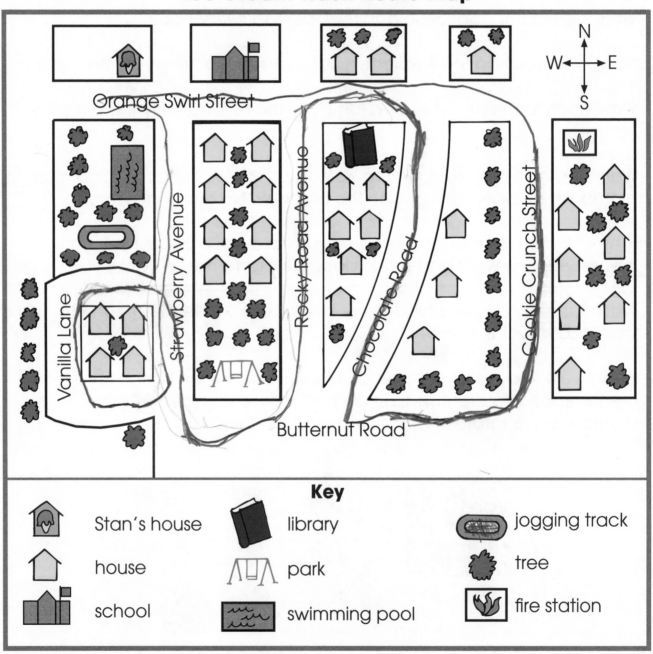

Key

🏠 Stan's house 📕 library ⬭ jogging track

🏠 house park 🌳 tree

🏫 school swimming pool 🔥 fire station

Ice Cream!

Draw Stan's route on the map on page 48. Read the information below. Use the map key and compass rose to help you.

1. Stan backs out of his driveway onto Orange Swirl Street.

2. He goes east.

3. Then, he turns south on Strawberry Avenue.

4. He drives past the swimming pool. After he passes the jogging track, he turns west on Vanilla Lane.

5. He drives around Vanilla Lane. Then, he drives east on Butternut Road past the park.

6. He turns and drives north along Rocky Road Avenue.

7. At the corner he turns and drives east on Orange Swirl Street.

8. He passes the library and drives south on Chocolate Road.

9. He turns east onto Butternut Road and drives past the row of trees.

10. Then, he turns north and drives along Cookie Crunch Street.

11. He passes the fire station and turns west and drives on Orange Swirl Street until he reaches his home.

Name

Secret Mission

Sam Superspy is on a mission. He must get the secret papers and deliver them to his boss as soon as possible. This is a map of where the mission is to take place. Follow the directions on page 51 to help Sam.

Key
- bench
- river
- bridge
- path
- tree
- swing
- jungle gym
- fountain
- duck pond
- trash can
- entrance

Secret Mission

Directions: Use a red crayon to mark the route Sam will take.

1. Enter the park through the entrance at the north end of the park.

2. Turn and walk east and then south past the swings and jungle gym.

3. Turn and go west to the fountain.

4. Walk to the bench south of the fountain.

5. You will find the papers Sam needs under the trash can to the west of the bench. Draw a red X to show where Sam finds the secret papers.

Now, Sam must deliver the secret papers to his boss. Use a blue crayon to mark the route Sam will take. Start at the red X you drew.

1. Walk south to the path.

2. Turn and walk east along the path to the trash can.

3. Turn and walk south near the duck pond.

4. Walk south to the path.

5. Turn and walk west toward the bridge.

6. There is a man standing under the tree north of the bridge. Sam hands the secret papers to him. Mission completed! Draw a blue X to show where Sam delivers the secret papers.

Connect the Dots

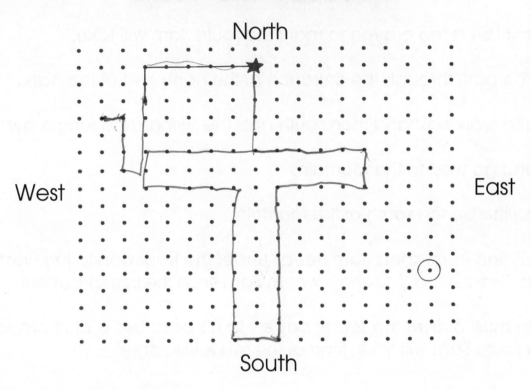

North

West

East

South

Directions: Follow the directions to complete a drawing. Begin at the star. The first two steps are done for you.

Draw a straight line . . .

1. five spaces west.
2. two spaces south.
3. four spaces east.
4. nine spaces south.
5. two spaces east.

6. nine spaces north.
7. four spaces east.
8. two spaces north.
9. five spaces west.
What letter did you draw? ____T ?____

Begin at the circle to complete another drawing.

Draw a straight line . . .

1. four spaces south.
2. one space west.
3. three spaces north.

4. one space west.
5. one space north.
6. two spaces east.
What number did you draw? 5 ?_____

Name ___Jada___

Finding Your Way Around Town

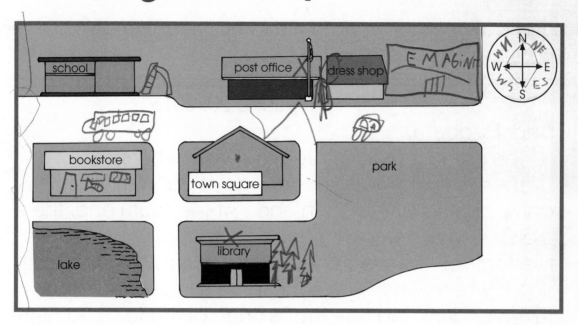

Directions: You are in the middle of the town square. Circle the correct answer to each question.

1. What direction is the library from you?   north   west   ~~south~~
2. What direction is the bookstore from you?   (west)   east   south
3. What direction must you go to reach the post office?   east   (north)   west
4. Which direction must you go to get to the park?   north   west   (east)

Use crayons or markers to complete the map.

1. Place a red X on the first place north of the library.
2. Place a black X on the place east of the post office.
3. Draw a red circle on the place west of the dress shop.
4. Draw a blue fish on the place south of the bookstore.
5. Draw three trees east of the library.

6. Draw a movie theater east of the dress shop.
7. Draw a car south of the dress shop.
8. Draw a slide east of the school and west of the post office.
9. Draw doors and windows on the first building north of the lake.
10. Draw a yellow bus south of the place that is west of the post office.

A Great Camp!

Read the letter. Then, draw a map to show what the camp looks like. Make a key for the map.

June 20, 2016

Dear Elizabeth,

This camp is great! I'll tell you what is here.

There is a big wooden gate as you come into the campground at the north end. At the south end, there is a lake where we swim and ride in boats. We sleep in five tents on the west side. A big log cabin on the east side is where we eat. We make necklaces and other things under a big tree that is north of the tents. At night we sing songs and tell stories around a campfire south of the log cabin.

Hope you are having fun at home. See you soon.

Your friend,
Sandy

Camp Map

N
W ← → E
S

Key

Making a Compass

A compass is a magnet that can identify geographic direction. It is very easy and a lot of fun to make your own compass!

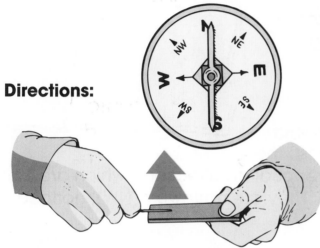

Directions:

You will need:
magnet
steel sewing needle
piece of thin plastic foam
    (from fast-food packaging)
shallow glass or plastic bowl
masking tape
water

1. Pull the sewing needle toward you across the magnet. Repeat this 20 times. Be sure to always pull in the same direction.

2. Test your needle on a steel object. If it is not yet magnetized, repeat step #1.

3. Tape the needle to a small piece of plastic foam.

4. Float your magnet in a dish of water.

What happened?

Wait for your floating needle to stop spinning. In what direction is it pointing?

_____

Try giving the floating needle a little spin. Wait for it to stop spinning.

Now what direction is it pointing? _____

Drawing a Compass Rose

The maps of the early explorers were beautiful pieces of art. Their maps would often have pictures of fire-breathing dragons and sea monsters to warn of the dangers at where they were traveling.

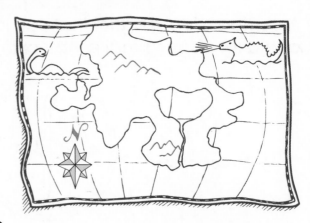

In a corner of an explorer's map would be a beautiful compass rose. The compass rose indicated the four cardinal directions—north, south, east, and west. The compass rose also indicated four intermediate directions, which are halfway between the four cardinal directions. They are northwest (NW), northeast (NE), southwest (SW), and southeast (SE).

Follow the steps to draw a **compass rose** in the upper right-hand corner of the map. Add the cardinal **directions** to your rose compass. Then, draw a map of your own make-believe land.

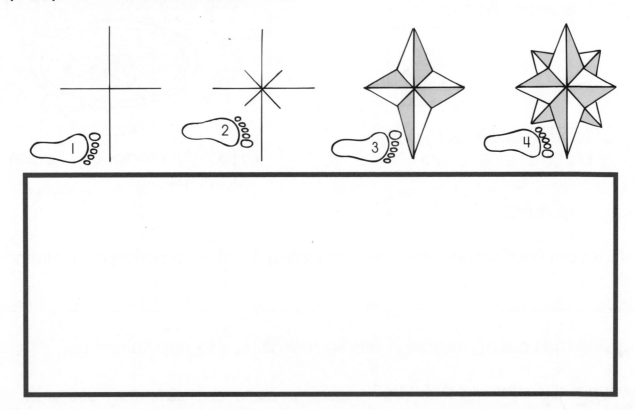

Spaceship Search

Gus Galactic needs help to identify these alien spaceships. Write a ship's letter in each blank to solve these riddles.

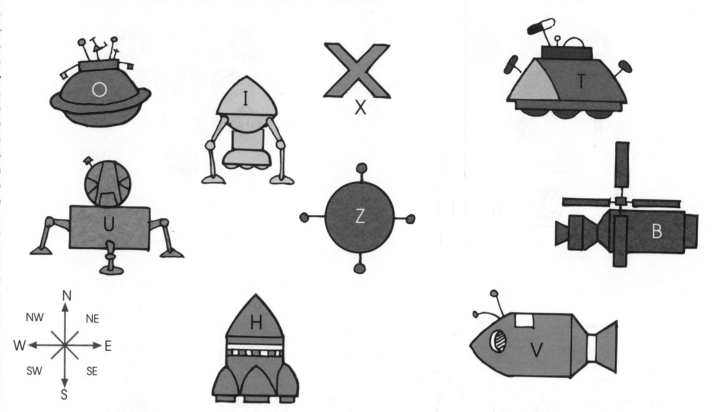

1. I am **N** of Ship **H**. _____
2. I am **E** of Ship **Z**. _____
3. I am **SE** of Ship **Z**. _____
4. I am **S** of Ship **O**. _____
5. I am **NW** of Ship **Z**. _____

6. I am **SW** of Ship **B**. _____
7. I am **NE** of Ship **Z**. _____
8. I am **NE** of Ship **I**. _____
9. I am **SE** of Ship **U**. _____
10. I am **NW** of Ship **B**. _____

Cosmic Challenge

Start at Ship H. Travel in the orbit given. Which ship will you dock with?

1. Go **NW** to Ship _____.
2. Go **NE** to Ship _____.
3. Go **NE** to Ship _____.
4. Go **S** to Ship _____.

5. Go **SE** to Ship _____.
6. Go **NE** to Ship _____.
7. Go **NW** to Ship _____.
This is your docking station.
Congratulations.

Name

Compass Rose Pool

Chalk your cue! Start with the numbered ball given. Follow the directions to find the mystery ball.

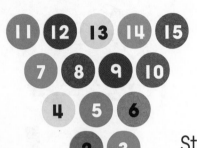

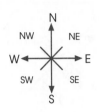

Start

3

1. NW _____   5. NW _____

2. NE _____   6. E _____

3. W _____   7. SE _____

4. W _____   8. NE _____

Start

15

1. W _____   5. NE _____

2. SW _____   6. W _____

3. SW _____   7. SW _____

4. E _____   8. SW _____

Start

7

1. E _____   5. E _____

2. E _____   6. NE _____

3. SW _____   7. NW _____

4. SW _____   8. NE _____

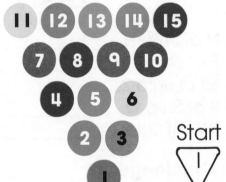

Start

1

1. NE _____   5. E _____

2. NE _____   6. NE _____

3. W _____   7. W _____

4. NE _____   8. SW _____

Name

The Sleuth Pooch

Help the Sleuth Pooch find his missing collar. Trace over the arrows given in order on his notepad. Then, color the Sleuth Pooch's collar.

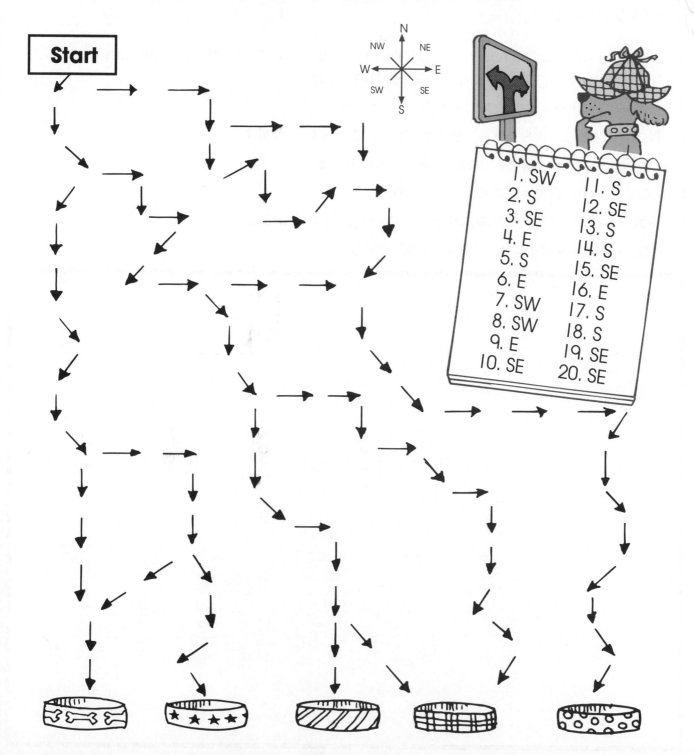

1. SW
2. S
3. SE
4. E
5. S
6. E
7. SW
8. SW
9. E
10. SE
11. S
12. SE
13. S
14. S
15. SE
16. E
17. S
18. S
19. SE
20. SE

Name

Draw Your Own Map

A cartographer makes maps. Try your hand at being a cartographer and make your own map by following these directions. Read all of the directions before you begin.

1. Draw a compass rose using both cardinal and intermediate directions in the bottom right-hand corner of the map.
2. Draw a lake in the center of the map.
3. Northwest of the lake, draw some ducks in flight.
4. Directly south of the lake, draw six trees.
5. East of the ducks, draw the sun.
6. Southwest of the lake, draw a playground area.
7. East of the lake, draw a picnic area.

Name _____

Acorn Park

Write the names of the intermediate directions on the lines.

NW is _____.   NE is _____.
SW is _____.   SE is _____.

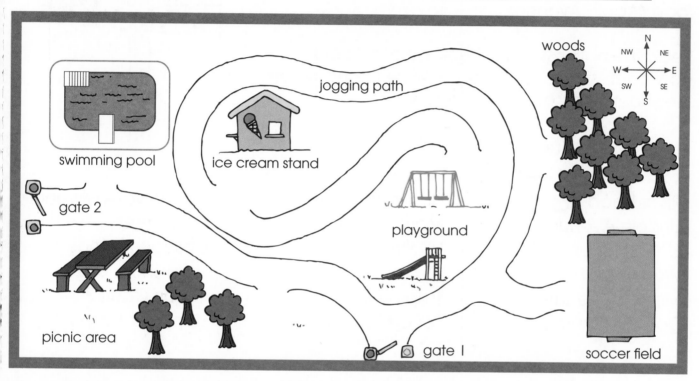

Directions: Use the names of cardinal and intermediate directions to complete these sentences about the map of Acorn Park.

1. The swimming pool is _____ of the playground.
2. The ice cream stand is _____ of the picnic area.
3. The soccer field is _____ of the swimming pool.
4. The playground is _____ of the picnic area.
5. The woods are _____ of the playground.
6. Gate 2 is on the _____ side of Acorn Park.
7. The swimming pool is _____ of the picnic area.
8. Gate 1 is on the _____ side of Acorn Park.
9. The woods are _____ of gate 1.

Name _____

Street Names

How did your street get its name? Was it named after a famous explorer like Columbus? Maybe it's named after a state, like Michigan Avenue. Perhaps it's named after a tree (Oak Street) or a food (Apple Avenue).

Read the names of the streets below. Decide how each street got its name. Write the name of the street in the correct category.

River Road
Lincoln Avenue
Church Street
Willow Road
Mexico Avenue
Dolphin Court

Flamingo Road
Market Avenue
Hill Street
Ohio Street
Tulip Lane
Jefferson Street

Pennsylvania Avenue
Oak Street
College Avenue
Lake Shore Drive
Edison Court
Elephant Avenue

Famous People	Places	Trees and Plants
_____	_____	_____
_____	_____	_____
_____	_____	_____

Land and Water Features	Human Institutions	Animals
_____	_____	_____
_____	_____	_____
_____	_____	_____

City Streets

Every town has some interesting street names. Streets can get their names in many different ways. They are often named after presidents, states, trees, and flowers. What are some street names in your town? Write each name in the correct category.

People's Names	Places	Funny Names
Human Institutions	Natural Features	Animals
Plants and Trees	Directions	Other

Near School

Geographers can tell us how places are the same and how they are different. Where you live is different from where your friend lives. Maybe you live southwest of your school while your friend lives north of the school.

Directions: Write the names and draw pictures of landmarks that are found near your school. Place each one on the chart in its correct location relative to your school.

Northwest	North	Northeast
West	School	East
Southwest	South	Southeast

A Walk Around Town

Take a walk around the town of Forest Grove. Use a marker or crayon to trace your route.

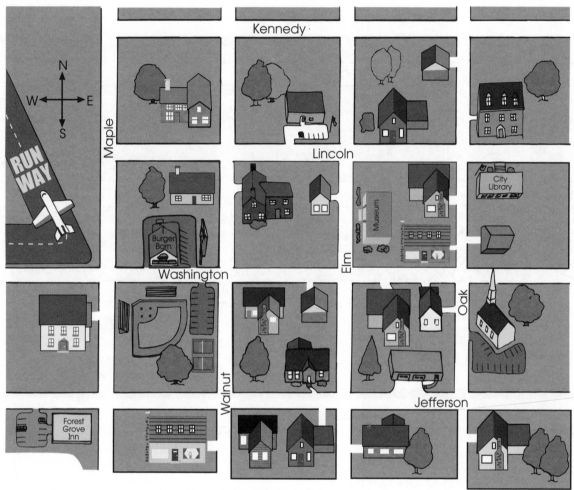

Directions:

1. Begin your walking tour at Forest Grove Inn.
2. Walk two blocks east to Elm Street.
3. Turn north on Elm Street. Walk to the Museum.
4. Go one-half block north to the corner of Elm and Lincoln.
5. Turn east on Lincoln. Walk until you come to the City Library.
6. Go south on Oak Street until you reach Washington Street.
7. Turn west on Washington and walk two and one-half blocks to the Burger Barn.
8. Lunch is over. Take the shortest way back to Forest Grove Inn.

Legends Help You Reach Maps

A legend is another word for a key. A map legend explains the symbols found in a map.

Star City

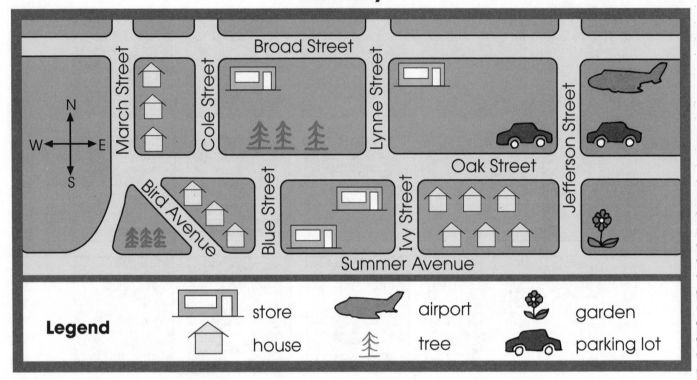

Directions: Use the map legend to answer the questions.

1. Does Star City have an airport? _____
2. How many houses are on Bird Avenue? _____
3. What is on the corner of Oak Street and Jefferson Street?_____
4. The garden is on the corner of Jefferson Street and _____.
5. How many stores are in Star City? _____
6. What direction is Summer Avenue from Oak Street? _____
7. Which street is directly west of Ivy Street? _____
8. How many trees are north of Oak Street? _____
9. How many houses are between Ivy Street and Jefferson Street?_____
10. How many stores are north of Summer Avenue?_____

Cartographers Use Symbols

Directions: On another sheet of paper, draw a map using the symbols and directions below.

1. Draw a compass rose in the lower right-hand corner of the page.

2. Draw a [road symbol] in the center of the map from west to east.

3. Draw 6 [house symbol] in the southwest corner of the map.

4. Draw 4 [tree symbol] east of the [house symbol].

5. Draw a [G grocery store symbol] north of the [road symbol].

6. Draw a [C clothing store symbol] west of the [G grocery store symbol].

7. Draw a [T movie theater symbol] south of the [road symbol].

8. Draw a [C clothing store symbol] north of the [house symbol].

On another sheet of paper, draw another map using the symbols and directions below.

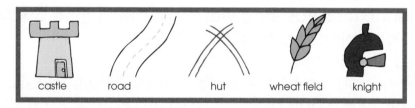

1. Draw a compass rose in the lower right-hand corner of the page.

2. Draw a castle in the center of the map.

3. Draw a road from the castle door southeast to the bottom of the map.

4. Draw 4 huts west of the castle.

5. Draw a knight on the east and west sides of the castle door.

6. Draw a wheat field east of the castle.

7. Draw a road east from the huts to the castle road.

Welcome to Crystal River

Crystal River is a great small town to live in. It has stores, parks, churches, schools, libraries, and more.

Complete the map of Crystal River on page 71. Use the directions below to draw the buildings and parks and to write the names of the streets and businesses on the map where they belong.

When you finish your map, share it with a friend. How are your maps alike? How are they different?

Directions:

1. Bridge Street crosses the Crystal River.
2. Diamond Avenue runs east and west. It is south of the Crystal River.
3. North Street is one block north of Park Street.
4. Elm Street runs directly into Park Street.
5. The Burger Barn is on the corner of Bridge and Park Streets.
6. The Crystal Library is a half block west of the Burger Barn.
7. Elm School is on the corner of Elm Street and Park Street.
8. Crystal Church is west of Elm School.
9. There are stores on the remainder of the north side of Park Street.
10. Bob's Bait Shop is on Bridge Street near the river.
11. The only buildings on North Street are houses.
12. The Crystal River flows through the middle of the city park.
13. The Crystal Airport is on the south edge of town.
14. Memorial Hospital is south of the river.
15. The fire station is on Bridge Street.

Name _____

Welcome to Crystal River

Use the directions on page 70 to complete the map of Crystal River.

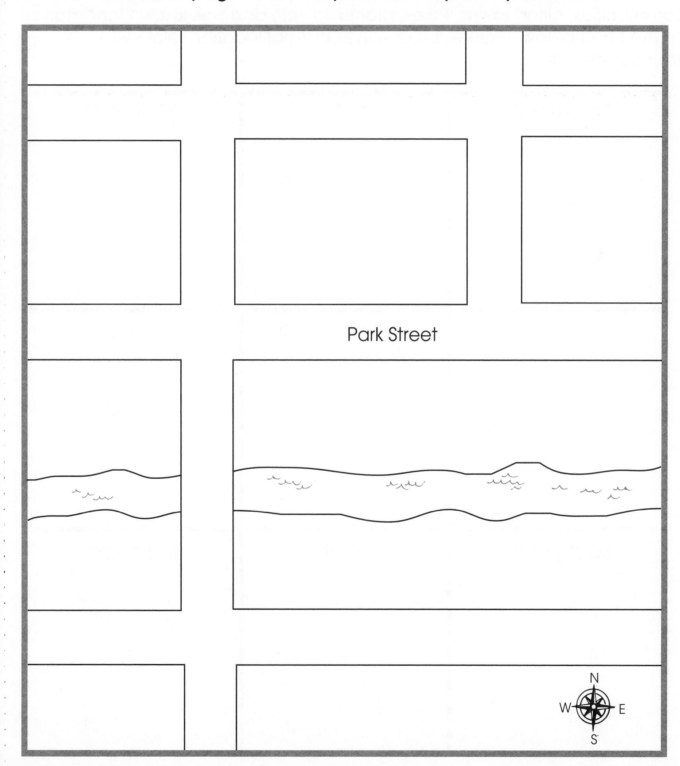

Park Street

Near My Community

Use a state map to locate your community. Then, write the names of other communities, cities, towns, lakes, places to visit, and well-known landmarks on the chart below. Write each one in its correct location relative to your community.

Northwest	North	Northeast
West	My Community	East
Southwest	South	Southeast

Tourist Map of Oldtown

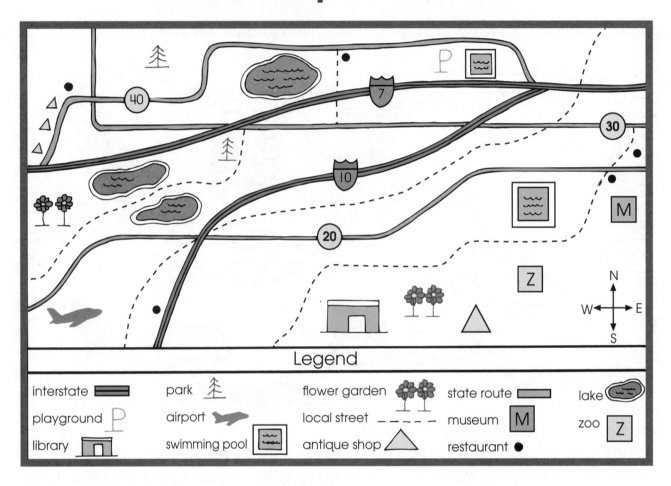

Legend

interstate ▬▬   park 🌲   flower garden 🌸   state route ▬▬   lake 🏞️

playground P   airport ✈️   local street – – –   museum M   zoo Z

library 🏛️   swimming pool 🔲   antique shop △   restaurant ●

1. The airport is located between Interstate_____and Route_____.

2. What attractions are north of Interstate 7? _____
_____

3. Could you take a local street from the airport to the library? _____

4. How many lakes are in Oldtown? _____

5. On which side of town is the museum located? _____

6. What is located at the point where Route 30 crosses Interstate 7? _____

7. Name the road that runs north of the playground. _____

8. How many swimming pools are in Oldtown? _____

9. How many antique shops are in the town? _____

10. Is there a local street between the zoo and the swimming pool? _____

Is It North, South, East, or West?

Direction words can help you locate places quickly on a map.

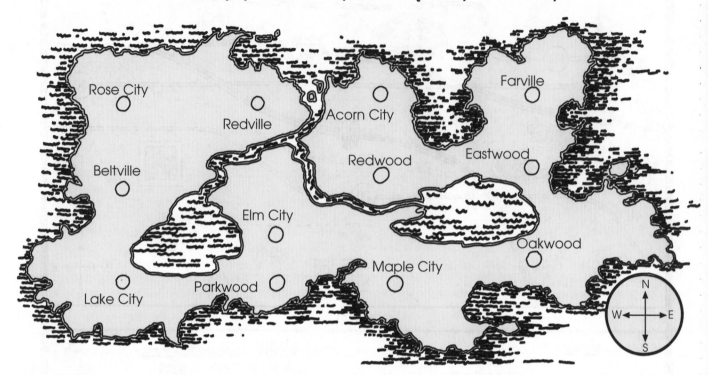

Directions: Circle the correct answer.

1. What city is south of Acorn City?	Rose City	Redwood	Farville
2. What city is north of Beltville?	Rose City	Redwood	Lake City
3. What city is east of Rose City?	Beltville	Lake City	Redville
4. What city is west of Maple City?	Redwood	Acorn City	Parkwood
5. What city is south of Farville?	Acorn City	Eastwood	Redville
6. What city is west of Redwood?	Eastwood	Maple City	Beltville
7. What city is north of Lake City?	Beltville	Maple City	Oakwood
8. What city is west of Farville?	Acorn City	Oakwood	Eastwood

Use crayons or markers to follow these directions.
1. Draw a line south from Farville to Eastwood.
2. Draw a line north from Maple City to Redwood.
3. Draw a line east from Beltville to Redwood.
4. Draw a line west from Redville to Rose City.
5. Place an A on the city directly south of Eastwood.
6. Place a B on the city east of Acorn City.

North, South, East, and West

You are flying in an airplane from
Chicago to Nashville. In what direction
are you traveling?

If you said "south" to the above question, you are correct!

Write the direction you would be traveling for each set of cities. Use the four
cardinal directions — north, south, east, and west.

Atlanta to Los Angeles   _____   Houston to Minneapolis   _____
Seattle to Los Angeles   _____   Miami to New York   _____
San Francisco to Nashville   _____   Detroit to New York   _____
Denver to Salt Lake City   _____   Boston to Minneapolis   _____
Cincinnati to Detroit   _____   Atlanta to Albuquerque   _____
Chicago to Boston   _____   Nashville to Miami   _____

Locating Cities

Directions: Use the compass rose to help you fill in each blank with the correct direction. Use the four cardinal directions — north, south, east, and west — and the four intermediate directions — northeast, northwest, southeast, and southwest.

1. El Paso, Texas, is _____ of Dallas, Texas.
2. Tulsa, Oklahoma, is _____ of Oklahoma City, Oklahoma.
3. Mobile, Alabama, is _____ of Baton Rouge, Louisiana.
4. Little Rock, Arkansas, is _____ of Nashville, Tennessee.
5. Houston, Texas, is _____ of New Orleans, Louisiana.
6. Jackson, Mississippi, is _____ of Memphis, Tennessee.
7. Dallas, Texas, is _____ of Austin, Texas.
8. The state of Louisiana is _____ of Arkansas.
9. The state of Alabama is _____ of Texas.
10. The state of Oklahoma is _____ of Tennessee.
11. The state of Georgia is _____ of Texas.
12. Atlanta, Georgia, is _____ of Savannah, Georgia.
13. The state of Tennessee is _____ of Arkansas.
14. Dallas, Texas, is _____ of Little Rock, Arkansas.
15. Mobile, Alabama, is _____ of Atlanta, Georgia.

Name_____

Scale Is Fun!

Scale measures distance on a map. Use the scale given to measure distances in this winter wonderland. Cut out the ruler. Use it to measure from ❄ to ❄ to answer the questions below.

1. On the scale, how many feet equal one inch? _____
2. How many feet is it from the shovel to the sleigh? _____
3. How many feet is the snow angel from the snowman? _____
4. How many feet is the igloo from the sleigh? _____
5. How many feet is it from the snowmobile to the skis and poles? _____
6. How many feet is the snow fort from the shovel? _____
7. It is _____feet from the sledding hill to the shovel.
8. It is _____feet from the skis and poles to the sleigh.
9. It is _____feet from the skis and poles to the igloo.

**Page is blank for cutting
exercise on previous page.**

Go the Distance

This map shows the route for the yearly Pedalville Bike-a-thon. At the bottom of the map is a scale.

Bike-a-thon Map

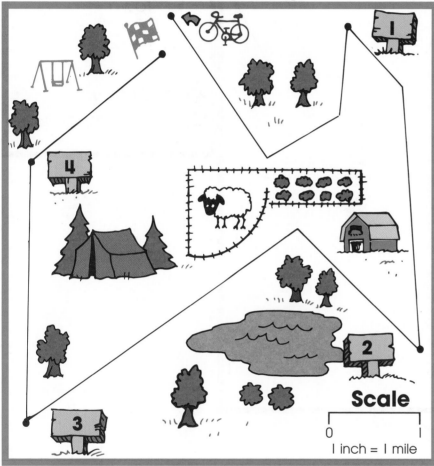

Scale

0 _____ 1

1 inch = 1 mile

Key

• checkpoint

race start

race end

— route

Directions: Use a ruler and the scale to measure the distances on the map.

1. How many miles are between "race start" and checkpoint 1?   _____
2. How many miles are between checkpoint 1 and checkpoint 2?   _____
3. How many miles are between checkpoint 2 and checkpoint 3?   _____
4. How many miles are between checkpoint 3 and checkpoint 4?   _____
5. How many miles are between checkpoint 4 and "race end"?   _____

Name_____

Are We There Yet?

Calvin is going on a vacation to Getaway Campground.

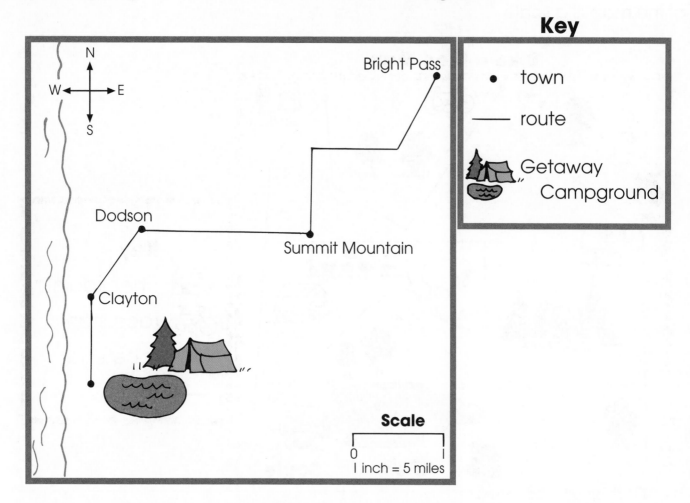

Directions: Use the scale and a ruler to answer the questions.

1. How many miles are between Bright Pass and Summit Mountain?

   _____

2. How far is it from Summit Mountain to Dodson? _____

3. How many miles are between Dodson and Clayton? _____

4. How far is it from Clayton to Getaway Campground? _____

5. How many miles in all are between Bright Pass and Getaway
   Campground? _____

Name_____

How Far is it?

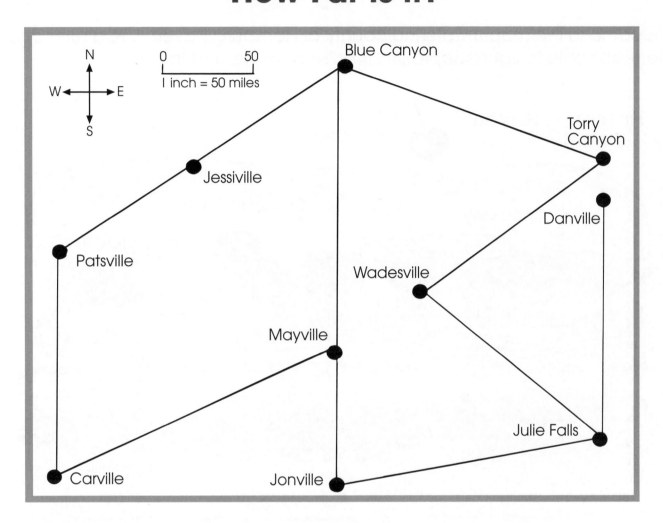

Directions: Measure these distances and answer the questions.

1. How far is it from Carville to Mayville? _____
2. How far is it from Wadesville to Torry Canyon? _____
3. If you travel from Blue Canyon to Jonville, how far will you travel?

_____

4. What town is between Patsville and Blue Canyon? _____
5. If you go through Wadesville, how far is it from Torry Canyon to Julie Falls?

_____

6. Which is longer—going from Carville to Patsville, or Carville to Mayville?

_____

Hamburg Haven

Welcome to the mouth-watering county of Hamburg Haven! Use a ruler and the map scale to figure approximate distances around this "burg."

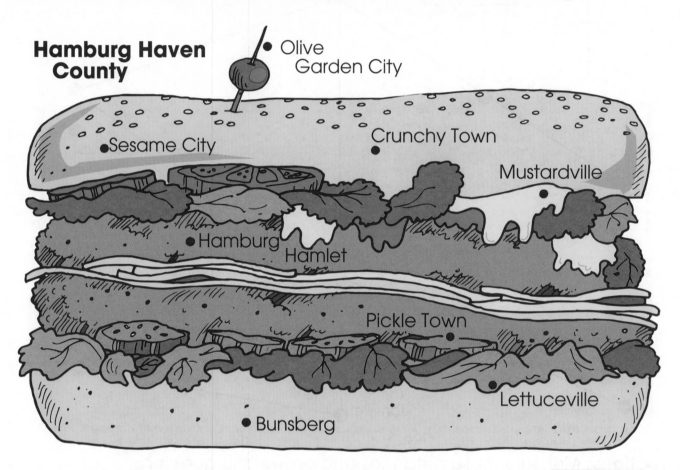

Hamburg Haven County

Olive Garden City

Sesame City

Crunchy Town

Mustardville

Hamburg Hamlet

Pickle Town

Lettuceville

Bunsberg

About how many miles is it? (Hint: Measure from dot to dot.)

0   5   10
1 inch = 10 miles

1. from Olive Garden City to Pickle Town? _____
2. from Bunsberg to Lettuceville? _____
3. from Crunchy Town to Mustardville? _____
4. from Mustardville to Pickle Town? _____
5. from Bunsberg to Sesame City? _____
6. from Hamburg Hamlet to Lettuceville? _____
7. from Crunchy Town to Bunsberg? _____

Camping in Nature Park

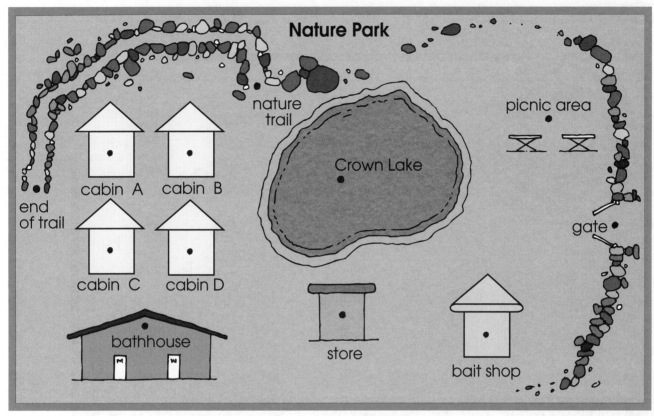

Nature Park

nature trail

picnic area

Crown Lake

cabin A   cabin B

end of trail

cabin C   cabin D

gate

bathhouse

store

bait shop

0   1

1 inch = 1 miles

Directions: Use a ruler to help you answer the questions.

1. How far is it from the center of Crown Lake to the bait shop? _____
2. How far is it from the picnic area to Crown Lake? _____
3. How far must you travel from cabin C to the bathhouse? _____
4. What is the distance from the beginning of the nature trail to Crown Lake? _____
5. Your family is staying in cabin A. How far must you travel from the gate to the cabin? _____
6. What is the approximate distance in miles from the beginning to the end of the nature trail? _____
7. How far must your family travel to the store if you are staying in cabin D? _____
8. How far is it from the store to cabin B? _____
9. The end of the nature trail is how far from the picnic area? _____
10. How far is the bathhouse from cabin A? _____

Flying from Place to Place

You are an airline pilot. You will need a ruler for this activity.

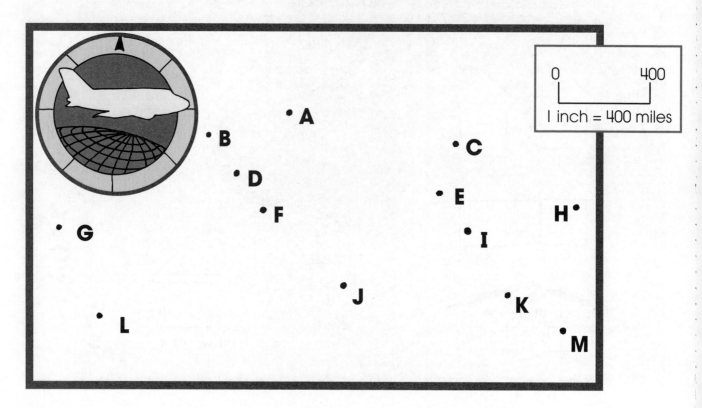

1. You need to file a flight plan from city **J** to city **C**. How far will the plane travel? _____

2. You must fly from city **D** to city **F** to city **E**. How many miles will you travel? _____

3. How far is it from city **H** to city **C**? _____

4. Is it closer to fly from city **I** to city **M** or from city **I** to city **A**? _____

5. If your plane holds enough fuel to fly 500 miles, can you fly from city **L** to city **G** without refueling? _____

6. With fuel for 500 miles, can you fly from city **A** to city **J**? _____

7. About how many miles is it from city **C** to city **M**? _____

8. What direction must you fly from city **H** to city **F**? _____

9. What direction must you fly from city **J** to city **K**? _____

Name _____

Amazing Arizona

Get to know Arizona, the 48th state. Below is a map showing the largest Indian reservations and cities located in or near them in Arizona. Use a ruler and the scale. Write the approximate distance in miles.

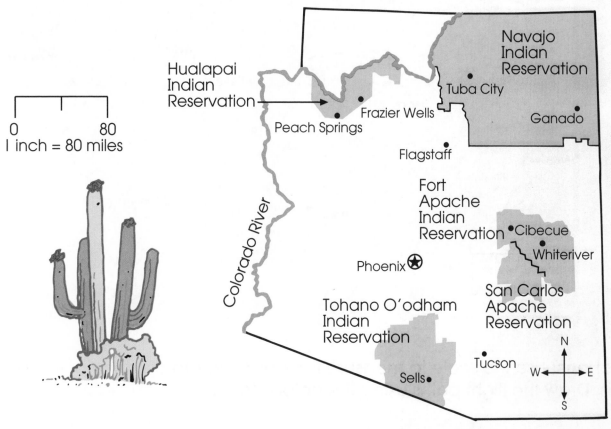

1. About how many miles from Phoenix to Peach Springs? _____

2. About how many miles from north to south on its eastern border? _____

3. About how many miles from Flagstaff to Ganado? _____

4. From Tucson to Flagstaff? _____

5. From Whiteriver to Ganado? _____

6. From Tuba City to Tucson? _____

7. From Peach Springs to Sells? _____

8. From Cibecue to Sells? _____

9. The Fort Apache Indian and San Carlos Apache Reservations north to south at their greatest distance. _____

10. The Navajo Indian Reservation from east to west at its greatest distance. _____

Name_____

Flight Path Frenzy

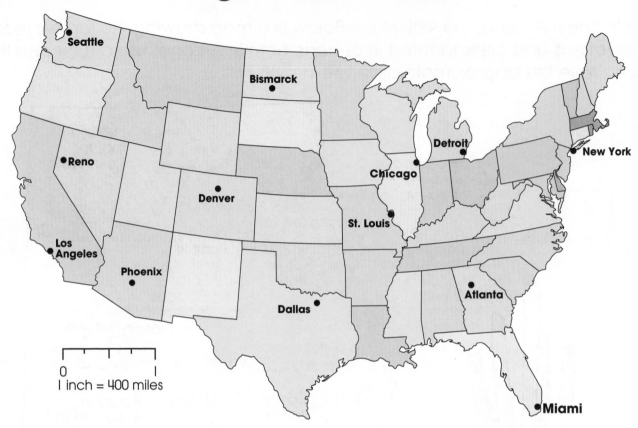

Seattle

Bismarck

Detroit

New York

Reno

Chicago

Denver

St. Louis

Los Angeles

Phoenix

Atlanta

Dallas

Miami

0
1 inch = 400 miles

Directions: Use the scale to measure the approximate distance of these flights. Draw the flight paths using the colors stated.

From:

1. Atlanta to Dallas_____miles (orange)
2. Denver to Chicago _____miles (purple)
3. Los Angeles to Phoenix_____miles (yellow)
4. Seattle to Dallas _____miles (green)
5. St. Louis to New York_____miles (brown)
6. Denver to Miami _____miles (red)
7. Reno to Detroit _____miles (dark blue)
8. Los Angeles to New York_____miles (pink)
9. Seattle to St. Louis_____miles (black)
10. Chicago to Miami_____miles (light blue)

Name _____

Traveling on Different Roads

Use a ruler to measure distances on this map and answer the questions below. Don't forget to use the compass rose and the legend.

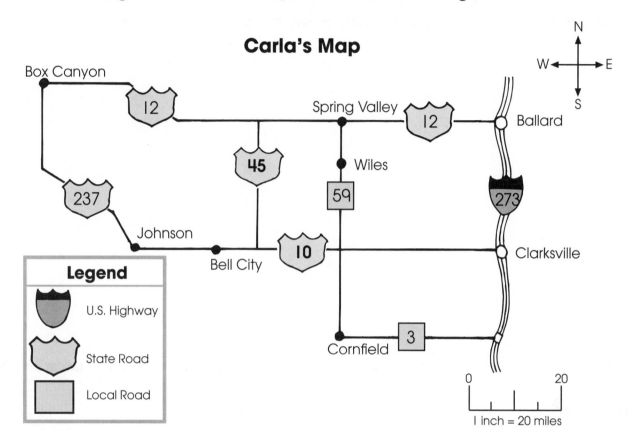

1. What U.S. highway would Carla travel on from Clarksville to Ballard? _____
2. If Carla travels from Bell City to Clarksville, what state road will she use?

   _____

3. How far is it from Johnson to Bell City? _____
4. Does Carla take a state or local road to travel from Wiles to Spring Valley?

   _____

5. Cornfield is located at the junction of which two local roads?

   _____

6. What direction is Johnson from Bell City? _____
7. If Carla drives from Clarksville to Ballard, what direction and about how many miles will she travel? _____

Name _____

Recreation Location

You are the planner for a new recreation center. Use a ruler and the map scale to measure and draw its features, following the directions below.

0   20
I inch = 20 feet

Directions:

1. Draw a 20 ft. square in the SE corner of the map.
2. Draw a rectangle N of the square 25 ft. wide by 45 ft. long.
3. Draw a rectangle in the SW corner, measuring 60 ft. long by 25 ft. wide.
4. Draw a 20 ft. square in the NW corner of the map.
5. Draw another 20 ft. square east of the square you drew in #4.

Add details to your shapes to transform the shapes into
1. a racquetball court.
2. a basketball court.
3. a swimming pool.
4. a golf driving range.
5. a baseball batting cage.

Write a name for the recreation center in the middle of the map.

Name_____

How Many People?

This map uses symbols to show how many people live in each town. Use the map and the legend to answer the questions below.

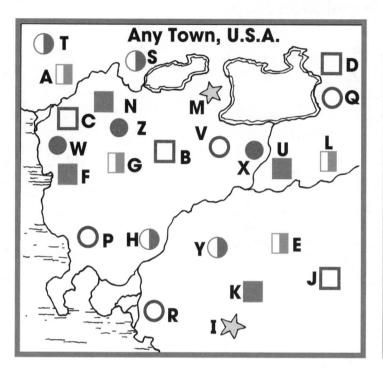

1. How many people live in a town that has this symbol ■ ?_____

2. What does ☆ mean on the map? _____

3. Name the four towns with 0-500 people. _____

4. How many towns have 1,000-5,000 people? _____

5. How many people live in town G? _____

6. Circle the town with the most people.   A   B   I

7. Circle the town with the fewest people.   L   K   J

8. Name the towns with 1,000-5,000 people. _____

9. How many towns have over 100,000 people? _____

10. Name the towns with 50,000-100,000 people. _____

11. Draw a circle around the towns with 500-1,000 people.

12. Draw a large **X** on the towns with 25,000-50,000 people.

Name _____

What is the Population?

Use this map of an imaginary state to answer the following questions.

Population Map

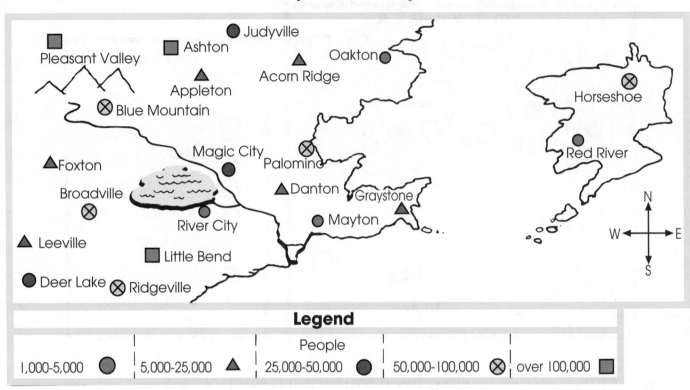

Legend

			People					
1,000-5,000 ●	5,000-25,000 ▲	25,000-50,000 ●	50,000-100,000 ⊗	over 100,000 ■

1. Name the five cities with a population of 50,000-100,000. _____
   _____

2. Would you choose Foxton or Ashton for a baseball stadium that seats 50,000 people? _____

3. Name the three cities with a population over 100,000. _____

4. Which is bigger—Pleasant Valley or Mayton? _____

5. Which town has more people—River City or Magic City? _____

6. Which town has more people—Judyville or Danton? _____

7. Which is larger—Little Bend or Ridgeville? _____

8. Which city is smaller—Blue Mountain or Deer Lake? _____

9. How many towns have 1,000-5,000 people? _____

10. How many towns have 5,000-25,000 people? _____

Section 2
United States Geography

Crossing the States

Use the map of the United States on pages 93 and 95 and the compass rose to fill in the puzzle.

Across:

2. the state east of Indiana

6. the state west of North Dakota

8. the smaller state east of Connecticut

10. the state south of Georgia

11. the state west of Utah

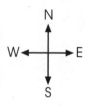

Down:

1. the state west of New Hampshire

2. the state south of Washington

3. the state north of Missouri

4. the state east of Arizona

5. the larger state south of New York

7. the state north of South Dakota

9. the state south of Arkansas

The crossword puzzle filled in:

		V						
E		R	O	h	i	O		
N		M	r			w		
E		O	E			a		
W		N	G					P
M	O	N	T	A	N	A		E
E	N		O					N
X	R	H	O	D	E	I	S	L A N D
I	T						O	S Y
C	H		LAKE AREA				U	Y L
O	D						I	L V
	D						S	A
	K		F	L	O	R	I D A	N
	O						A	I A
	T						N	
	A	N E V A D A					A	

11. N E V A D A

Postcard Geography

Use this postcard to tell a friend about a place within the United States where you are vacationing. Design your own stamp and write in your friend's address.

To:

See the States

Use the map of the United States on pages 93 and 95. Color the van at the bottom of this page. Cut it out along the dashed line. Use a piece of tape to attach it to your pencil.

Now your van is packed and you are ready to start your trip. Read the sentences below. Move your pencil where the directions lead you to find answers to the questions below.

Directions:

1. Start in Ohio.

2. Go west to Iowa. Which states did you pass through?

   _____

3. Go south to Louisiana. Which states did you pass through?

   _____

4. Go west to California. Which states did you pass through?

   _____

5. Turn and go north to Washington. What state did you pass through?

   _____

6. It's time to head home to Ohio. In which direction will you travel?

   _____

What a Vacation!

This is a map of the United States. It shows where four children went on their family vacations. Use this map and the key on page 101 to find out where each child went.

What a Vacation!

Key

→ → →   David's trip

• • • • •   Becky's trip

•••••••   Adam's trip

— · — · —   Sheila's trip

☆   home

National Baseball Hall of Fame and Museum

Fossil Butte National Monument

Dahlonega Gold Museum

Sea World

Grand Canyon

U.S. Space and Rocket Center

Grasshopper Glacier

Naismith Memorial Basketball Hall of Fame

Virginia City (old mining town)

1. Use a yellow crayon to trace David's route.

2. Use a blue crayon to trace Becky's route.

3. Use a red crayon to trace Adam's route.

4. Use a green crayon to trace Sheila's route.

5. Which person traveled the farthest west? _____

6. Which person probably likes sports? _____

7. Which person traveled the farthest south? _____

8. Write the names of the places Sheila saw on her vacation.

    _____

    _____

9. Where did Becky go in Florida? _____

Flying Cross-Country

Pretend you are on an airplane that is flying cross-country. Name the states that you would fly over if the plane flew in a straight line from the first city to the second.

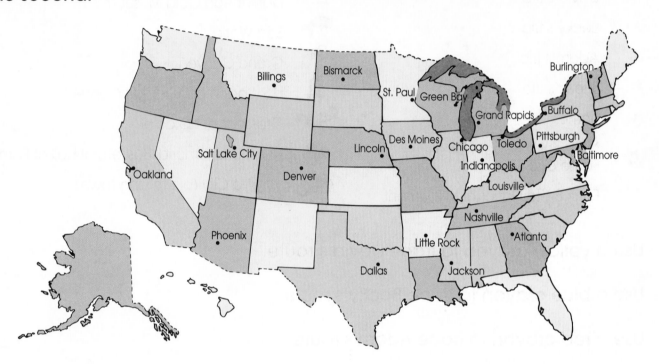

Atlanta, Georgia to Jackson, Mississippi   _____

Grand Rapids, Michigan to St. Paul, Minnesota   _____

Bismarck, North Dakota to Lincoln, Nebraska   _____

Oakland, California to Salt Lake City, Utah   _____

Phoenix, Arizona to Dallas, Texas   _____

Little Rock, Arkansas to Chicago, Illinois   _____

Toledo, Ohio to Green Bay, Wisconsin   _____

Pittsburgh, Pennsylvania to Burlington, Vermont   _____

Denver, Colorado to Billings, Montana   _____

Nashville, Tennessee to Indianapolis, Indiana   _____

Des Moines, Iowa to Louisville, Kentucky   _____

Baltimore, Maryland to Buffalo, New York   _____

Play Ball!

In the spring, you can hear the umpire shout, "Play Ball!" In North America, there are 30 Major League baseball teams. Most of the teams are named after the city in which they play, but four teams are named after their states. One of the teams is in Canada.

Write the name of the state or province where each team plays. You get bonus points if you can give the team name. Then, complete the map on page 106.

American League

City	State/Province	Team name
Baltimore	_____	_____
Boston	_____	_____
Los Angeles	California	_____
Chicago	_____	_____
Cleveland	Ohio	_____
Detroit	_____	_____
Kansas City	_____	_____
Minneapolis	Minnesota	_____
New York	_____	_____
Oakland	_____	_____
Seattle	_____	_____
Arlington	Texas	_____
Tampa Bay	_____	_____
Toronto	_____	_____

National League

City	State/Province	Team name
Chicago	_____	_____
Cincinnati	_____	_____
Denver	Colorado	_____
Miami	Florida	_____
Houston	_____	_____
Los Angeles	_____	_____
Milwaukee	_____	_____
Washington	_____	_____
New York	_____	_____
Philadelphia	_____	_____
Phoenix	Arizona	_____
Pittsburgh	_____	_____
San Diego	_____	_____
San Francisco	_____	_____
St. Louis	_____	_____
Atlanta	_____	_____

Play Ball!

Label the cities where the Major League baseball teams play. Label the American League cities red and the National League cities blue.

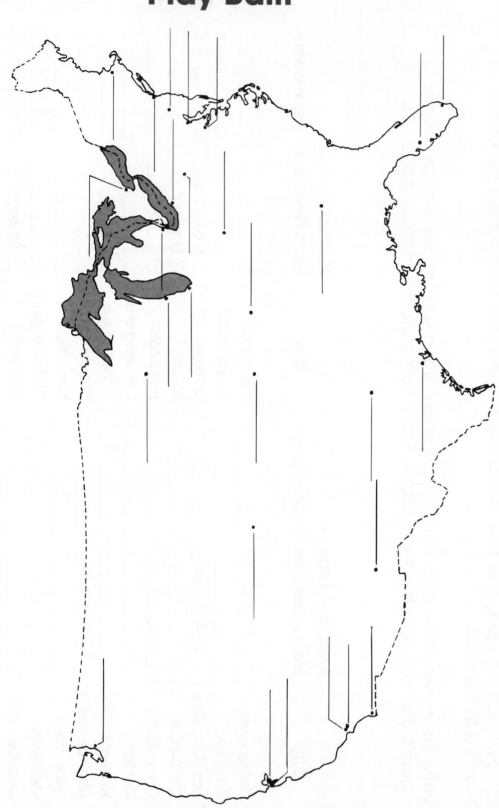

Name_____

Mystery States I

Can you identify these state shapes? Use a U.S. map to help you. Write the name of each state and its capital city ☆ .

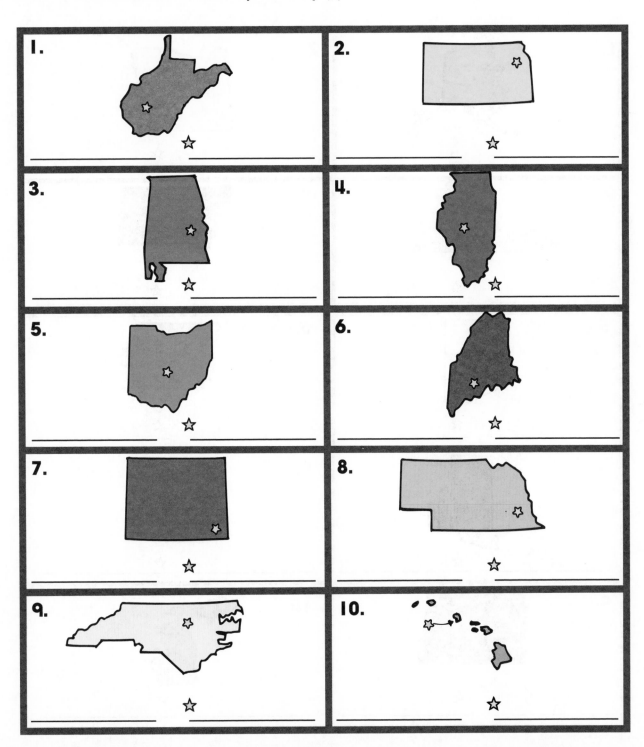

1. _____ ☆ _____

2. _____ ☆ _____

3. _____ ☆ _____

4. _____ ☆ _____

5. _____ ☆ _____

6. _____ ☆ _____

7. _____ ☆ _____

8. _____ ☆ _____

9. _____ ☆ _____

10. _____ ☆ _____

Mystery States II

Can you identify these state shapes? Use a U.S. map to help you. Write the name of each state and its capital city ☆.

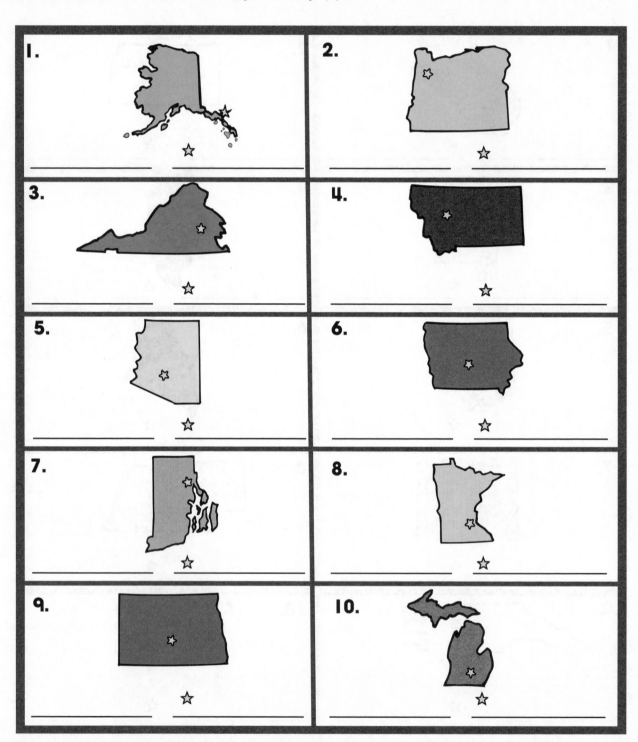

Mystery States III

Can you identify these state shapes? Use a U.S. map to help you. Write the name of each state and its capital city ☆.

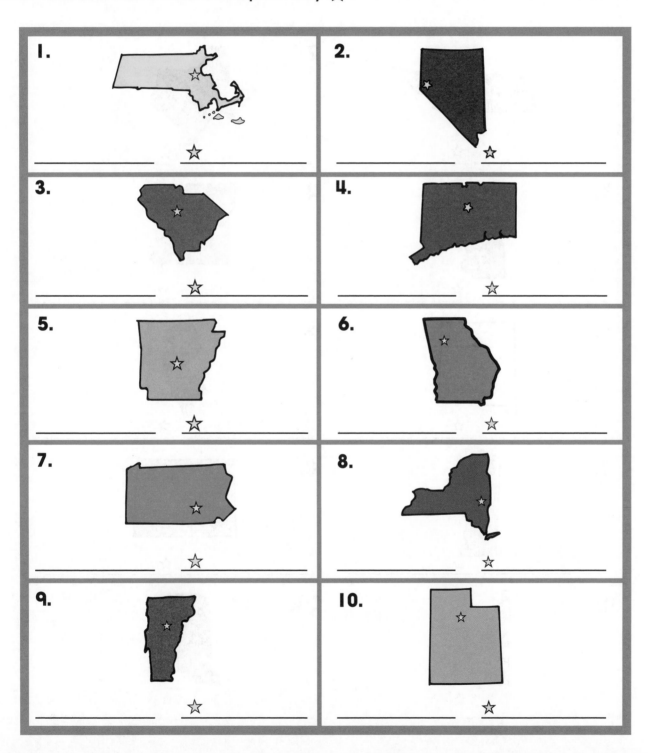

1. _____ ☆ _____

2. _____ ☆ _____

3. _____ ☆ _____

4. _____ ☆ _____

5. _____ ☆ _____

6. _____ ☆ _____

7. _____ ☆ _____

8. _____ ☆ _____

9. _____ ☆ _____

10. _____ ☆ _____

Mystery States IV

Can you identify these state shapes? Use a U.S. map to help you. Write the name of each state and its capital city ☆.

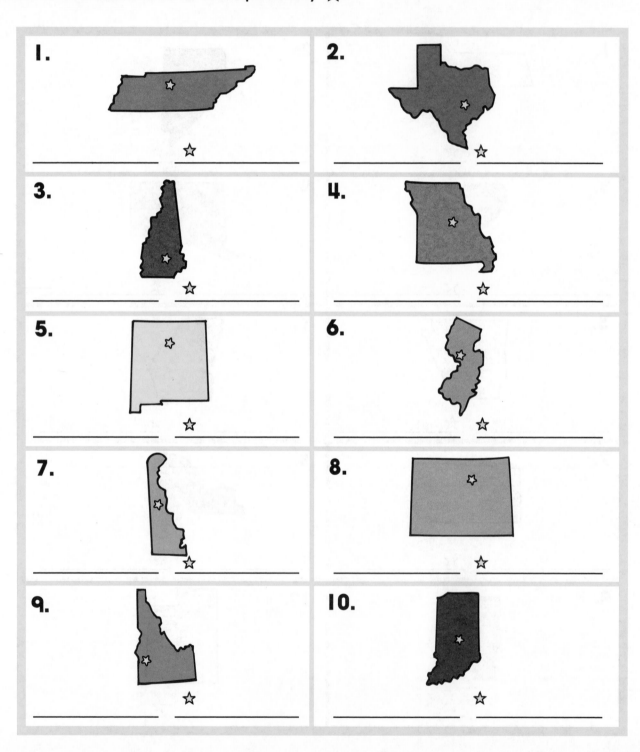

Mystery States V

Can you identify these state shapes? Use a U.S. map to help you. Write the name of each state and its capital city ☆.

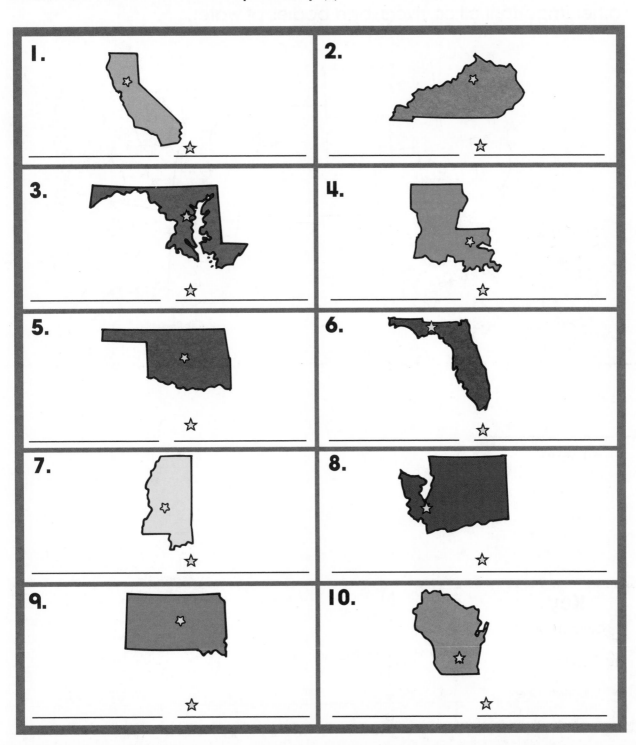

1. _____ ☆ _____

2. _____ ☆ _____

3. _____ ☆ _____

4. _____ ☆ _____

5. _____ ☆ _____

6. _____ ☆ _____

7. _____ ☆ _____

8. _____ ☆ _____

9. _____ ☆ _____

10. _____ ☆ _____

My Hometown

Find and color your state on the United States map. Then, draw an outline map of your state in the space below. Label your hometown, capital, and any other important cities, rivers, and bodies of water.

My State

Key

😊 Hometown

☆ Capital

● Important Cities

N
W ← → E
S

Name_____

Near My State

Use a map of the United States to locate your state. Write the names of any bordering states, countries, or bodies of water on the chart below. Write each one in its correct location relative to your state.

Northwest	North	Northeast
West	**My State**	**East**
	Draw an outline of your state.	
Southwest	**South**	**Southeast**

"We're Going Places" Mileage Chart

Let's take a trip around your state. On the left side of the chart, fill in the names of five cities in your state. The first one should be your hometown. Then, write the names of five additional cities or places to visit in your state across the top. Use a state highway map or other source to find the number of miles between each place. Complete the chart.

Places to Visit in My State

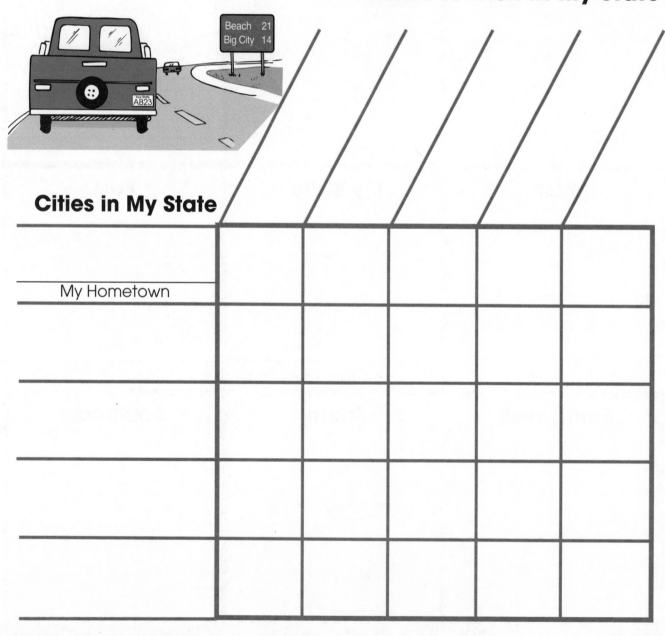

Cities in My State

My Hometown

Boundary Bonanza

Directions: Use the United States map on page 116 to answer these questions about boundaries.

1. Which state is made of islands?   _____

2. Which state is south of Utah?   _____

3. Which state is northeast of Idaho? _____

4. Which states are east of Ohio?   _____

5. Which state is west of Arkansas?   _____

6. Which state lies between Colorado and Missouri?   _____

7. Which three states are just south of Michigan?   _____

8. Which states touch New York on its eastern border?

_____, _____, _____.

9. Which state is in the northeast corner of the United States? _____

10. Which state is south of Oklahoma?   _____

11. Which states border the Gulf of Mexico? _____,

_____, _____, _____, _____ .

12. The only state that borders Maine is _____.

13. Four states that border Texas are _____,

_____, _____ and _____.

14. The state south of North Dakota is _____.

15. The state southwest of Nebraska is _____.

Across the Line

This is a map of the United States. The lines show the boundaries (the lines that separate one state from another) of each state. Use this map with pages 115 and 117.

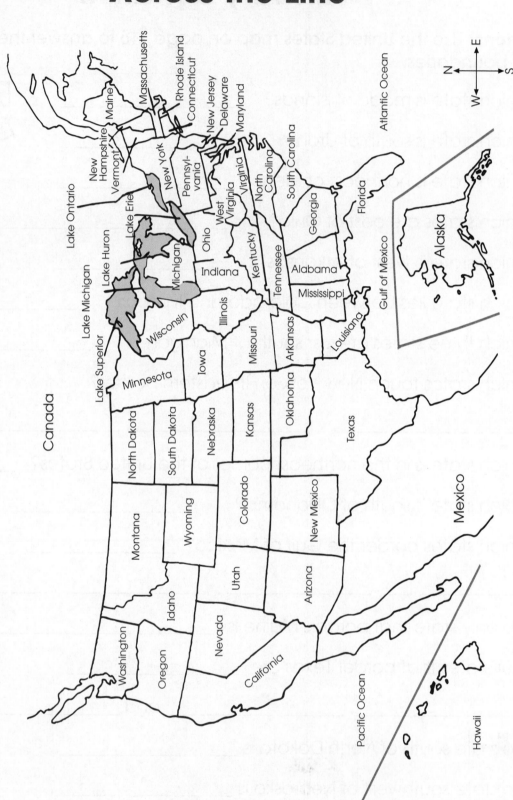

Across the Line

Directions: Use the United States map on page 116 to complete the following.

1. What is the name of the state in which you live? _____

2. Draw a blue line along the boundary lines of the state where you live.

3. What country is north of the United States? _____

4. Draw a green line along the northern boundary of the United States.

5. What country is south of the United States? _____

6. Draw an orange line along the southern boundary of the United States.

7. Find the state, country, or body of water that is the

    a. northern boundary of your state.
        Color it green.

    b. eastern boundary of your state.
        Color it blue.

    c. southern boundary of your state.
        Color it yellow.

    d. western boundary of your state.
        Color it red.

Water Watch

Some of the largest lakes in the United States are shown on the map. Find and color them blue. Then, go on to page 119.

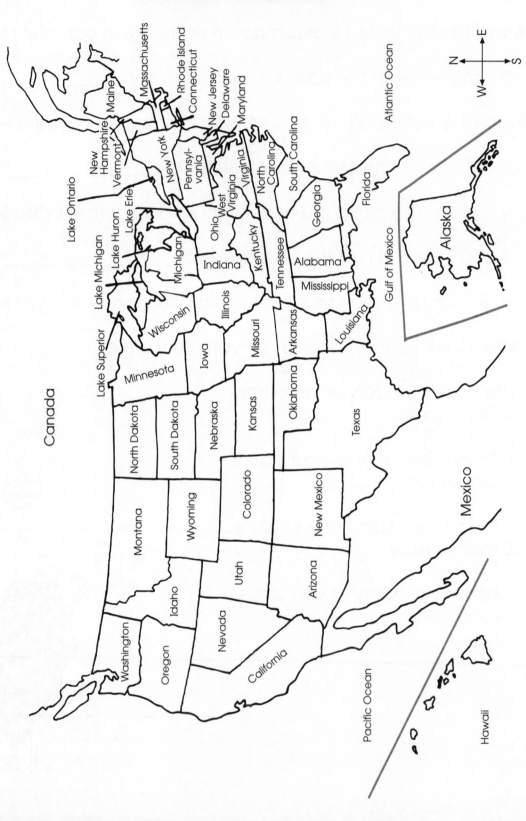

Name _____

Water Watch

Directions: Use the United States maps on pages 118 and 120 to answer the questions.

1. The lakes along the northern border of the United States are called the Great Lakes. Write the names of these five lakes.

   _____

   _____

2. Which river flows along the border between Canada and Minnesota?

   _____

3. What two rivers flow through Utah?

   _____

4. Which river flows along the border between Washington and Oregon?

   _____

5. Circle the name of the river that flows along the border between Mexico and the United States.

   Mississippi River   Rio Grande River   Yukon River   Missouri River

6. Circle the name of the river that flows through the state of Alaska.

   Mississippi River   Rio Grande River   Yukon River   Missouri River

7. How many states does the Mississippi River flow through or past? _____

Rivers Run Through It

This map shows the United States' major rivers. Trace the rivers in blue. Then, use the map to answer the river riddles on page 121.

Hudson R.

St. Lawrence R.

Allegheny R.

Potomac R.

Roanoke R.

Ohio R.

Tennessee R.

Alabama R.

Illinois R.

Rainy R.

Mississippi R.

Missouri R.

Arkansas R.

Red R.

Yellowstone R.

Green R.

Rio Grande R.

Colorado R.

Snake R.

Columbia R.

Sacramento R.

Yukon R.

N NE E SE S SW W NW

Rivers Run Through It

Directions: Use the United States map on page 120 to answer the questions.

1. I form the southwest border of Texas. _____

2. I am the Ohio River. I form the southern borders for which three states?

    _____

3. I separate Oregon and Washington. _____

4. I am located between the Great Lakes and the Gulf of St. Lawrence.

    _____

5. I cut through Colorado, Kansas, Oklahoma and Arkansas.

    _____

6. I flow into the Colorado River in Utah. _____

7. I am a New York river. _____

8. I run across the state of Idaho._____

9. I am located mainly in Pennsylvania and flow into the Ohio River.

    _____

10. I begin in Wyoming and run into the Missouri River._____

11. I flow through the state of Virginia. _____

12. I run from Chicago to St. Louis._____

13. I form the northeast border of Texas._____

14. I am located in northern California. _____

15. What rivers are near your home? Write about them. _____

    _____

    _____

River Boundaries

Directions: Write the number from the United States map by the name of each river.

____ Colorado River   ____Mississippi River   ____Columbia River   ____Ohio River

Use the map above to answer the questions.

1. The Columbia River forms a natural boundary between which two states?

   _____ and _____

2. The Mississippi River forms all or part of the eastern borders of these states:

   _____, _____, _____,

   _____, and _____.

3. The Ohio River forms the southern borders of which three states?

   _____, _____, and _____

4. The Colorado River forms a short border between _____

   and _____.

Up the Lazy River

"The steamboat is coming!" was a cry heard in the many small river towns in the 1800s. Steamboats carried people and packages along the waterways before the faster railroads were developed.

The shipping tags below tell where each package is beginning and ending its journey. Use a map, atlas, or the Internet to find the river on which the steamboat will be traveling. Some steamboats may have to travel on more than one river.

Directions: Write the name of the river route on each shipping tag.

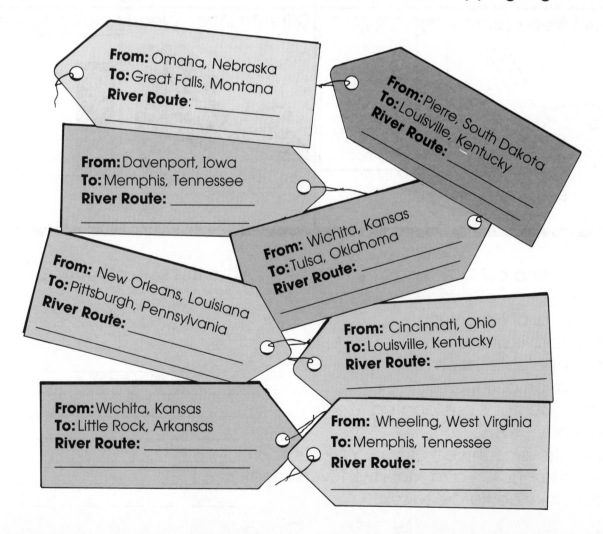

From: Omaha, Nebraska
To: Great Falls, Montana
River Route: _____
_____

From: Pierre, South Dakota
To: Louisville, Kentucky
River Route: _____

From: Davenport, Iowa
To: Memphis, Tennessee
River Route: _____
_____

From: Wichita, Kansas
To: Tulsa, Oklahoma
River Route: _____
_____

From: New Orleans, Louisiana
To: Pittsburgh, Pennsylvania
River Route: _____
_____

From: Cincinnati, Ohio
To: Louisville, Kentucky
River Route: _____

From: Wichita, Kansas
To: Little Rock, Arkansas
River Route: _____
_____

From: Wheeling, West Virginia
To: Memphis, Tennessee
River Route: _____
_____

Name_____

Focusing on Four

Shown are four kinds of maps.

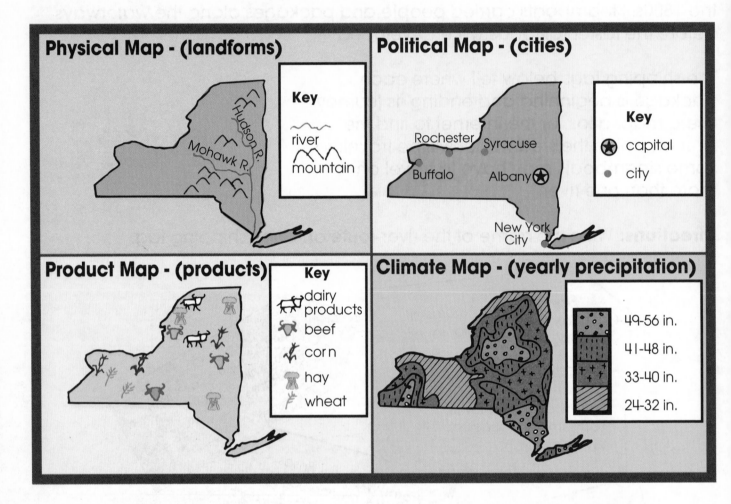

To find out . . .   Use this kind of map . . .

1. the capital of New York   _____
2. where corn is grown   _____
3. inches of precipitation   _____
4. the location of Buffalo   _____
5. where mountains are located   _____
6. where hay grows   _____
7. if Syracuse is northwest of New York City _____
8. where the Hudson and Mohawk Rivers meet _____
9. where dairy cattle are raised   _____

Political Maps

Political maps not only show where cities are located, they also show boundary lines between states and between countries.

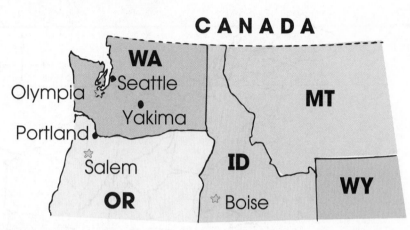

Key

State boundary _____
International boundary _ _ _ _
Cities •
State capitals ⭐

Use a map, atlas, or other resource to help you label the names of the states and cities on the political map of the United States on page 126. Use the states' postal abbreviations. As you complete the map, cross off each state in the list below.

States

Alabama	AL	Louisiana	LA	Ohio	OH
Alaska	AK	Maine	ME	Oklahoma	OK
Arizona	AZ	Maryland	MD	Oregon	OR
Arkansas	AR	Massachusetts	MA	Pennsylvania	PA
California	CA	Michigan	MI	Rhode Island	RI
Colorado	CO	Minnesota	MN	South Carolina	SC
Connecticut	CT	Mississippi	MS	South Dakota	SD
Delaware	DE	Missouri	MO	Tennessee	TN
Florida	FL	Montana	MT	Texas	TX
Georgia	GA	Nebraska	NE	Utah	UT
Hawaii	HI	Nevada	NV	Vermont	VT
Idaho	ID	New Hampshire	NH	Virginia	VA
Illinois	IL	New Jersey	NJ	Washington	WA
Indiana	IN	New Mexico	NM	West Virginia	WV
Iowa	IA	New York	NY	Wisconsin	WI
Kansas	KS	North Carolina	NC	Wyoming	WY
Kentucky	KY	North Dakota	ND		

Cities and State Capitals

Chicago, Illinois
Los Angeles, California
Atlanta, Georgia
Seattle, Washington

New York City, New York
Miami, Florida
Washington D.C.
Boston, Massachusetts

Philadelphia, Pennsylvania
Detroit, Michigan
Denver, Colorado
St. Louis, Missouri

United States Maps

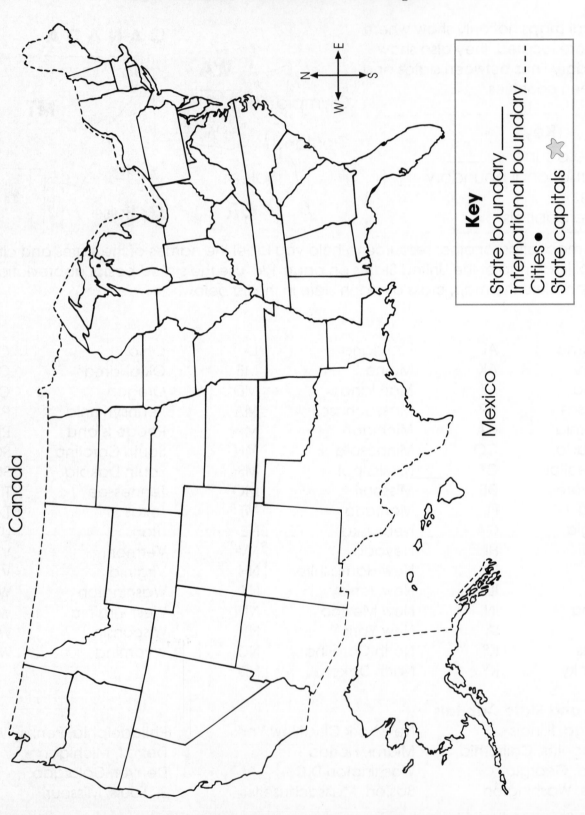

Key
State boundary
International boundary
Cities •
State capitals ⭐

Canada

Mexico

State Smart

Use this map of some of the states to answer the questions below.

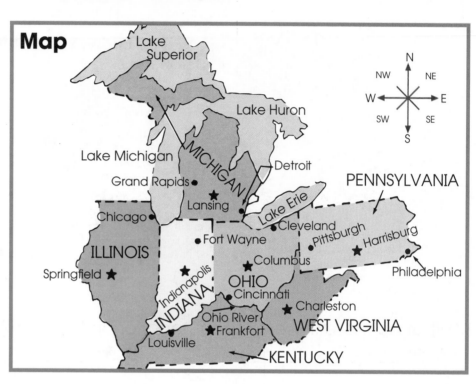

Key
- ★ state capital
- • city
- ~ river
- --- state

1. What state is west of Ohio? _____

2. The capital of West Virginia is _____.

3. Pittsburgh is a city in the state of _____.

4. What Ohio city is on the Ohio River? _____

5. Which state is southwest of Michigan? _____

6. What lake is west of Michigan? _____

7. Frankfort is the capital of _____.

8. What is the capital of Indiana? _____

9. Springfield is the capital of _____.

10. Chicago is _____ of Springfield, Illinois.

11. What Ohio city is northeast of Columbus? _____

12. Grand Rapids is _____ of Lansing, Michigan.

13. What state is east of Illinois? _____

14. What lake forms part of the northern border of Ohio? _____

What is a Political Map?

Midwestern United States

Legend
capital cities ★
cities ●
state boundaries --------

1. What do these three symbols stand for on this map?

   A. ★ _____   B. ● _____

   C. _ _ _ _ _ _ _ _____

2. The _____ forms the boundary between Missouri and Illinois.

3. _____ forms part of the boundary between Wisconsin and Michigan.

4. The eastern boundary of North Dakota is formed by the _____.

5. Ohio's western boundary is shared by the state of_____.

6. The southern part of Iowa is bordered by the state of _____.

7. What are the capital cities of these states?

   A. Kansas   _____   D. North Dakota _____

   B. Indiana   _____   E. Michigan   _____

   C. Wisconsin _____   F. Illinois   _____

8. The _____ River is north of Indianapolis.

9. Name the four lakes shown on this map. _____
   _____

10. Name the river which cuts South Dakota in half. _____

11. The northeastern border of Michigan is formed by Lake_____.

12. Chicago is on the coast of Lake _____.

Counties in Arizona

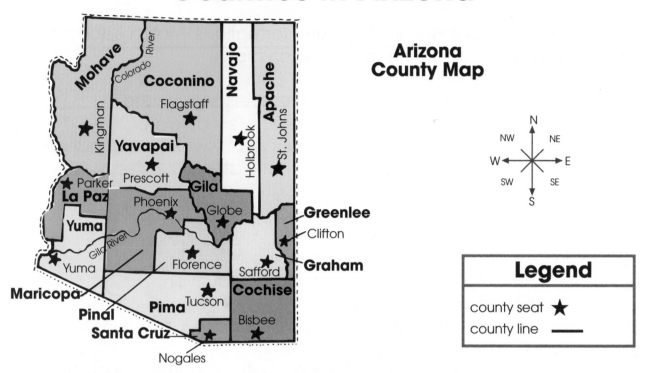

Arizona County Map

Legend

county seat	★
county line	——

1. What do these symbols stand for on the map?

   A. ★ _____   B. —— _____

2. What county is located in the southwest corner of the state?_____

3. Is Pima County in the northern or southern part of Arizona? _____

4. Name the county seat for each county listed.

   A. Cochise _____   D. Yuma _____

   B. Mohave _____   E. Coconino _____

   C. Greenlee _____   F. Navajo _____

5. Is Cochise east or west of Pima County? _____

6. The county directly north of Yuma is _____.

7. What is the county seat for Santa Cruz? _____

8. Name the county that is south of Graham County. _____

9. What is the smallest county in Arizona? _____

10. Name the river that flows through Yuma County. _____

11. The county seat of Pinal is _____.

12. Which county and county seat have the same name? _____

Natural Wonders

The earth's physical features are its natural formations. Match each formation with its definition by writing a number in each blank.

_____ river	1. land rising high above the land around it
_____ bay	2. land surrounded completely by water
_____ island	3. piece of land surrounded by water on all but one side
_____ gulf	4. inlet of a large body of water that extends into the land; smaller than a gulf
_____ mountain	5. an opening in the earth's crust that spills lava, rock, and gases
_____ plain	6. large inland body of water
_____ lake	7. lowland between hills or mountains
_____ peninsula	8. long, narrow body of water
_____ valley	9. large area of flat grasslands
_____ volcano	10. vast body of salt water
_____ ocean	11. large area of a sea or ocean partially enclosed by land

Directions: Write each feature's number on the map.

Features Map

Landforms and Physical Features

Look at the different landforms and physical features found in the picture.

Label the ten landforms on the picture. Then, write the name of each landform next to its definition below.

mountain   lake   peninsula   basin   canyon
plain   plateau   hill   island   river

• a large area of flat or gently sloping land _____

• a body of land completely surrounded by water _____

• a deep valley with steep sides_____

• a body of land surrounded by water on three sides_____

• an area of flat land that is higher than the surrounding land_____

• a low region surrounded by higher land_____

• a large stream of water that flows into a larger body of water_____

• a natural elevation smaller than a mountain _____

• a body of water that is completely surrounded by land _____

• a very high hill _____

Land Regions

Physical maps show natural features of the earth such as water, mountains, deserts, and high and low regions. Follow the directions to complete the map.

Physical Map

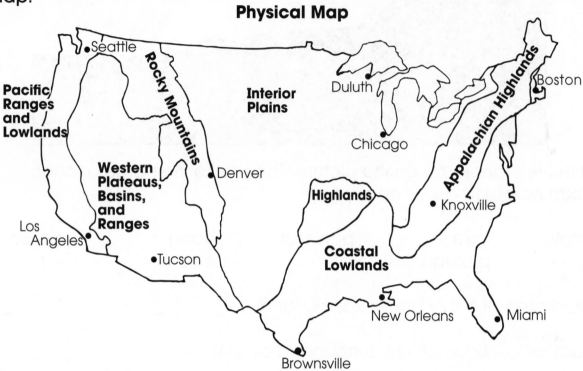

1. Draw brown ⌒ in the mountain and highland regions.

2. Draw orange ⹀ on the Pacific Ranges and Lowlands.

3. Color the 5 Great Lakes blue.

4. Draw green ⌇ on the Coastal Lowlands.

5. Draw red ///////// in the Western Plateaus, Basins, and Ranges.

6. Color the Interior Plains yellow.

7. Name one city found in the mountains. _____

8. Name one city found in the Coastal Lowlands. _____

Physical Features of the United States

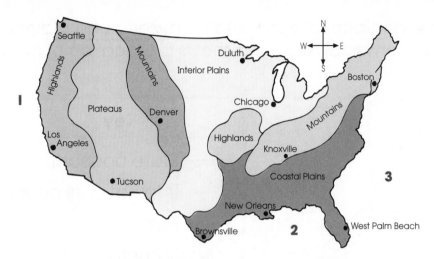

Directions: Use the map to answer the questions below.

1. Name the two cities on the map found in mountain areas.

   _____

2. Name the three cities found on coastal plains.

   _____

3. Seattle and Los Angeles are found on which coast—east or west? _____

4. Name the two cities located on the interior plains.

   _____

5. Your home state is located on which type of land? _____

Use a map of North America and the map above to answer these questions.

1. Identify the bodies of water marked with numbers on the map above.
   (1) _____ (2) _____ (3) _____

2. The mountains on the eastern side of the United States are the

   _____.

3. The _____ Mountains are in the western part of the United States.

Physical Maps

Maps that show landforms like mountains, deserts, and plains are called physical maps. A physical map also shows the location of rivers, lakes, and oceans.

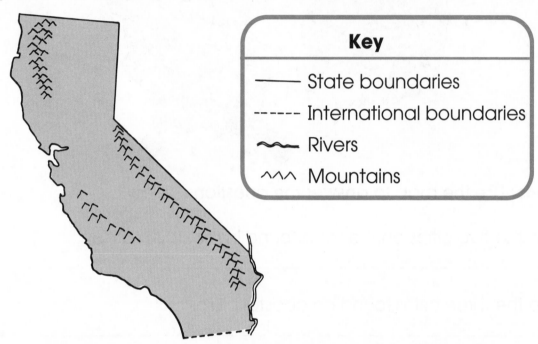

Key

——— State boundaries

------ International boundaries

∿∿ Rivers

⋀⋀⋀ Mountains

Use a map, atlas, or the Internet to help you locate the physical features listed below. Find them on the Physical Map of the United States on page 132.

Rivers
Mississippi River
Missouri River
Colorado River
Ohio River
Hudson River
Arkansas River

Lakes
Great Salt Lake
Lake Michigan
Lake Superior
Lake Huron
Lake Erie
Lake Ontario

Oceans and Sea
Pacific Ocean
Atlantic Ocean
Gulf of Mexico

Mountains
Sierra Nevada Mountains
Cascade Mountains

Land Regions
Great Plains
Mojave Desert
Great Basin

Types of Land

Directions: Use this map of the United States and another map, atlas, or the Internet to answer the questions.

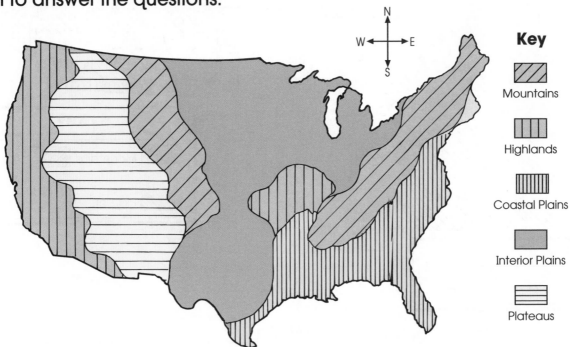

1. The western coast of the United States is composed of _____.

2. The central part of the United States is _____.

3. The northeastern part of the United States has_____.

4. What does the symbol ▤ stand for on the map? _____

5. In which part of the United States will you find coastal plains?_____

6. The state of California is mostly _____.

7. Florida is composed of _____.

8. The southwestern part of Texas is _____.

9. What symbol is used to show mountains? _____

Comparing Two States

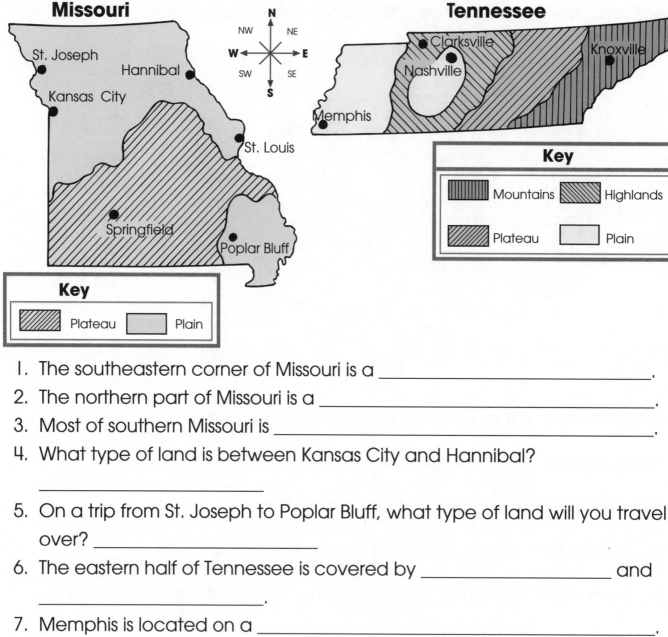

Missouri

Tennessee

Key
- Mountains
- Highlands
- Plateau
- Plain

Key
- Plateau
- Plain

1. The southeastern corner of Missouri is a _____.

2. The northern part of Missouri is a _____.

3. Most of southern Missouri is _____.

4. What type of land is between Kansas City and Hannibal?

   _____

5. On a trip from St. Joseph to Poplar Bluff, what type of land will you travel over? _____

6. The eastern half of Tennessee is covered by _____ and

   _____.

7. Memphis is located on a _____.

8. What two features do Tennessee and Missouri share?

   _____ and _____

9. The central part of Tennessee is mostly _____.

10. What types of land will you cross between Memphis and Knoxville?

    _____

11. Which state is almost half plateau? _____

Alaska and New York

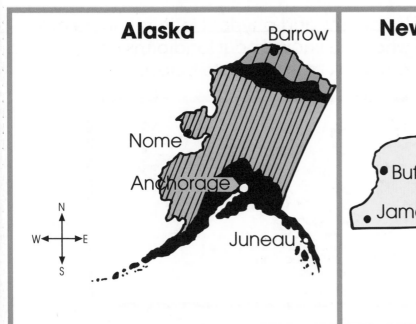

Key

/////	Arctic Region (tundra)
■	Mountains
/////	Plateaus and Lowlands

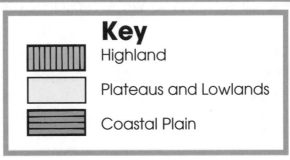

Key

‖‖‖	Highland
☐	Plateaus and Lowlands
▭	Coastal Plain

1. Barrow is part of the_____ Region.
2. Most of Alaska is covered with _____.
3. The southern part of Alaska is _____.
4. What type of land would you travel over from Barrow to Juneau?

   _____
5. The northeastern part of New York is mostly _____.
6. Both New York and Alaska have _____and lowlands.
7. Plattsburgh, New York, is located in which part of the state—southwest or
   northeast? _____
8. The western half of New York is composed of _____.
9. The extreme northern part of New York is a _____.
10. Is Nome on the eastern or western coast of Alaska? _____

Poetic Forms

Just as there are many kinds of landforms and physical features, there are also many forms of poetry. Use what you know about landforms and physical features to write a diamanté poem. Look at the sample below.

Michigan
Swimming, skiing, and sailing
Home of automobiles, cereal, and furniture
Green, sandy, beautiful
Peninsula

Follow the directions to write a diamanté poem about a place:

line one	_____	place name
line two	_____	2 or 3 things to do there
line three	_____	3 or 4 words telling what it is known for
line four	_____	2 or 3 adjectives describing it
line five	_____	landform or physical feature

Now it's your turn to write a diamanté. Choose a place with a special landform or physical feature. It might have a cape, island, peninsula, mountain, canyon, or desert.

_____

_____

_____

_____

_____

Natural Wonders of the United States

Listed below are ten natural physical features found in the United States. Use an encyclopedia, atlas, or the Internet to complete the chart. Write the number of each feature on the U.S. Products and Natural Resources Map on page 140.

Natural Feature	State	Description
1. Devil's Tower		
2. Grand Canyon		
3. Denali		
4. Everglades		
5. Mount St. Helens		
6. Kilauea		
7. Carlsbad Caverns		
8. Cape Cod		
9. Badlands National Park		
10. Mojave Desert		

U.S. Products and Natural Resources

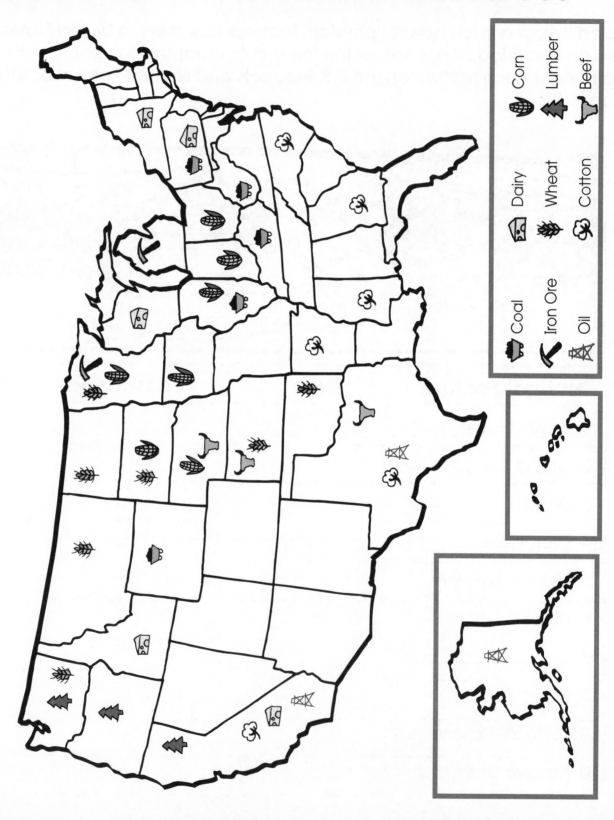

Use with page 139 and page 141.

U.S. Products and Natural Resources

The United States is one of the world's largest producers of manufactured goods because it is very rich in natural resources.

Look at the U.S. Products and Natural Resources map to see which states are the chief suppliers of certain products and natural resources.

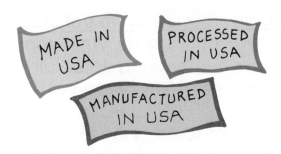

Directions: For each product or natural resource listed below, use the map on page 140 to name the states that are major suppliers.

Coal

_____

_____

_____

_____

Iron Ore

_____

_____

_____

_____

Oil

_____

_____

_____

_____

Corn

_____

_____

_____

_____

Wheat

_____

_____

_____

_____

Cotton

_____

_____

_____

_____

Dairy

_____

_____

_____

_____

Lumber

_____

_____

_____

_____

Beef

_____

_____

_____

_____

Grocery Store Geography

Many foods that we eat are not grown in our own communities. While some foods come from neighboring states, others come from countries halfway around the world.

Look at some of the foods in your cupboard and refrigerator at home. Check the labels to find out where they came from. Then, go to a grocery store and look at the labels on some other foods. Where did they come from? Look at the fruits and vegetables in the produce area. Many of them probably came from far away. Ask the grocer or produce manager where some of the fruits and vegetables are from.

Directions: Complete the chart.

Food	Where It Was Grown	Kind of Transportation Used to Ship the Food

On a map, locate where these foods were grown.

Which food was shipped the greatest distance? _____

How far did it travel to reach your grocery store? _____

Grocery Store Geography

Many foods are shipped long distances. Create a display to show how far some have traveled.

You will need:
Grocery Store Geography (page 142)
an outline of the United States
a large piece of posterboard or paper
markers or crayons
glue

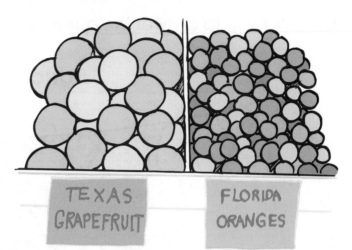

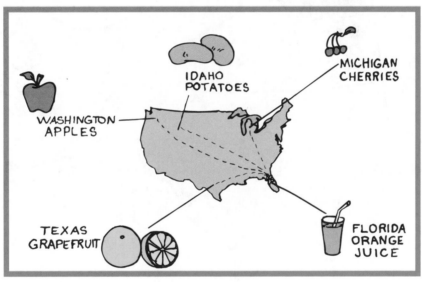

Directions:

1. Glue the outline map of the United States in the middle of your posterboard.
2. Label and color the states where each type of food on your food chart comes from.
3. Draw a picture of each food or cut out pictures from magazines to glue around the border of the poster. Draw a line from the food to where it is grown.
4. Label your community on the map with a star.
5. Draw a dotted line from the product source to your community.

Tilling the Soil

Use this map to answer the questions on page 145.

Agriculture Map

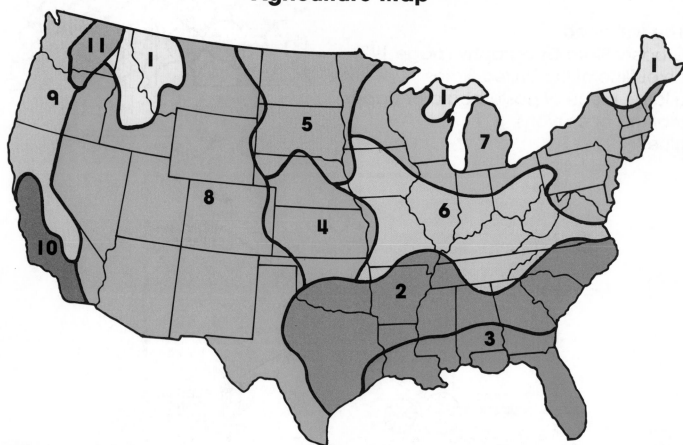

Legend

1. Timber	**5.** Spring wheat	**9.** Pacific hay, pasture, and timber
2. Cotton	**6.** Corn and livestock	
3. Sub-tropical fruits, vegetables	**7.** Dairy, hardy crops	**10.** Pacific fruits and vegetables
4. Winter wheat	**8.** Livestock ranching	**11.** Wheat

Tilling the Soil

Directions: Use the map on page 144 to answer the questions below.

1. The far northeastern corner of the United States has _____.
2. What types of crops are found on the Pacific Coast?
   _____
3. What is a common crop grown in many southern states? _____
4. What two types of wheat are grown in 4 and 5?_____
5. Much of the land in the western part of the United States is used for
   _____.
6. What is most of the land in your state used for? _____

Use the map on page 144 and a political map of the United States to help you answer the questions.

1. What crops are grown in Florida? _____
2. Name the states where cotton is a major crop. _____
   _____
   _____
3. The major crop in Kansas is _____.
4. The eastern part of Washington grows _____.
5. Southwestern California grows _____.
6. North and South Dakota are major producers of _____.
7. Which of these states is a major producer of corn—Maine, Illinois, or
   California? _____
8. What is done in western Texas? _____
9. Michigan and Wisconsin produce _____.
10. Most of Nebraska produces winter _____.
11. Hay, pasture, and timber are produced in _____California.

Natural Resource Riddles

U.S. Products and Natural Resources—Leading States

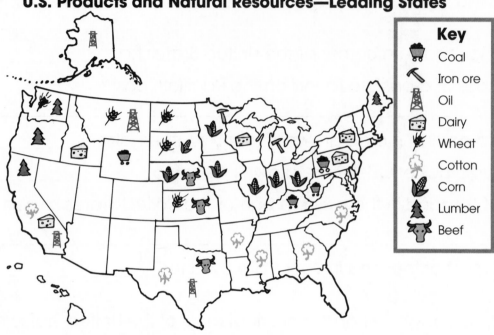

Key
- Coal
- Iron ore
- Oil
- Dairy
- Wheat
- Cotton
- Corn
- Lumber
- Beef

1. I am found in Alaska. _____

2. Montana is a leading producer of me. _____

3. New York produces me. _____

4. Illinois, Indiana, and Ohio are all leading producers of me._____

5. My name is lumber. Which states are leading suppliers of me?

   _____

6. Michigan is a leading supplier of me. _____

7. I am Texas. Name the products I produce. _____

   _____

8. I am Nebraska. Name my products._____

Products in California

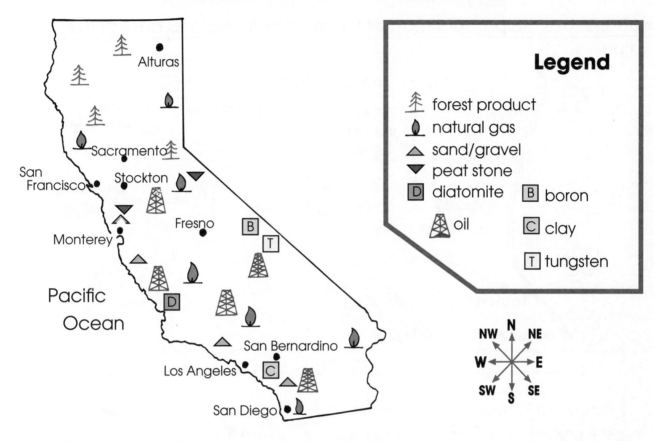

Legend

🌲 forest product
🔥 natural gas
▲ sand/gravel
▼ peat stone
D diatomite   B boron
🛢 oil   C clay
                T tungsten

1. Northwestern California produces mostly _____ products.

2. Southeast of San Diego natural _____ is produced.

3. Southeast of Stockton_____ is drilled.

4. North of Fresno _____ is mined.

5. On the map, the city southwest of Sacramento is _____ .

6. Is Monterey east or west of Fresno? _____

7. Name four products found east of Fresno. _____

8. Is San Bernardino east or west of Los Angeles? _____

9. What body of water is located west of California? _____

10. Is diatomite mined north or south of Los Angeles? _____

11. Is San Francisco northwest or southeast of Monterey? _____

12. Does California mine any gold near San Diego? _____

How Much Revenue?

Directions: Use the product map of this imaginary state to answer the questions.

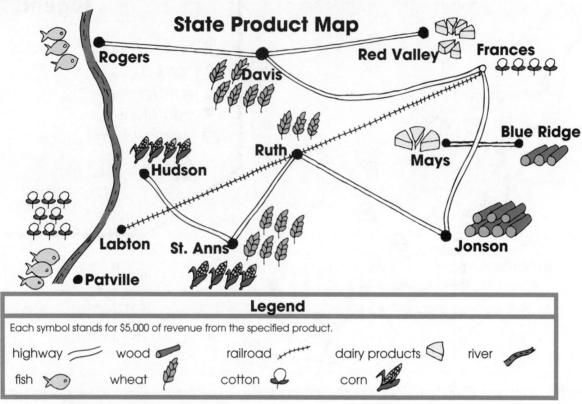

State Product Map

Legend

Each symbol stands for $5,000 of revenue from the specified product.

highway　⟋　　wood　🪵　　railroad　⊢⊢⊢　　dairy products　◁　　river　〰️

fish　🐟　　wheat　🌾　　cotton　✿　　corn　🌽

1. How much money, or revenue, does each symbol stand for? _____
2. How much does the state make from corn?_____
3. What product is grown near Jonson? _____
4. Does this state get more money from cotton or wood? _____
5. How much money does the state earn from fish? _____
6. Patville earns money by catching _____.
7. The town of Red Valley produces _____ products.
8. What is the shortest way to transport cotton from Labton to Rogers?
   _____
9. How much money does the corn grown at Hudson produce for the state?
   _____
10. How much money does wheat produce for the state? _____
11. What is grown near Ruth? _____

Products in the United States

Directions: Use the map and the legend to answer the questions below.

Legend

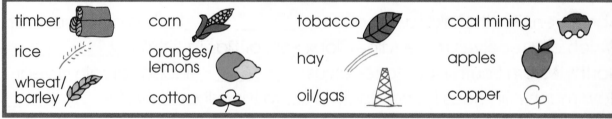

1. Which state grows apples?_____

2. How many states on this map grow oranges and lemons? _____

3. Both Arkansas and Louisiana grow _____.

4. Hay is grown in how many states? _____.

5. North and South Carolina both grow _____.

6. _____is produced in Maine.

7. Name the product grown in Alabama and Georgia. _____

8. Coal is mined in the states of _____.

9. Name the states that grow corn. _____

10. Name the products produced in California. _____

How Much Did it Rain?

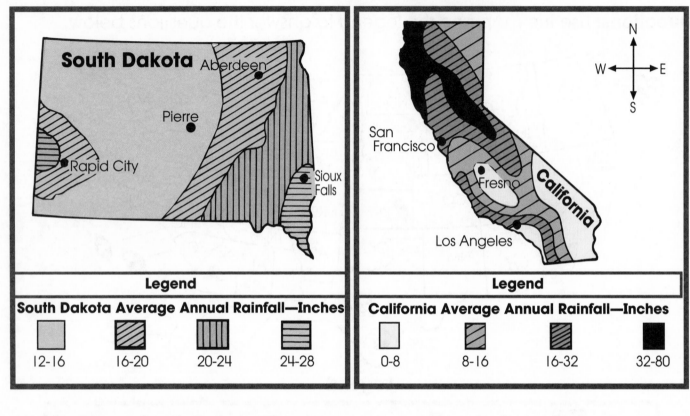

1. Aberdeen, South Dakota, receives _____inches of rain a year.

2. Which city receives more rain—Sioux Falls or Rapid City? _____

3. Northwestern South Dakota receives _____ inches of rain a year.

4. How much rain does Pierre, South Dakota, usually receive? _____

5. The southeastern corner of South Dakota receives _____inches of rain.

6. What does the symbol ☐ mean on the map of California? _____

7. Southeastern California receives_____inches of rain a year.

8. Los Angeles, California, receives an average of _____ inches of rain a year.

9. The northeastern part of California receives _____inches of rain.

10. What does this symbol ■ mean on the map of California? _____

11. Fresno, California, receives an average of _____inches of rain.

12. Which city receives more rain—Sioux Falls, South Dakota, or Fresno, California? _____

13. The extreme northwestern corner of California receives _____inches of rain a year.

Temperature Ranges

What is the average January temperature where you live? The average monthly temperature is figured using the daily temperatures for the whole month. This information can be found in most almanacs and encyclopedias. Why would it be helpful to know the average temperature of a city?

_____

_____

Directions: Use an almanac or encyclopedia fo find the average high and low temperatures for the cities listed below for January and July.

State	City	Average Monthly Temperatures (°F)			
		January High	Low	July High	Low
Alaska	Nome				
California	Los Angeles				
Colorado	Denver				
Florida	Tampa				
Iowa	Des Moines				
Michigan	Detroit				
New York	Syracuse				
North Dakota	Fargo				
South Carolina	Columbia				
Texas	Dallas				
Wisconsin	Madison				

Circle the highest temperature in each "high" column and the lowest temperature in each "low" column.

U.S. Climate Zones

The word climate is used to describe the weather in a particular place over a long period of time. Because the United States covers such a large area, it has a number of different climate zones. Some areas have long, cold winters and short, cool summers, while other areas are always warm in both the summer and the winter.

Key

1	☐ alpine	4	☐ mediterranean						
2	☐ steppe	5	☐ desert	7	☐ subtropical	9	☐ tropical		
3	☐ tundra	6	☐ continental	8	☐ marine	10	☐ subarctic		

Directions: Choose colors to color code the key and the climate zone map. Then, use the map to fill in the blanks.

* climate zone in which you live _____
* climate zone of the northeast _____
* climate zones of the Rocky Mountains _____
* three climate zones found in Alaska _____
* climate zones found in Texas _____
* climate zones of Florida _____
* climate zone of Michigan _____

Section 3
United States Regions

PACIFIC STATES

MOUNTAIN STATES

NORTH CENTRAL STATES

SOUTH CENTRAL STATES

MIDWEST STATES

NORTHEASTERN STATES

SOUTHEASTERN STATES

The Pacific States

The Pacific States is a region with majestic mountains, beautiful beaches and coastlines, thick green forests, and hot, dry deserts.

1. Washington

2. Oregon

3. California

4. Alaska

5. Hawaii

Name _____

Fill in the "Five Fundamental Themes of Geography" for each state. After "discovering" a state, fill in all the columns of the chart except **Regions**. When you have finished with all of the states in a section, fill in **Regions**.

Five Fundamental Themes of Geography					
Name of State	**Location** (Where is it?)	**Place** (What is it like?)	**People and Environment** (What do the people do?)	**Movement** (How do people, goods, and ideas move?)	**Regions** (What are some of the common features?)

Welcome to Washington

How Washington Became a State

Before the arrival of the Europeans, many Native American tribes lived in Washington, including the Nez Percé, Walla Walla, Spokane, Yakima, Makah, and Nooksak. In 1792, British naval officer, George Vancouver, mapped Puget Sound, and an American ship explored the Columbia River. By the early 1800s, Washington's rich wildlife and natural resources attracted British and American fur traders. The Columbia River offered easy access from the sea to the territory. The fur traders built their forts along the Columbia River. The Americans built Fort Okanogan, while the Canadians set up Spokane House. By 1824, the British Hudson's Bay Company had established Fort Vancouver.

State Flag

Soon, the first missionaries began arriving. Marcus Whitman founded a missionary settlement at Walla Walla in 1836. By 1846, the border with Canada was agreed upon. Within two years, hundreds of settlers came by way of the Oregon Trail. Washington became the forty-second state on November 11, 1889.

Famous Washingtonians

- Bing Crosby was a well-known singer and actor.
- Bill Gates founded Microsoft, a computer software company.
- Edward R. Murrow was a reporter and television news pioneer.
- Richard Hugo was an award-winning poet.
- Gary Larson created *The Far Side* cartoons.
- Henry M. Jackson was an important U.S. senator.
- Judy Collins is a singer and songwriter.

State Greats

- The Boeing airplane plant in Everett is the largest building in the United States. It covers 98 acres.
- Olympic National Park protects the North American seashore and temperate rainforest.
- Mount St. Helens, a volcano, erupted in 1980.
- Microsoft's headquarters near Seattle has made Washington a leading state in computer software technology.
- Mount Rainier has more glaciers than any other single peak in the United States. It is Washington's highest mountain.
- The state's trees are an important resource. Timber from Washington is shipped all over the country.

Name _____

Washington: The Evergreen State

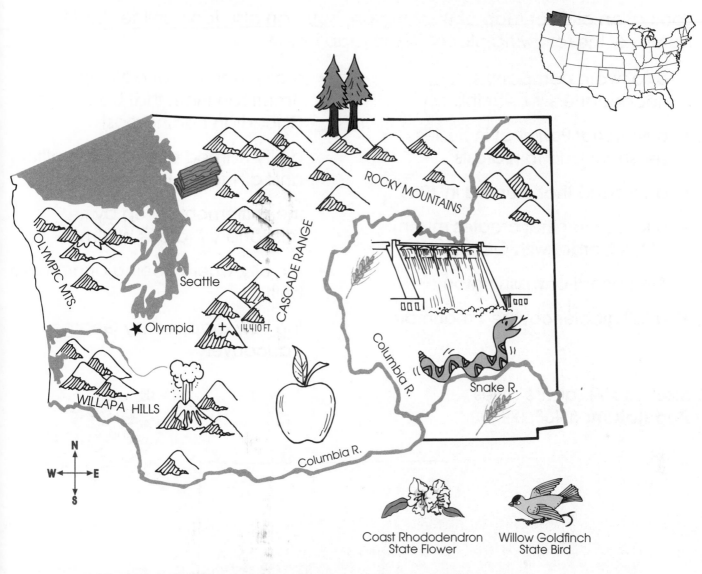

Coast Rhododendron
State Flower

Willow Goldfinch
State Bird

- named for the first president—George Washington
- nicknamed the Evergreen State for the abundance of evergreen trees

 Mount Rainier—14,410 ft.

 Mount St. Helens—erupted on May 18, 1980

 Grand Coulee Dam—largest concrete dam in United States

 Apples—leads the states in apple production

Circle the capital city. Locate the landmarks found in the above key. Color them on the map.

Washington: The Evergreen State

Look at an atlas or map of Washington. You can also look online. Add the names of the following places to the map below.

- a software company's headquarters is near this city

- a National Park that includes seashore and rainforests

- a volcano that erupted in 1980

- a large river that creates much of the border with Oregon

- the capital of Washington

- a tall glacier-covered mountain

- a city, named for a Native American tribe, that began as a Canadian trading post

- a city named after a British officer and a Hudson Bay fort

- the settlement set up by missionary Marcus Whitman

- the city where Boeing aircraft are built

- the bay mapped by George Vancouver

Size: 68,139 square miles
Population: 6,468,424

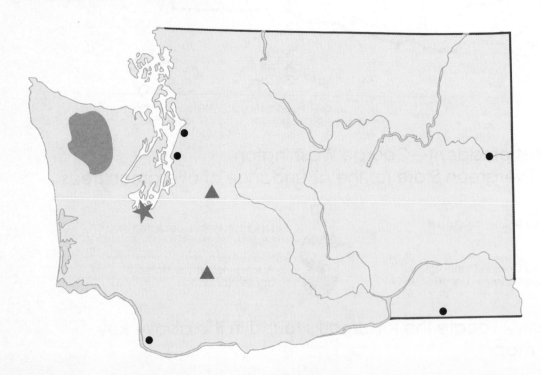

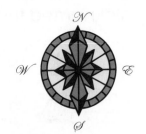

Washington: The Evergreen State

Complete the crossword puzzle below.

Across

1. the capital city
3. an American fort
6. the name of a British explorer and a modern city
8. a famous cartoonist
9. a television pioneer

Down

2. the name of a Native American tribe
4. the Hudson's Bay Company and the Americans wanted this
5. Mount St. Helens is one, and so is Mount Rainier
7. an important forest resource

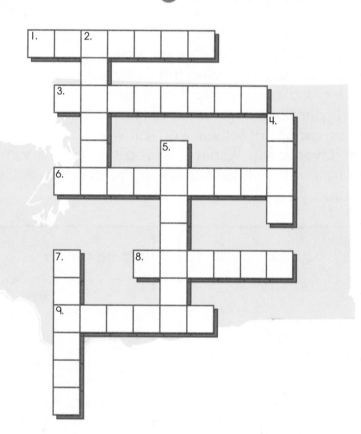

How many of Washington's larger cities were built along the Columbia River? Write about why you think settlers chose to live along the river.

_____

_____

_____

_____

Name_____

Welcome to Oregon

How Oregon Became a State

The Cascade Mountain Range runs from north to south across Oregon, creating a green forested coastline to the west and dry plateaus to the east. Before the first Europeans arrived, both areas were inhabited by Native Americans. The territory was home to over 100 different tribes, including the Nez Percé, Chinook, Cayuse, and Yakima. Once Captain Robert Gray sailed up the mighty Columbia River in 1792, explorers and fur traders soon followed.

State Flag

In 1805, the famous explorers Lewis and Clark traveled overland from the east and traveled along the Columbia River. Not realizing how close they were to the ocean, they built a shelter and spent a terrible winter at Fort Clatsop. By 1834, the first groups of settlers were arriving in the fertile Willamette River valley. Within nine years, large wagon trains of people were following the Oregon Trail west, in hopes of finding land and wealth. Oregon became the thirty-third state on February 14, 1859.

Famous Oregonians

- Barbara Roberts was Oregon's first female governor.
- Raymond Carver was an author and poet.
- Chief Joseph was a great Nez Percé leader.
- Phil Knight co-founded Nike, Inc.
- Gary Payton is a former professional basketball player.
- Mark Hatfield was governor and U.S. senator.
- Linus Pauling won Nobel prizes for chemistry and peace.
- Beverly Cleary won the Newbery Medal for children's literature.

State Greats

- A volcanic explosion of Mount Mazama created Crater Lake. Crater Lake is 1,943 feet deep, the deepest lake in the United States.
- Oregon Dunes National Recreation Area contains miles of seaside sand dunes for family enjoyment.
- Hells Canyon on the Snake River is 7,993 feet deep—deeper than the Grand Canyon.
- Ashland is home to an annual Shakespearean Festival.
- More than 75 percent of birds migrating along the Pacific "Flyway" stop in the national wildlife refuges near Upper Klamath Lake.

Name_____

Oregon: The Beaver State

Read the clues. Complete the words about Oregon.

an explorer's fort   __ __ __ __ __ O __

a children's author   __ __ __ __ R __

Chief Joseph's tribe   __ __ __   __ E __ __ __

he explored the Columbia River   G __ __ __

Pauling won two of these prizes   __ O __ __ __

a shoe man   __ N __ __ __ __

The Oregon state flag is the only American flag with two different sides. The front shows a heart shaped shield to stand for early Oregon. The back shows a beaver. On a sheet of paper, design a new Oregon flag. What would you use to stand for Oregon?

_____

_____

_____

_____

Oregon: The Beaver State

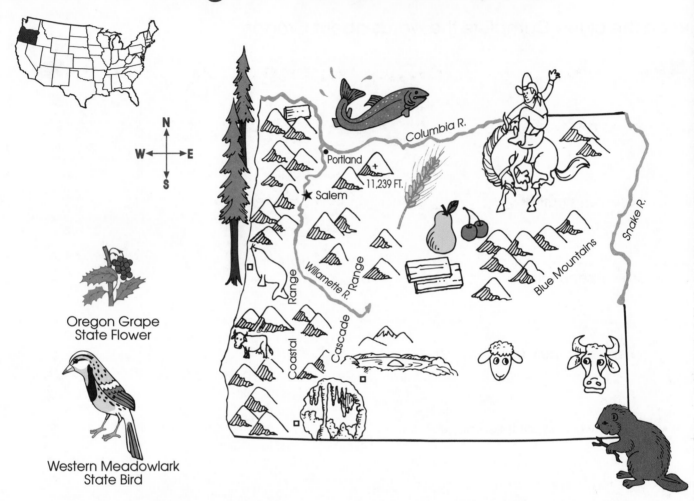

Oregon Grape
State Flower

Western Meadowlark
State Bird

- name originated from the French word ouragan, meaning hurricane
- nicknamed the Beaver State because the area supplied thousands of beaver skins during early fur trading

Mount Hood—11,239 ft.

Pendleton Round-Up

Sea Lion Caves

Oregon Caverns

Crater Lake—deepest lake in the United States

Circle the capital city. Locate the landmarks found in the above key. Color them on the map.

Name_____

Oregon: The Beaver State

Look at an atlas or map of Oregon. You can also look online. Add the names of the following places to the map below.

- Portland, the largest city and a port of the Columbia River

- a lake created when a volcano blew its top

- the deepest canyon in the United States

- the river found by Captain Robert Gray

- the state capital

- the location of Lewis and Clark's 1805–1806 winter camp

- the city that hosts a Shakespearean festival

- a family recreation area of beach sand dunes

- the mountain range that divides the state

- this river's valley was home to the first settlers

Size: 98,379 square miles
Population: 3,970,239

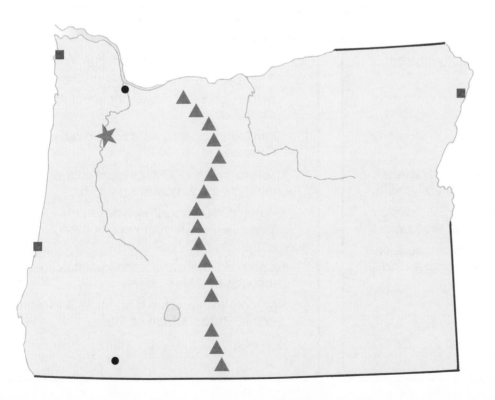

Welcome to California

State Flag

How California Became a State

When Portuguese explorer Juan Rodríguez Cabrillo sailed by the Californian coast for Spain in 1542, he claimed the area for Spain. At that time, more than 100 Native American tribes were living in California. In 1579, the British explorer Sir Francis Drake claimed California for England. The Spanish soon realized that they must settle California or lose their land. However, it was not until almost 200 years later, in 1769, that Father Junípero Serra built a mission in San Diego. It was the first of 21 missions. California was ruled by Spain until 1821, when Mexico won its independence. California was then a province of Mexico. American trappers and settlers settled in California around this time. Later, the United States declared war against Mexico and, in 1848, California became a United States territory. That same year, gold was found at Sutter's Mill near Sacramento. The gold rush brought people from all over the world to search for gold. On September 9, 1850, California became the thirty-first state.

Famous Californians

- Richard M. Nixon was the thirty-seventh president.
- John Steinbeck was a writer who set most of his novels in California.
- Sally Ride was the first American woman in space.
- Shirley Temple Black was a child actress and representative to the United Nations.
- General George Smith Patton, Jr., was a famous military leader during World War II.
- Ronald Reagan was our fortieth president and also governor of California. He had been an actor in films as well.

State Greats

- Disneyland, Walt Disney's first theme park, is located in a suburb of Los Angeles.
- Hollywood is the movie capital of the world.
- San Francisco is famous for its Golden Gate Bridge.
- Sequoia National Park's giant sequoia trees are the largest living things.
- Yosemite National Park is home to Yosemite Falls, the nation's highest waterfall.
- Death Valley contains the lowest point in the Western Hemisphere.
- Mount Whitney is the highest peak in the United States outside of Alaska.

California: The Golden State

Look at an atlas or map of California. You can also look online. Add the names of the following places to the map below.

- the capital city of California

- the place near where the Gold Rush started

- the city where Disneyland is located

- the place where the first mission was built

- the city where the Golden Gate Bridge is located

- the location of Yosemite Falls

- the highest mountain in the lower 48 states

- the location of the giant sequoia trees

- the lowest point in the Western Hemisphere

- the country that owned California until 1821

Size: 163,695 square miles
Population: 38,802,500

California: The Golden State

Read the clues. Unscramble the words about California.

★ the state flower   YPPOP   _ _ _ _ _

★ the tallest mountain in California TYHNIWE   _ _ _ _ _ _ _

★ the lowest place in California   EATDH AYLLVE _ _ _ _ _ _ _ _ _ _ _

★ a famous national park   OSMTYEIE   _ _ _ _ _ _ _ _

★ the Spanish built 21 of them   SISMNIOS   _ _ _ _ _ _ _ _

★ the movie capital of the world   LLDOOHYOW   _ _ _ _ _ _ _ _ _

★ the state nickname   OGDLNE   _ _ _ _ _ _

In the past, California was known as "The Bear Flag Republic." There is a grizzly bear on California's state seal and flag today. Draw a picture of the flag and write about why a grizzly bear might have been chosen.

_____

_____

_____

_____

The state seal has the word "Eureka" on it, which means "I have found it." Write about the things that were found in California.

_____

_____

_____

_____

California: The Golden State

California Valley Quail
State Bird

Golden Poppy
State Flower

- named by early explorers, possibly referring to a treasure island in a Spanish story
- nicknamed the Golden State, possibly for its gold fields, its golden pastures, and its sunshine

Mount Whitney—the highest point in the contiguous United States—14,494 ft.

Joshua Tree National Park

Golden Gate Bridge

Death Valley National Park

Lassen Volcanic National Park

Redwood National Park—contains world's tallest known tree

Circle the capital city. Locate the landmarks found in the above key. Color them on the map.

Alaska: The Last Frontier

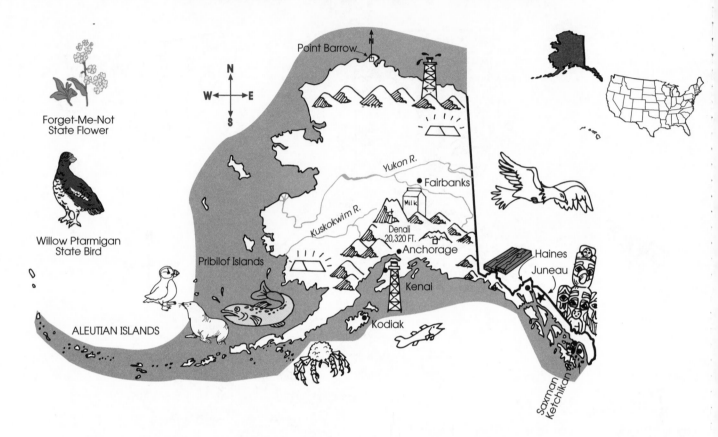

Forget-Me-Not State Flower

Willow Ptarmigan State Bird

N
W — E
S

Point Barrow

Yukon R.

Fairbanks

Kuskokwim R.

Milk

Denali 20,320 FT.

Anchorage

Pribilof Islands

Kenai

Haines

Juneau

Kodiak

ALEUTIAN ISLANDS

Saxman Ketchikan

- name came from the Aleutian word meaning *great land*, which refers to Alaska's size and its abundance of natural resources
- nickname the Last Frontier reflects the fact that much of the region is unsettled

 Point Barrow—northernmost point of the United States

 Saxman and Ketchikan—world's largest collection of totem poles

 Malaspina—North America's largest glacier

 Kenai and Kodiak—major salmon processing areas

 Kodiak and Aleutian Islands—known for their catches of Alaskan King Crab

 Pribilof Islands—colonies of puffins and world's largest herd of northern fur seals

 Greens Creek Mine—largest silver mine in the United States

 Denali—20,320 ft.

 Aleutian Islands —longest range of active volcanoes in the US

 Bald Eagles—greater number of bald eagles gather north of Haines than any other place in the world

Circle the capital city. Locate the landmarks found in the above key. Color them on the map.

Name_____

Alaska: The Last Frontier

Look at an atlas or map of Alaska. You can also look online. Add the names of the following places to the map below.

- a chain of islands crossing into the eastern hemisphere

- the highest mountain in North America

- a gold rush town and Alaska's second largest city

- the state capital where Chief Kowee first found gold

- a narrow waterway between Alaska and Russia, named for a Danish explorer

- the northern beginning of the Trans-Alaska Pipeline

- the northernmost point in the United States

- the Trans-Alaska Pipeline ends at Valdez and this large area of water

- the island first settled by Russians

- the city named after the man who purchased Alaska

Size: 665,384 square miles
Population: 736,732

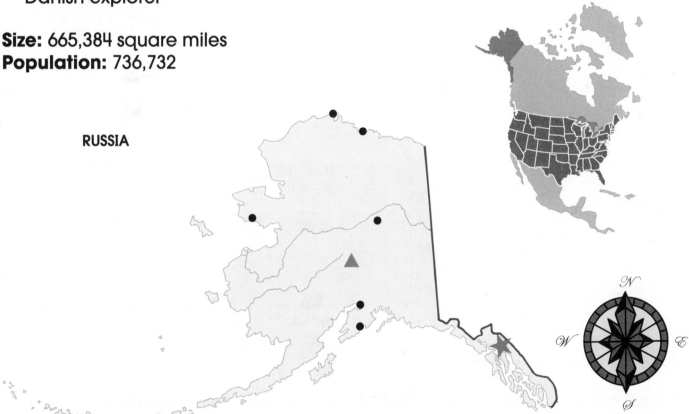

RUSSIA

Hawaii: The Aloha State

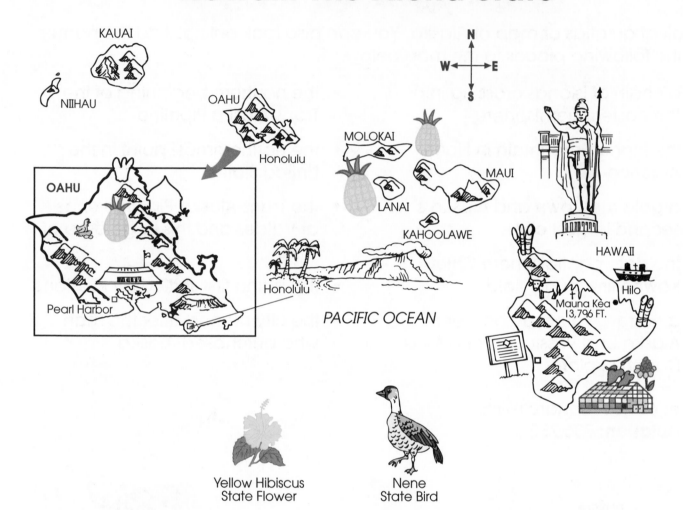

KAUAI

NIIHAU

OAHU

Honolulu

OAHU

Pearl Harbor

Honolulu

MOLOKAI

LANAI

MAUI

KAHOOLAWE

PACIFIC OCEAN

HAWAII

Mauna Kea 13,796 FT.

Hilo

N
W E
S

Yellow Hibiscus
State Flower

Nene
State Bird

 Mauna Kea—13,796 ft.

 Hilo—largest port on the Big Island of Hawaii

 Haleakala—on Maui, the world's largest inactive volcano crater

 U.S.S. Arizona Memorial—in Pearl Harbor, honors those who died aboard the *U.S.S. Arizona* when Japanese attacked on December 7, 1941

 King Kamehameha—statue of Hawaii's greatest ruler

 Pu'uhonua o Honaunau National Historical Park—on Hawaii Island, explains history and culture of early Hawaiians

 National Memorial Cemetery of the Pacific—on Oahu in the Punchbowl crater

 Diamond Head—on Oahu, an extinct volcano

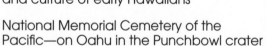 Polynesian Cultural Center on Oahu

 Waimea Canyon—on Kauai, gorges of many beautiful colors

Circle the capital city. Locate the landmarks found in the above key.
Color them on the map.

Hawaii: The Aloha State

- name believed to come from Hawaiian word *Havaiki*, which was the name of a Pacific Island on which the Hawaiian people had resided earlier

- nickname the Aloha State refers to the Hawaiian word *aloha*, which means *love* and is used for greetings of *hello*, *welcome*, and *goodbye*

Hawaii consists of 132 islands. There are 8 main islands.

1. Hawaii—nickname the Big Island refers to it being the largest island

2. Lanai—nickname the Pineapple Island refers to the island being one large pineapple plantation

3. Kahoolawe—smallest of the main islands and is uninhabited

4. Molokai—nickname the Friendly Island refers to how graciously the people welcome visitors and treat one another

5. Kauai—nickname the Garden Island refers to its beautiful gardens and numerous green plants

6. Oahu—nickname the Gathering Place refers to it being the largest island by population

7. Maui—nickname the Valley Island refers to the canyons cut into the two volcanoes that form the island

8. Niihau—nicknamed the Forbidden Island because no one can visit the island without the owners' permission

Hawaii: The Aloha State

Look at an atlas or map of Hawaii. You can also look online. Add the names of the following places to the map below.

- Honolulu, the capital city of the islands

- Hawaii, the "big island"

- the island of Maui

- the location of Volcanoes National Park

- the island where the Polynesian Cultural center is located

- Pearl Harbor

- the "Pineapple Island" of Lanai

- the "Friendly Island" of Molokai

- the "Forbidden Island" of Niihau

Size: 10,970 square miles
Population: 1,419,561

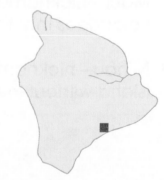

Name _____

The Mountain States

The Mountain States' major feature is the majestic Rocky Mountains that stretch from north to south in this region. The Mountain States are known for their high plateaus, deep canyons, and desert regions.

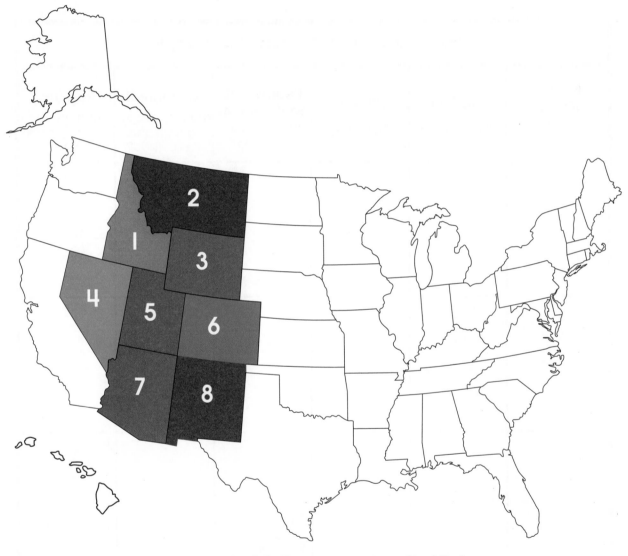

1. Idaho   5. Utah

2. Montana   6. Colorado

3. Wyoming   7. Arizona

4. Nevada   8. New Mexico

Name_____

The Mountain States

Fill in the "Five Fundamental Themes of Geography" for each state. After "discovering" a state, fill in all the columns of the chart except **Regions**. When you have finished with all of the states in a section, fill in **Regions**.

Five Fundamental Themes of Geography					
Name of State	**Location** (Where is it?)	**Place** (What is it like?)	**People and Environment** (What do the people do?)	**Movement** (How do people, goods, and ideas move?)	**Regions** (What are some of the common features?)

The Mountain States

Five Fundamental Themes of Geography					
Name of State	Location (Where is it?)	Place (What is it like?)	People and Environment (What do the people do?)	Movement (How do people, goods, and ideas move?)	Regions (What are some of the common features?)

Idaho: The Gem State

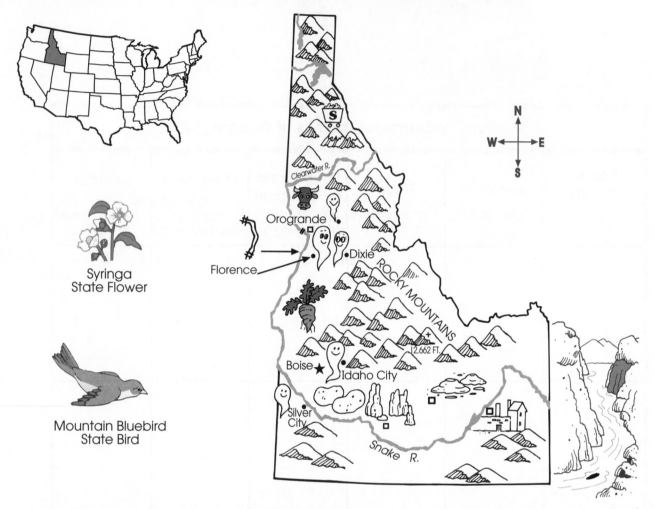

Syringa
State Flower

Mountain Bluebird
State Bird

- name originated from the Shoshone Indian word *ee-dah-how*, which means *sun coming down the mountain* or *daybreak*
- nicknamed the Gem state for the gold, silver, and other minerals in the area that brought a mining boom

 Borah Peak—12,662 ft.

Craters of the Moon
National Monument

Cities of Rock
National Reserve

 Ghost Towns—Silver City,
Florence, Idaho City, Dixie,
and Orogrande

Pocatello—contains Old
Fort Hall, a reconstruction
of a trading post on the
Oregon Trail

 Hells Canyon—
the nation's
deepest canyon

 Potatoes—grows
more than any
other state

Circle the capital city. Locate the landmarks found in the above key.
Color them on the map.

Idaho: The Gem State

Look at an atlas or map of Idaho. You can also look online. Add the names of the following places to the map below.

- the city where Philo Farnsworth invented the television
- the oldest town in Idaho
- the capital of Idaho
- site of the first trading post in Idaho
- the site of the Bear River Massacre

- Lake Coeur d'Alene
- Craters of the Moon National Park
- The Birds of Prey Natural Area is on this river
- Borah Peak, Idaho's tallest mountain
- Hells Canyon National Park

Size: 83,569 square miles
Population: 1,634,464

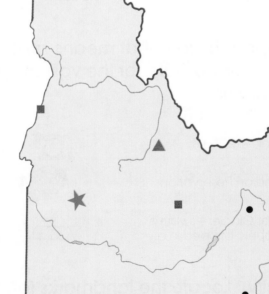

Montana: The Treasure State

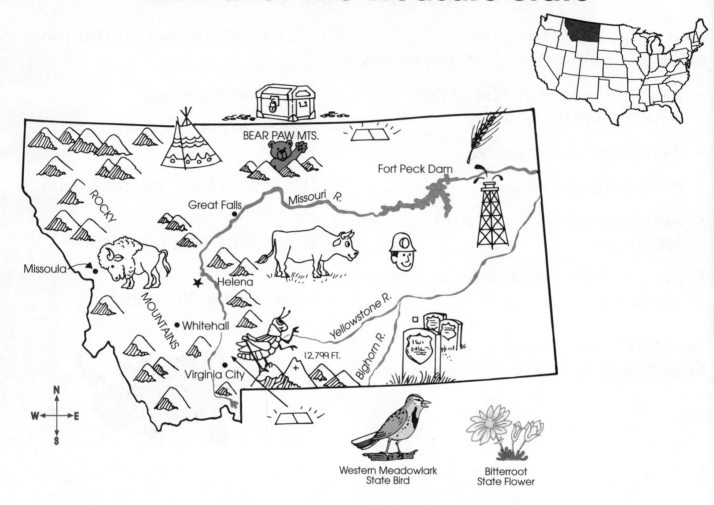

Western Meadowlark
State Bird

Bitterroot
State Flower

- named for the Spanish word that means *mountainous*
- nicknamed the Treasure State for the vast amounts of gold and silver found in its mountains

Granite Peak—12,799 ft.

Little Bighorn Battlefield National Monument

Blackfeet Indian Reservation

National Bison Range

Grasshopper Glacier—swarms of grasshoppers trapped in a glacier

Virginia City—site of one of richest gold deposits in 1863

Circle the capital city. Locate the landmarks found in the above key. Color them on the map.

Name _____

Montana: The Treasure State

Look at an atlas or map of Montana. You can also look online. Add the names of the following places to the map below.

- mountain range in the western part of the state

- the country to the north of the state

- the capital of Montana

- one of the biggest dams in the world

- the river where Lt. Col. Custer was defeated

- the National Park with year-round snow

- the city near the site of 1,000-year-old cave drawings

- the place near where Jeannette Rankin was born

- where silver was discovered

- the city where gold was discovered in a gulch

Size: 147,040 square miles
Population: 1,023,579

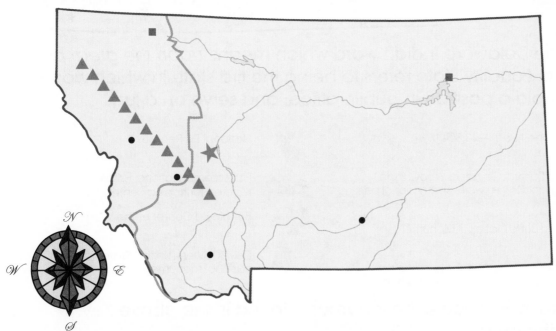

Name_____

Wyoming: The Equality State

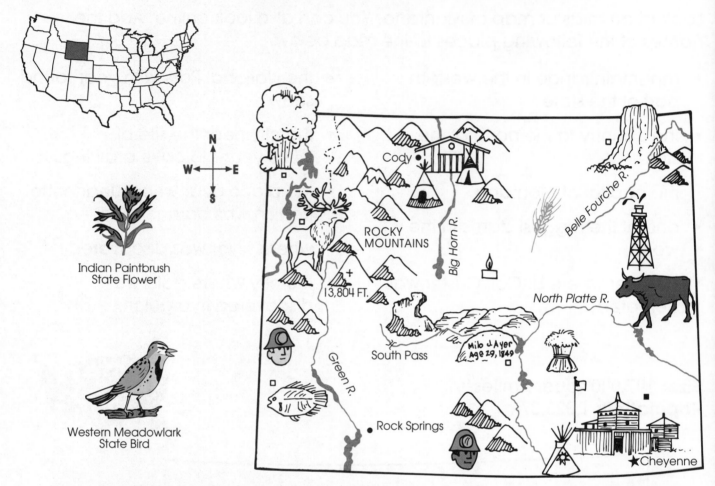

Indian Paintbrush
State Flower

Western Meadowlark
State Bird

- named for the Delaware Indian word which means *upon the great plain*
- nickname the Equality State refers to being the first state in which women could vote, hold a position in public office, and serve on a jury

 Gannett Peak—13,804 ft.

 Old Faithful Geyser in Yellowstone National Park—world's 1st national park

 Fossil Butte National Monument

 Independence Rock—hundreds of pioneers carved their names here

 National Elk Refuge

 Fort Laramie National Historic Site—restored fur trading center

 Buffalo Bill Center of the West

 Devils Tower—United States' first national monument

Circle the capital city. Locate the landmarks found in the above key. Color them on the map.

Wyoming: The Equality State

Look at an atlas or map of Wyoming. You can also look online. Add the names of the following places to the map below.

- this city is just east of central Wyoming

- the capital of Wyoming

- a city in northwest Wyoming

- this river passes through the Grand Teton National Park

- the first national park

- these beautiful mountains are in their own national park

- this river passes by Casper

- a city near Cheyenne

- this state is to the west and borders Montana

- this mountain range divides North America

- this state is to the east and borders Colorado

- the Continental Divide

Size: 97,813 square miles
Population: 584,153

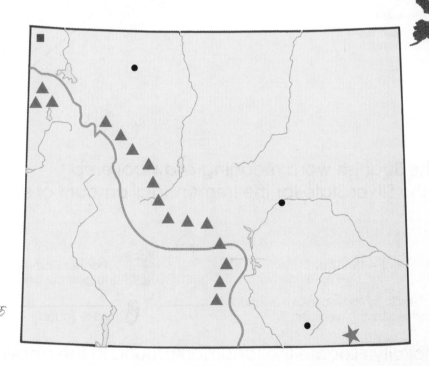

Nevada: The Silver State

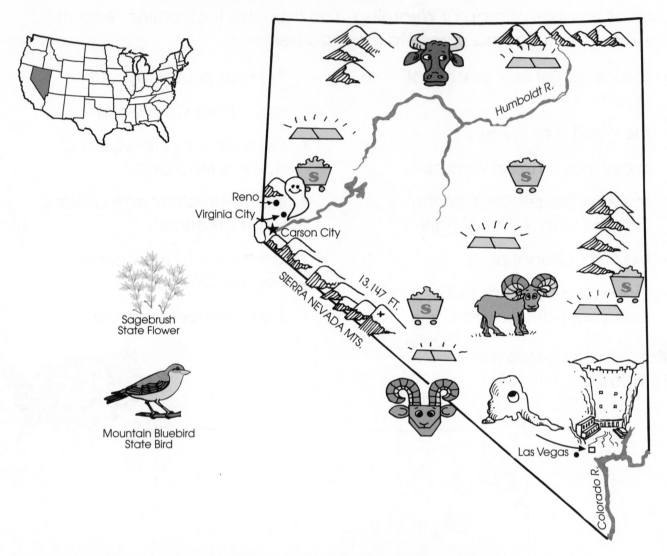

Sagebrush
State Flower

Mountain Bluebird
State Bird

Reno

Virginia City

★ Carson City

SIERRA NEVADA MTS.

13,147 FT.

Humboldt R.

Las Vegas

Colorado R.

- named for the Spanish word meaning *snow-covered*
- nicknamed the Silver State for the tremendous amount of silver that was mined

 Boundary Peak—13,147 ft.

 Valley of Fire State Park—contains Elephant Rock, formed by the weather

 Hoover Dam—one of the world's largest concrete dams

 Lake Tahoe

Circle the capital city. Locate the landmarks found in the above key. Color them on the map.

Nevada: The Silver State

Look at an atlas or map of Nevada. You can also look online. Add the names of the following places to the map below.

- the capital of Nevada

- a very large dam

- this town is Nevada spelled backward

- Waddie Mitchell was born here

- this is Nevada's tallest mountain

- this river forms a small part of Nevada's border with Arizona

- odds are you can find gamblers in this southern city

- this lake is near the Hoover Dam

- this state shares Nevada's eastern border

- this is the biggest mountain lake

- this desert is in southeastern Nevada

Size: 110,572 square miles
Population: 2,839,099

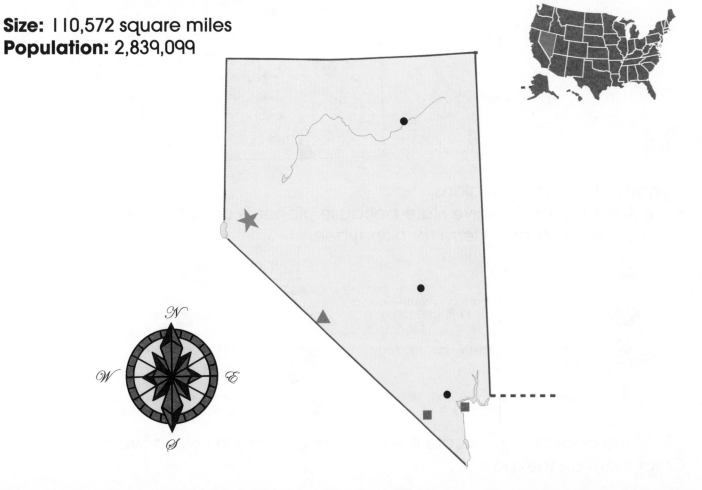

Name_____

Utah: The Beehive State

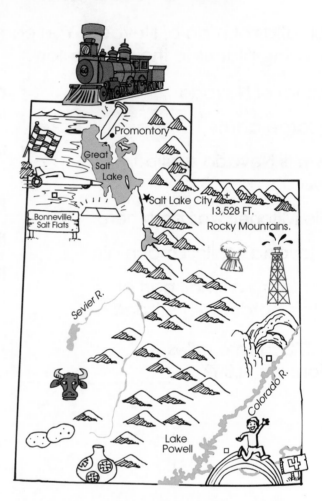

N
W ← → E
S

Sego Lily
State Flower

California Seagull
State Bird

- named for the Ute Indians
- nicknamed the Beehive State because pioneers called the region *Deseret*—a Mormon term for *honeybee*

 King's Peak—13,528 ft.

 Hovenweep National Monument—housed Anasazi Indians about A.D. 1200-1300

 International Speedway—cars race on flat salt beds

 Promontory—first transcontinental railroad completed in 1869

 Four Corners Monument—where Utah, Arizona, New Mexico, and Colorado meet

 Bonneville Salt Flats

 Arches National Park

 Rainbow Bridge National Monument—one of the world's largest natural stone bridges

Circle the capital city. Locate the landmarks found in the above key.
Color them on the map.

Utah: The Beehive State

Look at an atlas or map of Utah. You can also look online. Add the names of the following places to the map below.

- Merlin Olsen is from here
- the other states making the "four corners"
- Utah's capital
- a freshwater lake
- where racecar records are set

- a town near Utah Lake
- many Western movies are filmed here
- you can float in this lake
- see dinosaur bones here

Size: 84,898 square miles
Population: 2,942,902

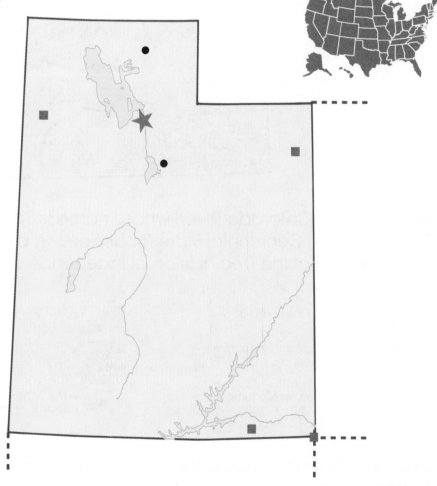

Name_____

Colorado: The Centennial State

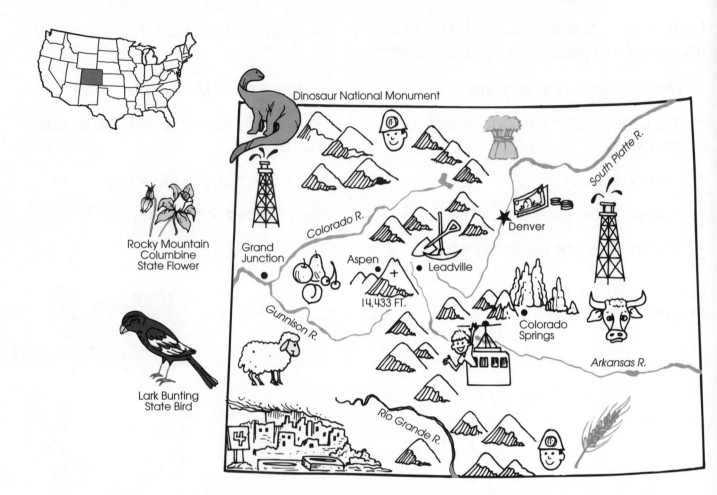

- named for the Colorado River, whose name is Spanish for *colored red*
- nicknamed the Centennial State for becoming a state in 1876, which was the centennial of the Declaration of Independence

 Mount Elbert—14,433 ft.

 Mesa Verde National Park— 1,000-year-old-cliff dwellings

 Four Corners Monument—place where Utah, Arizona, Colorado, and New Mexico meet

 Garden of the Gods—giant formations of red sandstone

 Royal Gorge Bridge

 U.S. Mint—millions of coins made yearly

Circle the capital city. Locate the landmarks found in the above key. Color them on the map.

Name_____

Colorado: The Centennial State

Look at an atlas or map of Colorado. You can also look online. Add the names of the following places to the map below.

- an astronaut's hometown

- the state capital

- the Colorado River

- the highest city in America

- the site that inspired "America the Beautiful"

- the home of the U.S. Air Force Academy

- the national park that preserves the cliff dwellings

- a ski community whose population grows by almost five times on winter weekends

- the mining town of Pueblo

- the Rio Grande

- Dinosaur National Monument

Size: 104,094 square miles
Population: 5,355,866

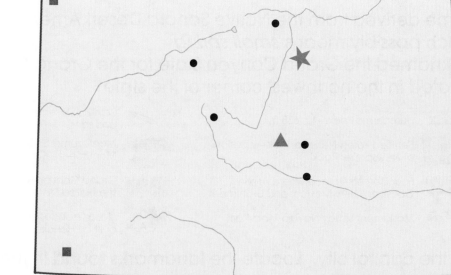

Name _____

Arizona: The Grand Canyon State

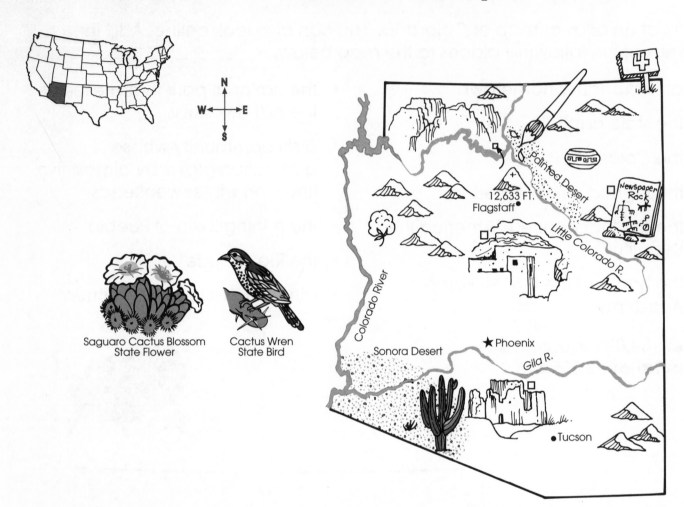

- name derived from the Native Sonora Desert American word *arizonac*, which possibly means *small spring*
- nicknamed the Grand Canyon State for the Grand Canyon, which is located in the northwest corner of the state

 Humphreys Peak—12, 633 ft.

 Petrified Forest National Park—location of Newspaper Rock

 Four Corners—place where Arizona, Colorado, New Mexico, and Utah meet

 Monument Valley Navajo Tribal Park

 Painted Desert—layers of colorful rock and sand

 Montezuma Castle National Monument—five-story cliff-dwelling ruin

 Grand Canyon National Park—one of the United States' most famous scenic wonders

 Casa Grande Ruins National Monument—built by Hohokum Indians about A.D. 1350

Circle the capital city. Locate the landmarks found in the above key. Color them on the map.

Name _____

Arizona: The Grand Canyon State

Look at an atlas or map of Arizona. You can also look online. Add the names of the following places to the map below.

- the river named for the state of Colorado

- the country to the south that once owned Arizona

- the town where Wyatt Earp was Deputy U.S. Marshal

- the river named after the poisonous lizard

- the city named after a flag pole

- the capital of Arizona

- the largest canyon in the United States

- the place where the corners of four states meet

- the dam named after Herbert Hoover

- the Indian reservation that has the oldest village

- the city that is home to Arizona State University

Size: 113,990 square miles
Population: 6,731,484

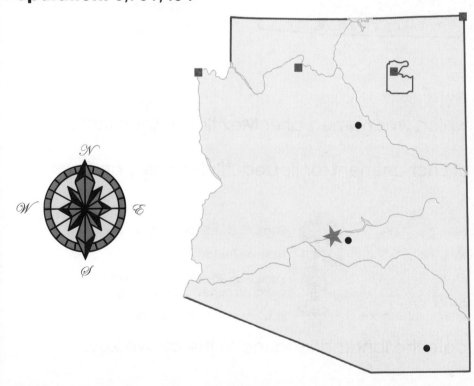

New Mexico: Land of Enchantment

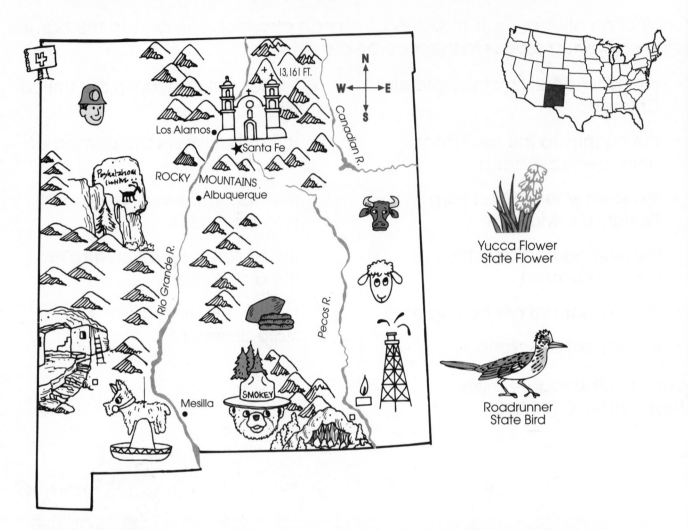

- named after Mexico, which was named after Mexitli, an Aztec Indian war god
- nicknamed the Land of Enchantment for its beautiful scenery and rich history

Wheeler Peak—13,161 ft.

Four Corners Monument

San Miguel Mission

Carlsbad Caverns National Park— one of the world's great natural wonders

Gila Cliff Dwellings National Monument

Historic Mesilla

Inscription Rock National Monument—has petroglyphs never deciphered

Smokey Bear Historical Park

Circle the capital city. Locate the landmarks found in the above key. Color them on the map.

New Mexico: Land of Enchantment

Look at an atlas or map of New Mexico. You can also look online. Add the names of the following places to the map below.

- the capital of New Mexico

- the city started by Francisco Cuervo y Valdes

- the river whose name means "Big" or "Grand" river in Spanish

- the river that shares its name with the city of San Francisco

- the city where the first atomic bomb was developed

- the place where the atomic bomb was tested

- the country to the south of New Mexico

- the place where you can walk a three-mile underground trail

- the city near Taos Pueblo

- the place where Maria Montoya Martinez grew up

Size: 121,590 square miles
Population: 2,085,572

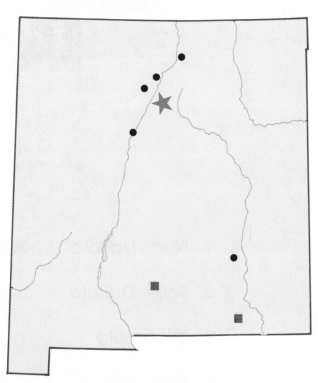

Name_____

The North Central States

Look around the North Central states and you will see why they are also called the Plains states. The plains have rich soil that makes this area famous for growing wheat and corn.

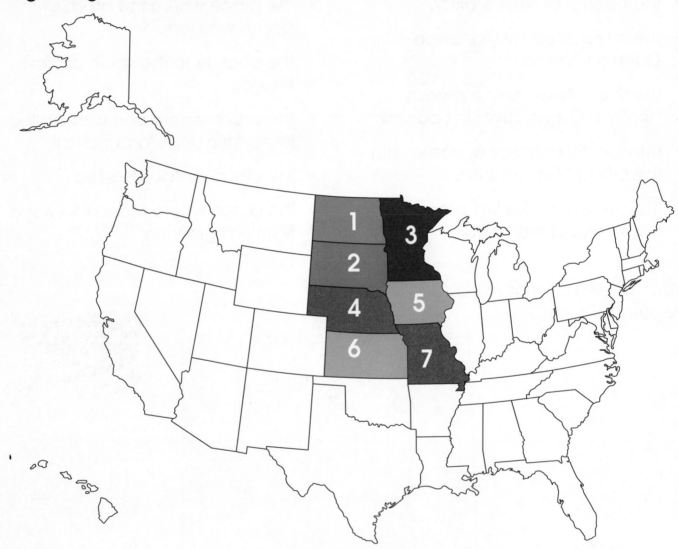

1. North Dakota   5. Iowa

2. South Dakota   6. Kansas

3. Minnesota   7. Missouri

4. Nebraska

Fill in the "Five Fundamental Themes of Geography" for each state. After "discovering" a state, fill in all the columns of the chart except **Regions**. When you have finished with all of the states in a section, fill in **Regions**.

Five Fundamental Themes of Geography					
Name of State	Location (Where is it?)	Place (What is it like?)	People and Environment (What do the people do?)	Movement (How do people, goods, and ideas move?)	Regions (What are some of the common features?)

Name _____

Five Fundamental Themes of Geography

Name of State	Location (Where is it?)	Place (What is it like?)	People and Environment (What do the people do?)	Movement (How do people, goods, and ideas move?)	Regions (What are some of the common features?)

North Dakota: Peace Garden State

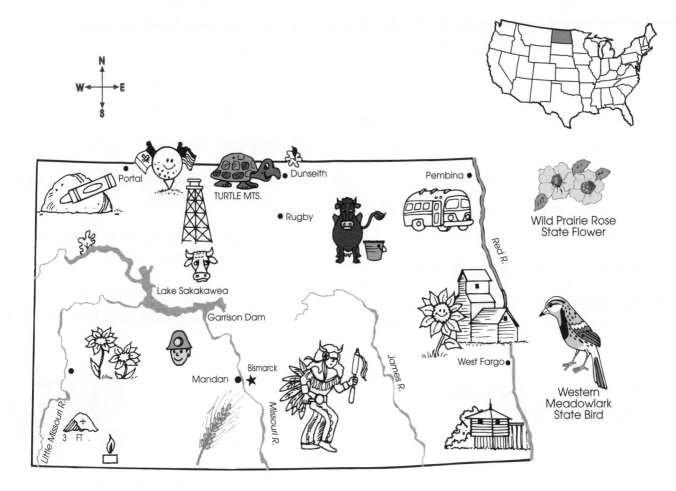

- named for Sioux Indians who called themselves Dakota or Lakota
- nicknamed the Peace Garden State

 White Butte—3,506 ft.

 Sunflowers—top producer of seeds

 Bonanzaville—preserved pioneer buildings in a diverse village

 United Tribes Powwow

 Pembina—large plant produces motor coaches

 International Peace Garden—symbolizes friendship between U.S. and Canada

 Writing Rock—boulder with ancient Indian picture writing

 International Golf Course—spans two countries; tee for the 9th hole in Canada and cup in the U.S.

 Fort Abercrombie— 1st U.S. military post in North Dakota

• Rugby—geographic center of North America

Circle the capital city. Locate the landmarks found in the above key. Color them on the map.

North Dakota: Peace Garden State

Look at an atlas or map of North Dakota. You can also look online. Add the names of the following places to the map below.

- the capital

- the river that shares a name with a state

- the country to the north

- the city where Lewis and Clark built a fort

- the first European settlement

- the cities with the two United States Strategic Air Commands

- the National Park to honor Theodore Roosevelt

- the city near Writing Rock

- the town that hosts "Pioneer Days at Bonanzaville"

- the lake named for Lewis and Clark's guide

- the state to the south that was once part of the Dakota Territory

Size: 70,698 square miles
Population: 739,482

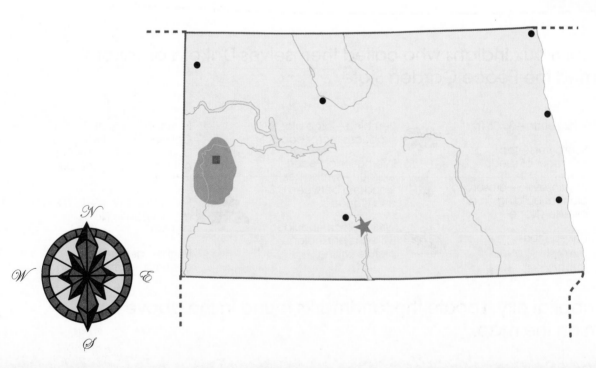

South Dakota: Mount Rushmore State

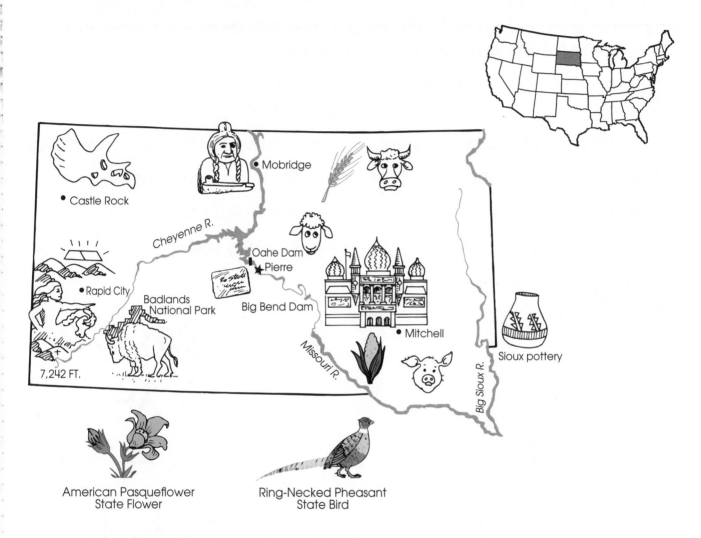

American Pasqueflower
State Flower

Ring-Necked Pheasant
State Bird

- named for Sioux Indians who called themselves Dakota or Lakota
- nicknamed the Mount Rushmore State

Harney Peak—7,242 ft.

Mobridge—sculpture marking the
burial site of Sioux leader Sitting Bull

Triceratops Fossil—found in 1927 in
Harding County and now on display

Custer State Park

Castle Rock—geographic center of the
50 United States

Lead Plate—buried by the La Vérendrye
brothers in 1743—discovered in 1913

Circle the capital city. Locate the landmarks found in the above key.
Color them on the map.

South Dakota: Mount Rushmore State

Look at an atlas or map of South Dakota. You can also look online. Add the names of the following places to the map below.

- A part of Citibank headquarters is here

- two of the world's longest caves

- home of Allen Neuharth

- Yankton Reservation

- Badlands National Park

- the world's largest drugstore is here

- Devil's Gulch, a 20-foot wide canyon

- hometown of Hubert Humphrey

- South Dakota's capital

- Wounded Knee Creek

- Waubay Lake

Size: 77,116 square miles
Population: 853,175

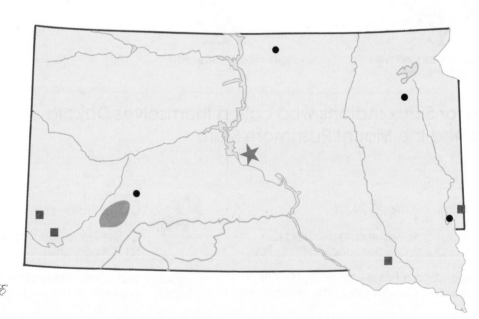

Minnesota: The Gopher State

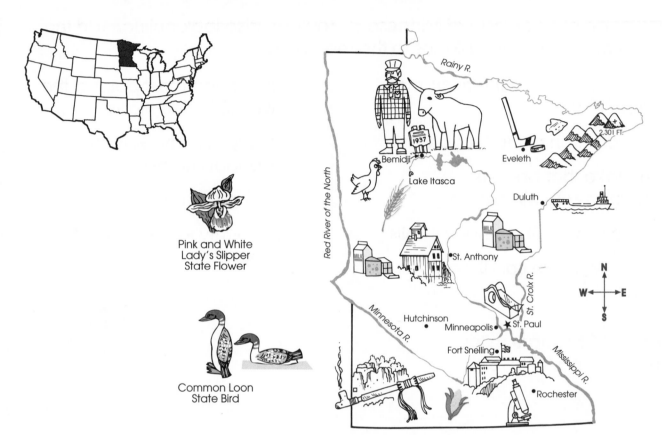

Pink and White
Lady's Slipper
State Flower

Common Loon
State Bird

- name derived from Sioux Indian words meaning *sky-tinted water*
- nicknamed the Gopher State for the vast numbers of gophers that inhabited its prairie

 Eagle Mountain—2,301 ft.

 Arrowhead Country—northeastern tip shaped like an arrowhead

 Bemidji—Paul Bunyan and Babe

 St. Paul—where transparent tape was invented

 Historic Fort Snelling—1820s restored military post

 Lake Itasca—beginning of the Mississippi River

 Mayo Clinic—one of the world's most famous medical centers

 U.S. Hockey Hall of Fame Museum

 Falls of St. Anthony—first flour mill in Minnesota, in 1823

 Duluth—farthest inland port in U.S.

 Pipestone National Monument—Indians used red pipestone found here to make ceremonial pipes

Circle the capital city. Locate the landmarks found in the above key. Color them on the map.

Name_____

Minnesota: The Gopher State

Look at an atlas or map of Minnesota. You can also look online. Add the names of the following places to the map below.

- Fort Snelling and the rivers that meet there
- the location of the Mayo Clinic
- the lake that borders northeastern Minnesota
- the city near St. Anthony's Falls
- the city where Bob Dylan was born

- the northernmost point of the lower 48 United States
- the city of Judy Garland's childhood home
- the capital of Minnesota
- the county to the north of Minnesota

Size: 86,935 square miles
Population: 5,457,173

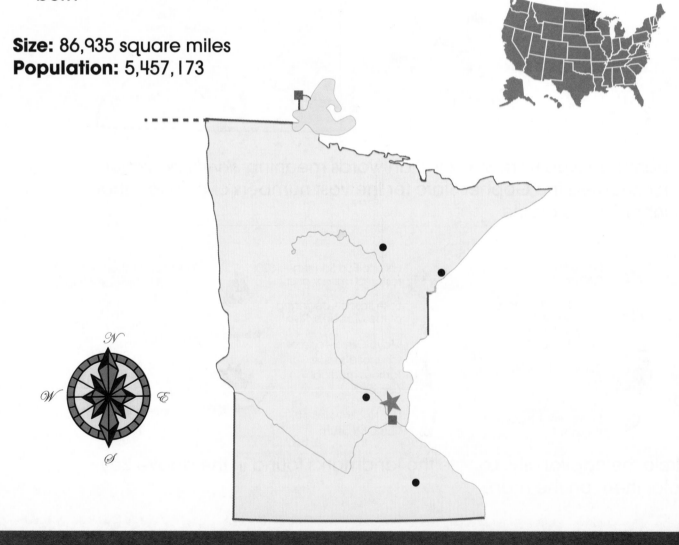

Nebraska: The Cornhusker State

Carhenge

Niobrara R.

Missouri R.

SAND HILLS

5,426 FT.

Wellfleet

Kearney

Grand
Island

Platte R.

Omaha

Lincoln★

Nebraska
City

Western Meadowlark
State Bird

Goldenrod
State Flower

- named for the Oto Indian word *nebrathka*, meaning *flat water*, which was the Indian name for the Platte River
- nicknamed the Cornhusker State for the state's leading crop of corn

 Toadstool Geologic Park—in the Badlands, has rock formations resembling toadstools

 Wellfleet—largest mammoth fossil ever found

 National Museum of Roller Skating

 Arbor Lodge State Historical Park—home of Julius Sterling Morton, founder of Arbor Day

Chimney Rock National Historic Site

 Carhenge—replica of Stonehenge made of cars

 Cranes—about 500,000 stop along the Platte River every spring as they migrate north

 Buffalo Bill's State Historical Park—wild west showman's ranch house and barn

 Homestead National Monument of America—site of one of the first pieces of land claimed under the Homestead Act

Circle the capital city. Locate the landmarks found in the above key. Color them on the map.

Nebraska: The Cornhusker State

Look at an atlas or map of Nebraska. You can also look online. Add the names of the following places to the map below.

- the North Platte river flows from this state

- Omaha is on this river

- this state is to the east of Nebraska

- the capital of Nebraska

- this state shares Nebraska's northern border

- this area makes up most of Nebraska

- this state cuts into southwest Nebraska

- Nebraska shares this area with Iowa

- this river passes by Grand Island and flows into the Missouri River

- this state is due south of Nebraska

- Malcolm X's birthplace

Size: 77,347 square miles
Population: 1,881,503

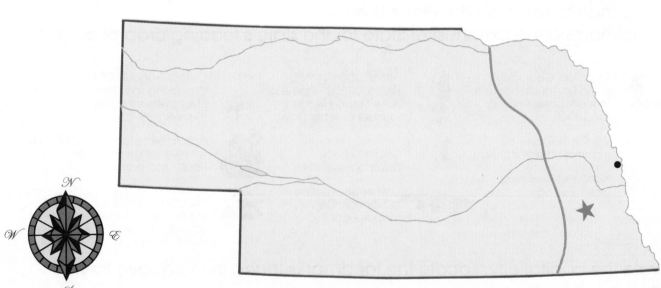

Iowa: The Hawkeye State

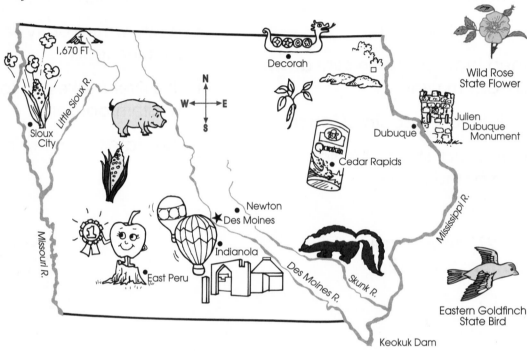

- named after the Sioux Indian tribe Ayuhwa
- nicknamed the Hawkeye State in honor of Chief Black Hawk, a Sauk and Fox Indian leader

 Vesterheim Museum— Norwegian-American culture exhibits

 Julien Dubuque Monument—burial site of the first permanent white settler in Iowa

 National Balloon Museum and U.S. Ballooning Hall of Fame

 Cedar Rapids—one of the largest cereal mills in the U.S.

 East Peru—red delicious apple was developed here in the 1880s

 Sioux City—one of the largest popcorn processing plants in U.S.

 Effigy Mounds National Monument—earthen mounds shaped like animals, built by prehistoric Indians

Circle the capital city. Locate the landmarks found in the above key. Color them on the map.

Iowa: The Hawkeye State

Look at an atlas or map of Iowa. You can also look online. Add the names of the following places to the map below.

- this city is known for making popcorn

- the capital of Iowa

- mined lead could be sent down this eastern river

- the state to the south of Iowa

- the river that shares the same name as the capital

- this town celebrates Capt. James T. Kirk's birthday each year

- a city where early settlers came to mine lead

- this river makes up Iowa's western border

- the state to the north of Iowa

Size: 56,273 square miles
Population: 3,107,126

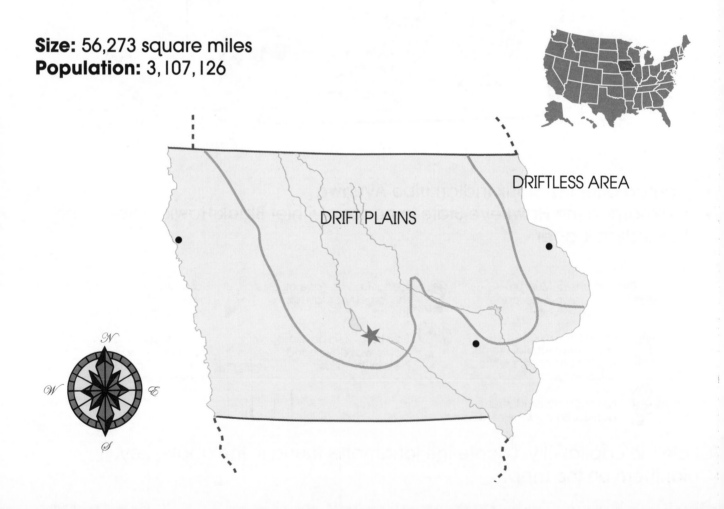

Kansas: The Sunflower State

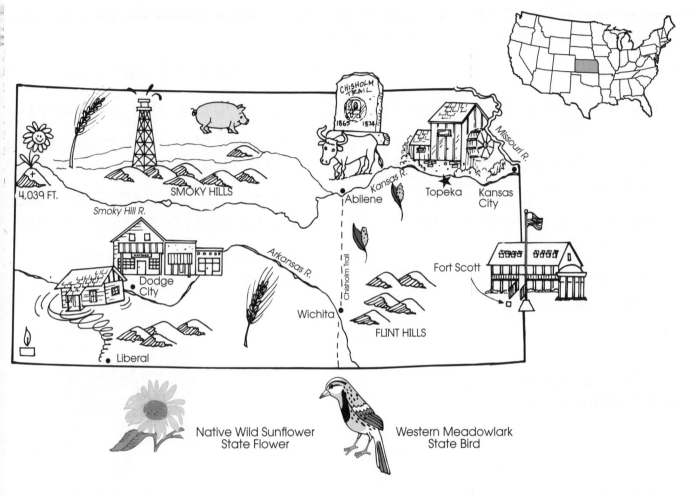

SMOKY HILLS

4,039 FT.

Smoky Hill R.

Abilene

Kansas R.

Topeka   Kansas City

Missouri R.

Arkansas R.

Dodge City

Chisholm Trail

Wichita

Fort Scott

FLINT HILLS

Liberal

CHISHOLM TRAIL 1865 — 1874

Native Wild Sunflower
State Flower

Western Meadowlark
State Bird

- named for the Kansa, or Kaw, Indians, whose name means *people of the south wind*
- nicknamed the Sunflower State for the abundance of sunflowers

 Mount Sunflower—4,039 ft.

Liberal—home of the original model of Dorothy's house from the 1939 film *The Wizard of Oz*

Old flour mill—represents the many flour mills in the Kansas City and Topeka area today

 Frontier town on Santa Fe Trail, famous for cattle drives

 Chisholm Trail—used for herding cattle from Texas to Abilene for shipment to the East

 Fort Scott National Historic Site—restored 1840's military post

Circle the capital city. Locate the landmarks found in the above key.
Color them on the map.

Kansas: The Sunflower State

Look at an atlas or map of Kansas. You can also look online. Add the names of the following places to the map below.

- the state capital
- the city that has the same name as the state
- the river that separates Kansas and Missouri
- the place where salt was first produced
- the birthplace of Melissa Etheridge

- the states that border Kansas
- the birthplace of Amelia Earhart
- the city that was an important site in the Underground Railroad
- Location of Dwight D. Eisenhower Presidential Library and Museum
- the city that produces small aircraft

Size: 82,278 square miles
Population: 2,904,021

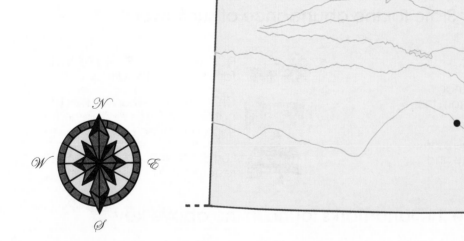

Missouri: The Show Me State

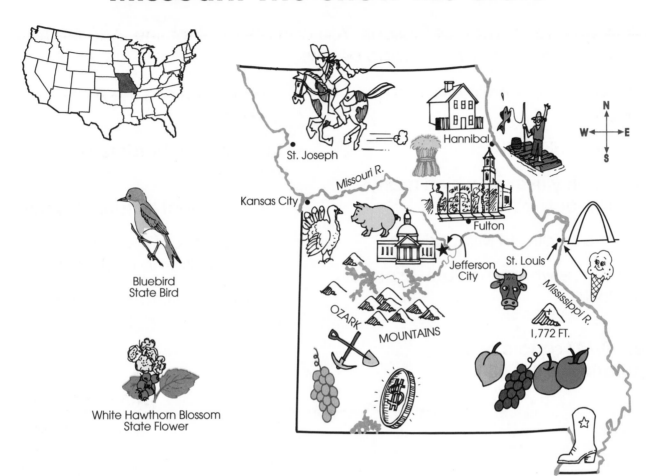

Bluebird
State Bird

White Hawthorn Blossom
State Flower

- named for an Indian word meaning *town of the long canoes*
- nickname the Show Me State related to an 1899 speech by Congressman Vandiver in which he indicated he was unimpressed with speeches and wanted to be shown results

 Taum Sauk Mountain—1,772 ft.

 Pony Express—carried mail from St. Joseph, Missouri to Sacramento, California from 1860 to 1861

 Mark Twain Boyhood Home and Museum—author of *Tom Sawyer*

 National Churchill Museum—has a 1990 sculpture using eight Berlin Wall sections

 Gateway Arch—tallest monument in U.S.

 Bootheel Country—named because the shape resembles a boot heel

 Silver Dollar City—theme park

 First ice cream cone—at Louisiana Purchase Exposition in St. Louis in 1904

Circle the capital city. Locate the landmarks found in the above key. Color them on the map.

Missouri: The Show Me State

Look at an atlas or map of Missouri. You can also look online. Add the names of the following places to the map below.

- the lake where Bagnell Dam is located

- the capital of Missouri

- the mighty river on which many steamboats traveled

- the mountains in Missouri

- the place where the Pony Express started

- the city that has the same name as Kansas

- the river that borders Missouri on the west

- the states that border Missouri

- the location of the Harry S. Truman home and library

- the boyhood home of Mark Twain

Size: 69,707 square miles
Population: 6,063,589

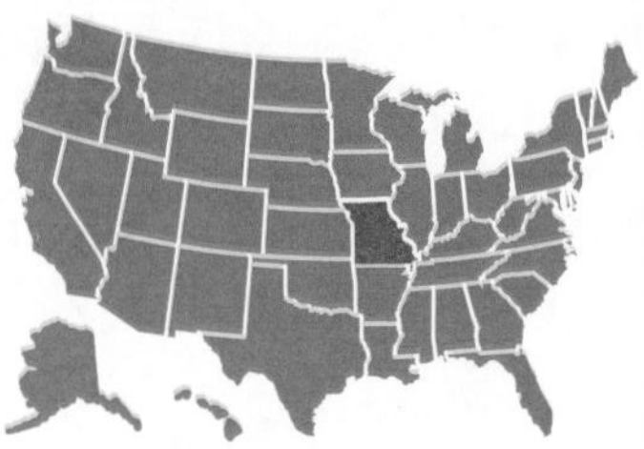

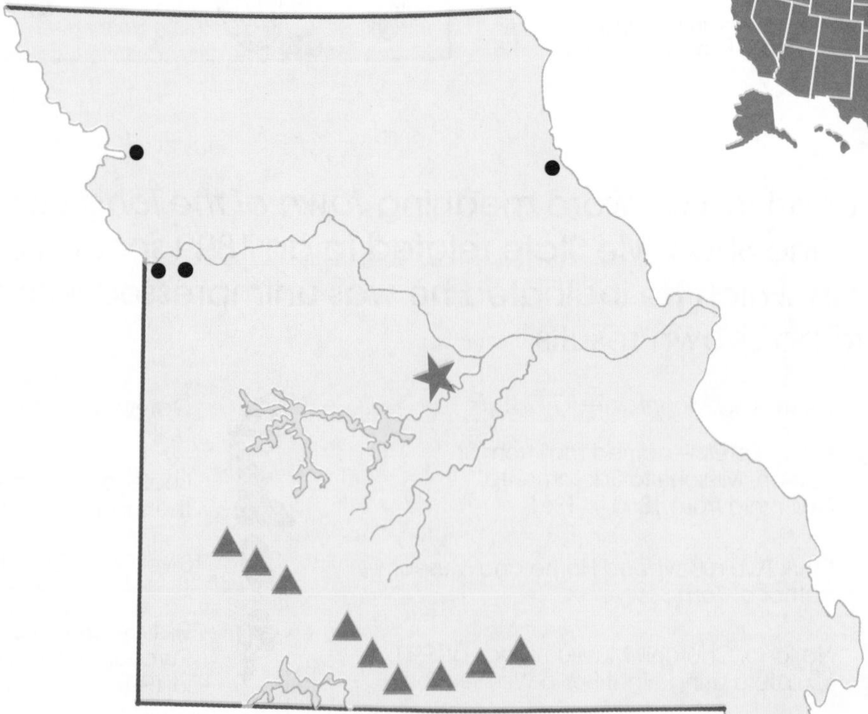

The South Central States

The South Central states is a region with large areas of flat land good for raising cattle and growing cotton. This region is also known for its rich deposits of oil that are found beneath the surface of the land and ocean floor.

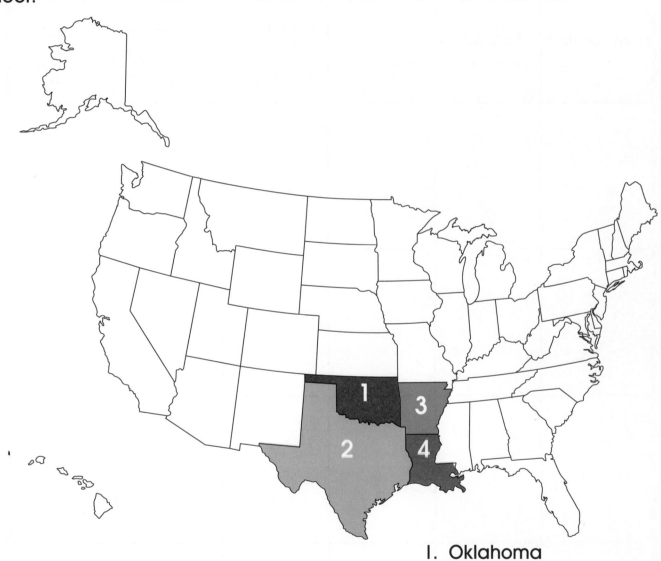

1. Oklahoma

2. Texas

3. Arkansas

4. Louisiana

Fill in the "Five Fundamental Themes of Geography" for each state. After "discovering" a state, fill in all the columns of the chart except **Regions**. When you have finished with all of the states in a section, fill in **Regions**.

Five Fundamental Themes of Geography					
Name of State	Location (Where is it?)	Place (What is it like?)	People and Environment (What do the people do?)	Movement (How do people, goods, and ideas move?)	Regions (What are some of the common features?)

Oklahoma: The Sooner State

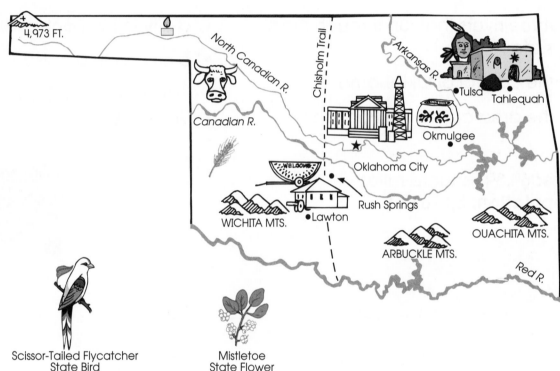

Scissor-Tailed Flycatcher
State Bird

Mistletoe
State Flower

- name derived from the Chocotaw Indian words *okla*, meaning *people*, and *homma*, meaning red
- nicknamed the Sooner State for the settlers who arrived before the land was opened for settlement

Black Mesa—4,973 ft.

Oklahoma City—only state capital with working oil wells on its site

Fort Sill National Historic Landmark and Museum—historical site built in 1869

 Rush Springs—annual Watermelon Festival celebrates the local harvest

Circle the capital city. Locate the landmarks found in the above key.
Color them on the map.

Oklahoma: The Sooner State

Look at an atlas or map of Oklahoma. You can also look online. Add the names of the following places to the map below.

- the states that border Oklahoma

- the river that separates Texas and Oklahoma

- three rivers that run through the state

- the capital of Oklahoma

- the area called the Panhandle

- Tulsa, the second largest city

- the location of the University of Oklahoma

- a city in the Panhandle

- a city north of Tulsa

- the location of Oklahoma State University

Size: 69,899 square miles
Population: 5,878,051

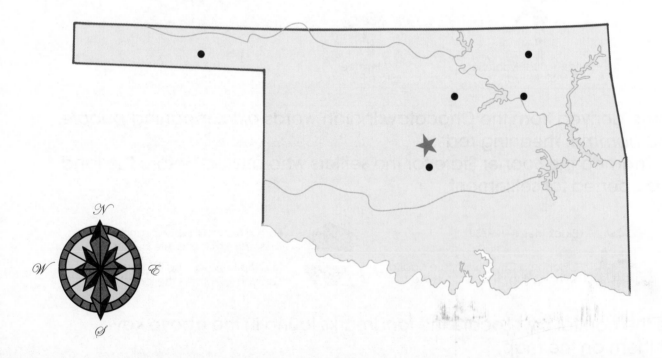

Texas: The Lone Star State

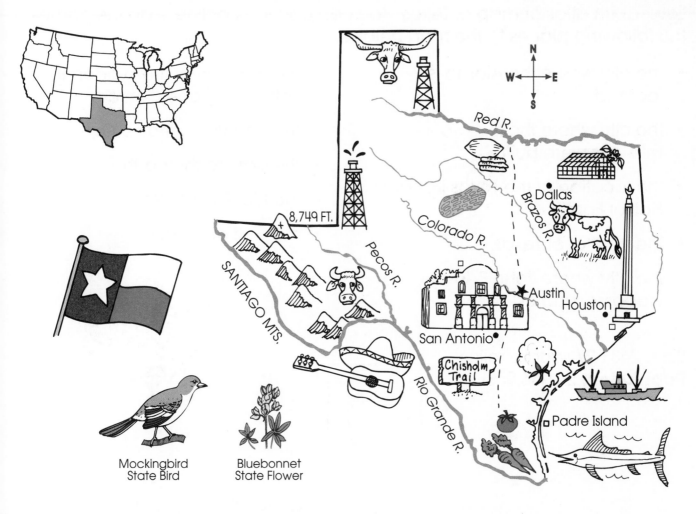

Mockingbird
State Bird

Bluebonnet
State Flower

- name comes from the Spanish pronunciation of the Indian word *tejas*, which means *allies* or *friends*
- nickname the Lone Star State comes from having only one star on its state

 Guadalupe Peak—8,749 ft.

San Jacinto Monument—honors Texans who fought and won the battle for independence from Mexico

 The Alamo—a famous San Antonio battle site

 Chisholm Trail—begins here

 Padre Island National Seashore

 Mexican culture and influence seen throughout the state

Circle the capital city. Locate the landmarks found in the above key.
Color them on the map.

Texas: The Lone Star State

Look at an atlas or map of Texas. You can also look online. Add the names of the following places to the map below.

- the city where the Alamo is located

- the city where the first two missions were built

- the location of the Texas Rangers Hall of Fame

- the capital of Texas

- the city where John F. Kennedy was assassinated

- the location of the Lyndon B. Johnson Space Center

- the country to the south

- the state to the north

- the Rio Grande River

- the Gulf of Mexico

Size: 268,597 square miles
Population: 26,956,958

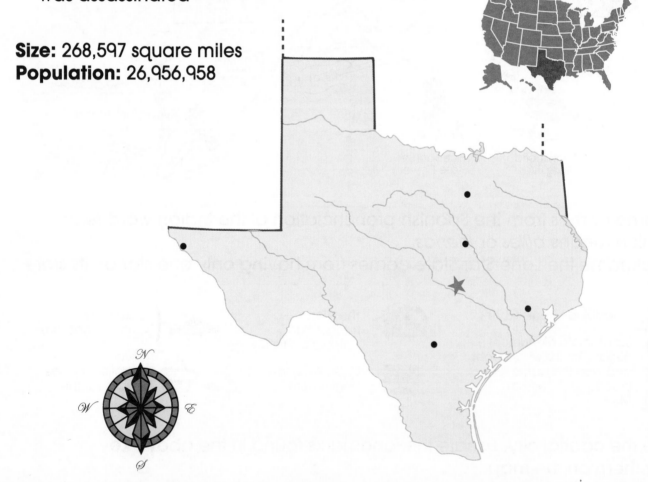

Arkansas: The Natural State

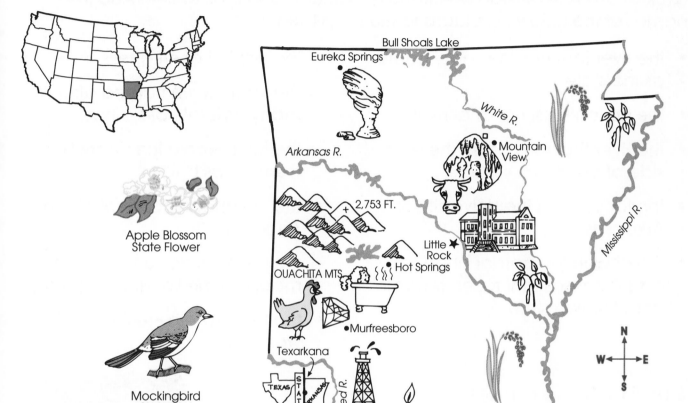

Apple Blossom
State Flower

Mockingbird
State Bird

- named for a Sioux Indian tribe named Arkansa, which means *downstream people*
- nickname the Natural State refers to the abundance of lakes, streams, forests, and wildlife.

    Magazine Mountain—2,753 ft.

Pivot Rock—balances on a small base

MacArthur Park—honors military commander, General Douglas MacArthur

Crater of Diamonds State Park— diamond mine which tourists can visit

 Hot Springs National Park—minerals and hot springs believed to be helpful for certain illnesses

 Blanchard Springs Caverns

 Texarkana—town on the border between Texas and Arkansas

Circle the capital city. Locate the landmarks found in the above key. Color them on the map.

Arkansas: The Natural State

Look at an atlas or map of Arkansas. You can also look online. Add the names of the following places to the map below.

- the river that has the same name as the state

- the nation's first national river

- the river that runs down the east side of the state

- the location of the University of Arkansas

- the city on the border of Texas and Arkansas that takes its name from the two states

- the capital of Arkansas

- the tourist town named after its many natural hot springs

- the town where the Ozark Folk Center was built

- the childhood home of Maya Angelou

- the town where surveyors began mapping the Louisiana territory

- the town where President Clinton was born

Size: 53,179 square miles
Population: 2,966,369

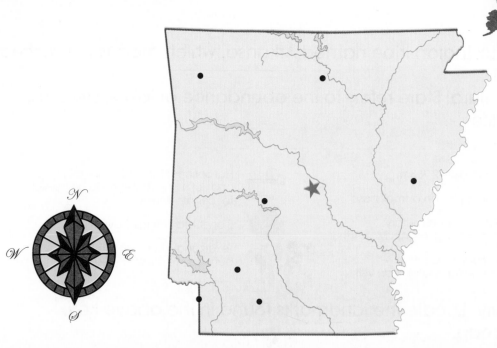

Louisiana: The Pelican State

Magnolia
State Flower

Brown Pelican
State Bird

- named for the French King, Louis XIV
- nicknamed the Pelican State for the many brown pelicans that reside along the coast

 Driskill Mountain—535 ft.

 Poverty Point National Monument—ancient Indian earthen mounds built between 1700 and 700 B.C.

 Avery Island—chili peppers grown here to make Tabasco sauce

 Egrets—three of the world's largest egret sanctuaries

 Preservation Hall—famous for its jazz bands

 Bald cypress swamps

 Jean Lafitte National Historical Park & Preserve—area where pirate Jean Lafitte helped Andrew Jackson in the 1815 Battle of New Orleans

 Acadian Village—features historic Cajun food and culture

 Mardis Gras—annual carnival celebration features dancing, parties, and parades

Circle the capital city. Locate the landmarks found in the above key. Color them on the map.

Louisiana: The Pelican State

Look at an atlas or map of Louisiana. You can also look online. Add the names of the following places to the map below.

- the river that creates the border between Texas and Louisiana
- Tensas River National Wildlife Refuge
- hometown of Jerry Lee Lewis
- home of the tallest capitol building in the country
- Chandeleur Island archipelago

- Terry Bradshaw's birthplace
- Bayou Lafourche
- Lake Pontchartrain
- Oil City
- New Orleans
- the longest river in the U.S.
- Barataria Bay

Size: 52,375 square miles
Population: 4,649,676

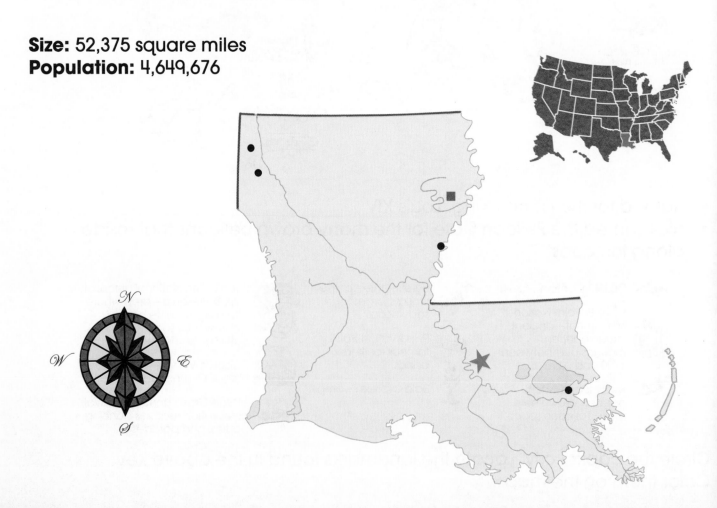

The Midwest States

The Midwest States is a region with beautiful freshwater lakes, deep green forests, and fertile farmland.

1. Wisconsin

2. Michigan

3. Illinois

4. Indiana

5. Ohio

The Midwest States

Fill in the "Five Fundamental Themes of Geography" for each state. After "discovering" a state, fill in all the columns of the chart except **Regions**. When you have finished with all of the states in a section, fill in **Regions**.

Five Fundamental Themes of Geography					
Name of State	Location (Where is it?)	Place (What is it like?)	People and Environment (What do the people do?)	Movement (How do people, goods, and ideas move?)	Regions (What are some of the common features?)

Wisconsin: The Badger State

Wood Violet
State Flower

Robin
State Bird

Hayward

Brule R.

Menominee R.

St. Croix R.

1,951 FT.

MILK

Mississippi R.

Wisconsin R.

TISSUE

NFL

Green Bay

Neenah

Baraboo

★ Madison

Mt. Horeb   Milwaukee

Racine

- name comes from the Miami Indian word Meskousing, meaning *river running through a red place*
- nickname the Badger State used to describe the lead miners of the 1820s who lived in caves dug into the hillsides

Timms Hill—1,951 ft.

Circus World Museum

Racine—malted milk invented here in 1887

Green Bay Packers Hall of Fame

Neenah—facial tissue invented here in the early 1900s

National Freshwater Fishing Hall of Fame and Museum

Circle the capital city. Locate the landmarks found in the above key. Color them on the map.

Wisconsin: The Badger State

Look at an atlas or map of Wisconsin. You can also look online. Add the names of the following places to the map below.

- this is a "super" Great Lake

- the capital of Wisconsin

- this bay feeds into Lake Michigan

- this state is between Wisconsin and Canada

- this state is to the south

- this city is home to a professional football team

- a large lake in Wisconsin

- this river makes up the southwestern border

- a large city on the banks of Lake Michigan

- part of this state is wedged between the Great Lakes and Wisconsin

- the only Great Lake to be entirely in the United States

Size: 65,496 square miles
Population: 5,757,564

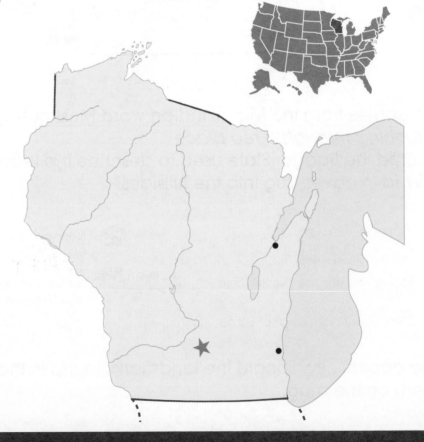

Michigan: The Wolverine State

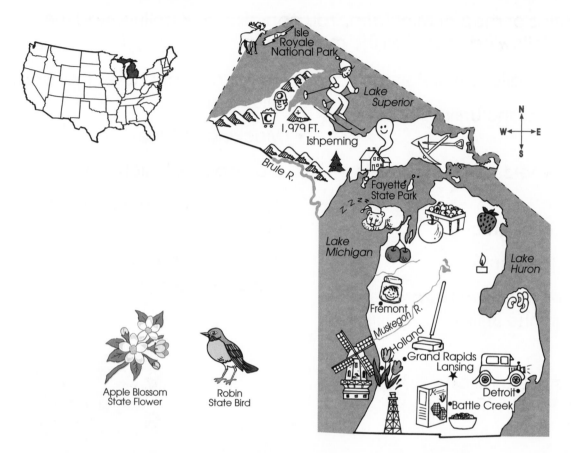

  Apple Blossom
State Flower

 Robin
State Bird

- named for the Indian word for Lake Michigan, *Michigama*, meaning *great lake*
- nicknamed the Wolverine State for wolverines that were trapped by fur traders and Battle Creek sold at trading posts

 Mount Arvon—
1,979 ft.

 United States Ski and
Snowboard Hall of Fame

Gerber—largest
baby food plant in
the U.S.

Fayette Historic
State Park—iron-ore
smelting village
from 1867 to 1891

Isle Royale National
Park—has one of the
largest herds of moose
in the United States

 Grand Rapids—first
carpet sweeper
invented here in 1876
by M.R. Bissel

 Battle Creek—
produces the most
breakfast cereal in the
world

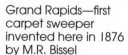 Sleeping Bear Dunes National
Lakeshore—features sand dune
shaped like a sleeping bear

Keweenaw Peninsula—one of the
world's few sources of pure copper

 Windmill Island Municipal Park—has
the only authentic and operational
Dutch windmill in the U.S.

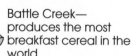 Detroit—nicknamed Motor City for its
large concentration of car and
truck production

Circle the capital city. Locate the landmarks found in the above key.
Color them on the map.

Michigan: The Wolverine State

Look at an atlas or map of Michigan. You can also look online. Add the names of the following places to the map below.

- a city named after Chief Pontiac
- the location of the University of Michigan
- the place where corn flakes were invented
- the Upper Peninsula
- the Lower Peninsula
- the lake where Oliver Hazard Perry fought the British

- the other Great Lakes that border Michigan
- Mackinac Island
- the capital of Michigan
- the center of the automobile industry
- the place where Father Jacques Marquette started his mission

Size: 96,713 square miles
Population: 9,909,877

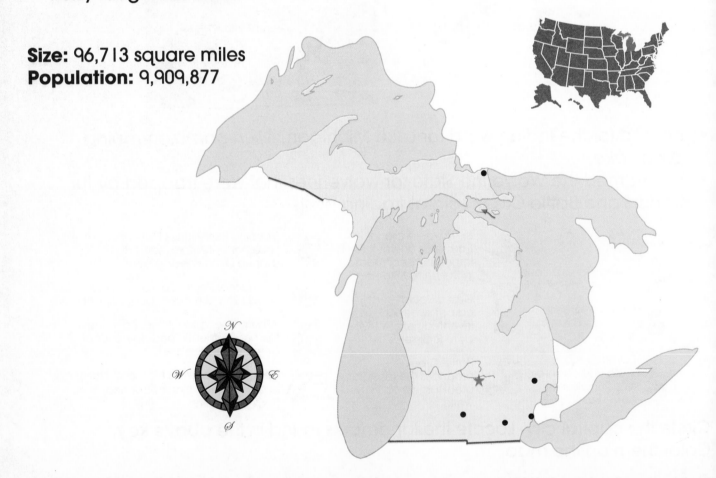

Illinois: The Land of Lincoln

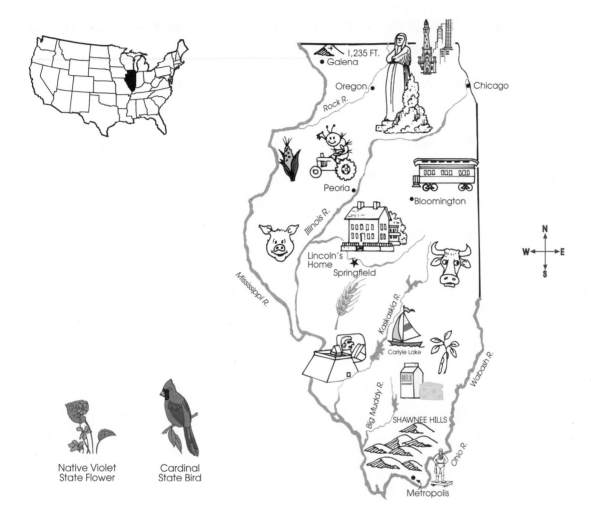

1,235 FT.
• Galena

Oregon

Rock R.

Chicago

Peoria

Bloomington

Illinois R.

Lincoln's
Home
Springfield

Mississippi R.

Kaskaskia R.

Carlyle Lake

MILK

Big Muddy R.

Wabash R.

SHAWNEE HILLS

Ohio R.

Metropolis

N
W   E
S

Native Violet
State Flower

Cardinal
State Bird

- named for the Illini Indians who called themselves *Illiniwek*, meaning *superior men*
- nicknamed the Land of Lincoln after Abraham Lincoln, who lived much of his life in the state

  Charles Mound—1,235 ft.

 Cahokia Mounds State Historic Site

 Peoria—international headquarters of Caterpillar Inc.

Lowden Memorial State Park—statue of Chief Black Hawk honors the area's Indians

 Metropolis—town celebrated as Superman's hometown

The Historic Water Tower— survived the Great Chicago Fire in 1871

 Bloomington—the first pullman sleeping car prototypes were made here in 1858

Circle the capital city. Locate the landmarks found in the above key.
Color them on the map.

Illinois: The Land of Lincoln

Look at an atlas or map of Illinois. You can also look online. Add the names of the following places to the map below.

- this city has one of the world's tallest skyscrapers

- this city sits on the Illinois river

- one settler thought this city was opposite from China

- this river links the Mississippi to the Illinois and Michigan Canal

- this lake is the largest wholly within the United States

- the capital of Illinois

- where Native Americans built a large structure

- this river forms the western border of Illinois

- a large city in the north

- Abraham Lincoln lived here as a boy

- boats use this man-made waterway to reach Chicago

Size: 57,914 square miles
Population: 12,880,580

Indiana: The Hoosier State

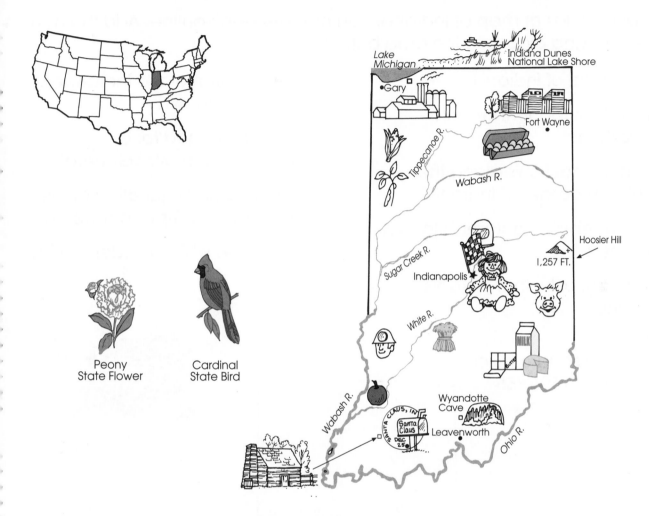

Peony
State Flower

Cardinal
State Bird

- name likely means *land of the Indians*
- nickname the Hoosier State may have come from a southern term for *rough hill people*

Indianapolis 500—car race

Indianapolis—Raggedy Ann doll created here in 1914

Santa Claus—remails many letters with its postmark at Christmastime

Wyandotte Cave—one of the largest caverns in the U.S.

Historic Fort Wayne—reconstructed 1816 military-trading post

Gary—has some of nation's largest steel mills

Lincoln Boyhood National Memorial—original cabin where Abraham Lincoln lived from ages 7-21

Circle the capital city. Locate the landmarks found in the above key. Color them on the map.

Indiana: The Hoosier State

Look at an atlas or map of Indiana. You can also look online. Add the names of the following places to the map below.

- the capital of Indiana

- the first permanent French settlement

- the river that flows along the southern border of Indiana

- the Studebaker automobile was built here

- the Great Lake that borders Indiana

- the location of the Indianapolis Motor Speedway

- the city named for a Revolutionary War General

- a city near the junction of the Wabash and Tippecanoe Rivers

- the states which border Indiana

Size: 36,420 square miles
Population: 6,596,855

Ohio: The Buckeye State

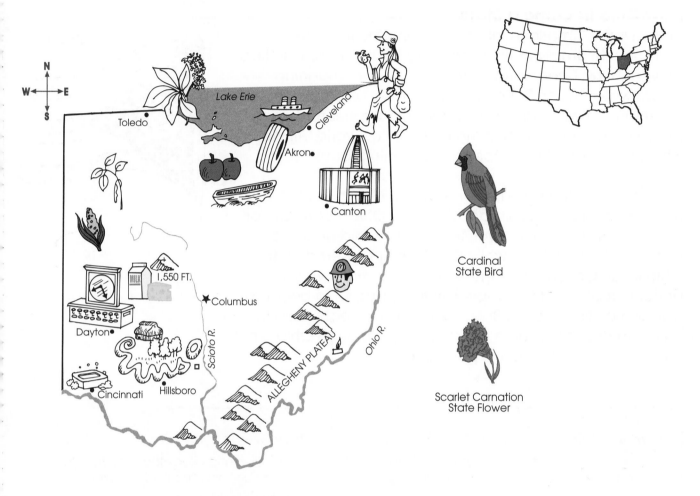

Cardinal
State Bird

Scarlet Carnation
State Flower

- name derived from Iroquois Indian word meaning *great water*
- nicknamed the Buckeye State for its abundance of buckeye trees

 Campbell Hill—1,550 ft.

 Dayton—first cash register invented here in 1878

 Serpent Mound National Historic Landmark— prehistoric Indian ceremonial mound, resembles a snake

 Ancient Dugout Canoe—from about 1600 B.C.; discovered in Ashland County

 Cincinnati—contains the largest soap factory in the U.S.

 Professional Football Hall of Fame

 Port of Cleveland—shipping port

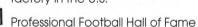 Johnny Appleseed—traveled through state, planting orchards

Akron—for many years, the largest producer of tires

Circle the capital city. Locate the landmarks found in the above key.
Color them on the map.

Welcome to Ohio

How Ohio Became a State

Many Native American tribes, including the Iroquois, Shawnee, Miami, and Wyandot lived in Ohio before settlers arrived. "Ohio" comes from an Iroquois word meaning "great water." John D. Rockefeller built his oil empire in Cleveland. Akron was home to rubber factories that once made more tires than anywhere else in the world. All the while, corn and other crops grew on Ohio's farms.

State Flag

Ohio became the seventeenth state on March 1, 1803. It was easy to travel and to ship goods on the Ohio waterways of Lake Erie and the Ohio River. Soon, Cleveland became a major port on the lake, while Cincinnati prospered on the Ohio River. Columbus, in the center of the state, was the perfect location for the capital. In the 1970s, Ohio became polluted by its factories. But now, Ohio has cleaned up the environment and people are returning. Although Ohio is not a large state, it has a large population.

Famous Ohioans

- John Glenn was the first American to orbit Earth. He also returned to space when he was 77.

- Presidents Ulysses S. Grant, Rutherford B. Hayes, James A. Garfield, Benjamin Harrison, William McKinley, William Howard Taft, and Warren G. Harding came from Ohio.

- Steven Spielberg makes movies, such as *E.T., Minority Report,* and *Raiders of the Lost Ark.*

- Neil Armstrong was the first person to walk on the Moon.

- Maya Lin sculpted the Vietnam Veterans Memorial in Washington, D.C.

State Greats

- The Cincinnati Red Stockings, now the Reds, became the first professional baseball team.

- Akron was once known as the "Rubber Capital of the World."

- The Rock and Roll Hall of Fame and Museum is located in Cleveland.

- The Pro Football Hall of Fame is located in Canton.

- The Cuyahoga River, near Lake Erie, was once so polluted that it caught fire. Today, it is a clean river.

- Oberlin College was the first to educate men and women together.

Ohio: The Buckeye State

Look at an atlas or map of Ohio. You can also look online. Add the names of the following places to the map below.

- state to the north

- this river empties into Lake Erie

- you can buy tires here

- this city celebrates famous music and musicians

- the city that boasts the birth of professional baseball

- state to the west

- Ohio's capital

- this river forms much of the Ohio border

- the major city in the northwest

- state to the east

- on one side of this lake is Ohio, on the other is Canada

Size: 44,026 square miles
Population: 11,594,163

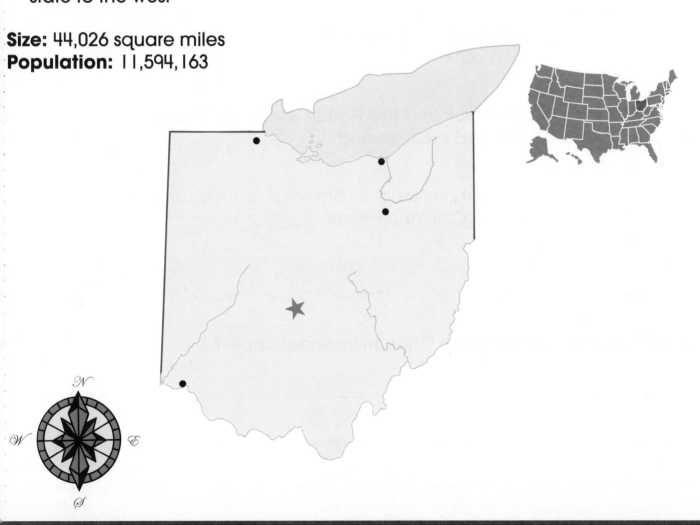

Ohio: The Buckeye State

Next to each sentence write a T if the statement is true or an F if the statement is false.

_____ The Ohio River forms the northern border of Ohio.

_____ The three largest cities in Ohio all start with "C."

_____ The Ohio River once caught fire.

_____ Toledo was known as an important producer of rubber.

_____ The Rock and Roll Hall of Fame and Museum is located in Cleveland.

_____ The first professional baseball team is now known as the Cincinnati Reds.

What industries helped make Ohio an important state?

_____

_____

_____

Name_____

The Northeastern States

The Northeastern States is a region with many natural harbors along the Atlantic Ocean. Inland, you will find rugged mountains and dense forests.

1. Maine

2. New Hampshire

3. Vermont

4. Massachusetts

5. Connecticut

6. Rhode Island

7. New Jersey

8. Delaware

9. Pennsylvania

10. New York

Fill in the "Five Fundamental Themes of Geography" for each state. After "discovering" a state, fill in all the columns of the chart except **Regions**. When you have finished with all of the states in a section, fill in **Regions**.

Five Fundamental Themes of Geography					
Name of State	**Location** (Where is it?)	**Place** (What is it like?)	**People and Environment** (What do the people do?)	**Movement** (How do people, goods, and ideas move?)	**Regions** (What are some of the common features?)

Five Fundamental Themes of Geography					
Name of State	Location (Where is it?)	Place (What is it like?)	People and Environment (What do the people do?)	Movement (How do people, goods, and ideas move?)	Regions (What are some of the common features?)

Maine: The Pine Tree State

Chickadee
State Bird

White Pine
Cone and Tassel
State Flower

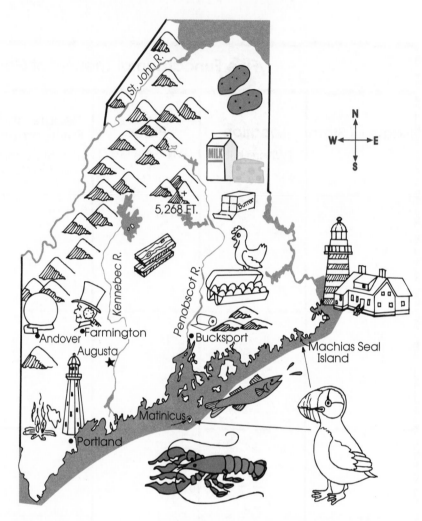

- name believed to have originated from the English explorers who used the term *main* to refer to the mainland, as opposed to the islands
- nicknamed the Pine Tree State for the abundance of pine tree forests

 Mount Katahdin—5,268 ft.

 Matinicus Island—sanctuary for puffins and other seabirds

 Satellite Earth Station— sends and receives orbiting satellites' signals

 Sebago Lake—Camp Fire Girls originated here in 1910

 Farmington—Earmuff Capital of the World, first earmuffs patented here in 1877

 West Quoddy Head Light—located on land that is the most easterly point of U.S.

 Portland Head Light— among the best known lighthouses in the U.S.

Circle the capital city. Locate the landmarks found in the above key. Color them on the map.

Maine: The Pine Tree State

Look at an atlas or map of Maine. You can also look online. Add the names of the following places to the map below.

- the capital of Maine

- the place where many lobster boats dock

- the country that borders Maine

- the one state that borders Maine

- the site where the L.L. Bean Company is located

- the town where Stephen King lives

- the coastal town that was closest to one of the first Revolutionary War naval battles

- the name of the body of water off the southern coast of Maine

- Penobscot River

- the Longfellow Mountains

Size: 35,380 square miles
Population: 1,330,089

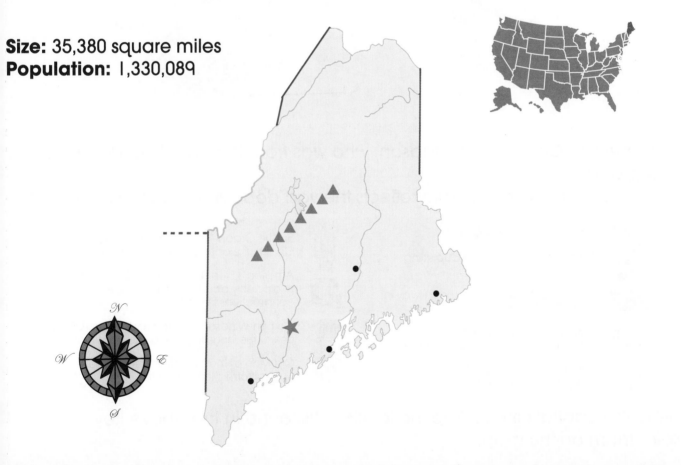

New Hampshire: The Granite State

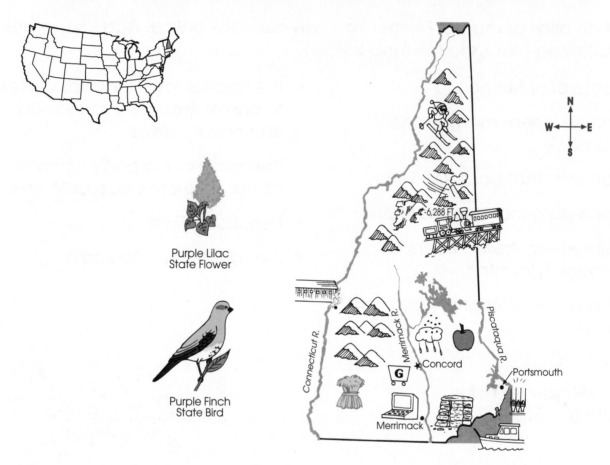

Purple Lilac
State Flower

Purple Finch
State Bird

- named by Captain John Mason, who was from the county of Hampshire in England
- nickname the Granite State reflects the vast deposits of granite in the state

 Mount Washington—6,288 ft.

 Waterville Valley—World Cup skiing competitions

 Mount Washington—first cog railway in the United States

 Merrimack—one of the largest computer companies in the U.S. located here

Concord—first place artificial rain was used to fight a forest fire

 Brattle Organ—in St. John's Episcopal Church, the oldest pipe organ in the U.S.

 America's Stonehenge—one of the largest and possibly oldest man-made stone constructions in the U.S.

 Cornish-Windsor Covered Bridge—at 450 ft., one of the longest covered bridges in the world

Old Man of the Mountain Historic Site—natural formation of granite

Circle the capital city. Locate the landmarks found in the above key.
Color them on the map.

New Hampshire: The Granite State

Look at an atlas or map of New Hampshire. You can also look online. Add the names of the following places to the map below.

- the site where the treaty of the Russo-Japanese war was signed

- the capital of New Hampshire

- the location of the Old Man of the Mountain

- the place where some of the fastest winds were recorded

- Lake Winnipesaukee

- the town where the MacDowell Colony is located

- the state that once claimed New Hampshire

- the birthplace of Daniel Webster

- the home of Robert Frost

- the Connecticut River

Size: 9,279 square miles
Population: 1,315,828

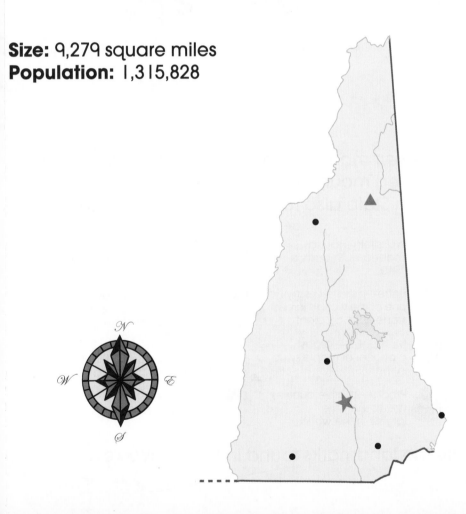

Vermont: The Green Mountain State

Hermit Thrush
State Bird

Red Clover
State Flower

- name from the French words *vert mont*, meaning *green mountain*, which describe the green, tree-covered mountains
- nickname the Green Mountain State also refers to forested mountains

 Mount Mansfield—4,393 ft.

 Cabot Creamery Cooperative—claims to make the best cheddar cheese in the world

 The Concord Academy—first school for training teachers

 UVM Morgan Horse Farm—has statue of the first of the breed of Morgan horses

 Waitsfield—round-shaped barn build in 1910

 Barre—granite quarry has one of the world's largest stone-finishing plant

 Montpelier—largest producer of maple syrup in the U.S.

 Proctor—marble quarries are among the largest in the world

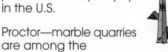 *Spirit of Ethan Allen*—replica of sternwheeler, cruises Lake Champlain

 Cornish-Windsor Covered Bridge—at 450 ft., one of the largest covered bridges in the world

Bennington Battle Monument—one of the United States' tallest monuments, honors colonists who defeated the British

Circle the capital city. Locate the landmarks found in the above key.
Color them on the map.

Vermont: The Green Mountain State

Look at an atlas or map of Vermont. You can also look online. Add the names of the following places to the map below.

- a lake named after an explorer

- the capital of Vermont

- a place near the first English-speaking settlement

- a site where granite is quarried

- the Green Mountains

- the state which once claimed Vermont and now borders it to the east

- the place where the Green Mountain Boys met

- the state's largest city

- the river that forms the border between New Hampshire and Vermont

- Mount Mansfield

- the birthplace of Chester Arthur

Size: 9,616 square miles
Population: 626,562

Massachusetts: The Bay State

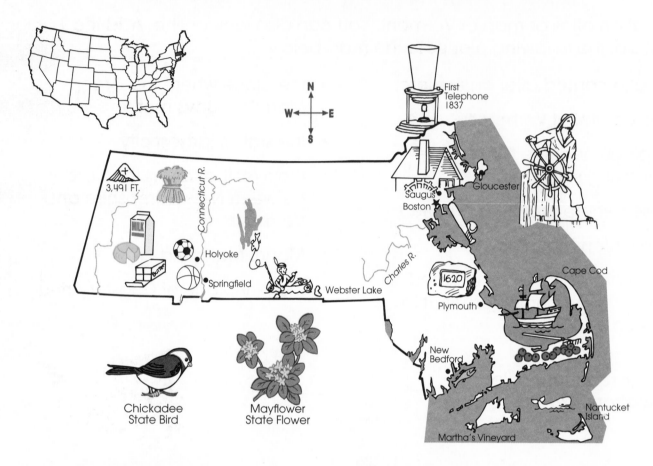

- name taken from the Massachusett Indian tribe, whose name means *near the great hill*
- nickname the Bay State refers to Massachusetts Bay, where Puritans established their colony

 Mount Greylock—3,491 ft.

 Holyoke—volleyball was developed here in 1895

 Saugus Iron Works National Historic Site—made and exported iron in the 1600s

 Nantucket Island—resort area that was once a whaling port

 Springfield—basketball invented here in 1891, contains Naismith Memorial Basketball Hall of Fame

Boston—first World Series played here in 1903

Gloucester—statue built to honor all of its people who have died at sea

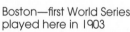 Plymouth Rock—marks where the Pilgrims landed according to tradition

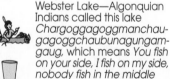 Cape Cod National Seashore—Pilgrims landed here before going on to Plymouth

 Webster Lake—Algonquian Indians called this lake *Chargoggagoggmanchau-gagoggchaubunagungam-gaug,* which means *You fish on your side, I fish on my side, nobody fish in the middle*

 First Telephone—1876 in Boston

Circle the capital city. Locate the landmarks found in the above key. Color them on the map.

Massachusetts: The Bay State

Look at an atlas or map of Massachusetts. You can also look online. Add the names of the following places to the map below.

- the capital of Massachusetts

- the birthplace of basketball

- Cape Cod

- the city with the oldest college in the United States

- a town named for Francis Cabot Lowell

- the place where the Pilgrims landed

- the town where Emily Dickinson wrote her poems

- the two sites where the first fighting of the Revolutionary War took place

- the Berkshires

- the place where Paul Revere began his ride

- Martha's Vineyard

Size: 10,554 square miles
Population: 6,745,408

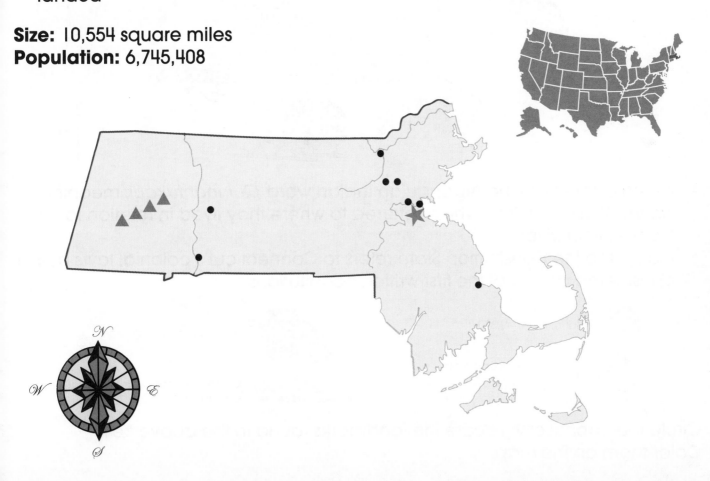

Connecticut: The Constitution State

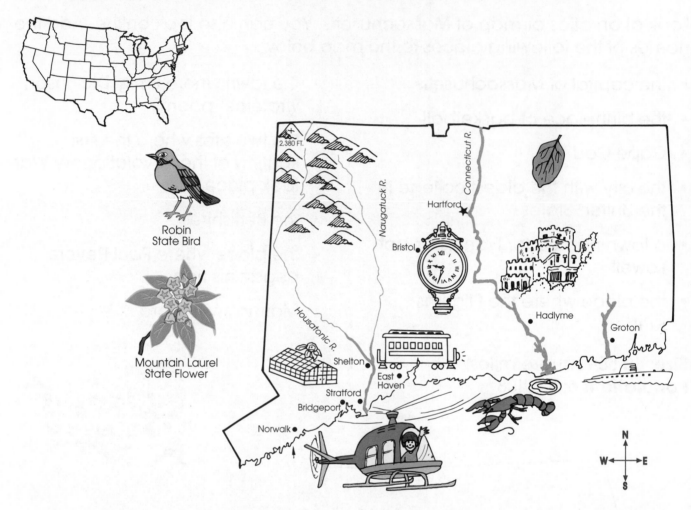

- name came from the Algonquian Indian word *Quinnehtukqut*, meaning *on the long tidal river*, which referred to where they lived in relation to the Connecticut River
- nickname the Constitution State refers to Connecticut's colonial laws being considered as one of the first written constitutions

Mount Frissel—2,380 ft.

American Clock and Watch Museum

Gillette Castlle State Park

Groton—United States Naval Submarine Base

Circle the capital city. Locate the landmarks found in the above key. Color them on the map.

Connecticut: The Constitution State

Look at an atlas or map of Connecticut. You can also look online. Add the names of the following places to the map below.

- the place where visitors can tour the *U.S.S. Nautilus*
- the site of Yale University
- the town where the first helicopter was developed
- the state capital
- Long Island Sound
- the Connecticut River

- the town known as "Park City"
- a city that takes its name from London, England
- Block Island Sound
- the former fishing town of Norwalk
- a popular vacation spot

Size: 5,543 square miles
Population: 3,596,677

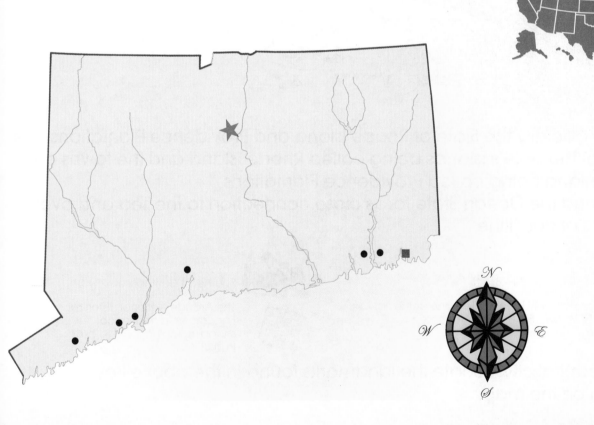

Rhode Island: The Ocean State

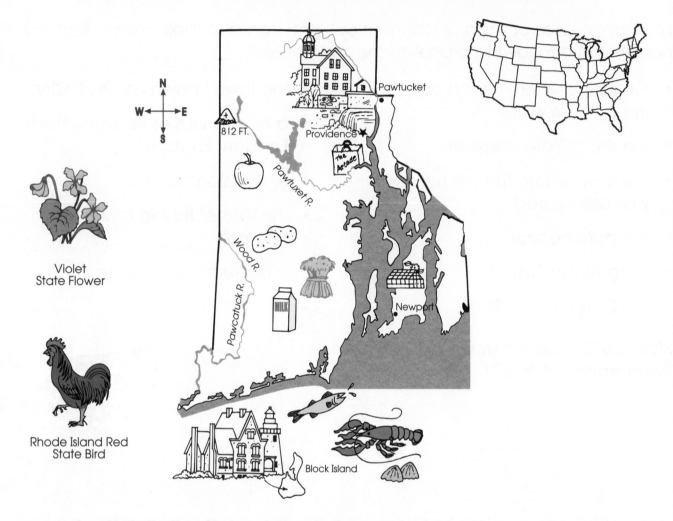

Violet
State Flower

Rhode Island Red
State Bird

Pawtucket

Providence

The Arcade

Pawtuxet R.

Wood R.

Pawcatuck R.

MILK

Newport

Block Island

- name is officially the State of Rhode Island and Providence Plantations, the largest of the state's islands being called Rhode Island and the towns on the mainland being called Providence Plantations
- nicknamed the Ocean State for its close connection to the sea and over 400 miles of coastline

 Jerimoth Hill—812 ft.

Slater Mill Historic Site—one of the first
textile mills in North America

Southeast Lighthouse

 The Arcade National Historical
Landmark—oldest indoor
shopping mall in the U.S., built
in 1828

Circle the capital city. Locate the landmarks found in the above key.
Color them on the map.

Rhode Island: The Ocean State

Look at an atlas or map of Rhode Island. You can also look online. Add the names of the following places to the map below.

- the site of America's first successful cotton mill

- the capital of Rhode Island

- Narragansett Bay

- many wealthy families built mansions here

- Block Island

- Warwick, one of Rhode Island's first towns

- the state that borders Rhode Island on the west

- Block Island Sound

- the ocean to the south

- Pawtuxet River

- Blackstone River

Size: 1,545 square miles
Population: 1,055,173

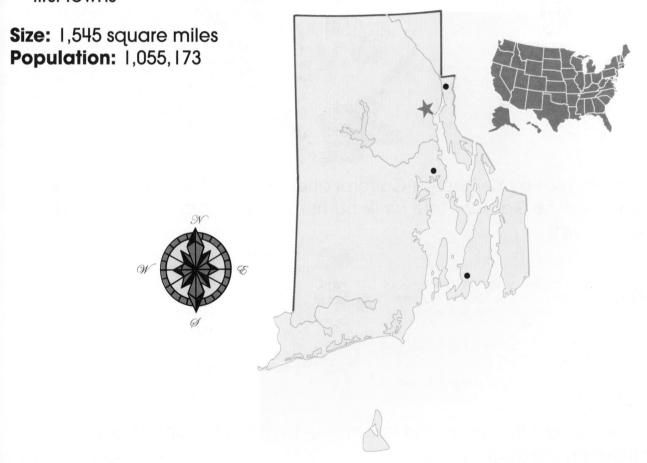

New Jersey: The Garden State

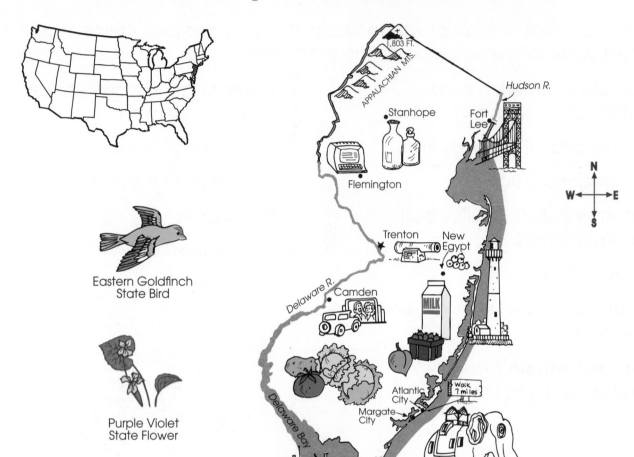

- named in 1664 by Sir George Carteret after the Isle of Jersey in England
- nicknamed the Garden State for its numerous truck farms, flower gardens, and orchards

 High Point—1,803 ft.

 Lucy, the Margate Elephant National Historic Landmark—built in 1881, the oldest roadside attraction in the United States

 Flemington—leader in machinery and computer assembly

 George Washington Bridge—thousands use this to commute from New Jersey to New York City

 Old Barracks Museum—British and Irish lived here during the French and Indian Wars

 Camden—first drive-in theater opened here on June 6, 1933

 New Egypt—Ocean Spray first made

 Atlantic City—boardwalk and casinos make this popular for tourists

 Waterloo Village State Historic Site—a 19th century restored town of the 1700s

Circle the capital city. Locate the landmarks found in the above key. Color them on the map.

New Jersey: The Garden State

Look at an atlas or map of New Jersey. You can also look online. Add the names of the following places to the map below.

- the state capital

- the river that flows between New Jersey and Pennsylvania

- the southernmost point of New Jersey

- the location of one of America's leading universities

- the largest city in New Jersey

- the states that border New Jersey

- the mountains in northern New Jersey

- the city on the coast that shares its name with an ocean

- the ocean bordering eastern New Jersey

- the place where Samuel Morse invented the telegraph

Size: 8,723 square miles
Population: 8,938,175

Delaware: The First State

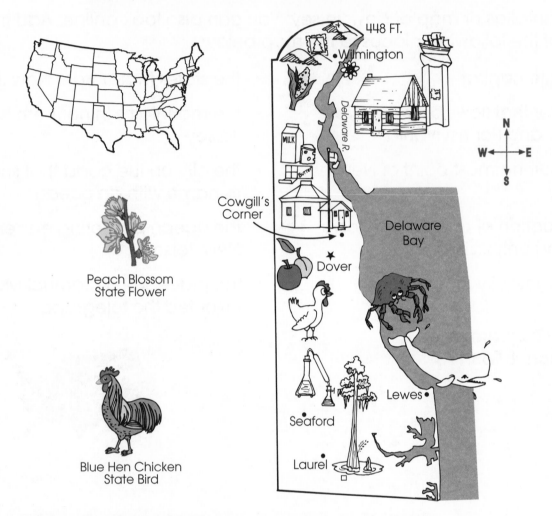

448 FT.

Wilmington

Delaware R.

MILK
BUTTER

Cowgill's Corner

Delaware Bay

Dover

Lewes

Seaford

Laurel

N
W — E
S

Peach Blossom
State Flower

Blue Hen Chicken
State Bird

- named for the governor of Virginia, Baron De La Warr
- nicknamed the First State for being the first state to approve the United States Constitution

 Wilmington—nicknamed Chemical Capital of the World

 Great Cypress Swamp—10,000 acres of wetland and forest

 The Octagonal School opened in 1836

Seaford-Nylon Capital of the World—nylon first made by Du Pont Company in 1939

Lewes—whaling colony settled by the Dutch in 1631

 First Christmas Seals—sold in Wilmington Post Office in 1907

 Fort Christina National Historical Landmark—site of the first permanent settlement of Swedes and Finns in Delaware

Circle the capital city. Locate the landmarks found in the above key. Color them on the map.

Delaware: The First State

Look at an atlas or map of Delaware. You can also look online. Add the names of the following places to the map below.

- the home of E.I. du Pont de Nemours and Company

- the place where the Town Hall of Hoorn was built

- the state capital

- the river where three countries started settlements

- Nanticoke River

- the state that shares a rounded border with Delaware

- the ocean that borders Delaware to the east

- the two communities that are in both Delaware and Maryland

- the bay that is named for Delaware

- the town that was once called New Amstel

Size: 2,489 square miles
Population: 935,614

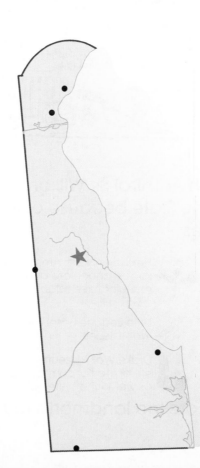

Pennsylvania: The Keystone State

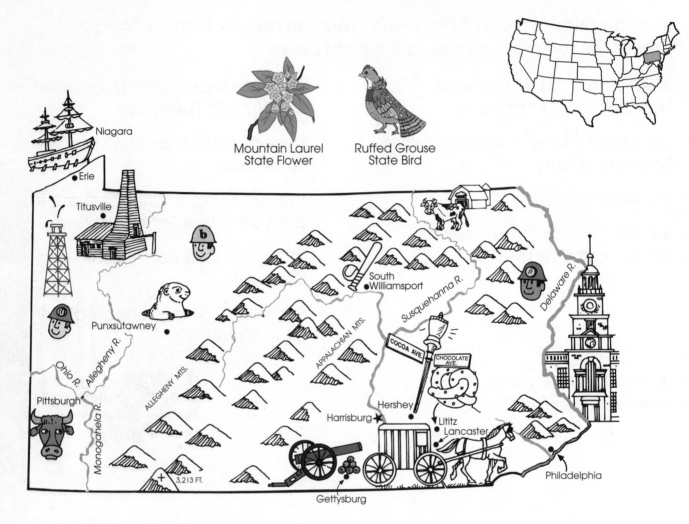

Mountain Laurel
State Flower

Ruffed Grouse
State Bird

- named in 1681 for British Admiral Sir William Penn, means *Penn's Woods*
- nicknamed the Keystone State because of its location in the center of the thirteen original colonies

 Mount Davis—3,213 ft.

 U.S. Brig Niagara— used by Oliver Perry to defeat the British in War of 1812

 Lititz—first pretzel bakery opened in 1861

 Hershey—North America's largest chocolate and cocoa manufacturer, established in 1905

 Little League Baseball World Series

 Drake Well Museum— site of the first commercial oil well in the United States

 Groundhog Day Festivities

 Landis Valley Village and Farm Museum

 Independence Hall— Declaration of Independence signed here in 1776

Circle the capital city. Locate the landmarks found in the above key. Color them on the map.

Name _____

Pennsylvania: The Keystone State

Look at an atlas or map of Pennsylvania. You can also look online. Add the names of the following places to the map below.

- the great lake that borders northwest Pennsylvania

- the river that separates Pennsylvania and New Jersey

- the capital

- the town that founded Little League baseball

- the city where the Continental Congress met

- coal was discovered near this city

- the city where Lincoln gave his famous speech

- General Marshall's hometown

- the city named after the Duke of York

- the site of one of the largest chocolate factories

Size: 46,054 square miles
Population: 12,787,209

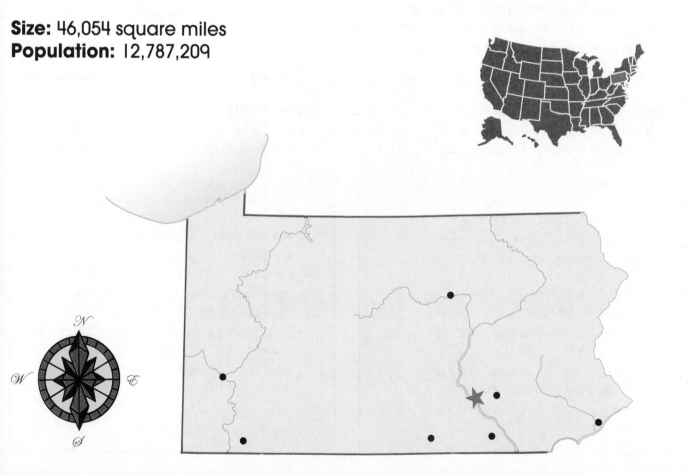

Welcome to New York

How New York Became a State

The first people living in the land that became New York were the Native American tribes, including the Iroquois and Algonquin. The first European explorer to visit New York was Giovanni da Verrazano in 1524. In 1609, the land was explored by Henry Hudson of the Netherlands and Samuel de Champlain of France. The Netherlands claimed the area for their own, but they did not settle it. In 1624, the Dutch built the first town, Fort Orange. This town would later become Albany. The next year, New Amsterdam was built.

State Flag

In 1664, England took control of the land and renamed New Amsterdam New York City. The French returned and joined forces with the Native Americans. The French attacked the English at Schenectady in 1690. England finally defeated the French in 1763. Despite the English victory, many people did not want to be part of England. In 1776, the United States declared its independence from England. New York became the eleventh state on July 26, 1788.

Bluebird
State Bird

Rose
State Flower

Famous New Yorkers

- Hiawatha was an Iroquois leader and peacemaker, who helped set up the Iroquois Federation.

- Franklin D. Roosevelt was born in Hyde Park and became the thirty-second president of the United States.

- James Baldwin wrote books about African-Americans and lived in New York City.

- Woody Allen directs and acts in many movies about New York.

- George Gershwin wrote music for orchestras.

- Elizabeth Ann Seton was a saint and founded the Sisters of Charity.

- Herman Melville is famous for writing the book *Moby Dick*.

State Greats

- From 1892 to 1954, millions of people came to America through Ellis Island. It is now a museum.

- More than 500,000 gallons of water flow over Niagara Falls every second. It is one of the largest, most famous falls in the world. It is in both Canada and the U.S.

- The first American women's rights convention was held in Seneca Falls.

- The Kodak camera was invented by George Eastman in Rochester.

- New York City has the country's largest art museum, the Metropolitan Museum of Art.

- New York City was the first capital city of the United States.

Name_____

New York: The Empire State

Read each clue. Use the code to find the answers.

1-A	5-E	9-I	13-X	17-K	21-U	25-Y
2-G	6-J	10-P	14-D	18-R	22-V	26-F
3-C	7-B	11-M	15-O	19-Z	23-W	
4-N	8-H	12-L	16-S	20-T	24-Q	

first name of New York's famous actor and director

◯ __ __ __ __
23 15 15 14 25

a river named for an explorer

◯ __ __ __ __ __
8 21 14 16 15 4

first name of first explorer

__ ◯ __ __ ◯ __ __ __
2 9 15 22 1 4 4 9

used to be called Fort Orange

◯ __ __ ◯ __ __
1 12 7 1 4 25

home of George Eastman

__ __ __ ◯ __ __ ◯ __ __
18 15 3 8 5 16 20 5 18

Unscramble the circled letters to write the name of the famous Iroquois leader.

__ __ __ __ __ __ __ __

The Statue of Liberty was the first thing many immigrants saw when they came to Ellis Island and entered New York Harbor. The Statue of Liberty stands for freedom.

If you built a new statue to welcome people to New York, what would it look like? Draw a picture of your statue and write about what it stands for.

_____
_____
_____
_____
_____
_____

New York: The Empire State

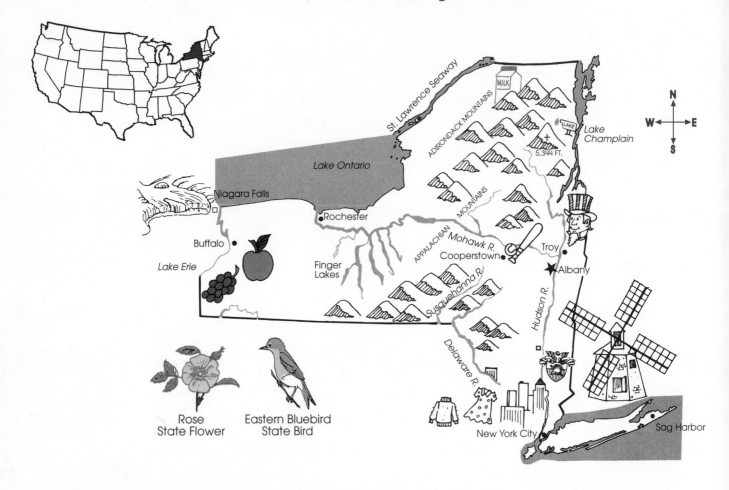

- name was originally New Netherland when a colony claimed by the Dutch; was then claimed by the English and the name was changed to New York to honor the Duke of York
- nickname the Empire State possibly related to George Washington in a 1785 letter when he described New York as "the seat of the empire"

Mount Marcy—5,344 ft.

New York City—a center of publishing industry and home of the fashion industry's Garment District

West Point—U.S. Military Academy

Niagara Falls—most famous waterfall in the world

Lake Placid—world famous resort with a glacial lake

National Baseball Hall of Fame and Museum

Sag Harbor—windmill once used here as a major source of energy

Uncle Sam—symbol originated in Troy

Circle the capital city. Locate the landmarks found in the above key. Color them on the map.

Welcome to Washington, D.C.

How Washington, D.C. Became the Capital

The Revolutionary War ended in 1783. The new United States of America named New York, then Philadelphia, as its capital. However, many people thought the capital should not belong to one state. In 1790, Congress said they would build a federal city in the wilderness. It would lie between Maryland and Virginia. They called the land the District of Columbia, or "D.C."

President George Washington chose Pierre Charles L'Enfant to plan the city in 1791. Congress held a contest to design the Capitol building and the President's House, later called the White House. William Thornton had the best plan for the Capitol. James Hoban had the best plan for the President's House. However, planning the capital was not easy. People disagreed about how the city should be laid out. L'Enfant quit halfway through the project. Andrew Ellicott took over to finish the job in 1792. In 1800, the federal city was named the Capital. In 1801, it was renamed Washington in honor of George Washington.

Official Flag

Wood Thrush
Official Bird

American
Beauty Rose
Official Flower

Famous Washingtonians

- Duke Ellington was a famous jazz and blues musician.

- John Foster Dulles was a secretary of state.

- Edward Brooke was the first African-American senator elected by popular vote.

- J. Edgar Hoover directed the Federal Bureau of Investigation (FBI).

- John Philip Sousa was a bandmaster and composer who was famous for his marches.

Capital Greats

- The National Mall is a grassy area between the Capitol and the Potomac River. Most of the national museums and many of the monuments are on the Mall.

- The Washington Monument is a hollow tower that stands 554 feet and 7 inches tall.

- The Lincoln Memorial contains a large statue of President Lincoln created by Daniel Chester French.

- George Washington University is a leading university in D.C.

- The Theodore Roosevelt memorial is the only D.C. memorial on an island. The island is in the Potomac River.

Washington, D.C.: The Nation's Capital

Look at an atlas or map of Washington, D.C. You can also look online. Add the names of the following places to the map below.

- the house built for the president
- the state to the southwest
- the state to the northeast
- the government building designed by William Thornton
- the river that divides D.C. from Virginia

- the grassy area filled with national museums
- a leading university
- the monument that honors George Washington
- the memorial that honors Abraham Lincoln
- the memorial on an island

Size: 68 square miles
Population: 601,723

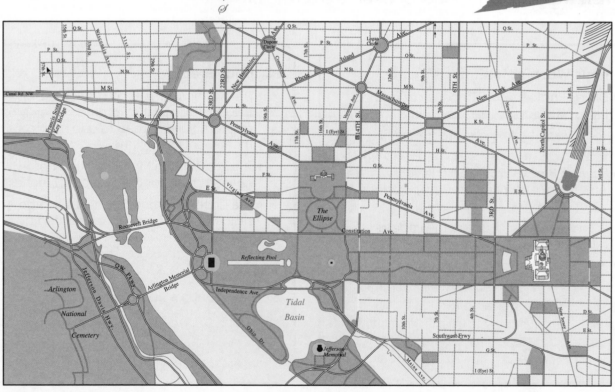

Washington, D.C.: The Nation's Capital

Andrew wants to work for the FBI one day. He wants to use codes to protect government secrets. This is Andrew's list of the best things to see in D.C. Use his code to find out what he likes best about D.C.

What to See in D.C.:

the tall, 554-foot tower   _____ _____

the road that connects the Capitol
and the White House   _____ _____

the monument honoring Lincoln   _____ _____

the rectangular body of water   _____ _____

To find Andrew's favorite area of the city, follow these decoding steps.

1 Write the first letter of each answer word on the line. _____

2 Cross out the W, M, P, R, and P. Write the remaining letters on the line. _____

3 Rewrite the remaining letters on the line. Add an L. _____

4 Unscramble to the letters to find Andrew's favorite place in D.C. _____

If Washington, D.C. were to become a state, it would need a new state flag. What would it look like? Design your own flag to honor D.C. Explain your design.

_____

_____

_____

_____

The Southeastern States

The Southeastern States is a region with many different kinds of land formations. It has long jagged coastlines, rugged mountains, deep pine forests, steep valleys, and beautiful rivers.

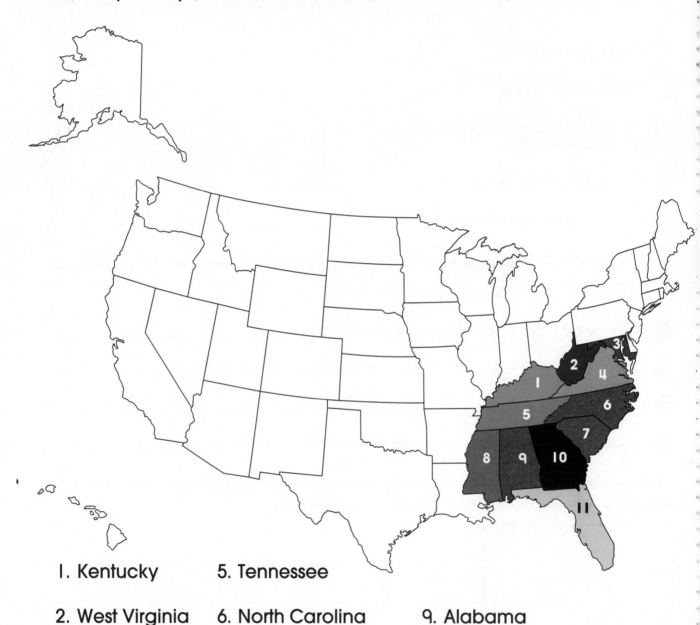

1. Kentucky

2. West Virginia

3. Maryland

4. Virginia

5. Tennessee

6. North Carolina

7. South Carolina

8. Mississippi

9. Alabama

10. Georgia

11. Florida

Fill in the "Five Fundamental Themes of Geography" for each state. After "discovering" a state, fill in all the columns of the chart except **Regions**. When you have finished with all of the states in a section, fill in **Regions**.

Five Fundamental Themes of Geography					
Name of State	Location (Where is it?)	Place (What is it like?)	People and Environment (What do the people do?)	Movement (How do people, goods, and ideas move?)	Regions (What are some of the common features?)

Five Fundamental Themes of Geography

Name of State	Location (Where is it?)	Place (What is it like?)	People and Environment (What do the people do?)	Movement (How do people, goods, and ideas move?)	Regions (What are some of the common features?)

Kentucky: The Bluegrass State

Goldenrod
State Flower

Cardinal
State Bird

- name possibly derived from the Cherokee Indian word *kentake*, which means *meadow* or *pasture*
- nicknamed the Bluegrass State for the blueish buds on the grass of this region

 Black Mountain—4,145 ft.

 Fort Boonesborough State Park—reconstructed fort founded by Daniel Boone

 Fort Knox—the United States Bullion Depository protects nation's gold reserves

 Kentucky Derby—at Churchill Downs race track; oldest horse racing event in U.S.

 Mammoth Cave National Park—world's longest known continuous cave system

 Lexington—thousands of thoroughbred horses raised on horse farms here

Cumberland Falls—nicknamed Niagara of the South

Circle the capital city. Locate the landmarks found in the above key.
Color them on the map.

Kentucky: The Bluegrass State

Look at an atlas or map of Kentucky. You can also look online. Add the names of the following places to the map below.

- the home of the Kentucky Derby

- the capital of Kentucky

- the location of the gold reserve

- the river which flows along the northern border of Kentucky

- the river which forms a part of the western boundary of Kentucky

- the longest cave in the world

- the home of the Corvette plant

- the seven states that border Kentucky

Size: 40,408 square miles
Population: 4,413,457

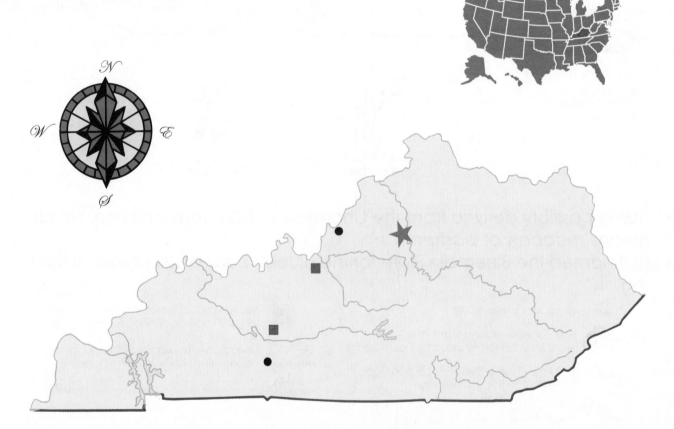

West Virginia: The Mountain State

Cardinal
State Bird

Rhododendron
State Flower

- named when northwestern counties separated from Virginia during the Civil War and sided with the North
- nicknamed the Mountain State for its rugged mountains, steep hills, and narrow valleys

 Spruce Knob—4,863 ft.

 Grave Creek Mound—largest conical burial mound, built 2,000 years ago by the Adena people

 Marshall County—underground salt mines

 Huntington—famous histoically for its glassware and pottery

 Shepherdstown—monument to James Rumsey, engineer and a steamboat inventor

 Paden City—glass marble manufacturer

 National Radio Astronomy Observatory

Circle the capital city. Locate the landmarks found in the above key. Color them on the map.

West Virginia: The Mountain State

Look at an atlas or map of West Virigina. You can also look online. Add the names of the following places to the map below.

- a one-time capital of West Virginia

- the state to the north and west of West Virginia

- West Virginia used to be a part of this state

- beautiful mountains in the east

- city near Kentucky

- the capital of West Virginia

- the states to the north and east

- this river forms a border between West Virginia and Ohio

- a onetime Confederate state to the south and west

- John Brown raided this place

Size: 24,230 square miles
Population: 1,850,326

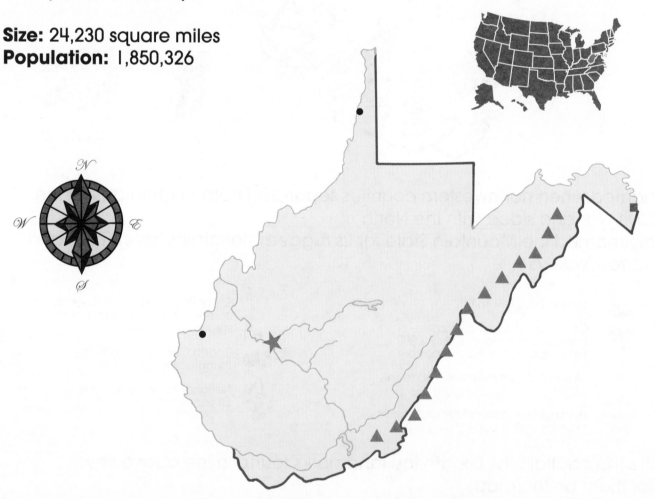

Maryland: The Old Line State

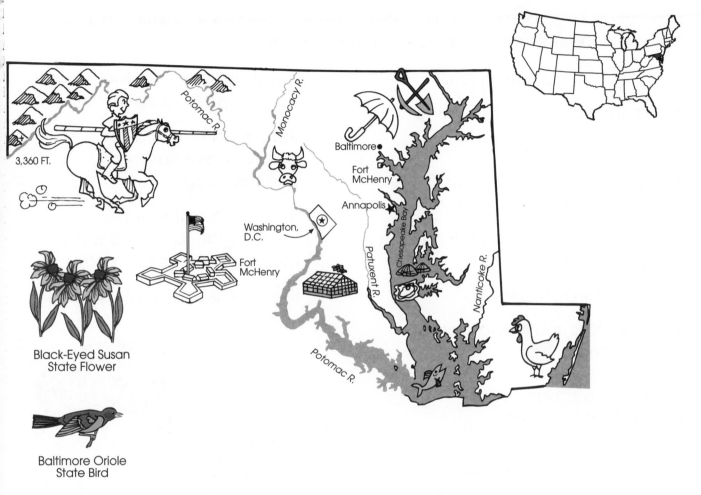

3,360 FT.

Potomac R.

Monocacy R.

Baltimore

Fort McHenry

Annapolis

Washington, D.C.

Fort McHenry

Patuxent R.

Chesapeake Bay

Nanticoke R.

Potomac R.

Black-Eyed Susan
State Flower

Baltimore Oriole
State Bird

- named in 1632 for Henrietta Maria, the wife of England's King Charles I
- nicknamed the Old Line State in honor of the troops from Maryland who fought so bravely on the line during the Revolutionary War

Backbone Mountain—3,360 ft.

Fort McHenry National Monument and Historic Shrine—Frances Scott Key wrote the "Star-Spangled Banner" here during the War of 1812

State Jousting Championship—held each year

Baltimore—first umbrella factory in the U.S., established in 1828

Washington, D.C.—George Washington chose this spot for the nation's capital

Circle the capital city. Locate the landmarks found in the above key. Color them on the map.

Maryland: The Old Line State

Look at an atlas or map of Maryland. You can also look online. Add the names of the following places to the map below.

- a city named after a lord

- this state is west of Maryland

- the state capital

- this waterway was a reason settlers came to Maryland

- the line that separated the North from the South

- the nation's capital

- this state is south and west of Maryland

Size: 12,406 square miles
Population: 5,976,407

- this state is on the other side of the Mason-Dixon line

- this river drains into the Chesapeake Bay from Pennsylvania

- this river cuts through Washington, D.C. and forms Maryland's western border

- this state is east of Maryland

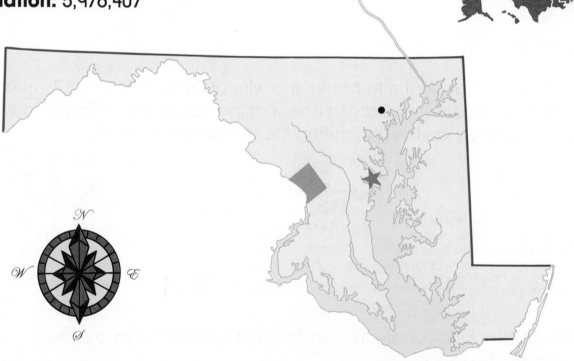

Virginia: The Old Dominion

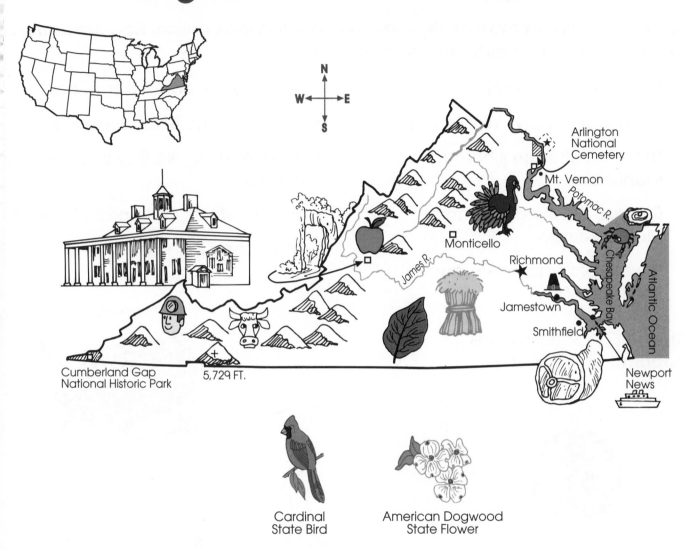

Cardinal
State Bird

American Dogwood
State Flower

- named for England's Queen Elizabeth I, who was called the Virgin Queen because she never married
- nicknamed the Old Dominion by Charles II because Virginia was loyal to the crown during the English Civil War

 Mount Rogers—5,729 ft.

Washington, D.C.—George Washington chose this spot for the nation's capital

 Arlington National Cemetery—Tomb of the Unknown Soldier

Smithfield—famous for its hams

Circle the capital city. Locate the landmarks found in the above key.
Color them on the map.

Virginia: The Old Dominion

Look at an atlas or map of Virginia. You can also look online. Add the names of the following places to the map below.

- the capital of Virginia

- the site of the Civil War surrender

- Thomas Jefferson's home, Monticello

- George Washington's home, Mount Vernon

- the site of the first permanent English colony

- Arlington National Cemetery

- the site of the British surrender

- the Chesapeake Bay Bridge-Tunnel

- the five states that border Virginia

- the ocean to the east

Size: 42,775 square miles
Population: 8,326,289

Name _____

Tennessee: The Volunteer State

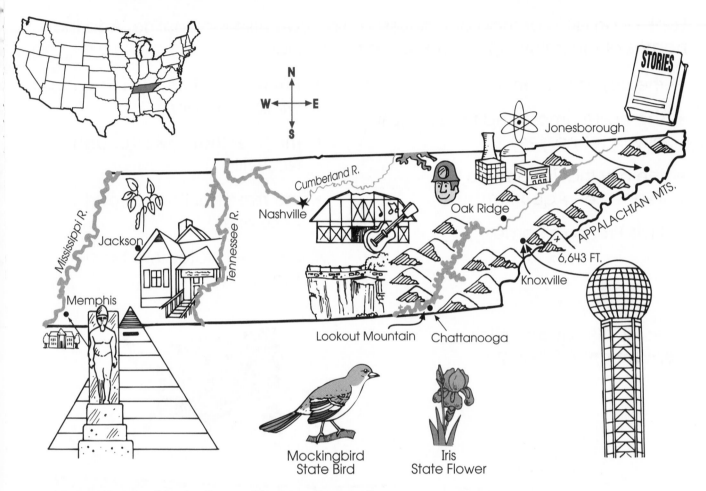

Nashville
Jackson
Memphis
Mississippi R.
Tennessee R.
Cumberland R.
Oak Ridge
Jonesborough
APPALACHIAN MTS.
6,643 FT.
Knoxville
Lookout Mountain
Chattanooga
STORIES

Mockingbird
State Bird

Iris
State Flower

- named for a Cherokee village, *Tanasie*
- nickname the Volunteer State refers to the large number of men who unhesitatingly volunteered for military service during the War of 1812 and the Mexican War

 Clingmans Dome— 6,643 ft.

 Casey Jones Home and Railroad Museum

 Sunsphere—266-foot tower built for 1982 World's Fair

 American Museum of Science and Energy

 The Pyramid—32-story stainless steel retail and entertainment complex

 Graceland—estate of Elvis Presley

 Lookout Mountain

 National Storytelling Festival

 Grand Ole Opry

Circle the capital city. Locate the landmarks found in the above key. Color them on the map.

Tennessee: The Volunteer State

Look at an atlas or map of Tennessee. You can also look online. Add the names of the following places to the map below.

- the capital of Tennessee

- the easternmost and third largest city in Tennessee

- the city that is home to the Tennessee Aquarium

- Elvis Presley's home

- the river that creates Tennessee's western border

- the river that flows through Nashville

- the river that flows through Knoxville

- the eight states that border Tennessee

Size: 42,144 square miles
Population: 6,549,352

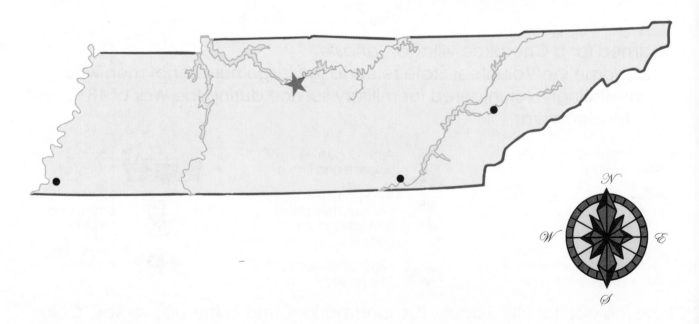

North Carolina: The Tar Heel State

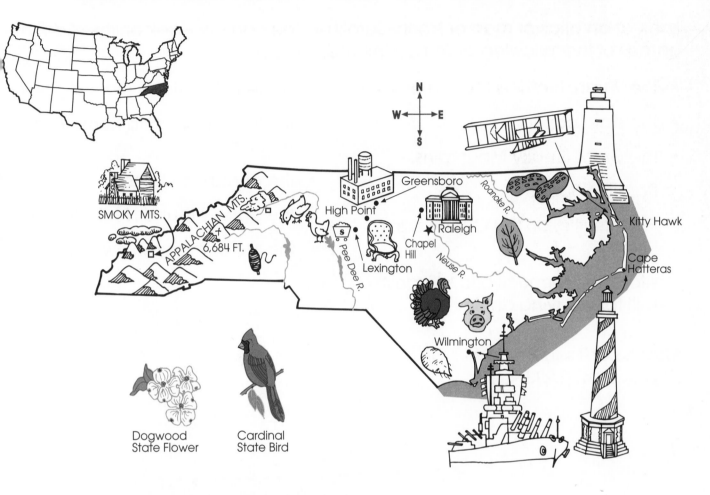

SMOKY MTS.

APPALACHIAN MTS.

6,684 FT.

Pee Dee R.

Lexington

High Point

Greensboro

Raleigh

Chapel Hill

Roanoke R.

Neuse R.

Kitty Hawk

Cape Hatteras

Wilmington

Dogwood
State Flower

Cardinal
State Bird

- named for King Charles I of England
- nickname the Tar Heel State refers to the large amount of tar produced which made North Carolina the leading colony in the naval store industry

 Mount Mitchell—6,684 ft.

 Morehead Planetarium and Science Center

 High Point—often called the Furniture Capital of the World

 Lexington—rich silver discovered, mine incorporated in 1838

 Gaston County—spins more yarn than any other U.S. county

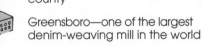 Greensboro—one of the largest denim-weaving mill in the world

 Cape Hatteras Lighthouse—guards the Graveyard of the Atlantic

 Wright Brothers National Memorial

 Cherokee Indian Reservation—has replica of a 1700's Indian village

 Grandfather Mountain—resembles an old man sleeping

 U.S.S. North Carolina—took part in every major Pacific Ocean battle in WWII

Circle the capital city. Locate the landmarks found in the above key. Color them on the map.

North Carolina: The Tar Heel State

Look at an atlas or map of North Carolina. You can also look online. Add the names of the following places to the map below.

- the Wright Brothers Monument

- the state capital

- the Great Smoky Mountains

- Pamlico Sound

- Fayetteville, on the Cape Fear River

- site of the former world's largest mill for weaving denim

- eastern America's highest peak

- the largest city and home to the Hornets

- the ocean to the east

- the states around North Carolina

- the site of many shipwrecks

Size: 53,819 square miles
Population: 9,943,964

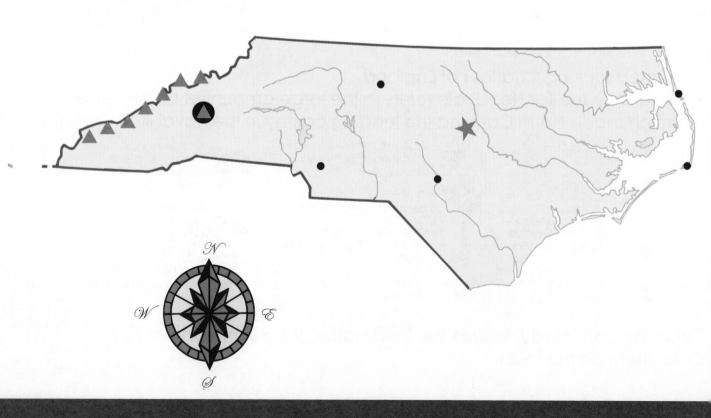

South Carolina: The Palmetto State

 Yellow Jessamine
State Flower

 Carolina Wren
State Bird

- named for King Charles I of England; "South" was added when the Carolinas separated
- nickname the Palmetto State may be the result of an incident during the Revolutionary War where soldiers fought from a palmetto log fort and smoke from a burning British ship resembled the state's palmetto tree

Sassafras Mountain—3,560 ft.

The Peachoid—a peach-shaped tank holding one million gallons of water

Fort Sumter National Monument—site of the beginning of the Civil War

Southern 500—stock car race

Middleton Place—one of Charleston's finest plantations and a National Historic Landmark

Hilton Head Island—popular vacation resort

Circle the capital city. Locate the landmarks found in the above key. Color them on the map.

South Carolina: The Palmetto State

Look at an atlas or map of South Carolina. You can also look online. Add the names of the following places to the map below.

- this is a popular seaside spot

- the ocean to the east of South Carolina

- this large city is in the northwestern part of the state

- an island near the southern border

- a big city on the ocean

- the capital of South Carolina

- a large lake between Columbia and Charleston

- historic shots were fired here

- the state south and west of South Carolina

- the state to the north

Size: 32,020 square miles
Population: 4,832,482

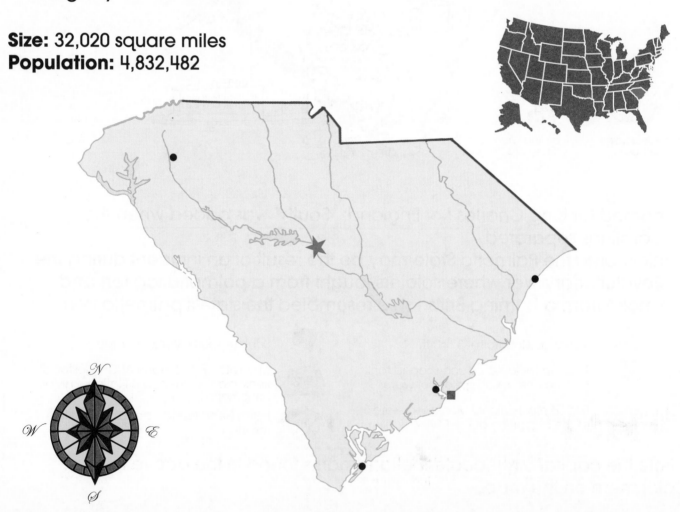

Mississippi: The Magnolia State

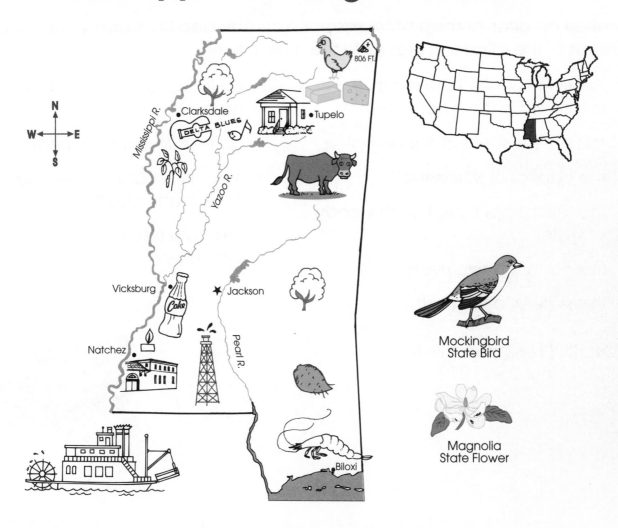

Mockingbird
State Bird

Magnolia
State Flower

- name taken from two Indian words, *misi* and *sipi* meaning *big river* or *great water*
- nickname the Magnolia State refers to the many magnolia trees that grow in the state

 Woodall Mountain—806 ft.

 Delta Blues Museum— dedicated to blues musicians and music

 Shrimp Festival—chief shrimp-packing port

 Elvis Presley Birthplace Park—site of famous rock 'n' roll singer's first home

 Vicksburg—site where Coca-Cola was first bottled in 1894

 Delta Queen— built in 1926, tours the Mississippi River

 Natchez—oldest permanent European settlement on the Mississippi River

Circle the capital city. Locate the landmarks found in the above key.
Color them on the map.

Mississippi: The Magnolia State

Look at an atlas or map of Mississippi. You can also look online. Add the names of the following places to the map below.

- this river is one of the most important in the whole country

- this state is south of Mississippi

- the capital of Mississippi

- the Mississippi flows into this body of water

- this connects two rivers

- this state is to the north

- an important battle was fought here

- go east to get to this state

- this city is named after the Native Americans who lived there

- this state is to the northwest of Mississippi

Size: 48,441 square miles
Population: 2,994,079

Name _____

Alabama: The Heart of Dixie

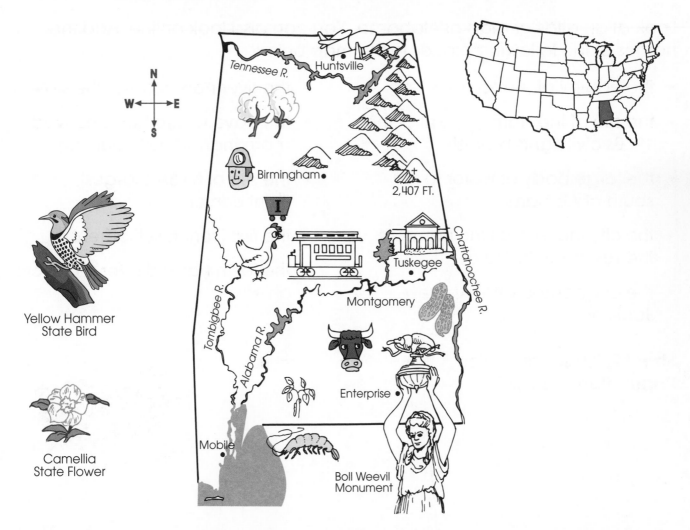

Tennessee R.
Huntsville
Birmingham
2,407 FT.
Tuskegee
Chattahoochee R.
Tombigbee R.
Alabama R.
Montgomery
Enterprise
Mobile
Boll Weevil
Monument

N
W — E
S

Yellow Hammer
State Bird

Camellia
State Flower

- named for a Creek Indian tribe, the Alibamu, whose name means *clearers of the thickets*
- nickname the heart of Dixie refers to its geographic location and the importance the state had during the Civil War

 Cheaha Mountain—
2,407 ft.

 U.S. Space and
Rocket Center

 Boll Weevil
Monument

 Montgomery—first electric trolley car system in the U.S. began operating here in 1886

 George Washington Carver Museum—honors Carver's discovery of many new uses for peanuts and sweet potatoes, helping farmers vary and improve their crops

Circle the capital city. Locate the landmarks found in the above key.
Color them on the map.

Alabama: The Heart of Dixie

Look at an atlas or map of Alabama. You can also look online. Add the names of the following places to the map below.

- the capital of Alabama

- the site of the starting point of the 1960s civil rights protests

- the large body of water to the south of Alabama

- the city that shares the name of the Tuskegee Institute

- the city named after Andrew Jackson

- the river named after the state

- the cave where humans lived more than 10,000 years ago

- the site of NASA's largest flight center

- the first French settlement

- the town named after a Choctaw chief

Size: 52,420 square miles
Population: 4,849,377

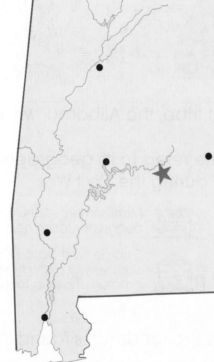

Georgia: The Peach State

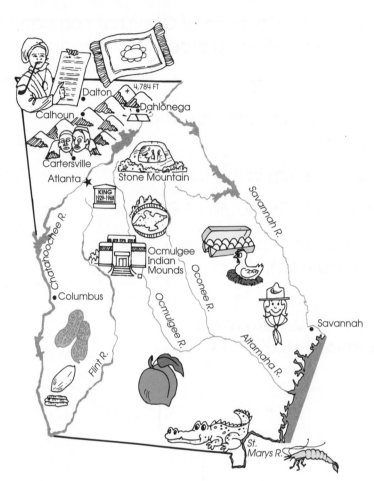

Cherokee Rose
State Flower

Brown Thrasher
State Bird

- named for King George II of England
- nickname the Peach State

 Brasstown Bald
Mountain—4,784 ft.

 Dahlonega Gold
Museum—located at
the site of the first gold
rush in the U.S.

 Etowah Mounds—built
by prehistoric Indians
around 1000 A.D.

 Savannah—Juliette
Gordon Lowe, founder
of the Girl Scouts of the
U.S.A., lived here

 Calhoun—statue honors
Sequoyah, who developed
Cherokee written
language

 Ocmulgee National
Monument—contains
remains of Indian mounds

 Dalton—produces more
carpeting than any other
place in the U.S.

 Atlanta—birthplace and
burial site of Martin Luther
King, Jr.

 Okefenokee Swamp—
national wildlife refuge,
which is known as
America's greatest
botanical garden

 Stone Mountain—
sculpture in huge granite
stone depicts Jefferson
Davis, Robert E. Lee and
Stonewall Jackson

 Rock Eagle Effigy—6,000-
year-old monument made
by prehistoric Indians

Circle the capital city. Locate the landmarks found in the above key.
Color them on the map.

Name_____

Georgia: The Peach State

Look at an atlas or map of Georgia. You can also look online. Add the names of the following places to the map below.

- capital of Georgia

- The Girl Scouts were founded in this city

- you can swim in this ocean

- the state to the south of Georgia

- Georgia shares these mountains with South Carolina

- Georgia's eastern border is shared with this state

- the large city in central Georgia

- "Land of the Trembling Earth"

- a city on the border with Alabama

- you can see Confederate heroes here

Size: 59,425 square miles
Population: 10,097,343

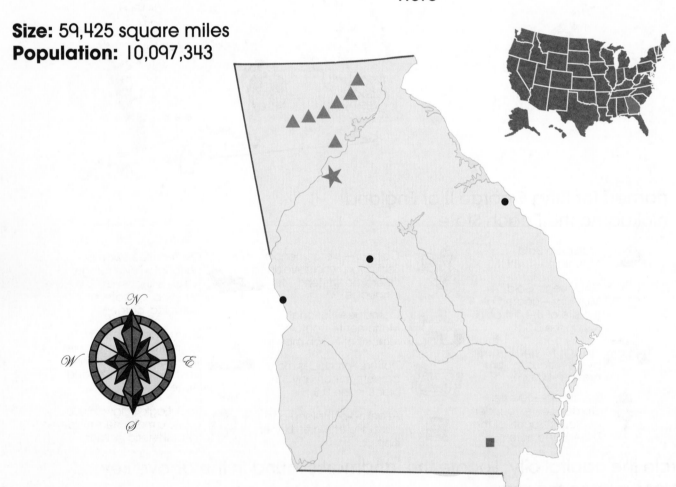

Florida: The Sunshine State

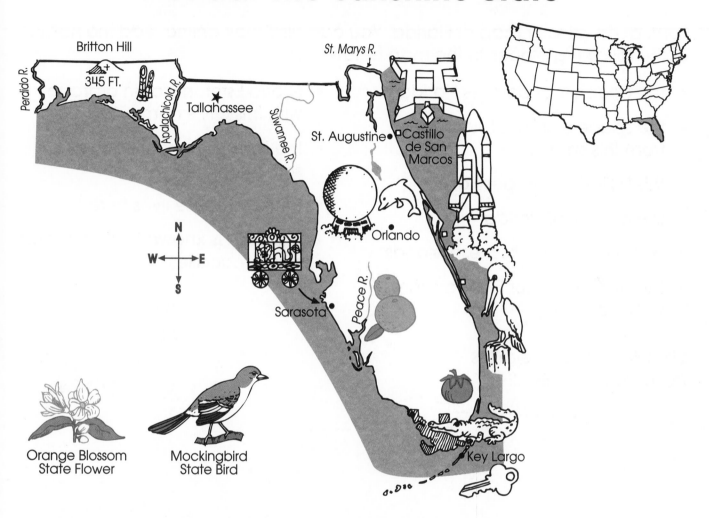

Orange Blossom
State Flower

Mockingbird
State Bird

- named from the Spanish word *florida*, meaning *flowery*, by Spanish explorer Juan Ponce de León
- nicknamed the Sunshine State for its warm and sunny climate

 Sea World—a popular tourist attraction featuring killer whales and dolphins

 Pelican Island National Wildlife Refuge—first federal wildlife refuge

 EPCOT Center—displays future technology

John and Mable Ringling Museum—Museum of Art and Circus Galleries

Cape Canaveral—Kennedy Space Center

Everglades National Park—largest subtropical wilderness in U.S.

Castillo de San Marcos National Monument—oldest permanent military fortress in the United States

 John Pennekamp Coral Reef State Park—first underseas park in the continental United States

Circle the capital city. Locate the landmarks found in the above key. Color them on the map.

Florida: The Sunshine State

Look at an atlas or map of Florida. You can also look online. Add the names of the following places to the map below.

- the ocean that borders Florida

- the space shuttle is launched from this spot

- this is Florida's largest lake

- the capital of Florida

- a long bridge links these islands

- the body of water Florida shares with Alabama

- Gloria Estefan was in a group with this city's name

- the first permanent Spanish settlement

- Mickey Mouse lives here

- this area is known for its alligators and crocodiles

Size: 65,757 square miles
Population: 19,893,297

Abbreviate Those States!

When you mail something to someone, the state in the address is always abbreviated using two uppercase letters. See how many postal abbreviations you know!

_____ Alabama	_____ Louisiana	_____ North Dakota
_____ Alaska	_____ Maine	_____ Ohio
_____ Arizona	_____ Maryland	_____ Oklahoma
_____ Arkansas	_____ Massachusetts	_____ Oregon
_____ California	_____ Michigan	_____ Pennsylvania
_____ Colorado	_____ Minnesota	_____ Rhode Island
_____ Connecticut	_____ Mississippi	_____ South Carolina
_____ Delaware	_____ Missouri	_____ South Dakota
_____ Florida	_____ Montana	_____ Tennessee
_____ Georgia	_____ Nebraska	_____ Texas
_____ Hawaii	_____ Nevada	_____ Utah
_____ Idaho	_____ New Hampshire	_____ Vermont
_____ Illinois	_____ New Jersey	_____ Virginia
_____ Indiana	_____ New Mexico	_____ Washington
_____ Iowa	_____ New York	_____ West Virginia
_____ Kansas	_____ North Carolina	_____ Wisconsin
_____ Kentucky		_____ Wyoming

Page is intentionally blank

Section 4
North & South America

What Is Where in North and South America?

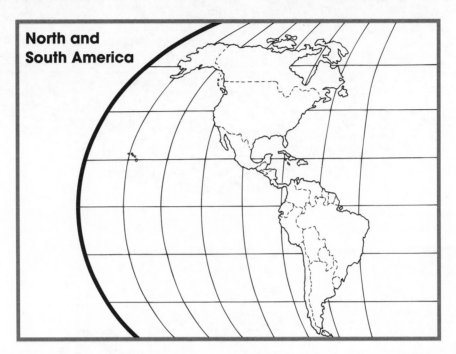

North and
South America

Directions: Follow these directions to complete the map. You may also use a
political map of North and South America.

1. Outline Canada in red.

2. Outline the United States in black.

   (Remember Alaska and Hawaii.)

3. Outline Mexico in orange.

4. Outline Brazil in brown.

5. Outline Chile in red.

6. Outline Argentina in orange.

7. Outline Paraguay in yellow.

8. Outline Colombia in black.

9. Outline Bolivia in red.

10. Color Peru yellow.

11. Color Ecuador orange.

12. Color Uruguay brown.

13. Color Venezuela purple.

14. Color Guyana pink.

15. Color Suriname orange.

16. Color French Guiana yellow.

17. Color the Gulf of Mexico green.

18. Color the Arctic Ocean blue.

19. Color the Pacific Ocean gray.

20. Color the Atlantic Ocean purple.

Neighboring Countries

Use a map of North America to locate your country. In the direction boxes, write the names of all the countries and/or bodies of water surrounding your country.

Northwest	North	Northeast
West	My Country	East
Southwest	South	Southeast

Draw an outline map of your country.

Within Continents

A continent is a large area of land.

This map shows two continents, North America and South America, and two oceans, the Atlantic Ocean and the Pacific Ocean. It also shows the countries that are on each continent. A solid line (——) shows the boundaries of each country. Use this map to answer the questions on page 291.

Within Continents

1. Write the names of the continents shown on the map.

_____

_____

2. Find the United States on the map. Color it green.

3. Find Alaska and Hawaii. They are part of the country of the United States.
   Color them green.

4. What country is north of the United States? Color it orange. _____

5. What large country is directly south of the United States? Color it red.

   _____

6. Which South American country is the biggest? _____

   _____

7. What long, skinny country is on the west coast of South America?

   _____

8. Which ocean is to the west of the continents of North America and South

   America? _____

9. In which direction would you go to travel from Canada to Chile?

   _____

O Canada!

Canada, the largest country in area in the Western Hemisphere, stretches across the North American Continent with its shores touching three oceans.

Canada has 10 provinces and 3 territories. A province is a political area that is very similar to a state.

You will need:
Political Map of Canada (page 293)
Canada map, atlas, or encyclopedia
colored pencils, crayons, or markers

Directions:

1. Complete a key with symbols for the national capital, province/territory capitals, and cities.

2. Label each of the ten provinces and three territories using uppercase letters.

3. Label the national capital and the capital of each province and territory.

4. Label these major cities:
   Calgary   Saskatoon   Windsor   Montreal   Vancouver

5. Label these bodies of water:
   Atlantic Ocean   Pacific Ocean   Arctic Ocean   Hudson Bay
   Labrador Sea   Baffin Bay

6. Color each province and territory a different color.

7. Color the bodies of water blue.

8. Color the United States one color.

Political Map of Canada

Use with page 292.

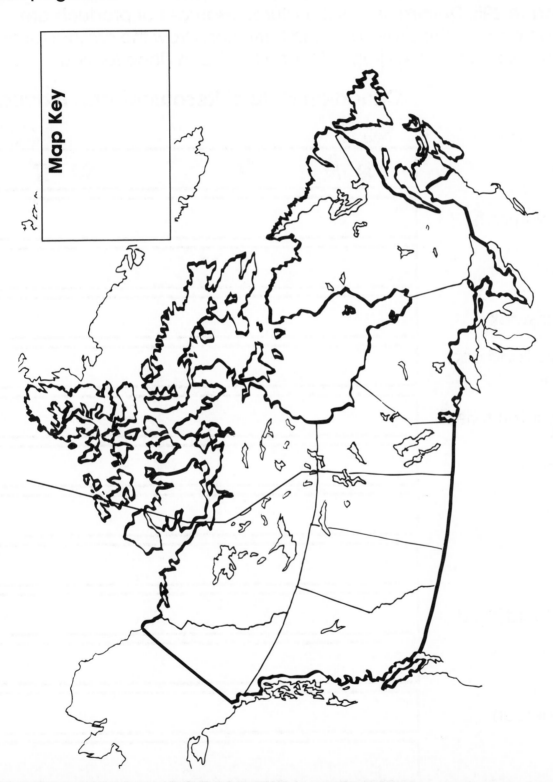

Map Key

Products and Natural Resources

Canada is rich in natural resources. Study the Products and Natural Resources map on page 295. Determine which natural resources or products are available in each of the provinces and territories. Draw the symbol for each product or resource on the graph. Alberta has been done for you.

Canadian Natural Resources and Products

	Moderate Producer			Major Producer

Alberta

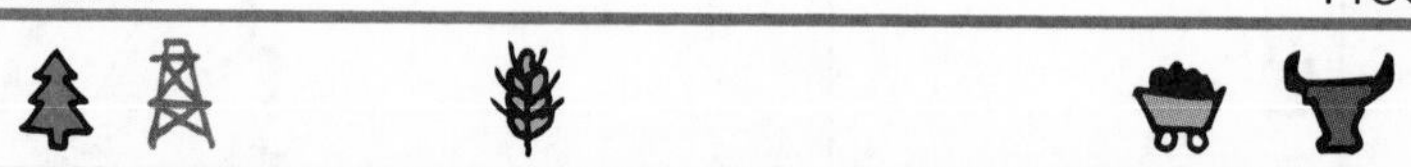

British Columbia

Manitoba

New Brunswick

Newfoundland and Labrador

Northwest Territories

Nova Scotia

Nunavut

Ontario

Prince Edward Island

Quebec

Saskatchewan

Yukon

Products and Natural Resources

Use with page 294.

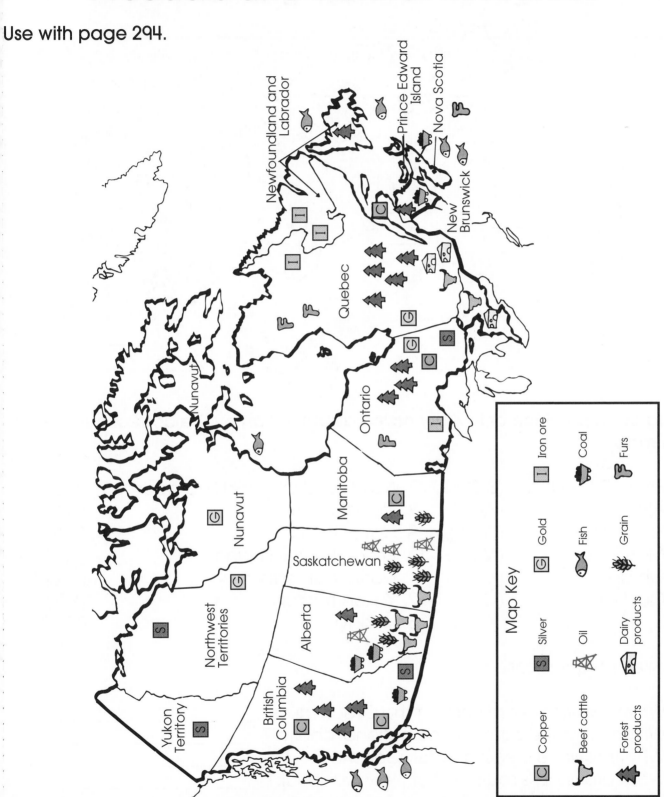

Northern Neighbors

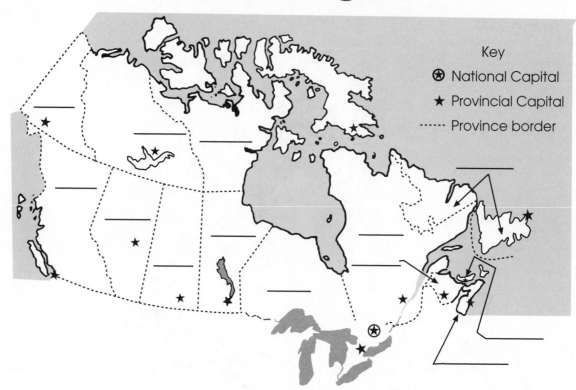

Write each province or territory name abbreviation by the correct number on the map.

1. British Columbia   (B.C.)
2. Alberta   (Alta.)
3. Saskatchewan   (Sask.)
4. Manitoba   (Man.)
5. Ontario   (Ont.)
6. Quebec   (Que.)

7. Newfoundland and Labrador   (N.L.)
8. New Brunswick   (N.B.)
9. Nova Scotia   (N.S.)
10. Prince Edward Island   (P.E.I.)
11. Northwest Territories   (N.W.T.)
12. Yukon Territory   (Y.T.)
13. Nunavut   (Nvt.)

Answer the questions.

1. Which provinces are north of the Great Lakes? _____
2. Which province contains the national capital? _____
3. What province is east of British Columbia? _____
4. What province is southeast of New Brunswick? _____
5. Manitoba is _____ of Saskatchewan.

Mexico

Mexico is the United States' neighbor to the south. The two countries share an almost 2,000-mile-long border. Mexico is the third most populated country in the Western Hemisphere. Only the United States and Brazil have more people.

Mexico is home to one of the largest cities in the world, Mexico City.

You will need:
copy of Physical and Political Map of Mexico (page 298)
physical and political map of Mexico, atlas, or encyclopedia
colored pencils, markers, or crayons

Directions:

1. Label and color-code the map key and color Mexico's six main land regions:

Pacific Northwest	Plateau of Mexico	Gulf Coastal Plain
Southern Uplands	Chiapas Highlands	Yucatan Peninsula

2. Draw and label the following mountain ranges. Use ∧∧∧ as symbols for mountains.

Sierra Madre Oriental	Sierra Madre del Sur	Sierra Madre Occidental

3. Label these large cities.

Mexico City	Monterrery	Guadalajara
Puebla	Chihuahua	Juarez
Tijuana	Acapulco	Tampico

4. Label these bodies of water.

Gulf of Mexico	Pacific Ocean	Gulf of California

Name

Physical and Political Map of Mexico

Use with page 297.

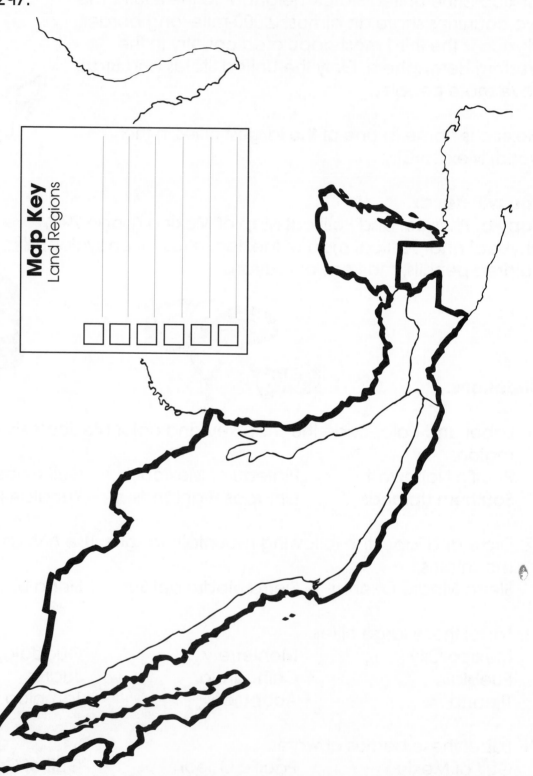

Map Key
Land Regions

Mexico

Area: 758,450 sq. mi.

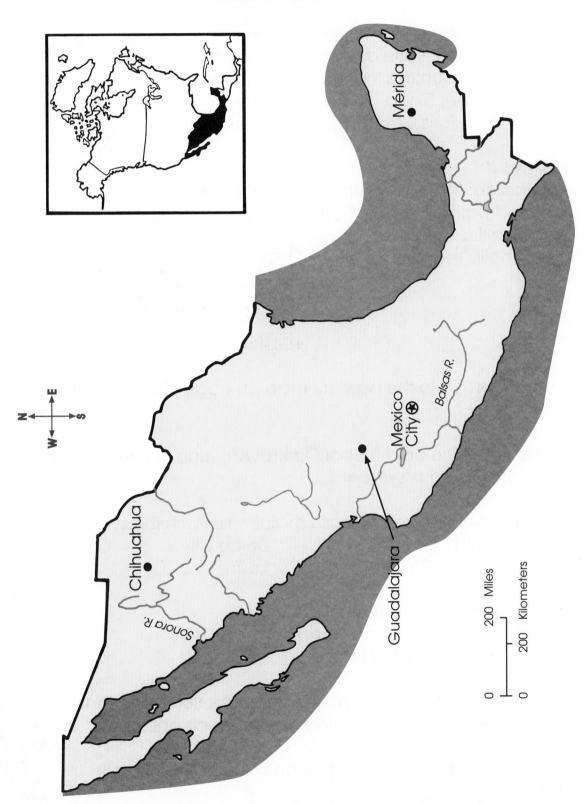

N
E
W
S

Mérida
•

Mexico
City ✪

Balsas R.

Chihuahua
•

Sonora R.

Guadalajara
•

200 Miles
200 Kilometers
0
0

Central America

Central America is the narrow isthmus, or strip of land, connecting North and South America. The seven small countries that make up Central America are Belize, Costa Rica, El Salvador, Guatemala, Honduras, Nicaragua, and Panama.

You will need:

copy of Political Map of Central America (page 301)
physical and political map of Central America, atlas, or encyclopedia
colored pencils, markers, or crayons

Directions: Complete the political map on page 305 using the information below.

1. Label each of the countries of Central America. Label and locate each of the capitals with this symbol ⭐.

2. Label and locate each of these major cities with this symbol ●.
   San Pedro Sula   Santa Ana   Belize City   Quezaltenango
   Colon   Limón   León

3. Label the following bodies of water:
   Pacific Ocean   Panama Canal
   Caribbean Sea   Gulf of Panama

4. On the Key, list all of the capitals in alphabetical order and write the letter-number coordinates after each one.

5. Color each of the Central American countries a different color.

Name _____

Political Map of Central America

Use with page 300.

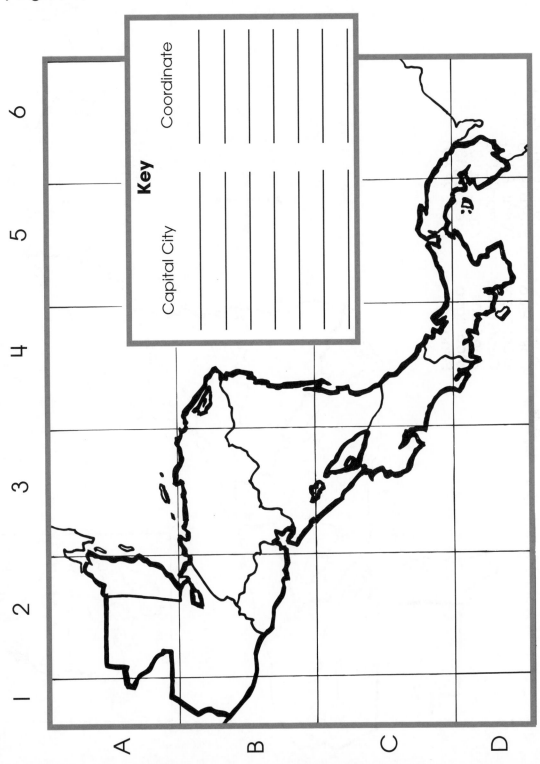

Central America

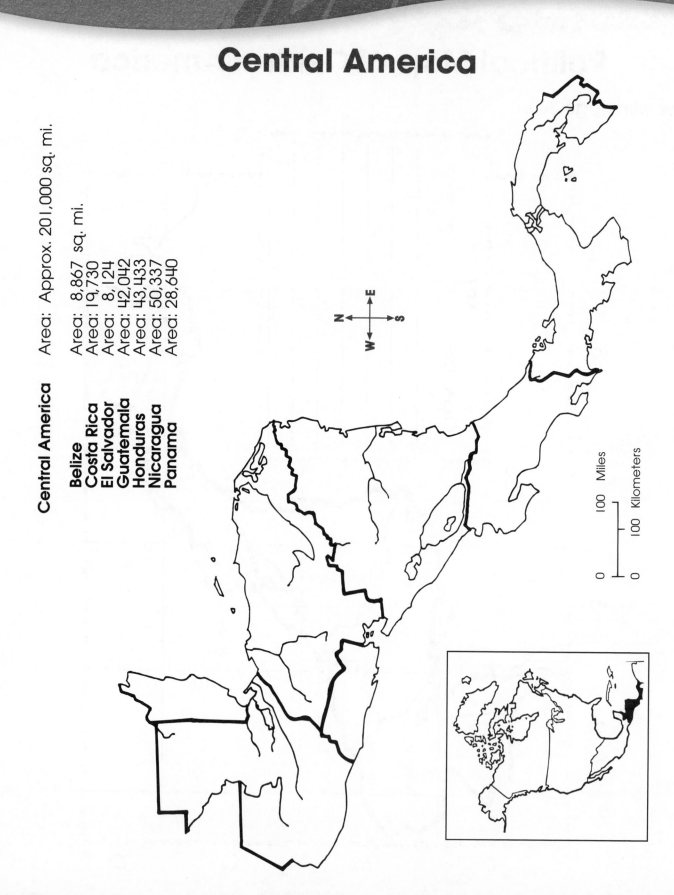

Central America   Area: Approx. 201,000 sq. mi.

Belize   Area: 8,867 sq. mi.
Costa Rica   Area: 19,730
El Salvador   Area: 8,124
Guatemala   Area: 42,042
Honduras   Area: 43,433
Nicaragua   Area: 50,337
Panama   Area: 28,640

100   Miles

100   Kilometers

South America

Venezuela Orinoco R.
Guyana
Suriname
French Guiana
Ecuador Colombia
Equator
Amazon R.
Brazil
Perû
Bolivia
Paraguay
Chile
Argentina Uruguay
Falkland Islands

Key
⊛ capital cities
⌒⌒ mountains
⌒ rivers

Directions: Answer the questions.

1. The equator passes through which countries? _____
   _____
   _____
   _____

2. Name the countries and dependency found north of the equator. _____
   _____
   _____
   _____

Refer to a political map of South America. Write the letter of each capital next to the name of its country.

_____ 1. Ecuador
_____ 2. Colombia
_____ 3. Venezuela
_____ 4. Guyana
_____ 5. Suriname
_____ 6. French Guiana
_____ 7. Brazil
_____ 8. Uruguay

_____ 9. Argentina
_____ 10. Chile
_____ 11. Bolivia

_____ 12. Peru
_____ 13. Paraguay
_____ 14. Falkland Islands

A. Buenos Aires	H. Lima
B. Sucre	I. Paramaribo
C. Brasília	J. Montevideo
D. Bogotá	K. Caracas
E. Quito	L. Santiago
F. Georgetown	M. Cayenne
G. Asunción	N. Stanley

Countries and Cities in South America

1. _____is the largest country in South America.

2. Which country shares Argentina's western border?_____

3. List three countries which share a border with Brazil.

   _____

4. Name the two countries that share the southern border of Colombia.

   _____

5. Name the country between Guyana and French Guiana. _____

6. _____is the capital of Venezuela.

7. Uruguay is between the countries of Argentina and _____.

8. The capital of Bolivia is _____.

9. _____ shares Peru's northwest border.

10. The capital of Paraguay is_____.

11. Cayenne is the capital of _____.

12. Name the country west of Guyana. _____

13. Name the three countries that share a border with Chile.

   _____

Name_____

Where Is It Raining?

South America—Precipitation Map

South America—Political Map

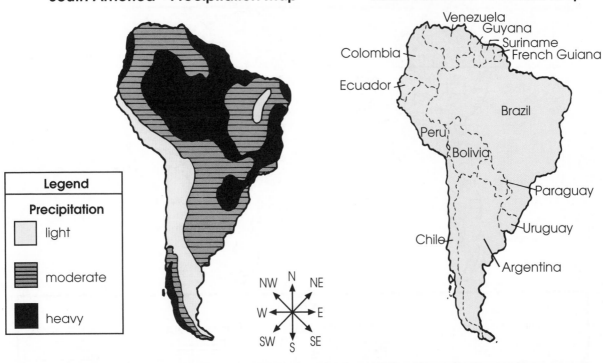

Legend

Precipitation

☐ light

▤ moderate

■ heavy

NW N NE
W ←→ E
SW S SE

Directions: Use both maps to answer these questions about South America.

1. What do these symbols stand for on the precipitation map?

   ☐ A. _____   ▤ B._____   ■ C._____

2. The lightest precipitation falls mainly on the _____ part of South America.

3. The heaviest precipitation falls mainly in the _____ part of South America.

4. Most of Argentina receives _____ precipitation.

5. The majority of South America receives _____ precipitation.

6. Most of Chile receives _____ precipitation.

7. The northwestern tip of Colombia receives _____ precipitation.

8. The western half of Ecuador receives _____ precipitation.

9. Most of Brazil receives _____ precipitation.

Land in South America

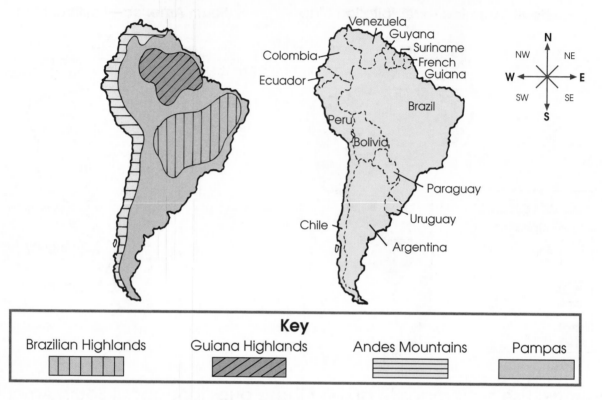

Key

| Brazilian Highlands | Guiana Highlands | Andes Mountains | Pampas |

1. Over half of the continent is covered by _____.

2. The _____ Mountains run from north to south on the western half of the continent.

3. In what part of the continent are the Guiana Highlands located? _____

4. In the eastern part of South America is an area called the _____ Highlands.

5. Most of Argentina is covered by _____.

6. Which country is covered completely by pampas—Uruguay or Venezuela? _____

7. Colombia's northeast border is shared by the country of _____.

8. Name the country that borders Argentina to the west. _____

9. Which country does not contain the Andes Mountains within its borders—Chile, Peru, or Uruguay? _____

Section 5
Grid Maps

Name_____

Numbers and Letters on a Map

This is a map of Red Falls.

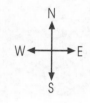

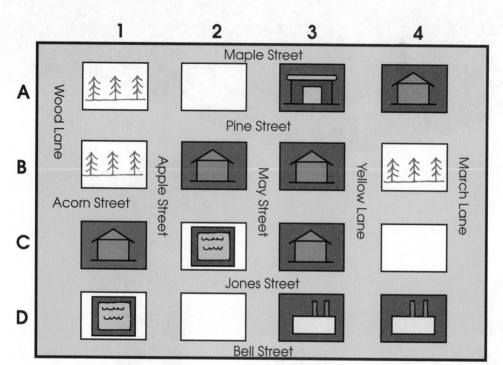

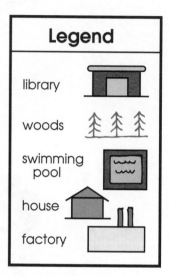

Directions: Use the numbers and letters to help you answer the questions.

1. Locate the blocks. Write what you see in each block.
   A1 _____   C1 _____
   D4 _____   D1 _____
2. Name the blocks with swimming pools. _____
3. Name the blocks with houses. _____
4. Name the blocks with woods. _____
5. Tell what is located in the first block south of A3. _____
6. What is in the block south of C1? _____
7. How many houses are in B2? _____
8. What is in the block east of B3? _____
9. What is in the block west of D4? _____
10. Draw a swimming pool in A2.
11. Draw a house in D2.
12. Draw a factory in C4.

Using a Grid

A map grid helps people locate places easily.

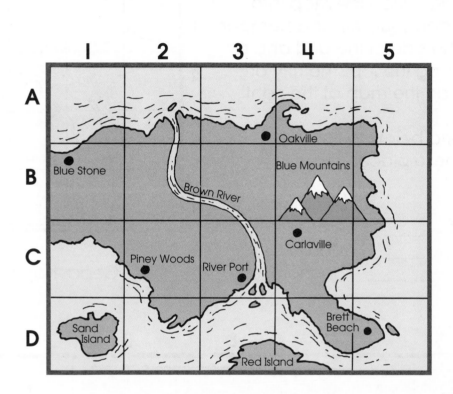

Directions: Use the numbers and letters to help you answer the questions below.

1. In which block is Brett Beach? _____
2. In which block is Blue Stone? _____
3. In which block is Piney Woods? _____
4. In which two blocks is Red Island? _____
5. In which four blocks is the Brown River? _____
6. In which block is Carlaville? _____
7. In which two blocks are the Blue Mountains? _____
8. Name the town located in A3. _____
9. Name the two islands found on the map. _____
10. In C5, add a town to the map.
11. In B2, add some trees.
12. In A5, add an island and name the island.

Name _____

A Little Gridwork

A grid makes it easier to find places on a map. The lines of a grid divide the map into imaginary squares. Each square has a number that appears along the side of the grid and a letter that appears along the top. The city of Detroit is found at D4 on the map at the right.

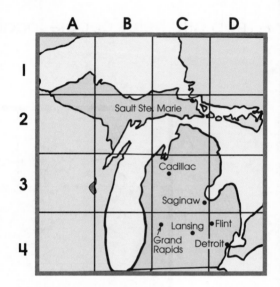

Directions: Use the grid below to find the location of each of these places.

_____ Sioux City	_____ Des Moines	
_____ Davenport	_____ Ames	
_____ Dubuque	_____ Mason City	
_____ Waterloo	_____ Council Bluffs	_____ Cedar Rapids

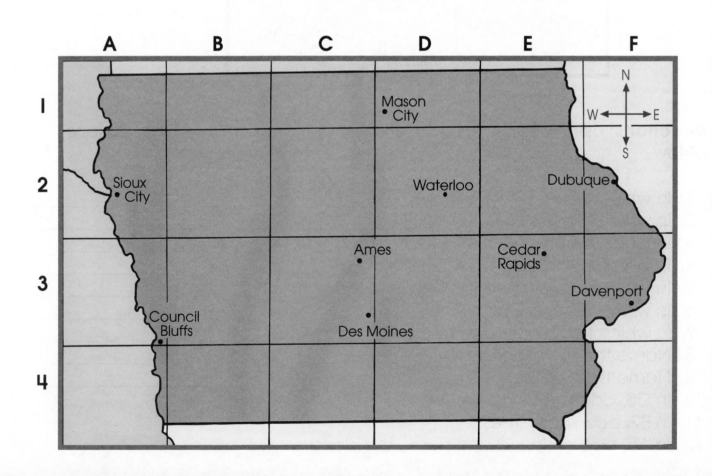

Name_____

Getting to Pirates' Island

You are a pirate captain on your way home to Pirates' Island.

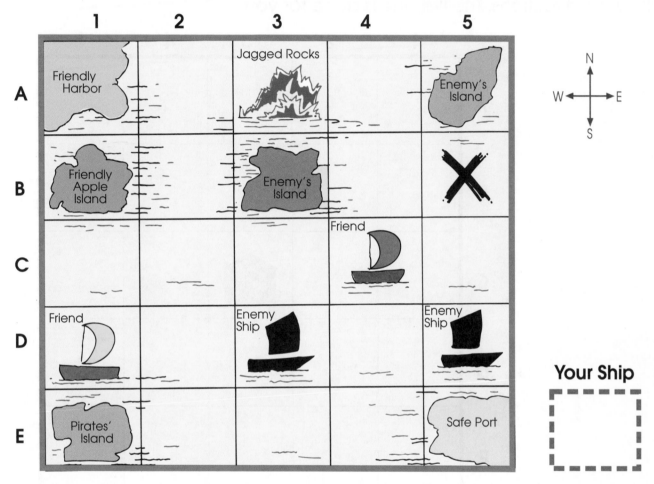

Directions: Draw a picture of your ship in the box and cut it out. Place the ship on the large **X**.

1. In which space is your ship located? _____
2. If you move your ship west two spaces, will you be safe? _____
3. Name another space where your ship will not be safe. _____
4. Move your ship from B5 to B2. Are you in a safe place? _____
5. Move your ship south three spaces from B2. What is your location?

   _____
6. If you move your ship from E2 to E1, where will you be? _____
7. Give the location for both enemy ships. _____
8. Can you safely move two spaces east of Friendly Apple Island? _____

Creating Your Own Grid Map

Create your own symbols for each object listed in the legend below. Then, follow the directions. The first one is done for you.

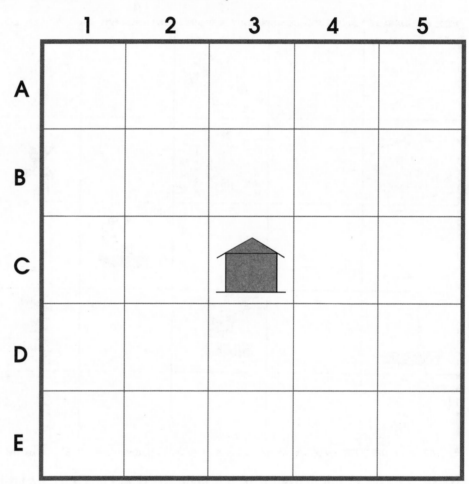

Legend

house		tree	flower
pond		bird	swing set

1. Draw a house in C3.
2. Draw a pond in D5 and in E5.
3. Draw two birds in A2.
4. Draw one bird in A4.

5. Draw a tree in C1 and in B1.
6. Draw a swing set in E3 and in E4.
7. Draw two flowers in D2.
8. Draw a tree in B5 and in C5.

Jumbo Gym

A new gym has been built in your city. Use the coordinates to name the location of the fitness features. The first one has been done for you.

Gym Grid Map

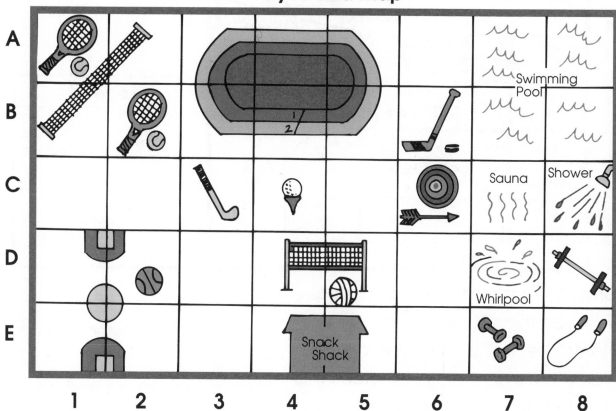

1. Archery ___C6___
2. Whirlpool_____
3. Swimming pool_____ ,_____ ,
   _____ ,_____
4. Golf driving range _____, _____
5. Floor hockey_____
6. Small weights room _____
7. Basketball court _____, _____,
   _____, _____
8. Track _____, _____, _____,
   _____, _____, _____
9. Snack Shack _____, _____
10. Volleyball court _____, _____
11. Weightlifting _____
12. Shower _____
13. Sauna_____
14. Rope jumping _____
15. Tennis courts _____, _____,
    _____, _____

The Southern States

Directions: Use the grid to help you locate places of the southern United States on this map.

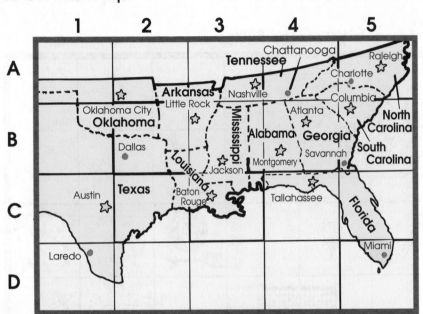
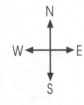
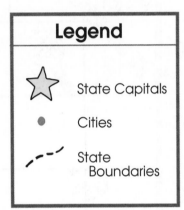

1. Draw the symbol for a state capital. _____

2. What do these lines - - - - stand for? _____

3. Name the Florida city located in D5. _____

4. Name the state capital located in A3. _____

5. Which state capital is located in A5? _____

6. What is the location of Atlanta, Georgia? _____

7. Name the state capital located in C3. _____

8. Give the location of Jackson, Mississippi. _____

9. What state capital is located in A2? _____

10. Give the location of Austin, Texas. _____

11. Name the cities located in B4. _____

12. Name a state located in A4 and A5. _____

13. Name the Tennessee city found in A4. _____

14. Name the two North Carolina cities located in A5.

_____   _____

We're Going Places

Directions: Draw an outline map of your state on the grid below. Label places or cities that are familiar to you. List them at the bottom of the page using the number and letter coordinates.

	A	B	C	D
1				
2				
3				
4				
5				

City or Place	Location	City or Place	Location
_____	_____	_____	_____
_____	_____	_____	_____
_____	_____	_____	_____
_____	_____	_____	_____

Name _____

Picture This!

Directions: Make a dot at each coordinate on the graph. Draw lines to connect the dots in order. Add details and color the fuzzy fellow you drew on the graph.

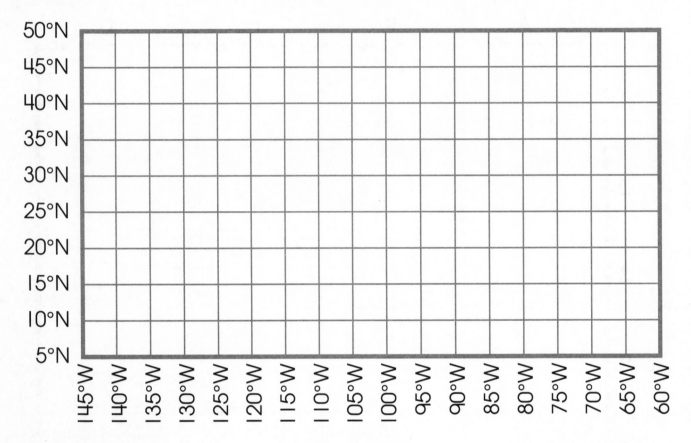

1.	5°N , 135°W	10.	50°N , 125° W	18.	35°N , 105° W
2.	15°N , 135°W	11.	50°N , 120° W	19.	35°N , 95° W
3.	15°N , 125°W	12.	45°N , 120° W	20.	25°N , 95° W
4.	25°N , 125°W	13.	45°N , 105° W	21.	25°N , 100° W
5.	25°N , 130°W	14.	50°N , 105° W	22.	15°N , 100° W
6.	35°N , 130°W	15.	50°N , 100° W	23.	15°N , 90° W
7.	35°N , 120°W	16.	45°N , 100° W	24.	5°N , 90° W
8.	45°N , 120°W	17.	45°N , 105° W	25.	5°N , 135° W
9.	45°N , 125°W				

Section 6
Global Geography

The Globe

A model of the earth is called a globe. It is a round map that shows land and water. It uses colors to show which is the land and which is the water.

Directions: Unscramble the letters below to find out the colors that are used on the globe.

Land is _____. e r g e n

Water is _____. e b u l

Color the land on the globe green.

Color the water on the globe blue.

It's a Round World

Use these maps with pages 320 and 321.

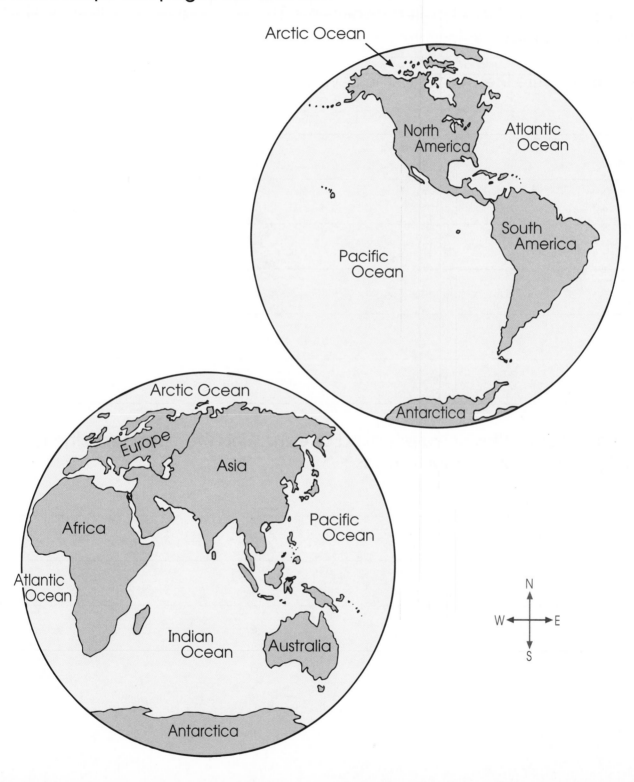

It's a Round World

The picture of the globe on page 319 shows both halves of the world. It shows the large pieces of land called continents. There are seven continents. Find them on the globe.

Directions: Write the names of the seven continents.

1. _____

2. _____

3. _____

4. _____

5. _____

6. _____

7. _____

There are four bodies of water called oceans. Find the oceans on the globe. Write the names of the four oceans.

1. _____

2. _____

3. _____

4. _____

A Global Guide

Use the globe on page 319. Read the clues below. Write the answers on the lines. Then, use the numbered letters to solve the riddle at the bottom of the page.

1. This direction points up.

___ ___ ___ ___ ___
 1   2   22   3

2. This direction points down.

___ ___ ___ ___ ___
 4   5   6

3. This direction points right.

___ ___ ___ ___
 7   8

4. This direction points left.

___ ___ ___ ___
 9   10

5. This ocean is west of North America.

___ ___ ___ ___ ___ ___ ___
11   12

___ ___ ___ ___ ___
13   14

6. This ocean is south of Asia.

___ ___ ___ ___ ___ ___
15   16   17

___ ___ ___ ___ ___

7. This ocean is east of South America.

___ ___ ___ ___ ___ ___ ___
    18   19

___ ___ ___ ___ ___
20   21

Riddle: What does a globe do? ___ ___ ___ ___ ___ ___ ___ ___
                                   15   6   4   11 15 21   8

___ ___ " ___ - ___ ___ ___ ___ ___ "
 5   10   12   22   2   5   21 16

___ ___ ___ ___ ___ ___ ___ ___ ___ .
13   5   22   11 19 14 17   7   18

Land and Water

Directions: Use the map below plus a wall map to do this activity.

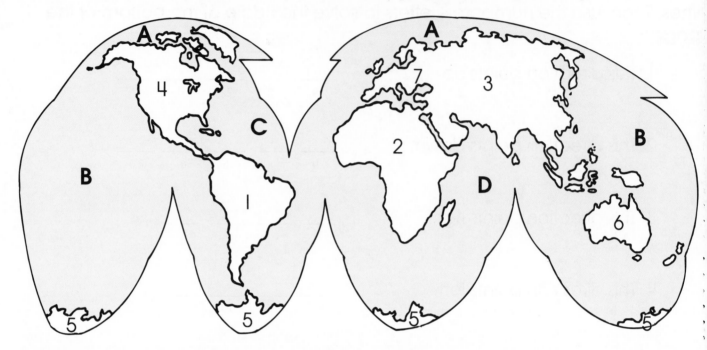

Write the name of each continent in the correct blank.

1. _____   5. _____
2. _____   6. _____
3. _____   7. _____
4. _____

Write the name of each ocean in the correct blank.

A. _____   C. _____
B. _____   D. _____

Use crayons or markers to follow these directions.

1. Color Australia green.   5. Color North America red.
2. Color Europe yellow.   6. Color South America brown.
3. Color Africa orange.   7. Color Asia purple.
4. Color Antarctica blue.

Color My World

Is it a city, state, country, continent, or body of water? Color each box according to the Color Key. Use an atlas for help.

Color Key

city—orange	state—green	country—yellow
water—blue	continent—purple	

Atlantic Ocean	India	Colorado	Miami
Peru	Antarctica	Lake Michigan	Hawaii
New Orleans	Spain	Europe	Gulf of Mexico
Vermont	Phoenix	Japan	Paris
East China Sea	Egypt	Wyoming	Sweden
Africa	London	Hudson Bay	Connecticut
Greece	Minnesota	South America	Dallas
Oakland	Great Salt Lake	Argentina	Arctic Ocean
North America	Canada	Chicago	Arkansas
Lake Victoria	Iowa	Asia	Venezuela
Lima	Persian Gulf	Mexico	Moscow
Pacific Ocean	Maryland	Cincinnati	Brazil

Where in the World is...

What is your global address? It's more than your street, city, state, and ZIP code.

What would your address be if you wanted to get a letter from a friend living in outer space?

Use an atlas, encyclopedia, science book, or other source to complete your global address.

Intergalactic Address Book

Name _____

Street _____

County or Parish _____

State or Province _____

Country _____

Continent _____

Hemisphere _____

Planet _____

Galaxy _____

Draw an **X** to mark the approximate place where you live.

Name_____

Where in the World?

Refer to the globe on page 319, a real globe, or a world map. Find the seven continents and four oceans. Now, you are ready to make your own globe using this page and pages 327 and 329.

Directions:

1. Cut out all the of continent and ocean labels.

2. Glue them where they belong in the boxes on the maps on pages 327 and 329.

3. Cut out all of the map circles along the outer lines.

4. Fold each circle in half along the dotted line. Keep the map side on the inside.

5. Be sure to keep the numbers on the circles at the top. Glue the back of the right half of circle **1** to the back of the left half of circle **2**.

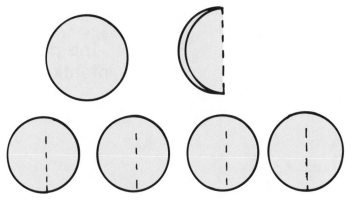

6. Glue the back of the right half of circle **2** to the back of the left half of circle **3**.

7. Glue the back of the right half of circle **3** to the back of the left half of circle **4**.

8. Complete the globe by gluing the back of the right half of circle **4** to the back of the left half of circle **1**.

This page has been
intentionally left blank.

Name_____

Where in the World?

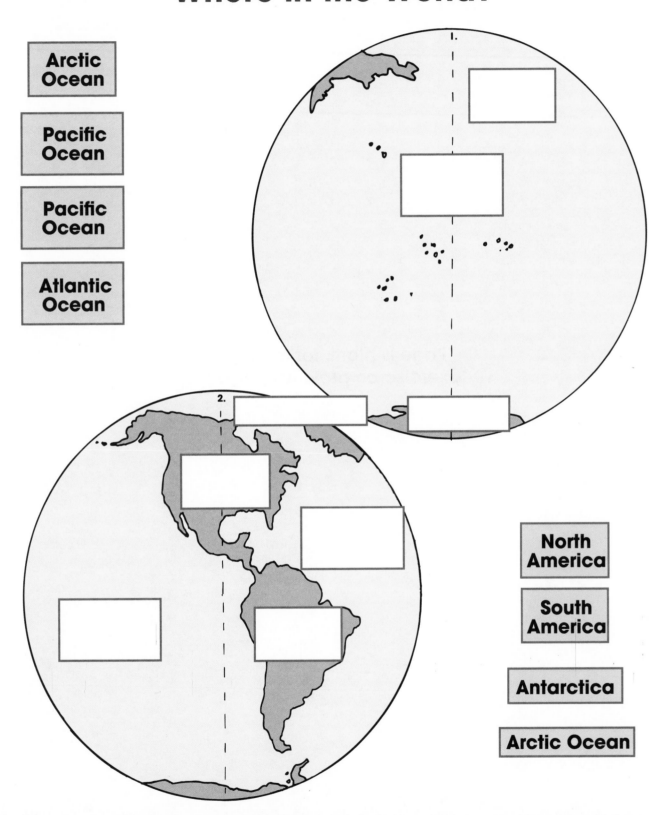

Arctic Ocean

Pacific Ocean

Pacific Ocean

Atlantic Ocean

North America

South America

Antarctica

Arctic Ocean

Page is blank for cutting exercise on previous page.

Where in the World?

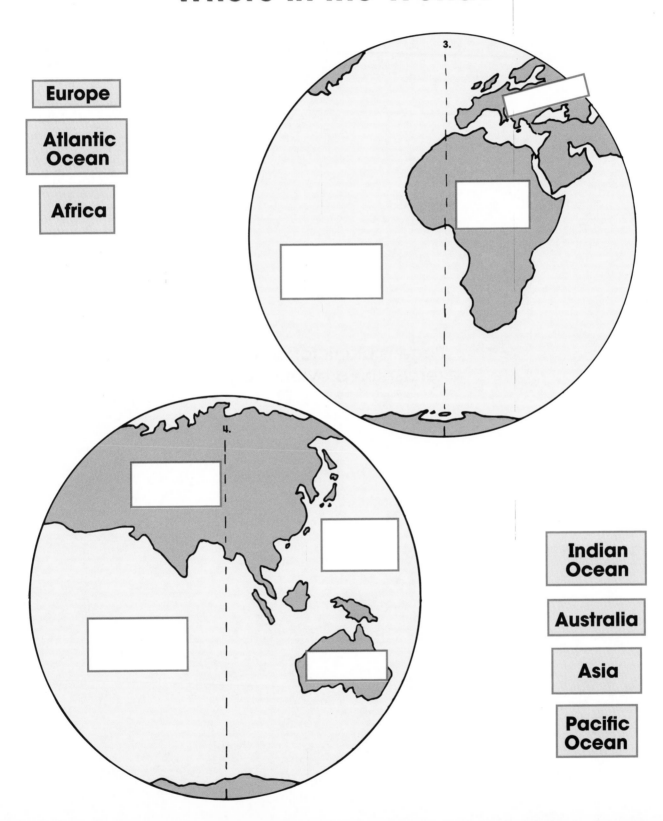

Europe

Atlantic Ocean

Africa

Indian Ocean

Australia

Asia

Pacific Ocean

**Page is blank for cutting
exercise on previous page.**

Near and Far

Below is a map of the world. It shows the seven continents. Around the map are pictures of animals that are native to the continents. The continent on which each animal can be found is written below the name of the animal.

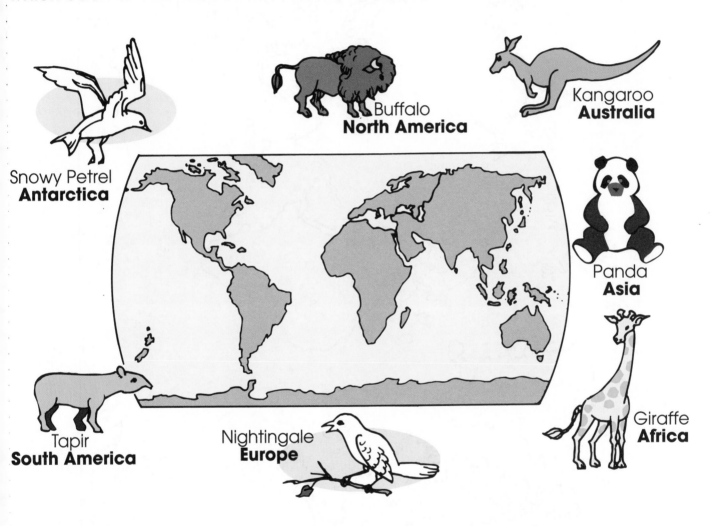

Snowy Petrel
Antarctica

Buffalo
North America

Kangaroo
Australia

Panda
Asia

Giraffe
Africa

Tapir
South America

Nightingale
Europe

Directions: Use a globe or world map to locate each continent. Draw a line from the picture of the animal to the continent where it is found.

1. Find the continent where you live.

2. Which animal lives on your continent? _____

3. Which animal lives on a continent far from you? _____

Let's Travel the Earth

Use with page 333.

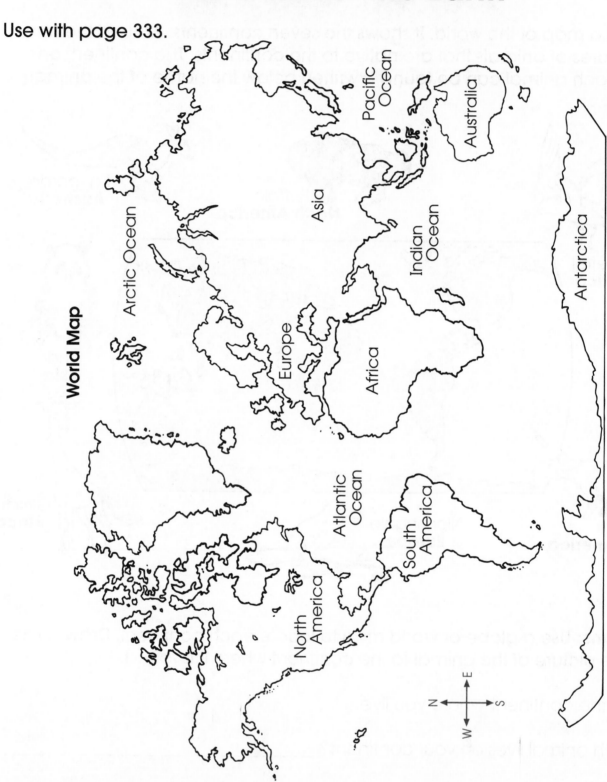

World Map

Arctic Ocean

Pacific Ocean

Australia

Asia

Indian Ocean

Europe

Africa

Antarctica

Atlantic Ocean

North America

South America

Let's Travel the Earth

Directions: Use the map on page 332 to answer the questions below. Circle the word that correctly completes each statement.

1. If you sail from North America to Antarctica, you will be on the . . .
   Arctic Ocean   Atlantic Ocean   Indian Ocean

2. If you fly east from Africa to Australia, you will fly over the . . .
   Indian Ocean   Pacific Ocean   Atlantic Ocean

3. To sail from Europe to South America, you will sail on the . . .
   Pacific Ocean   Arctic Ocean   Atlantic Ocean

4. To sail from North America to Europe, you will sail on the . . .
   Indian Ocean   Atlantic Ocean   Pacific Ocean

5. To travel from Europe to Asia, you must cross . . .
   the Pacific Ocean   the Indian Ocean   land

Fill in the blanks with the correct word.

1. The continent north of South America is _____.
2. The ocean directly south of Asia is the _____.
3. The ocean directly north of Asia is the _____.
4. The continent directly south of Europe is _____.
5. The continent directly south of Australia is _____.

Use a crayon or marker to follow these directions.

1. Draw a red line from North America to Africa.
2. Draw a green line from Asia to Antarctica.
3. Draw an orange line from Australia to Africa.
4. Draw a black line from Europe to South America.
5. Circle the names of all four oceans with blue.
6. Color North America green.
7. Draw a black dotted line (- - - - - -) around South America.

Hemispheres

The earth is a sphere. When the earth is cut in half horizontally along an imaginary line called the **equator**, the **Northern** and **Southern Hemispheres** of the earth are created.

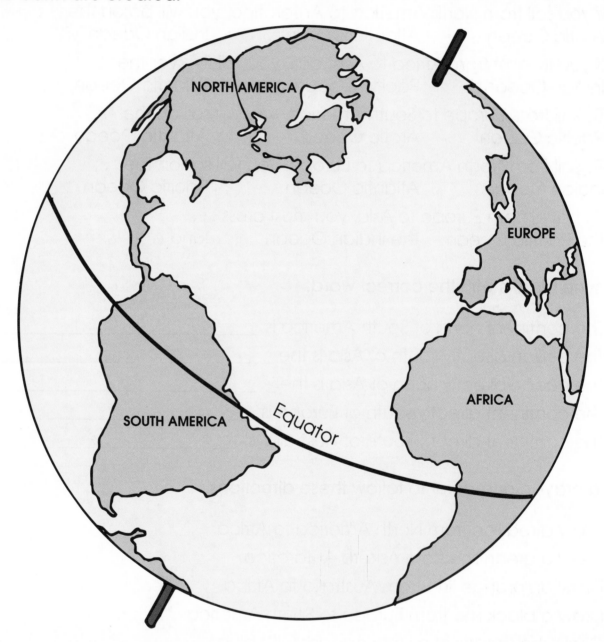

Trace the equator in orange.

Label the two hemispheres shown on the globe.

Name _____

Hemispheres

When the earth is cut in half vertically along an imaginary line called the **prime meridian**, the **Eastern** and **Western Hemispheres** of the earth are created.

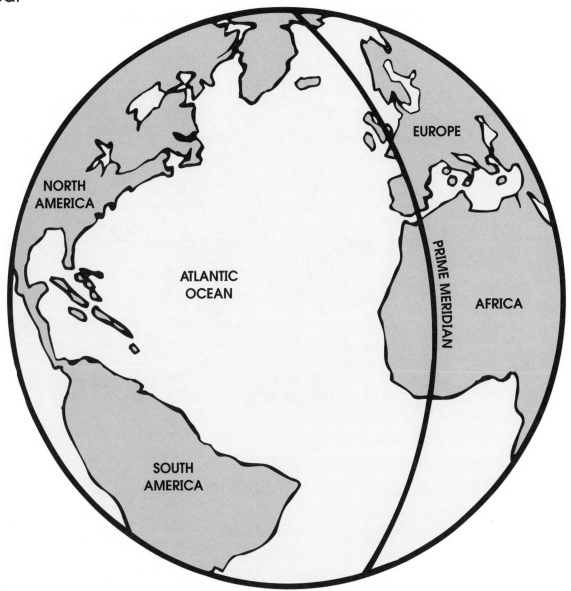

Trace the prime meridian in blue.

Label the two hemispheres shown on the globe.

Hemispheres

Directions: Examine the illustration below. Decide in which two hemispheres (Eastern or Western and Northern or Southern) each of the following continents or oceans is located. (Example: The United States is in the Northern and Western Hemispheres.) Write your answers in the spaces provided.

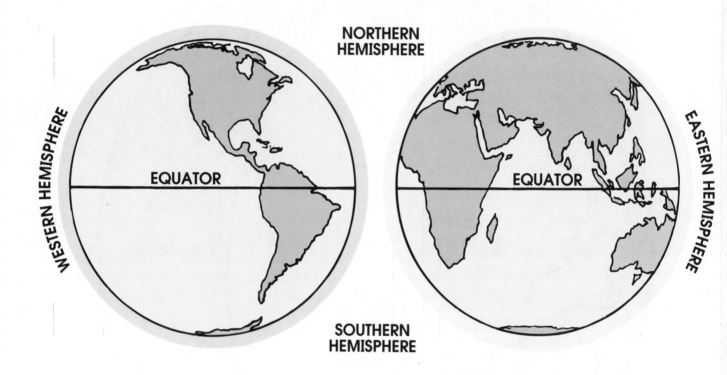

1. North America _____

2. Europe _____

3. South America _____

4. Pacific Ocean _____

5. Australia _____

6. Atlantic Ocean _____

7. Indian Ocean _____

8. Asia _____

9. Africa _____

10. Antarctica _____

11. Arctic Ocean _____

Name_____

Locating the Continents and Oceans

Directions: Use these maps and wall maps to complete this page.
Note: Some continents belong to more than one hemisphere.

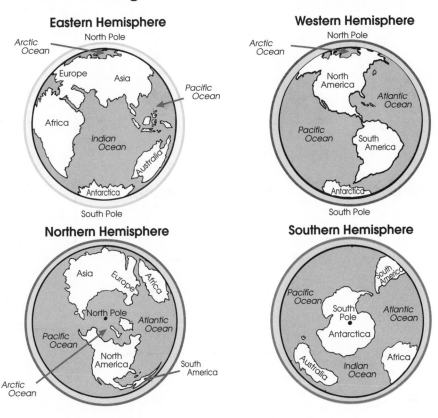

1. Which continents are found in both the Eastern and
   Western Hemispheres? _____

2. Which map does not show any part of Antarctica?
   _____

3. Which hemisphere does not include any part of Africa?
   _____

4. Color the continent located entirely in the Western and Northern
   Hemispheres red.

5. Color the continent located entirely in the Eastern and Southern
   Hemispheres green.

Happy Hemispheres

Write the name of each continent and ocean next to its number.

Western Hemisphere

1. _____
2. _____
3. _____
4. _____

Eastern Hemisphere

1. _____
2. _____
3. _____
4. _____
5. _____
6. _____

Northern Hemisphere

1. _____
2. _____
3. _____
4. _____
5. _____
6. _____

Southern Hemisphere

1. _____
2. _____
3. _____
4. _____
5. _____
6. _____
7. _____

Name_____

North to South

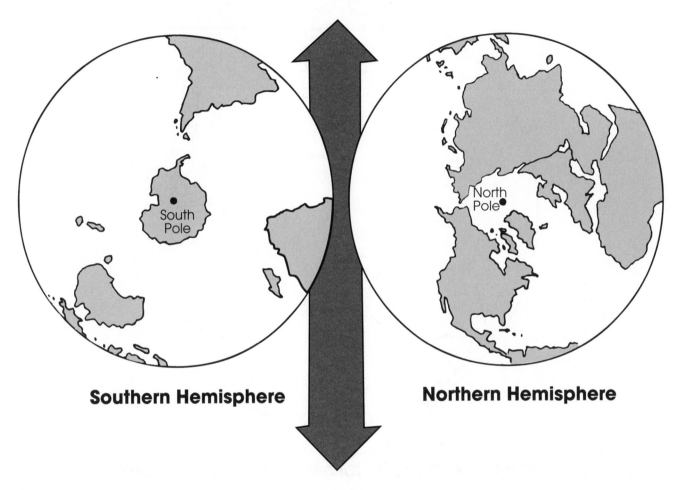

Southern Hemisphere   **Northern Hemisphere**

Directions: Label the continents on each hemisphere. Use the abbreviations below.

N.A. = North Ameria   **Ant.** = Antarctica
S.A. = South America   **Aust.** = Australia
Eur. = Europe   **Afr.** = Africa
As. = Asia

Color the oceans in each hemisphere using the colors and designs below.

(purple) Indian Ocean   (green) Atlantic Ocean

(blue) Pacific Ocean   (light green) Arctic Ocean

Name _____

Global Fun

Directions: Complete the globe by following the directions below.

1. Draw a whale in the Southern Hemisphere of the Pacific Ocean.

2. Trace the equator in orange.

3. Draw a shark in the Arctic Ocean.

4. Draw a smiling face near Antarctica.

5. Draw an ocean liner in the Northern Hemisphere of the Atlantic Ocean.

6. Color the axis poles red.

7. In North America, color Mexico yellow, Canada green, and the United States red.

8. Draw a yellow X in the Northern Hemisphere of Africa.

9. Color Europe purple.

10. Draw rainbow-colored diagonal stripes on South America.

11. Draw an orange circle on the Southern Hemisphere of Africa.

From East to West

Directions: Label the continents using the abbreviations below. Cut out the continents. Glue them onto the correct hemisphere in the proper places. Include Antarctica on each hemisphere.

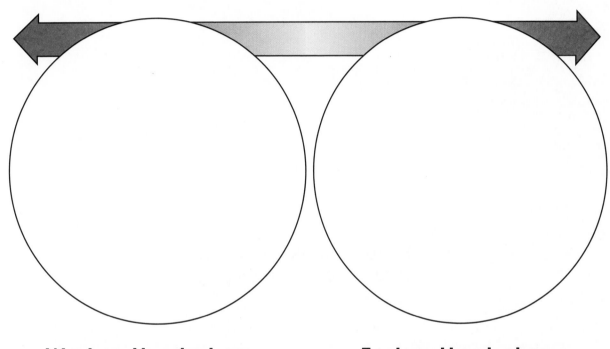

Western Hemisphere   Eastern Hemisphere

Abbreviations

N.A.   =   North America

Eur.   =   Europe

Aust. =   Australia

S.A.   =   South America

As.   =   Asia

Afr.   =   Africa

Ant.   =   Antarctica

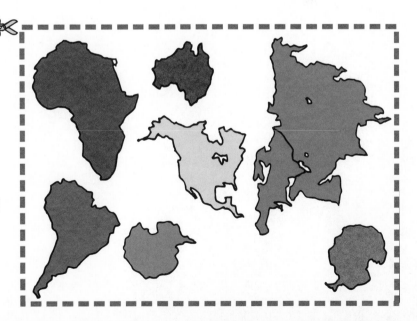

**Page is blank for cutting
exercise on previous page.**

The Long Lines

Lines of longitude on a globe run north and south. They are sometimes called **meridians**. Zero degrees longitude (0°) is an imaginary line called the **prime meridian**. It passes through Greenwich, England. Half of the lines of longitude are west of the prime meridian, and half are east of it.

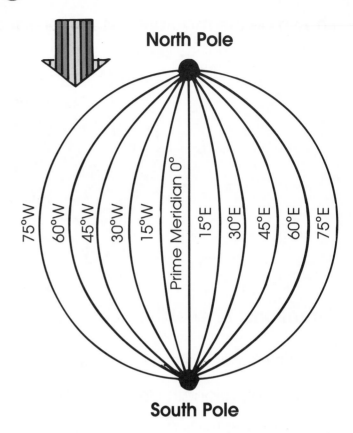

North Pole

South Pole

Directions: Answer the questions.

1. What is the name for the imaginary line at 0° longitude?

   _____

2. Lines to the left of the prime meridian are which direction?

   _____

3. Lines to the right of the prime meridian are which direction? _____

4. Where do lines of longitude come together?

   _____ and _____

5. What city does the prime meridian pass through? _____

6. Lines of longitude run in which directions?

   _____ and _____

7. Trace the prime meridian in red.

8. Trace the other meridians in blue.

Merry Meridians

Shown on the map are lines of longitude west of the prime meridian.

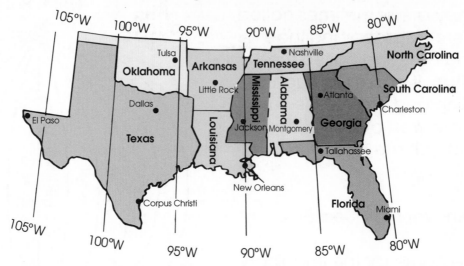

Directions: Answer the questions about these southeastern states.

1. Which two cities lie closest to 90°W? _____, _____

2. To which longitude line is Miami, Florida, closest? _____

3. Which cities lie between 80°W and 85°W? _____, _____, _____, _____.

4. Which city is closest to 95°W? _____

5. El Paso, Texas, is closest to which meridian? _____

6. Which two cities are closest to 85°W?_____, _____

7. Little Rock is between which two meridians? _____ and _____

8. Parts of which states lie between 85°W and 90°W?_____, _____, _____, _____, _____, _____, _____

9. Most of Florida lies between which meridians? _____

10. Corpus Christi lies between which meridians? _____ and _____

Where Is the Prime Meridian?

Meridians of longitude help people locate places east and west of the prime meridian and are measured in units called degrees (°).

Directions: Complete this page and page 346.

1. What do the letters N, S, E, and W stand for?
   _____

2. The _____ is 0° longitude.

3. Meridians of longitude are measured
   _____ and _____ of
   the prime meridian.

4. Where do all of the meridians meet?
   _____

5. Meridians of longitude are measured in units called
   _____.

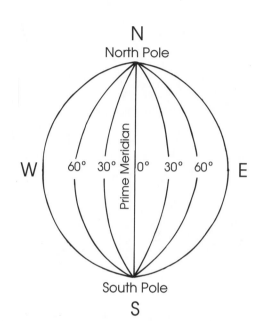

Follow the directions to complete this map.
Hint: The map above will help you.

A. Label the four cardinal directions.

B. Draw a meridian at 30°E and 30°W.

C. Draw a meridian at 60°E and 60°W.

D. Label the North and South Poles.

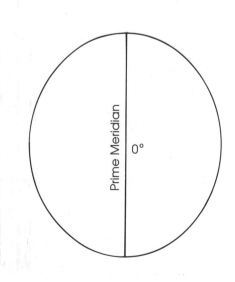

Where is the Prime Meridian?

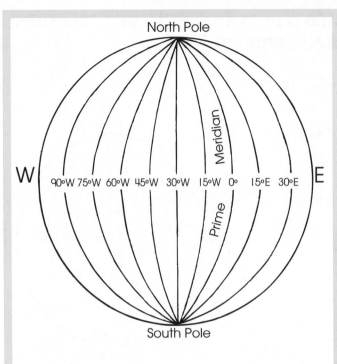

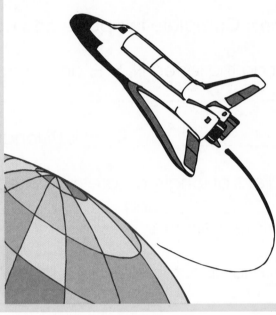

1. Is 15°E or 30°W farther from the prime meridian? _____

2. Is 60°W or 15°E closer to the prime meridian?_____

3. Name the two meridians east of the prime meridian.

   _____

4. How many meridians are west of the prime meridian?_____

5. What meridian is located between 15°W and 15°E?

   _____

6. Is 30°W or 15°E closer to the prime meridian?_____

7. Is 75°W or 90°W closer to the prime meridian? _____

8. Is 90°W or 15°E closer to 15°W?_____

9. Is 90°W or 75°W closer to the prime meridian? _____

10. Is 45°W or 30°E closer to the prime meridian?_____

11. Name the meridian west of 75°W. _____

12. Name the meridian east of 15°E. _____

Lines of Longitude

Directions: Use the meridians shown on the globe to answer the questions.

1. Lines of longitude are called
   _____.

2. They run in which directions?
   _____and _____

3. What does 0° longitude pass through?
   _____.

4. What is 0° longitude called?
   _____.

5. Degrees to the right of the prime
   meridian are which direction?
   _____.

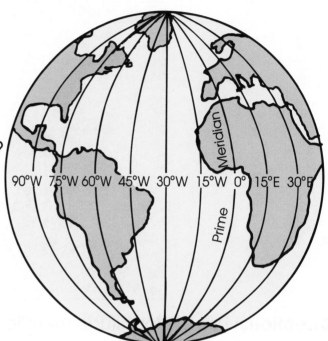

6. What meridian is west of 75°W? _____

7. Degrees to the left of the prime meridian are which direction? _____

8. Name the meridians east of 0° on this globe. _____

9. What meridian is east of 15°W? _____

10. Which meridians pass through the continent of Africa?
    _____

11. What meridian is west of 45°W? _____

12. Trace the prime meridian in orange.

13. Trace the other meridians in yellow.

Locating Cities

This map shows part of the northeastern United States. All longitude meridians on this map are west.

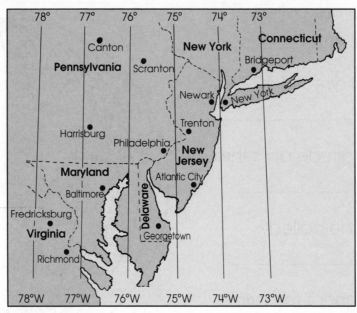

Directions: Use the longitude meridians to answer the questions.

1. Bridgeport, Connecticut, is closest to which meridian? _____

2. Trenton, New Jersey is closest to which meridian? _____

3. Name the meridians closest to these cities:

   Philadelphia _____   Georgetown _____

   Scranton _____   Newark _____

4. Name the seven states shown on this map. _____

   _____ _____ _____

   _____ _____ _____

5. Atlantic City is between _____ and _____ longitude.

6. Harrisburg is closest to which meridian? _____

7. Which is farther west—Harrisburg or Philadelphia? _____

8. Richmond is closest to _____ longitude.

North and South Dakota

Directions: Use this map to answer the questions. All longitude meridians are west.

1. Which meridian is closest to Eureka, South Dakota? _____

2. Which town is closer to 98°W—Platte, South Dakota or Lisbon, North Dakota? _____

3. Grenora, North Dakota is located almost exactly on the _____ meridian.

4. Is Deadwood, South Dakota north or south of Rapid City? _____

5. Which town is closer to 104°W—Bowman, North Dakota or Lemmon, South Dakota? _____

6. If you were traveling east from Rapid City, which meridian would you arrive at first? _____

7. Which meridian would you reach first when traveling east from Sioux Falls, South Dakota? _____

8. Bismarck is in the state of _____.

9. Lemmon, South Dakota is closest to the _____ meridian.

10. Name the North Dakota cities located east of 98°W longitude.

_____

_____

_____

Lines of Longitude

The lines of longitude tell how far east or west of the **prime meridian** (0°) a point is.

All lines of longitude are measured from the prime meridian in degrees. Everything west of the prime meridian is labeled **W** for **west**, and everything east of the prime meridian is labeled **E** for **east**.

Directions: Use a globe or map to find the longitude for each city. Remember to indicate both the number of degrees and whether it is east or west of the prime meridian.

NORTH POLE

SOUTH POLE

1. Los Angeles, USA _____

2. London, England _____

3. Wellington, New Zealand _____

4. Tokyo, Japan _____

5. Bangkok, Thailand _____

6. Santiago, Chile _____

7. Nairobi, Kenya _____

8. Tehran, Iran _____

9. Paris, France _____

10. Glasgow, Scotland _____

11. Rome, Italy _____

12. Buenos Aires, Argentina _____

13. Anchorage, Alaska _____

14. Calcutta, India _____

15. Cairo, Egypt _____

16. Shanghai, China _____

Locating Cities in Europe

Directions: Use this map to answer the questions. Pay particular attention to the location of the prime meridian.

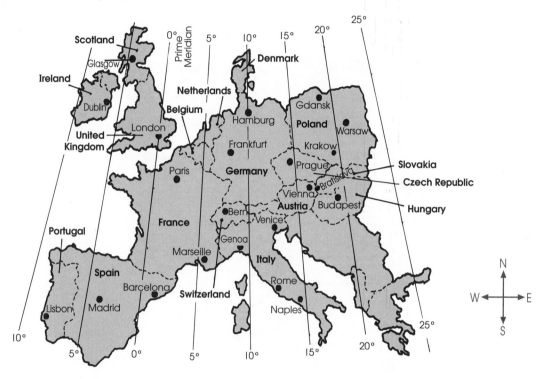

1. On the map, label each longitude meridian either east or west.
2. Rome, Italy, is located between the _____ and _____ meridians.
3. Which meridian passes through the western edge of Ireland?_____
4. Portugal is located between the _____ and _____ meridians.
5. Between which two meridians is most of Switzerland located? _____
6. Explain how you would decide which of the 5° meridians is east and which is west. _____
7. Warsaw is closest to the _____ meridian.
8. Marseille, France, is which direction from the 5°E meridian? _____
9. Gdansk is in the country of _____.
10. Prague is _____ of 15°E longitude.
11. Hamburg is on the _____ meridian.
12. Marseille is almost on the _____ meridian.

Lines of Latitude

Lines of latitude on a globe are called parallels. They run east and west. The equator is at 0° latitude. Use the map to answer the questions.

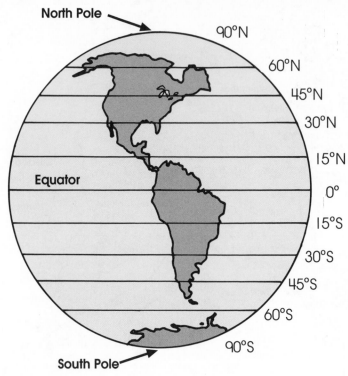

1. 0° latitude is called the _____.

2. Lines of latitude are called _____.

3. Parallels run in which directions? _____ and _____

4. The latitude of the North Pole is _____.

5. Which parallel runs through Florida? _____

6. What is located at 90°S latitude? _____

7. Which parallel runs through Canada? _____

8. Lines of latitude above the equator are labeled with which direction?

   _____

9. Below the equator, the parallels are labeled with which direction?

   _____

Name_____

Lateral Movement

Parallels measure the distance north or south from the equator. Zero degrees latitude (0°) is at the equator. Half of the parallels are north of the equator and half are south of it. The lines do not meet.

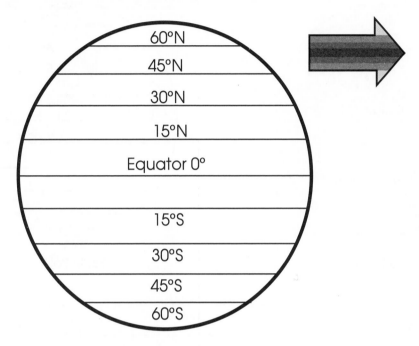

1. What is the symbol for degrees? _____

2. Latitude lines run _____ and _____.

3. Latitude lines are called _____.

4. Give the latitude of the equator. _____

5. The parallels above the equator are which direction? _____

6. The parallels below the equator are which direction? _____

7. Trace the equator parallel in orange.

8. Trace 15°N and 15°S in green.

9. Trace 30°N and 30°S in blue.

10. Trace 45°N and 45°S in red.

11. Trace 60°N and 60°S in purple.

Imaginary Lines

Directions: Answer the questions below using these maps.

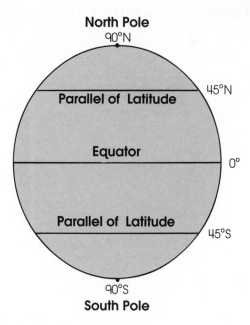

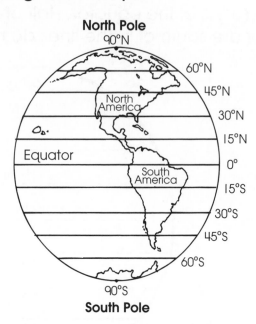

1. The _____ is 0° latitude.

2. The North Pole is _____ degrees north latitude.

3. Lines north and south of the equator are called _____.

4. The _____ is 90°S latitude.

5. Which line is closer to the equator—30°N or 15°S?_____

6. Which is closer to the South Pole—45°S or 30°S?_____

7. If you wanted to find a city located at 45°N, would you look above or
   below the equator? _____

8. Which continent on the map is entirely north of the equator?
   _____

9. South America lies between the parallels of latitude _____°N and 60°S.

10. The equator runs through the northern part of the continent of
    _____.

11. Color all of the land north of the equator red.

12. Color all of the land south of the equator green.

What's My Line?

There are several important lines of latitude on the globe which have special names.

Directions: Use a map, globe, or other resource to identify the special lines on the illustration of the globe below.

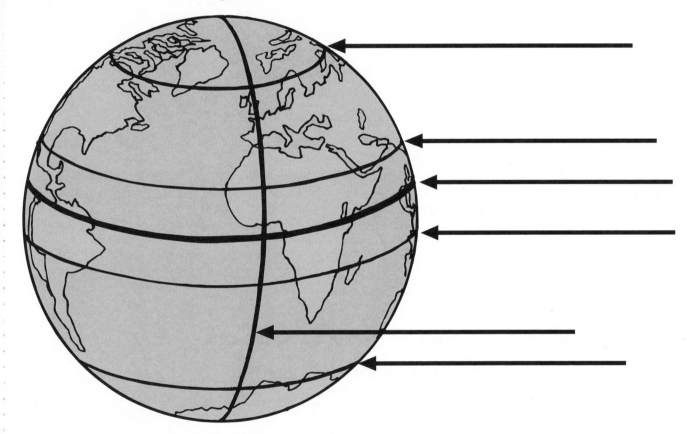

Name the imaginary line that . . .

passes through Mexico.   _____

is 0° latitude.   _____

passes through Alaska.   _____

is 0° longitude.   _____

divides the Northern and Southern Hemispheres.   _____

passes through Botswana.   _____

Across the USA

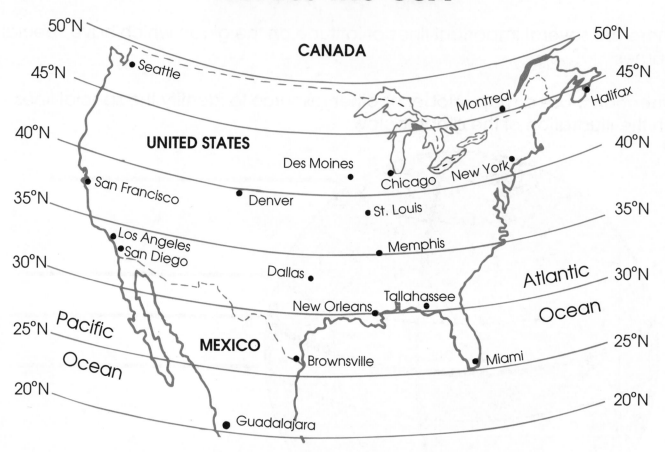

Directions: Use the map above to answer the questions.

1. Denver and New York are close to which parallel? _____

2. Which two cities are between 45°N and 50°N? _____

3. Los Angeles and Memphis are near which parallel? _____

4. Tallahassee is closest to which parallel? _____

5. St. Louis is between which parallels? _____ and _____

6. Which city is farthest north? _____ It is between which parallels? _____ and _____

7. Which city is farthest south? _____ It is between which parallels? _____ and _____

8. San Francisco is halfway between _____ and _____.

Name_____

Latitude in North America

Directions: Use the map on page 356 to answer the questions.

1. Is Chicago closer to 40°N or 45°N?_____

2. Name the three United States cities located between 25°N and 30°N.
   _____, _____, _____

3. New York is closest to the _____ parallel of latitude.

4. Name the eight United States cities located between 30°N and 40°N.
   _____, _____, _____, _____,
   _____, _____, _____, _____

5. The _____ Ocean is on the eastern side of the United States.

6. _____ is the country south of the United States.

7. Canada is the country _____ of the United States.

8. On the west, the United States is bordered by the _____ Ocean.

9. Montreal is in the country of _____.

10. Seattle is located closest to the _____ parallel of latitude.

11. Des Moines is located between the _____ parallel and the _____ parallel.

12. Is Dallas north or south of the 30°N parallel of latitude? _____

13. Name the four United States cities located between 40°N and 50°N.
    _____, _____, _____, _____

14. Denver is closest to the _____ parallel of latitude.

15. San Francisco is located south of _____ °N.

16. Which parallel of latitude goes through Florida? _____

17. Guadalajara is located in what country? _____

Parallels Help with Location

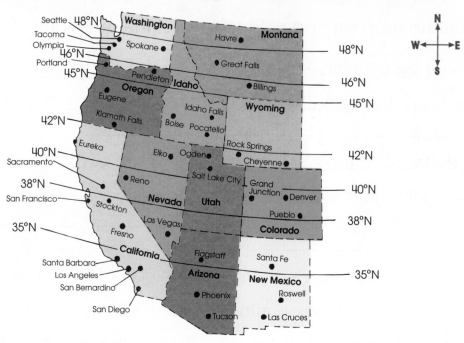

1. Billings, Montana is which direction from the 46°N parallel? _____

2. Pueblo, Colorado is almost directly on the _____ parallel of latitude.

3. The boundary between Oregon and California is formed by the _____ parallel.

4. The state of Wyoming is located between 40°N parallel and _____ parallel.

5. Name three cities in Idaho south of the 45°N parallel of latitude.

    _____   _____   _____

6. Which of these cities is south of the 35°N parallel—Flagstaff, Arizona or Roswell, New Mexico? _____

7. Name the three California cities located between the 35°N and 38°N parallels. _____   _____   _____

8. All of the cities shown in Washington are between the parallels of _____ and _____.

9. Which two Nevada cities are north of the 38°N parallel? _____ and _____

10. Klamath Falls, Oregon is almost directly on the _____ parallel.

Picture It!

Directions: Coordinates are sets of numbers that show where lines of latitude and longitude meet. Place a dot at each latitude / longitude coordinate on the graph. Draw lines to connect the dots in order.

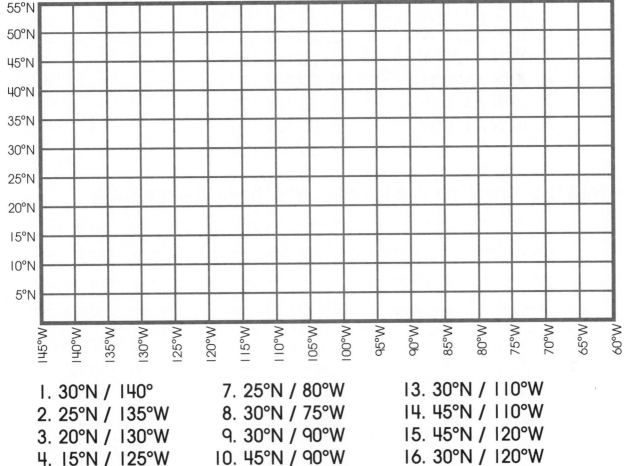

1. 30°N / 140°
2. 25°N / 135°W
3. 20°N / 130°W
4. 15°N / 125°W
5. 15°N / 90°W
6. 20°N / 85°W

7. 25°N / 80°W
8. 30°N / 75°W
9. 30°N / 90°W
10. 45°N / 90°W
11. 45°N / 100°W
12. 30°N / 100°W

13. 30°N / 110°W
14. 45°N / 110°W
15. 45°N / 120°W
16. 30°N / 120°W
17. 30°N / 140°W

Place a yellow X at each coordinate below. Do not connect the Xs.

1. 45°N / 140°W
2. 35°N / 135°W
3. 45°N / 130°W

4. 40°N / 80°W
5. 45°N / 70°W
6. 35°N / 65°W

Color the rest of the picture.

What Will They Be?

Directions: Place a dot at each of these latitude and longitude points on the graph.

1. 45°N / 105°W
2. 40°N / 110°W
3. 35°N / 115°W
4. 30°N / 120°W
5. 25°N / 125°W
6. 20°N / 120°N
7. 15°N / 115°W
8. 10°N / 110°W

9. 5°N / 105°W
10. 10°N / 100°W
11. 15°N / 95°W
12. 20°N / 90°W
13. 25°N / 85°W
14. 30°N / 90°W
15. 35°N / 95°W
16. 40°N / 100°W
17. 45°N / 105°W

Draw lines to connect the dots in order. What have you drawn? _____

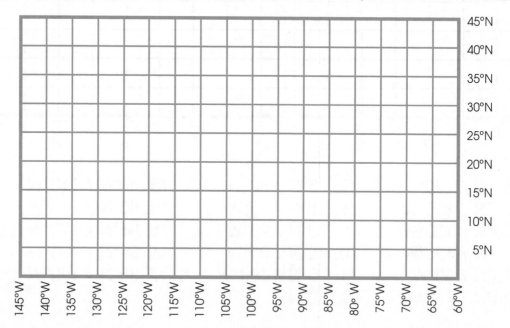

With a different color, place a dot at each of these latitude and longitude points.

1. 45°N / 85°W
2. 35°N / 85°W

3. 35°N / 65°W
4. 45°N / 65°W

Draw lines to connect the dots in order. What have you drawn?

_____

Name_____

Using Lines to Draw a State

Directions: Place a dot on the grid for each point given. The first two have been done for you.

1. 38°N / 99°W
2. 38° N / 102°W
3. 36°N / 102°W
4. 34°N / 102°W
5. 34°N / 104°W
6. 34°N / 106°W
7. 33°N / 105 1/2°W
8. 32 1/2°N / 105°W
9. 32°N / 104 1/2°W

10. 31°N / 104°W
11. 30°N / 104°W
12. 29 1/2°N / 103°W
13. 30°N / 102°W
14. 30°N / 101°W
15. 29°N / 101°W
16. 28°N / 100°W
17. 27 1/2°N / 99°W
18. 26 1/2°N / 97 1/2°W

19. 28°N / 97 1/2°W
20. 29°N / 96 1/2°W
21. 30°N / 95°W
22. 31°N / 94°W
23. 33°N / 94°W
24. 35°N / 94°W
25. 35°N / 96°W
26. 35°N / 99°W
27. 37°N / 99°W

Draw a line to connect all of the dots in order. What state did you draw?

_____

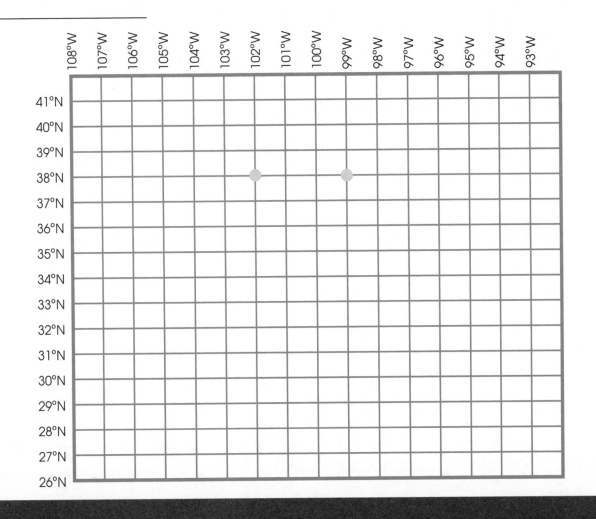

Casey's Island

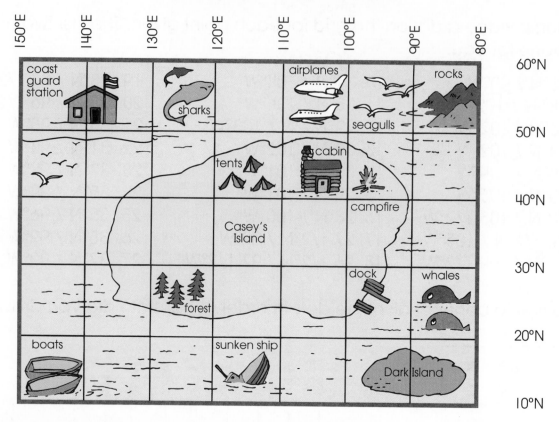

Directions: Use the map to answer the questions.

1. The whales are between which two latitude lines? _____

2. The coast guard station is located between which longitude lines?

   _____

3. If the whales try to go north to 55°N latitude, what will stop them?

   _____

4. The boats must cross what longitude lines to get to the sunken ship?

   _____

5. If you draw a latitude line at 35°N, what will you cross? _____

6. If the whales cross 90°E longitude, what will they reach?_____

7. Name the items that would be crossed by the 55°N latitude line.

   _____

8. Which longitude lines cross Casey's Island? _____

State Search

Which state is roughly between the coordinates given? After locating the state, color it on the map as directed.

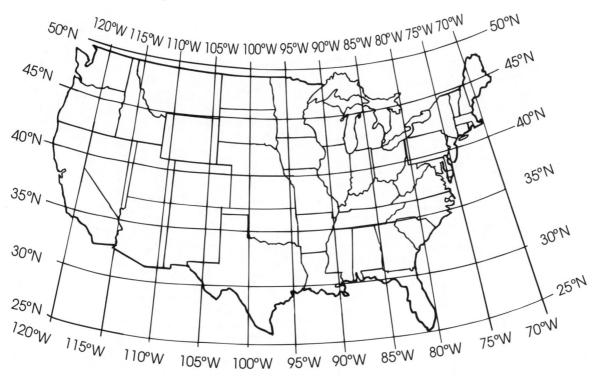

	Latitude	Longitude	State	Color
1.	45°N / 50°N	105°W / 115°W	_____	orange
2.	40°N / 45°N	75°W / 80°W	_____	tan
3.	44°N / 50°N	67°W / 70°W	_____	red
4.	25°N / 30°N	80°W / 85°W	_____	yellow
5.	40°N / 45°N	90°W / 95°W	_____	gray
6.	30°N / 35°N	85°W / 90°W	_____	green
7.	43°N / 47°N	87°W / 93°W	_____	blue
8.	31°N / 36°N	104°W / 109°W	_____	pink
9.	36°N / 38°N	82°W / 89°W	_____	light green
10.	36°N / 39°N	76°W / 84°W	_____	gold
11.	26°N / 34°N	94°W / 107°W	_____	purple
12.	41°N / 45°N	104°W / 111°W	_____	light blue
13.	36°N / 41°N	90°W / 95°W	_____	brown

See the USA

Use the coordinates to plan a trip across the USA.

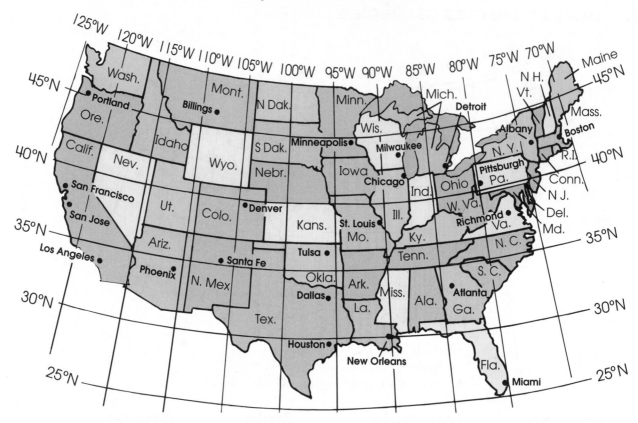

Directions: Write the name of the city closest to the intersection.

1. Your trip begins at 40°N / 105°W, the Mile-High City. _____

2. You fly over the Rocky Mountains to 45°N / 125°W. _____

3. Now, to 35°N / 105°W in New Mexico. _____

4. Next stop is Texas, the city near 30°N / 95°W. _____

5. It's Mardi Gras time at 30°N / 90°W. _____

6. Then, fun in the sun and the Atlantic Ocean at 25°N / 80°W. _____

7. To the Gateway Arch in the city of 40°N / 90°W. _____

8. The Steelers play football here—40°N / 80°W. _____

9. Next, to the capital of New York—43°N / 75°W. _____

Plotting North American Cities

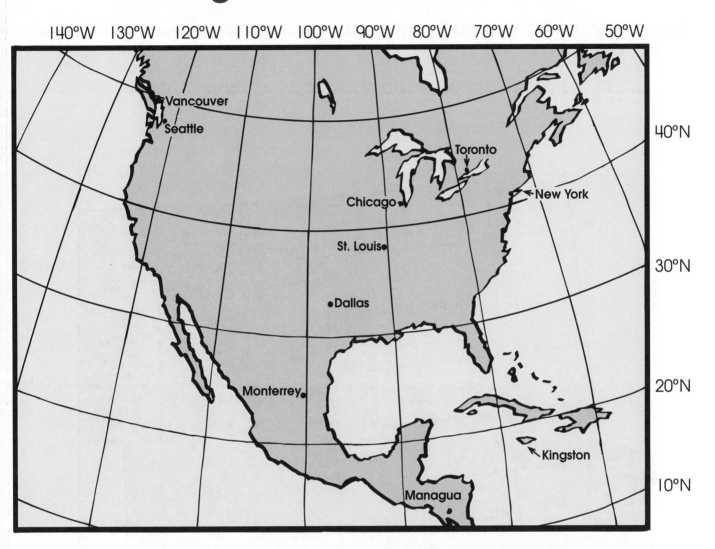

Directions: Use the lines of latitude and longitude to determine the approximate coordinates of the North American cities on the map above. Write the coordinates for each city in the blanks.

	Latitude	Longitude			Latitude	Longitude
1. Seattle	_____	_____		6. St. Louis	_____	_____
2. Kingston	_____	_____		7. Toronto	_____	_____
3. Dallas	_____	_____		8. New York	_____	_____
4. Vancouver	_____	_____		9. Monterrey	_____	_____
5. Managua	_____	_____		10. Chicago	_____	_____

Four States

Directions: Use this map to fill in the charts on page 367. Two answers have been done for you.

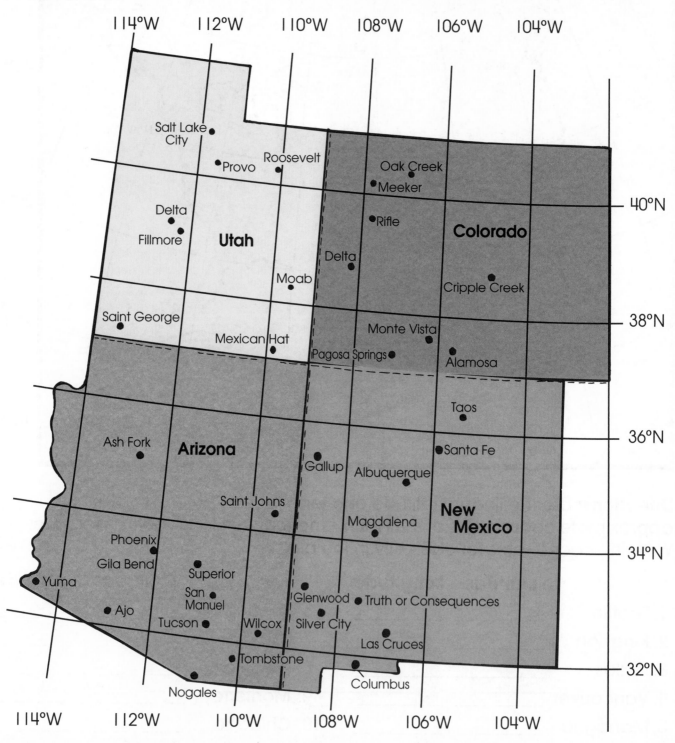

Four States

Use with page 366.

City	Coordinates
1. Salt Lake City, Utah	41°N / 112°W
2. Tucson, Arizona	
3. Santa Fe, New Mexico	
4. Oak Creek, Colorado	
5. Wilcox, Arizona	
6. Cripple Creek, Colorado	
7. Las Cruces, New Mexico	
8. Albuquerque, New Mexico	
9. Meeker, Colorado	
10. Saint George, Utah	

Coordinates	City
1. 33°N / 109°W	Glenwood, New Mexico
2. 41°N / 112°W	
3. 39°N / 108°W	
4. 31°N / 111°W	
5. 37°N / 110°W	
6. 40 1/2°N / 110°W	
7. 33 1/2°N / 107°W	
8. 39°N / 112 1/2°W	
9. 35 1/2°N / 108 1/2°W	
10. 33°N / 111°W	

Approximate Coordinates	State
32°N / 36°N and 110°W / 114°W	
36°N / 40°N and 110°W / 114°W	
32°N / 36°N and 104°W / 108°W	
36°N / 40°N and 104°W / 108°W	

Name _____

Name the City

Directions: Use the coordinates given below to locate each of the cities. The first one has been done for you.

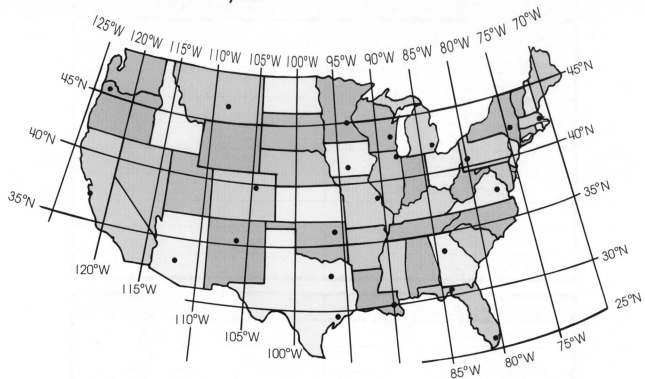

	Latitude	Longitude	City
1.	34°N	84°W	Atlanta
2.	26°N	80°W	
3.	40°N	80°W	
4.	36°N	96°W	
5.	37°N	122°W	
6.	33°N	112°W	
7.	39°N	90°W	
8.	46°N	108°W	
9.	43°N	88°W	
10.	42°N	94°W	
11.	43°N	74°W	
12.	45°N	93°W	
13.	33°N	97°W	
14.	30°N	95°W	

Locating Places in Western Europe

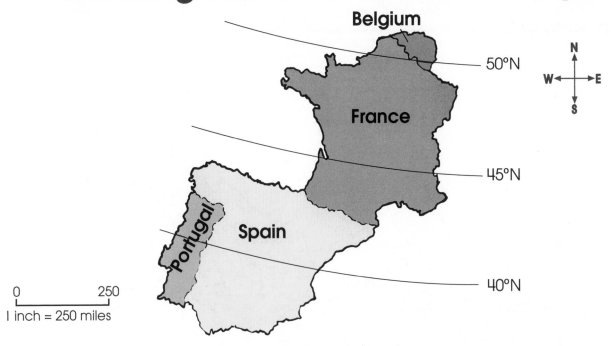

1. Name the four countries on this map.

   _____, _____, _____, _____

2. One inch equals _____ miles on the map.

3. Which parallel line crosses both Portugal and Spain? _____

4. Which two parallel lines cross France? _____ _____

5. Name the country directly north of France. _____

6. Place the city of Barcelona on the northeastern coast of Spain about
   225 miles south of the 45°N parallel.

7. Place the city of Paris in the north-central part of France about 75 miles
   south of the 50°N parallel.

8. Place Lisbon on the western coast of Portugal about 75 miles south of
   the 40°N parallel.

9. Place Madrid in the center of Spain about 50 miles north of the 40°N
   parallel.

10. Place Brussels near the north-central part of Belgium about 50 miles north
    of the 50°N parallel line.

11. Place Toulouse in the southwestern part of France 100 miles south of the
    45°N parallel.

Where in Europe?

Use with page 371.

Where in Europe?

Directions: Estimate and write the coordinates and countries for these European cities using the map on page 370. The first one has been done for you.

City	Latitude	Longitude	Country
1. London	52°N	0°	United Kingdom
2. Belgrade			
3. Warsaw			
4. Stockholm			
5. Athens			
6. Helsinki			
7. Paris			
8. Munich			
9. Copenhagen			
10. Oslo			
11. Glasgow			
12. Prague			
13. Bern			
14. Hamburg			
15. Dresden			
16. Dublin			
17. Rome			
18. Budapest			
19. Vienna			
20. Amsterdam			

Latitude and Longitude Lines

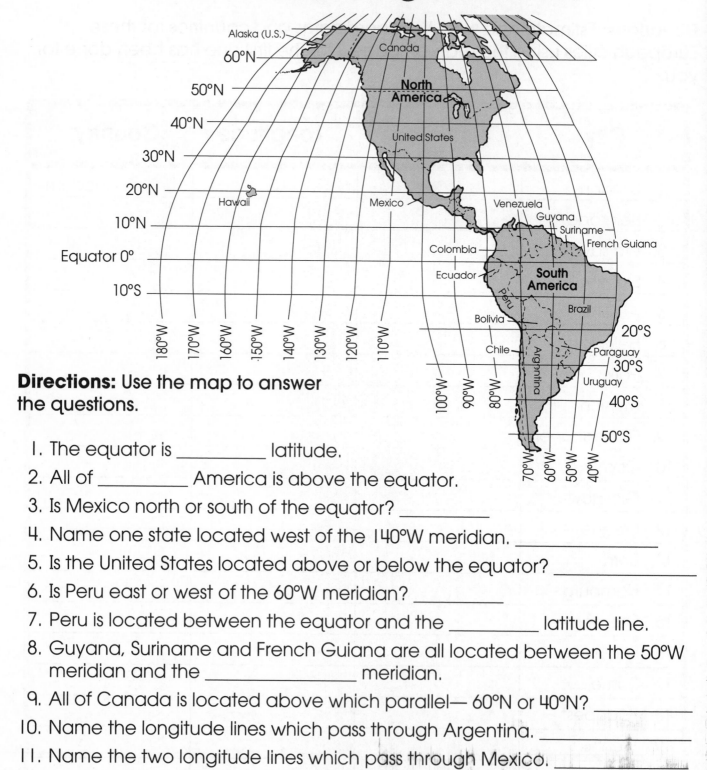

Directions: Use the map to answer the questions.

1. The equator is _____ latitude.

2. All of _____ America is above the equator.

3. Is Mexico north or south of the equator? _____

4. Name one state located west of the 140°W meridian. _____

5. Is the United States located above or below the equator? _____

6. Is Peru east or west of the 60°W meridian? _____

7. Peru is located between the equator and the _____ latitude line.

8. Guyana, Suriname and French Guiana are all located between the 50°W meridian and the _____ meridian.

9. All of Canada is located above which parallel— 60°N or 40°N? _____

10. Name the longitude lines which pass through Argentina. _____

11. Name the two longitude lines which pass through Mexico. _____

12. Is most of Colombia north or south of the equator? _____

Night and Day Difference

What causes the daily change from daylight to darkness? Day turns into night because the earth rotates, or spins, on its axis. The earth's axis is an imaginary line that cuts through the earth from the North Pole to the South Pole. The earth spins in a counterclockwise direction.

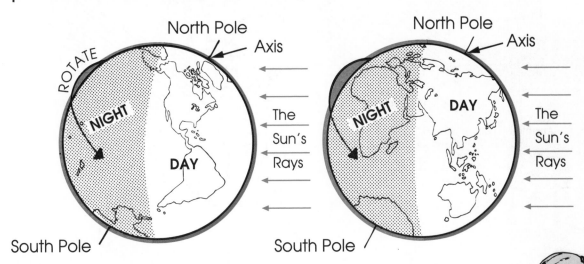

Demonstrate the difference between night and day. Ask a friend to help you.

You will need:
    globe
    flashlight

Directions:
    1. Set the globe on a table, as demonstrated in the picture. Make the room very dark.

    2. Standing five to ten feet away, aim the flashlight at the globe.

    3. Have the friend slowly rotate the globe counterclockwise on its axis.

    4. Discover what parts of the world are sleeping when it is daytime where you live.

Do You Have The Time?

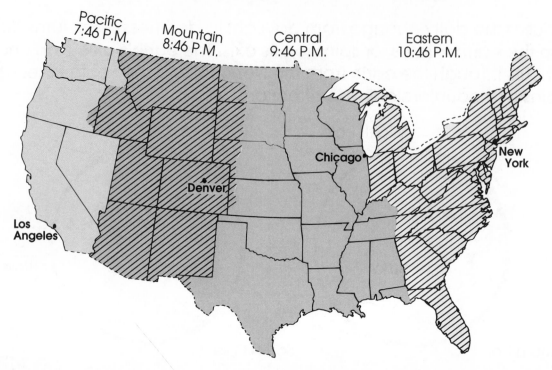

The earth spins on its axis in a west to east direction. This causes our day to begin with the sun rising in the east and setting in the west. Different areas of the United States can have different amounts of daylight at the same moment in time. For instance, when the sun is rising in New York, it is still dark in California.

A **time zone** is an area in which everyone has the same time. Every zone is one hour different from its neighbor. There are 24 time zones around the world. There are six time zones in the United States. The map above shows the four zones that cover the 48 contiguous, or touching, states.

When it is six o'clock in New York, what time is it in

Chicago? _____   Los Angeles? _____   Denver? _____

What is the name of the time zone in which you live? _____

Name three other states in your time zone.

_____

Name

World Time Zones

Use with page 376.

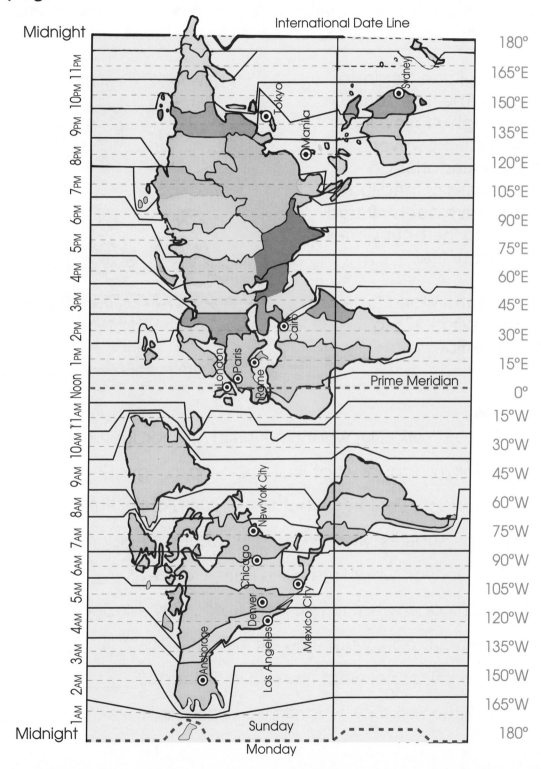

24-Hour Globe

The earth is divided into 24 standard time zones. These time zones are set so that large sections of the earth within each zone have the same time. In each time zone, people set their clocks and watches to the same time.

Every 15° of longitude begins a new time zone. The time zone boundaries roughly follow the lines of longitude. However, many of the boundaries do not follow the lines of longitude exactly. They have been altered to correspond to the boundaries of states and countries.

Directions: Use the World Time Zones map on page 375 to answer the questions.

If it is . . .

3:00 A.M. in New York City, what time is it in Anchorage, Alaska? _____

4:00 P.M. in Tokyo, Japan, what time is it in Cairo, Egypt?_____

1:00 P.M. in London, England, what time is it in Manila, Philippines? _____

3:00 P.M. in Los Angeles, what time is it in London, England?_____

10:00 A.M. in Denver, what time is it in Paris, France? _____

9:00 P.M. in Chicago, what time is it in Mexico City, Mexico? _____

4:00 A.M. in Anchorage, what time is it in Rome, Italy? _____

1:00 P.M. in Paris, France, what time is it in Chicago?_____

11:00 P.M. in New York City, what time is it in Paris, France? _____

Changing Times

A plane leaves Chicago at 5:30 P.M. heading for San Francisco. The flight takes three hours. At what time will it arrive in San Francisco?

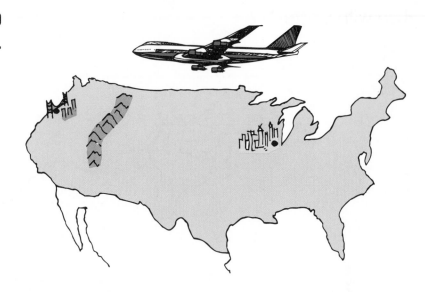

If you answered 8:30 P.M. to the above question, you are only partly correct. It would be 8:30 P.M. "Chicago time" but it would be 6:30 P.M. in San Francisco because the plane crossed two time zones.

Examine the time zones of the United States on the map on page 378. Notice that the time-zone boundaries do not always follow the state boundaries. Some states are in more than one time zone.

Directions: Use the United States Time Zones map on page 378 to answer the questions.

1. How many time zones are there in the United States? _____

2. How many time zones are there in the 48 contiguous (touching) states?

   _____

3. Name the time zones in all 50 states._____

4. If it is 3:30 P.M. in your state, what time is it in

   California? _____   Iowa?_____

   New York? _____   Colorado? _____

5. What time is it right now in

   Miami, Florida? _____   Portland, Oregon?_____

   Grand Rapids, Michigan? _____   Dallas, Texas? _____

United States Time Zones

Use with page 377.

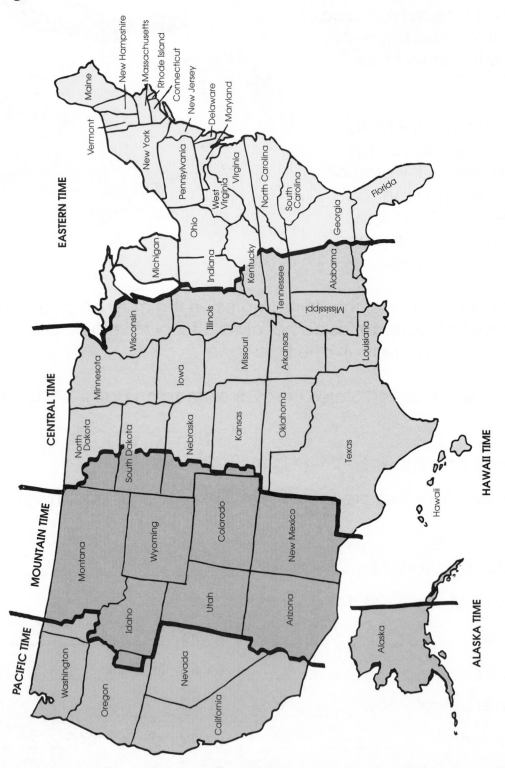

Carnac the Cartographer

A cartographer is a person who makes maps. Carnac the Cartographer was recently fired from his profession. Can you detect the errors he made on the map on page 380? Place a red **X** on all the mistakes that you see. Then, list corrections in the appropriate sections.

Continents	
Mistake	It should be...

Oceans/Seas	
Mistake	It should be...

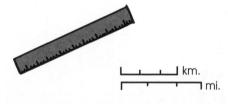

km.
mi.

Latitude /Longitude	
Mistake	It should be...

Direction Finder	
Mistake	It should be . . .

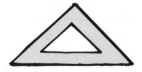

Name_____

Carnac the Cartographer

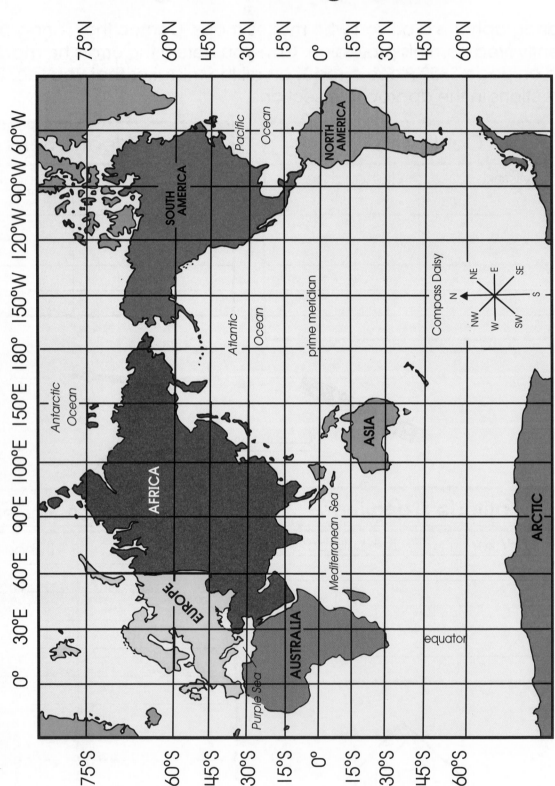

Page 6

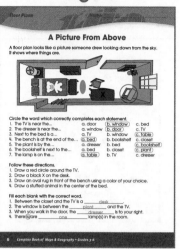

A Picture From Above

A floor plan looks like a picture someone drew looking down from the sky. It shows where things are.

Circle the word which correctly completes each statement.
1. The TV is near the...   a. door   **b. window**   c. bed
2. The dresser is near the...   a. window   **b. door**   c. TV
3. Next to the bed is a...   a. TV   b. window   **c. table**
4. The bench is at the end of the...   **a. bed**   b. bookshelf   c. closet
5. The plant is by the...   a. dresser   b. bed   **c. bookshelf**
6. The bookshelf is next to the...   a. bed   b. closet   **c. plant**
7. The lamp is on the...   **a. table**   b. TV   c. dresser

Follow these directions.
1. Draw a red circle around the TV.
2. Draw a black X on the desk.
3. Draw an oval rug in front of the bench using a color of your choice.
4. Draw a stuffed animal in the center of the bed.

Fill each blank with the correct word.
1. Between the closet and the TV is a _____ desk _____.
2. The window is between the _____ plant _____ and the TV.
3. When you walk in the door, the _____ dresser _____ is to your right.
4. There(is)are _____ one _____ lamp(s) in the room.

Page 7

The Mole Family

A floor plan shows where things are placed in a room. The Mole Family has just had all of their new living room furniture delivered. Now they have to arrange it. Help them decide where to put each piece of furniture. Color and cut out the pictures of the furniture. Glue the pictures on the drawing of the Mole Family's living room to make a floor plan.

Mole Family's Floor Plan

Answers will vary.

Page 9

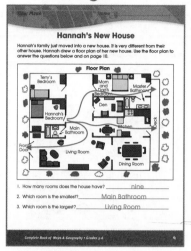

Hannah's New House

Hannah's family just moved into a new house. It is very different from their other house. Hannah drew a floor plan of her new house. Use the floor plan to answer the questions below and on page 10.

Floor Plan

1. How many rooms does the house have? _____ nine
2. Which room is the smallest? _____ Main Bathroom
3. Which room is the largest? _____ Living Room

Page 10

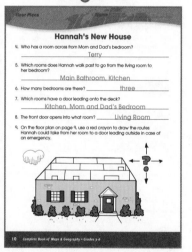

Hannah's New House

4. Who has a room across from Mom and Dad's bedroom?
_____ Terry

5. Which rooms does Hannah walk past to go from the living room to her bedroom?
_____ Main Bathroom, Kitchen

6. How many bedrooms are there? _____ three

7. Which rooms have a door leading onto the deck?
_____ Kitchen, Mom and Dad's Bedroom

8. The front door opens into what room? _____ Living Room

9. On the floor plan on page 9, use a red crayon to draw the routes Hannah could take from her room to a door leading outside in case of an emergency.

Page 11

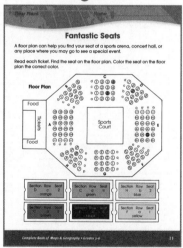

Fantastic Seats

A floor plan can help you find your seat at a sports arena, concert hall, or any place where you may go to see a special event.

Read each ticket. Find the seat on the floor plan. Color the seat on the floor plan the correct color.

Floor Plan

Food / Tickets / Food / Sports Court

Page 12

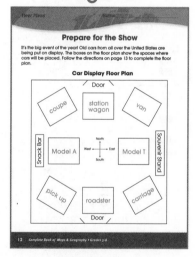

Prepare for the Show

It's the big event of the year! Old cars from all over the United States are being put on display. The boxes on the floor plan show the spaces where cars will be placed. Follow the directions on page 13 to complete the floor plan.

Car Display Floor Plan

Door

coupe / station wagon / van

Snack Bar / Model A / Model T / Souvenir Stand

pick up / roadster / carriage

Door

Page 15

Creating a Floor Plan

Pretend you are looking down at your classroom or a room in your home from the light on the ceiling. Draw how the room looks.

Answers will vary.

Page 16

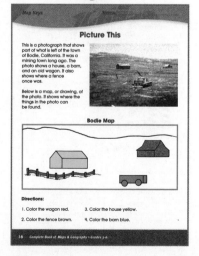

Picture This

This is a photograph that shows part of what is left of the town of Bodie, California. It was a mining town long ago. The photo shows a house, a barn, and an old wagon. It also shows where a fence once was.

Below is a map, or drawing, of the photo. It shows where the things in the photo can be found.

Bodie Map

Directions:
1. Color the wagon red.
2. Color the fence brown.
3. Color the house yellow.
4. Color the barn blue.

Page 17

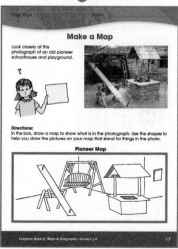

Make a Map

Look closely at this photograph of an old pioneer schoolhouse and playground.

Directions:
In the box, draw a map to show what is in the photograph. Use the shapes to help you draw the pictures on your map that stand for things in the photo.

Pioneer Map

Answer Key

Page 18

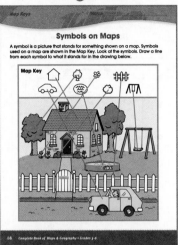

Page 19

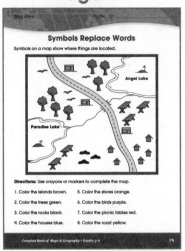

Page 20

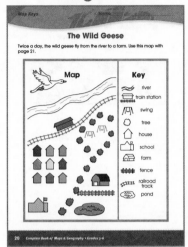

Page 21

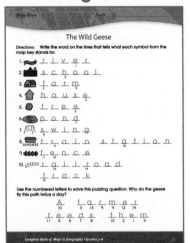

Page 22

Page 23

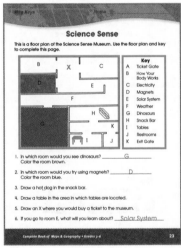

Page 24

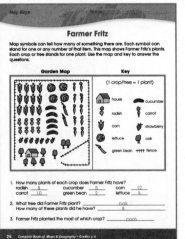

Page 25

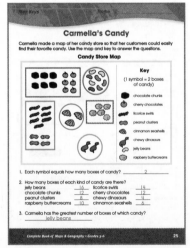

Page 26

Page 27

Time to Go Home

This map shows routes the dinosaur can take to get to its cave. Use the key to find each symbol on the map. Then, follow the directions.

Dinosaur Cave Map

Key
- volcano
- tree
- plant
- pond
- rocks
- mountains
- dinosaur cave

Directions:
1. Write the word **H O M E** on the dinosaur cave.
2. Color the volcano red.
3. Color the trees green.
4. Draw a blue line to show a route the dinosaur can take home that goes past the volcano.
5. Draw a yellow line to show a route the dinosaur can take home. Make it go past the rocks.

Page 28

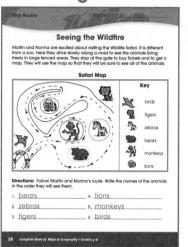

Seeing the Wildfire

Martin and Norma are excited about visiting the Wildlife Safari. It is different from a zoo. Here they drive slowly along a road to see the animals living freely in large fenced areas. They stop at the gate to buy tickets and to get a map. They will use the map so that they will be sure to see all of the animals.

Safari Map

Key
- birds
- tigers
- zebras
- bears
- monkeys
- lions

Directions: Follow Martin and Norma's route. Write the names of the animals in the order they will see them.

1. bears
2. zebras
3. tigers
4. lions
5. monkeys
6. birds

Page 29

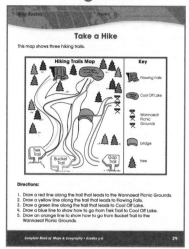

Take a Hike

This map shows three hiking trails.

Hiking Trails Map

Key
- Flowing Falls
- Cool Off Lake
- Wannaeat Picnic Grounds
- bridge
- tree

Directions:
1. Draw a red line along the trail that leads to the Wannaeat Picnic Grounds.
2. Draw a yellow line along the trail that leads to Flowing Falls.
3. Draw a green line along the trail that leads to Cool Off Lake.
4. Draw a blue line to show how to go from Trek Trail to Cool Off Lake.
5. Draw an orange line to show how to go from Bucket Trail to the Wannaeat Picnic Grounds.

Page 30

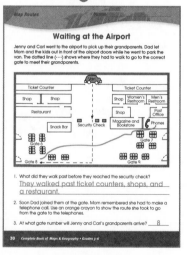

Waiting at the Airport

Jenny and Carl went to the airport to pick up their grandparents. Dad let Mom and the kids out in front of the airport doors while he went to park the van. The dotted line (- - -) shows where they had to walk to go to the correct gate to meet their grandparents.

1. What did they walk past before they reached the security check?
They walked past ticket counters, shops, and a restaurant.

2. Soon Dad joined them at the gate. Mom remembered she had to make a telephone call. Use an orange crayon to show the route she took to go from the gate to the telephones.

3. At what gate number will Jenny and Carl's grandparents arrive? 8

Page 31

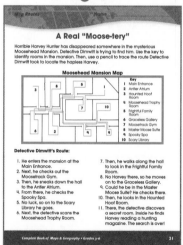

A Real "Moose-tery"

Horrible Harvey Hunter has disappeared somewhere in the mysterious Moosehead Mansion. Detective Dimwitt is trying to find him. Use the key to identify rooms in the mansion. Then, use a pencil to trace the route Detective Dimwitt took to locate the hapless Harvey.

Moosehead Mansion Map

Key
1. Main Entrance
2. Antler Atrium
3. Haunted Hoof Room
4. Moosehead Trophy Room
5. Frightful Family Room
6. Graceless Gallery
7. Moosetrack Gym
8. Master Moose Suite
9. Spooky Spa
10. Scary Library

Detective Dimwitt's Route:
1. He enters the mansion at the Main Entrance.
2. Next, he checks out the Moosetrack Gym.
3. Then, he sneaks down the hall to the Antler Atrium.
4. From there, he checks the Spooky Spa.
5. No luck, so on to the Scary Library he goes.
6. Next, the detective scans the Moosehead Trophy Room.
7. Then, he walks along the hall to look in the Frightful Family Room.
8. No Harvey there, so he moves on to the Graceless Gallery.
9. Could he be in the Master Moose Suite? He checks there.
10. Then, he looks in the Haunted Hoof Room.
11. Then, the detective discovers a secret room. Inside he finds Harvey reading a hunting magazine. The search is over!

Page 32

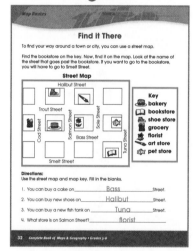

Find it There

To find your way around a town or city, you can use a street map.

Find the bookstore on the key. Now, find it on the map. Look at the name of the street that goes past the bookstore. If you want to go to the bookstore, you will have to go to Smelt Street.

Street Map

Key
- bakery
- bookstore
- shoe store
- grocery
- florist
- art store
- pet store

Directions:
Use the street map and map key. Fill in the blanks.

1. You can buy a cake on Bass Street.
2. You can buy new shoes on Halibut Street.
3. You can buy a new fish tank on Tuna Street.
4. What store is on Salmon Street? florist

Page 33

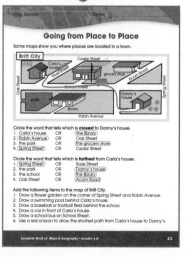

Going from Place to Place

Some maps show you where places are located in a town.

Circle the word that tells which is **closest** to Danny's house.
1. Carla's house OR (the library)
2. (Robin Avenue) OR Oak Street
3. the park OR (the grocery store)
4. (Spring Street) OR Cedar Street

Circle the word that tells which is **farthest** from Carla's house.
1. (Spring Street) OR Rose Street
2. the park OR (Danny's house)
3. the school OR (the library)
4. Oak Street OR (Acorn Road)

Add the following items to the map of Britt City.
1. Draw a flower garden on the corner of Spring Street and Robin Avenue.
2. Draw a swimming pool behind Carla's house.
3. Draw a baseball or football field behind the school.
4. Draw a car in front of Carla's house.
5. Draw a school bus on School Street.
6. Use a red crayon to draw the shortest path from Carla's house to Danny's.

Page 34

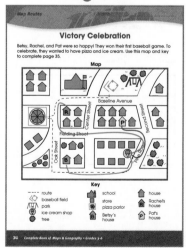

Victory Celebration

Betsy, Rachel, and Pat were so happy! They won their first baseball game. To celebrate, they wanted to have pizza and ice cream. Use this map and key to complete page 35.

Map

Key
- route
- baseball field
- park
- ice cream shop
- tree
- school
- pizza parlor
- Betsy's house
- house
- Rachel's house
- Pat's house

Page 35

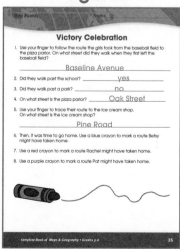

Victory Celebration

1. Use your finger to follow the route the girls took from the baseball field to the pizza parlor. On what street did they walk when they first left the baseball field?
Baseline Avenue

2. Did they walk past the school? yes
3. Did they walk past a park? no
4. On what street is the pizza parlor? Oak Street

5. Use your finger to trace their route to the ice cream shop. On what street is the ice cream shop?
Pine Road

6. Then, it was time to go home. Use a blue crayon to mark a route Betsy might have taken home.
7. Use a red crayon to mark a route Rachel might have taken home.
8. Use a purple crayon to mark a route Pat might have taken home.

Page 36

A New Puppy

Mike's dog had puppies. Jason and his parents are going to Mike's house to get one of the puppies. Use the street map and key to help you answer the questions.

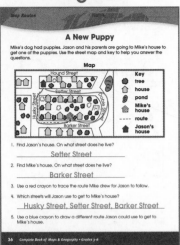

1. Find Jason's house. On what street does he live?
   Setter Street

2. Find Mike's house. On what street does he live?
   Barker Street

3. Use a red crayon to trace the route Mike drew for Jason to follow.

4. Which streets will Jason use to get to Mike's house?
   Husky Street, Setter Street, Barker Street

5. Use a blue crayon to draw a different route Jason could use to get to Mike's house.

Page 37

Places to Go

Mrs. Nelson needs to do many errands this afternoon. She only has a short time in which to do everything. Read Mrs. Nelson's list of things to do. Use the street map and key to help you answer the questions.

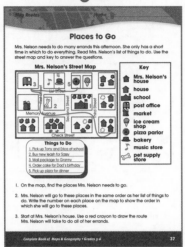

1. On the map, find the places Mrs. Nelson needs to go.

2. Mrs. Nelson will go to these places in the same order as her list of things to do. Write the number on each place on the map to show the order in which she will go to these places.

3. Start at Mrs. Nelson's house. Use a red crayon to draw the route Mrs. Nelson will take to do all of her errands.

Page 38

My Hometown

Complete the map by drawing the symbols from the key by each matching number on the map.

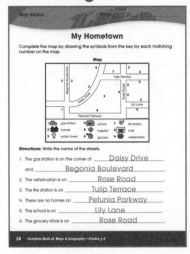

Directions: Write the name of the streets.

1. The gas station is on the corner of _____ **Daisy Drive**
   and _____ **Begonia Boulevard**
2. The veterinarian is on _____ **Rose Road**
3. The fire station is on _____ **Tulip Terrace**
4. There are no homes on _____ **Petunia Parkway**
5. The school is on _____ **Lily Lane**
6. The grocery store is on _____ **Rose Road**

Page 39

The Compass Rose

This is a compass rose. It tells the directions on a map. There are four arrows. Each arrow points in a different direction. These are called **cardinal** directions.

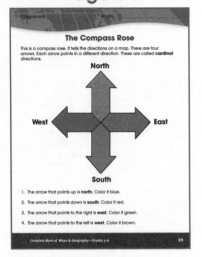

1. The arrow that points up is **north**. Color it blue.
2. The arrow that points down is **south**. Color it red.
3. The arrow that points to the right is **east**. Color it green.
4. The arrow that points to the left is **west**. Color it brown.

Page 40

Finding a Snack

The little bear cub is hungry for a snack. Read the clues. In each bear paw print, draw a picture of the snack he will find if he goes in that direction. Use the compass rose to help you.

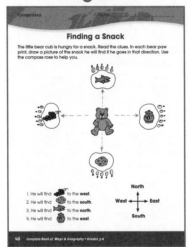

1. He will find _____ to the **west**.
2. He will find _____ to the **south**.
3. He will find _____ to the **north**.
4. He will find _____ to the **east**.

Page 41

Pirate's Booty

Sedgewick the Pirate must be able to find his buried treasure when he returns to the island. Read the sentences. Write the words **north**, **south**, **east**, and **west** in the blanks to help Sedgewick locate his treasure. Use the compass rose to help you.

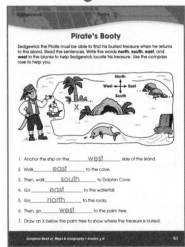

1. Anchor the ship on the _____ **west** _____ side of the island.
2. Walk _____ **east** _____ to the cave.
3. Then, walk _____ **south** _____ to Dolphin Cove.
4. Go _____ **east** _____ to the waterfall.
5. Go _____ **north** _____ to the rocks.
6. Then, go _____ **west** _____ to the palm tree.
7. Draw an X below the palm tree to show where the treasure is buried.

Page 42

Look to the Sky

Mr. McGill took his students on a field trip to the airport. A boy in his class drew this map of things they saw.

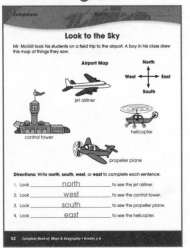

Directions: Write **north**, **south**, **west**, or **east** to complete each sentence.

1. Look _____ **north** _____ to see the jet airliner.
2. Look _____ **west** _____ to see the control tower.
3. Look _____ **south** _____ to see the propeller plane.
4. Look _____ **east** _____ to see the helicopter.

Page 43

Sign Search

Gina went for a hike. She found a piece of paper. There were strange directions written on it. Then, she looked around and saw pictures drawn on the rocks in the area. Aha! The paper she had found was a route to follow. Read the directions and draw the route on the map.

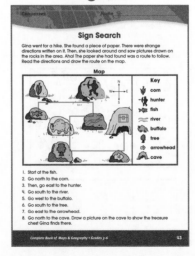

1. Start at the fish.
2. Go north to the corn.
3. Then, go east to the hunter.
4. Go south to the river.
5. Go west to the buffalo.
6. Go south to the tree.
7. Go east to the arrowhead.
8. Go north to the cave. Draw a picture on the cave to show the treasure chest Gina finds there.

Page 44

What Do Hikers See?

Follow the directions to complete this area map.

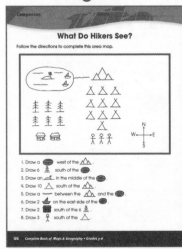

1. Draw a _____ west of the _____.
2. Draw 6 _____ south of the _____.
3. Draw an _____ in the middle of the _____.
4. Draw 10 _____ south of the _____.
5. Draw a _____ between the _____ and the _____.
6. Draw 2 _____ on the east side of the _____.
7. Draw 2 _____ south of the 6 _____.
8. Draw 3 _____ south of the _____.

Answer Key

Page 45

You're Invited

Liz sent out invitations to her birthday party. She drew a map to show how to go from school to her house.

Directions:
Write **north**, **south**, **east**, or **west** and the street name to complete the sentences.

1. Leave the school and go ___west___ on ___Oak Street___.
2. Turn ___south___ on ___Forest Road___.
3. Then, turn ___east___ on ___Petal Street___.

Page 46

Missing Diamonds

Mrs. Wently's diamonds are missing. Seth Sleuth has been hired to find them. He listens to Mrs. Wently's story. She had seen the robber run through the library and out onto the balcony. Then, he jumped to the ground and ran away. Seth Sleuth went to search the library. Perhaps the robber had hidden the diamonds in the library and planned to come back later to get them. This is a map of Mrs. Wently's library. Read more about the case on page 47.

Library Map

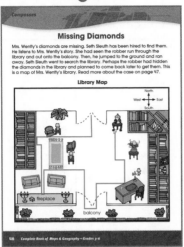

Page 48

Ice Cream!

Here comes the ice cream truck! On hot summer days, Stan drives his ice cream truck around the neighborhood. He takes the same route every day. This map shows the neighborhood where Stan drives. Follow the directions on page 49.

Ice Cream Truck Route Map

Page 50

Secret Mission

Sam Superspy is on a mission. He must get the secret papers and deliver them to his boss as soon as possible. This is a map of where the mission is to take place. Follow the directions on page 51 to help Sam.

Page 52

Connect the Dots

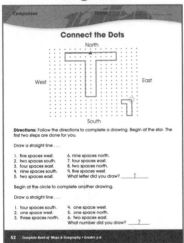

Directions: Follow the directions to complete a drawing. Begin at the star. The first two steps are done for you.

Draw a straight line . . .

1. five spaces west.
2. two spaces south.
3. four spaces east.
4. nine spaces south.
5. two spaces east.

6. nine spaces north.
7. four spaces east.
8. two spaces north.
9. five spaces west.
What letter did you draw? ___T___

Begin at the circle to complete another drawing.

Draw a straight line . . .

1. four spaces south.
2. one space west.
3. three spaces north.

4. one space west.
5. one space north.
6. two spaces east.
What number did you draw? ___7___

Page 53

Finding Your Way Around Town

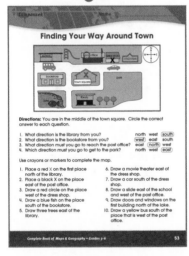

Directions: You are in the middle of the town square. Circle the correct answer to each question.

1. What direction is the library from you?   north   west   (south)
2. What direction is the bookstore from you?   (west) east   south
3. What direction must you go to reach the post office?   east (north) west
4. Which direction must you go to get to the park?   north   west   (east)

Use crayons or markers to complete the map.

1. Place a red X on the first place north of the library.
2. Place a black X on the place east of the post office.
3. Draw a red circle on the place west of the dress shop.
4. Draw a blue fish on the place south of the bookstore.
5. Draw three trees east of the library.

6. Draw a movie theater east of the dress shop.
7. Draw a car south of the dress shop.
8. Draw a slide east of the school and west of the post office.
9. Draw doors and windows on the first building north of the lake.
10. Draw a yellow bus south of the place that is west of the post office.

Page 54

A Great Camp!

Read the letter. Then, draw a map to show what the camp looks like. Make a key for the map.

June 20, 2016

Dear Elizabeth,
    This camp is great! I'll tell you what is here.
    There is a big wooden gate as you come into the campground at the north end. At the south end, there is a lake where we swim and ride in boats. We sleep in five tents on the west side. A big log cabin on the east side is where we eat. We make necklaces and other things under a big tree that is north of the tents. At night we sing songs and tell stories around a campfire south of the log cabin.
    Hope you are having fun at home. See you soon.
        Your friend,
        Sandy

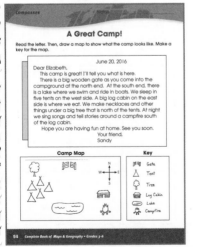

Page 55

Making a Compass

A compass is a magnet that can identify geographic direction. It is very easy and a lot of fun to make your own compass!

You will need:
magnet
steel sewing needle
piece of thin plastic foam (from fast-food packaging)
shallow glass or plastic bowl
masking tape
water

Directions:

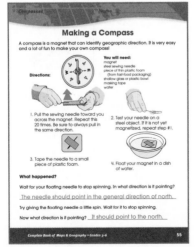

1. Pull the sewing needle toward you across the magnet. Repeat this 20 times. Be sure to always pull in the same direction.

2. Test your needle on a steel object. If it is not yet magnetized, repeat step #1.

3. Tape the needle to a small piece of plastic foam.

4. Float your magnet in a dish of water.

What happened?

Wait for your floating needle to stop spinning. In what direction is it pointing?

___The needle should point in the general direction of north.___

Try giving the floating needle a little spin. Wait for it to stop spinning.

Now what direction is it pointing? ___It should point to the north.___

Page 56

Drawing a Compass Rose

The maps of the early explorers were beautiful pieces of art. Their maps would often have pictures of fire-breathing dragons and sea monsters to warn of the dangers at where they were traveling.

In a corner of an explorer's map would be a beautiful compass rose. The compass rose indicated the four cardinal directions—north, south, east, and west. The compass rose also indicated four intermediate directions, which are halfway between the four cardinal directions. They are northwest (NW), northeast (NE), southwest (SW), and southeast (SE).

Follow the steps to draw a **compass rose** in the upper right-hand corner of the map. Add the cardinal **directions** to your rose compass. Then, draw a map of your own make-believe land.

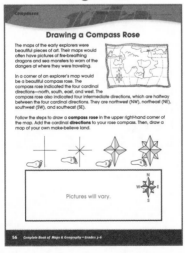

Pictures will vary.

Page 57

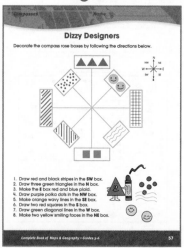

Dizzy Designers

Decorate the compass rose boxes by following the directions below.

1. Draw red and black stripes in the **SW** box.
2. Draw three green triangles in the **N** box.
3. Make the **E** box red and blue plaid.
4. Draw purple polka dots in the **NW** box.
5. Make orange wavy lines in the **SE** box.
6. Draw two red squares in the **S** box.
7. Draw green diagonal lines in the **W** box.
8. Make two yellow smiling faces in the **NE** box.

Page 58

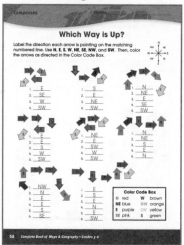

Which Way is Up?

Label the direction each arrow is pointing on the matching numbered line. Use **N, E, S, W, NE, SE, NW,** and **SW**. Then, color the arrows as directed in the Color Code Box.

Color Code Box			
N red		W	brown
NE blue		NW	orange
E purple		SW	yellow
SE pink		S	green

Page 59

Spaceship Search

Gus Galactic needs help to identify these alien spaceships. Write a ship's letter in each blank to solve these riddles.

1. I am **N** of Ship H. ___
2. I am **E** of Ship Z. ___
3. I am **SE** of Ship Z. ___
4. I am **S** of Ship O. ___
5. I am **NW** of Ship Z. ___
6. I am **SW** of Ship B. ___
7. I am **NE** of Ship Z. ___
8. I am **NE** of Ship L. ___
9. I am **SE** of Ship U. ___
10. I am **NW** of Ship X. ___

Cosmic Challenge
Start at Ship H. Travel in the orbit given. Which ship will you dock with?

1. Go **NW** to Ship ___
2. Go **NE** to Ship ___
3. Go **NE** to Ship ___
4. Go **S** to Ship ___
5. Go **SE** to Ship ___
6. Go **NE** to Ship ___
7. Go **NW** to Ship ___
This is your docking station. Congratulations.

Page 60

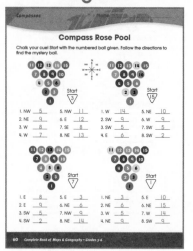

Compass Rose Pool

Chalk your cue! Start with the numbered ball given. Follow the directions to find the mystery ball.

1. NW _5_   5. NW _11_
2. NE _9_   6. E _9_
3. W _7_   7. SE _8_
4. W _7_   8. NE _13_

1. W _14_   5. NE _10_
2. SW _9_   6. W _9_
3. SE _8_   7. S _9_
4. E _9_   8. SW _2_

1. E _9_   5. E _10_
2. E _9_   6. NE _6_
3. NW _9_   7. W _14_
4. SW _2_   8. NE _14_

1. NE _9_   5. E _10_
2. NE _6_   6. NE _15_
3. NE _9_   7. W _9_
4. NE _9_   8. SW _14_

Page 61

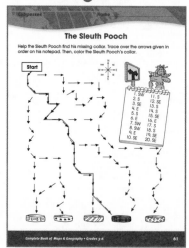

The Sleuth Pooch

Help the Sleuth Pooch find his missing collar. Trace over the arrows given in order on his notepad. Then, color the Sleuth Pooch's collar.

1. SW   11. S
2. S   12. SE
3. SE   13. S
4. E   14. S
5. S   15. SE
6. E   16. E
7. SW   17. S
8. SW   18. S
9. E   19. SE
10. SE   20. S

Page 62

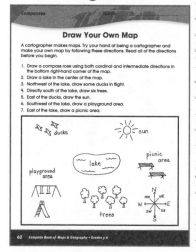

Draw Your Own Map

A cartographer makes maps. Try your hand at being a cartographer and make your own map by following these directions. Read all of the directions before you begin.

1. Draw a compass rose using both cardinal and intermediate directions in the bottom right-hand corner of the map.
2. Draw a lake in the center of the map.
3. Northwest of the lake, draw some ducks in flight.
4. Directly south of the lake, draw six trees.
5. East of the ducks, draw the sun.
6. Southwest of the lake, draw a playground area.
7. East of the lake, draw a picnic area.

Page 63

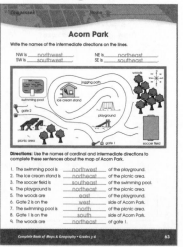

Acorn Park

Write the names of the intermediate directions on the lines.

NW is _northwest_   NE is _northeast_
SW is _southwest_   SE is _southeast_

Directions: Use the names of cardinal and intermediate directions to complete these sentences about the map of Acorn Park.

1. The swimming pool is _northwest_ of the playground.
2. The ice cream stand is _northeast_ of the picnic area.
3. The soccer field is _southeast_ of the swimming pool.
4. The playground is _northeast_ of the picnic area.
5. The woods are _east_ side of Acorn Park.
6. Gate 2 is on the _west_ side of Acorn Park.
7. The swimming pool is _north_ of the picnic area.
8. Gate 1 is on the _south_ side of Acorn Park.
9. The woods are _northeast_ of gate 1.

Page 64

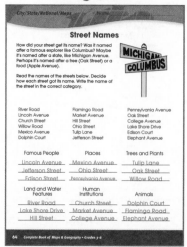

Street Names

How did your street get its name? Was it named after a famous explorer like Columbus? Maybe it's named after a state, like Michigan Avenue. Perhaps it's named after a tree (Oak Street) or a food (Apple Avenue).

Read the names of the streets below. Decide how each street got its name. Write the name of the street in the correct category.

River Road
Lincoln Avenue
Church Street
Willow Road
Mexico Avenue
Dolphin Court

Flamingo Road
Market Avenue
Hill Street
Ohio Street
Tulip Lane
Jefferson Street

Pennsylvania Avenue
Oak Street
College Avenue
Lake Shore Drive
Edison Court
Elephant Avenue

Famous People
Lincoln Avenue
Jefferson Street
Edison Street

Places
Mexico Avenue
Ohio Street
Pennsylvania Avenue

Trees and Plants
Tulip Lane
Oak Street
Willow Road

Land and Water Features
River Road
Lake Shore Drive
Hill Street

Human Institutions
Church Street
Market Avenue
College Avenue

Animals
Dolphin Court
Flamingo Road
Elephant Avenue

Page 65

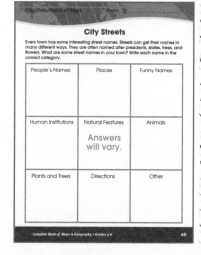

City Streets

Every town has some interesting street names. Streets can get their names in many different ways. They are often named after presidents, states, trees, and flowers. What are some street names in your town? Write each name in the correct category.

People's Names	Places	Funny Names
Human Institutions	Natural Features	Animals
	Answers will vary.	
Plants and Trees	Directions	Other

Page 66

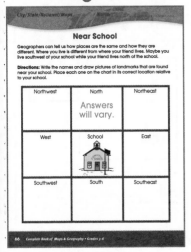

Near School

Geographers can tell us how places are the same and how they are different. Where you live is different from where your friend lives. Maybe you live southwest of your school while your friend lives north of the school.

Directions: Write the names and draw pictures of landmarks that are found near your school. Place each one on the chart in its correct location relative to your school.

Northwest	North	Northeast
	Answers will vary.	
West	School	East
Southwest	South	Southeast

Page 67

A Walk Around Town

Take a walk around the town of Forest Grove. Use a marker or crayon to trace your route.

Directions:

1. Begin your walking tour at Forest Grove Inn.
2. Walk two blocks east to Elm Street.
3. Turn north on Elm Street. Walk to the Museum.
4. Go one-half block north to the corner of Elm and Lincoln.
5. Turn east on Lincoln. Walk until you come to the City Library.
6. Go south on Oak Street until you reach Washington Street.
7. Turn west on Washington and walk two and one-half blocks to the Burger Barn.
8. Lunch is over. Take the shortest way back to Forest Grove Inn.

Page 68

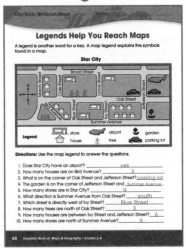

Legends Help You Reach Maps

A legend is another word for a key. A map legend explains the symbols found in a map.

Directions: Use the map legend to answer the questions.

1. Does Star City have an airport? _____ yes
2. How many houses are on Bird Avenue? _____ 3
3. What is on the corner of Oak Street and Jefferson Street? parking lot
4. The garden is on the corner of Jefferson Street and _____ Summer Avenue
5. How many stores are in Star City? _____ 4
6. What direction is Summer Avenue from Oak Street? _____ south
7. Which street is directly west of Ivy Street? _____ Blue Street
8. How many trees are north of Oak Street? _____
9. How many houses are between Ivy Street and Jefferson Street? _____ 6
10. How many stores are north of Summer Avenue? _____ 4

Page 71

Welcome to Crystal River

Use the directions on page 70 to complete the map of Crystal River.

Page 72

Near My Community

Use a state map to locate your community. Then, write the names of other communities, cities, towns, lakes, places to visit, and well-known landmarks on the chart below. Write each one in its correct location relative to your community.

Northwest	North	Northeast
West	My Community	East
	Answers will vary.	
Southwest	South	Southeast

Page 73

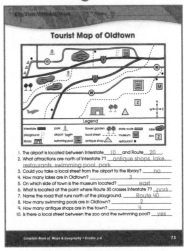

Tourist Map of Oldtown

1. The airport is located between Interstate _____ 10 and Route _____ 20.
2. What attractions are north of Interstate 7? _____ antique shops, lake, restaurants, swimming pool, park
3. Could you take a local street from the airport to the library? _____ no
4. How many lakes are in Oldtown? _____ 3
5. On which side of town is the museum located? _____ east
6. What is located at the point where Route 30 crosses Interstate 7? _____ park
7. Name the road that runs north of the playground. _____ Route 40
8. How many swimming pools are in Oldtown? _____ 2
9. How many antique shops are in the town? _____ 4
10. Is there a local street between the zoo and the swimming pool? _____ yes

Page 74

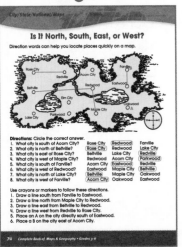

Is It North, South, East, or West?

Direction words can help you locate places quickly on a map.

Directions: Circle the correct answer.

1. What city is south of Acom City? Rose City **Redwood** Farville
2. What city is north of Bellville? **Rose City** Redwood Lake City
3. What city is east of Rose City? Bellville Lake City **Redville**
4. What city is west of Maple City? Redwood Acom City **Parkwood**
5. What city is south of Farville? Acom City **Eastwood** Redville
6. What city is west of Redwood? Eastwood Maple City **Bellville**
7. What city is north of Lake City? **Bellville** Maple City Oakwood
8. What city is west of Farville? **Acom City** Oakwood Eastwood

Use crayons or markers to follow these directions.

1. Draw a line south from Farville to Eastwood.
2. Draw a line north from Maple City to Redwood.
3. Draw a line east from Bellville to Redwood.
4. Draw a line west from Redville to Rose City.
5. Place an A on the city directly south of Eastwood.
6. Place a B on the city east of Acom City.

Page 75

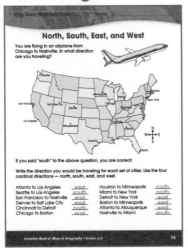

North, South, East, and West

You are flying in an airplane from Chicago to Nashville. In what direction are you traveling?

If you said "south" to the above question, you are correct!

Write the direction you would be traveling for each set of cities. Use the four cardinal directions — north, south, east, and west.

Atlanta to Los Angeles	west	Houston to Minneapolis	north
Seattle to Los Angeles	south	Miami to New York	north
San Francisco to Nashville	east	Detroit to New York	east
Denver to Salt Lake City	west	Boston to Minneapolis	west
Cincinnati to Detroit	north	Atlanta to Albuquerque	west
Chicago to Boston	east	Nashville to Miami	south

Page 76

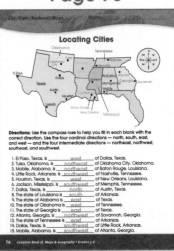

Locating Cities

Directions: Use the compass rose to help you fill in each blank with the correct direction. Use the four cardinal directions — north, south, east, and west — and the four intermediate directions — northeast, northwest, southeast, and southwest.

1. El Paso, Texas, is _____ west _____ of Dallas, Texas.
2. Tulsa, Oklahoma, is _____ northeast _____ of Oklahoma City, Oklahoma.
3. Mobile, Alabama, is _____ northeast _____ of Baton Rouge, Louisiana.
4. Little Rock, Arkansas, is _____ southwest _____ of Nashville, Tennessee.
5. Houston, Texas, is _____ west _____ of New Orleans, Louisiana.
6. Jackson, Mississippi, is _____ southwest _____ of Memphis, Tennessee.
7. Dallas, Texas, is _____ north _____ of Austin, Texas.
8. The state of Louisiana is _____ south _____ of Arkansas.
9. The state of Alabama is _____ east _____ of Texas.
10. The state of Oklahoma is _____ north _____ of Tennessee.
11. The state of Georgia is _____ east _____ of Texas.
12. Atlanta, Georgia, is _____ northwest _____ of Savannah, Georgia.
13. The state of Tennessee is _____ northwest _____ of Arkansas.
14. Dallas, Texas, is _____ southwest _____ of Little Rock, Arkansas.
15. Mobile, Alabama, is _____ southwest _____ of Atlanta, Georgia.

Page 77

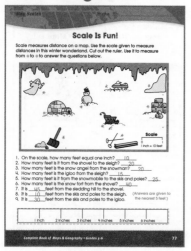

Scale Is Fun!

Scale measures distance on a map. Use the scale given to measure distances in this winter wonderland. Cut out the ruler. Use it to measure from ● to ● to answer the questions below.

Scale
1 inch = 10 feet

1. On the scale, how many feet equal one inch? __10__
2. How many feet is it from the shovel to the sleigh? __20__
3. How many feet is the snow angel from the snowman? __20__
4. How many feet is the igloo from the sleigh? __15__
5. How many feet is it from the snowmobile to the skis and poles? __25__
6. How many feet is the snow fort from the shovel? __40__
7. It is __45__ feet from the sledding hill to the shovel.
8. It is __10__ feet from the skis and poles to the sleigh. (Answers are given to the nearest 5 feet.)
9. It is __30__ feet from the skis and poles to the igloo.

| 1 inch | 2 inches | 3 inches | 4 inches | 5 inches | 6 inches |

Page 79

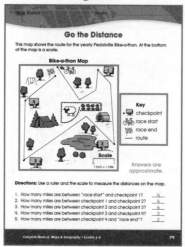

Go the Distance

This map shows the route for the yearly Pedalville Bike-a-thon. At the bottom of the map is a scale.

Bike-a-thon Map

Key
🏁 checkpoint
🚲 race start
🏁 race end
— route

Scale
1 inch = 1 mile

Answers are approximate.

Directions: Use a ruler and the scale to measure the distances on the map.

1. How many miles are between "race start" and checkpoint 1? __4__
2. How many miles are between checkpoint 1 and checkpoint 2? __4__
3. How many miles are between checkpoint 2 and checkpoint 3? __6__
4. How many miles are between checkpoint 3 and checkpoint 4? __3__
5. How many miles are between checkpoint 4 and "race end"? __2__

Page 80

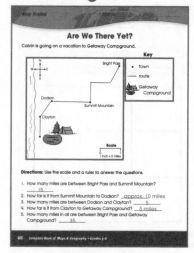

Are We There Yet?

Calvin is going on a vacation to Getaway Campground.

Key
● town
— route
🏕 Getaway Campground

Scale
1 inch = 5 miles

Directions: Use the scale and a ruler to answer the questions.

1. How many miles are between Bright Pass and Summit Mountain? __15__
2. How far is it from Summit Mountain to Dodson? __approx. 10 miles__
3. How many miles are between Dodson and Clayton? __5__
4. How far is it from Clayton to Getaway Campground? __5 miles__
5. How many miles in all are between Bright Pass and Getaway Campground? __35__

Page 81

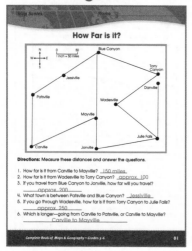

How Far is it?

Scale: 1 inch = 50 miles

Directions: Measure these distances and answer the questions.

1. How far is it from Carville to Mayville? __150 miles__
2. How far is it from Wadesville to Torry Canyon? __approx. 100__
3. If you travel from Blue Canyon to Jonville, how far will you travel? __approx. 200__
4. What town is between Patsville and Blue Canyon? __Jessiville__
5. If you go through Wadesville, how far is it from Torry Canyon to Julie Falls? __approx. 250__
6. Which is longer—going from Carville to Patsville, or Carville to Mayville? __Carville to Mayville__

Page 82

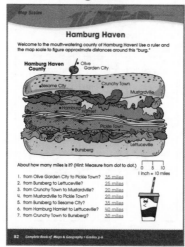

Hamburg Haven

Welcome to the mouth-watering county of Hamburg Haven! Use a ruler and the map scale to figure approximate distances around this "burg."

Hamburg Haven County

Scale: 1 inch = 10 miles

About how many miles is it? (Hint: Measure from dot to dot.)

1. from Olive Garden City to Pickle Town? __35 miles__
2. from Bunsberg to Lettuceville? __25 miles__
3. from Crunchy Town to Mustardville? __20 miles__
4. from Mustardville to Pickle Town? __20 miles__
5. from Bunsberg to Sesame City? __35 miles__
6. from Hamburg Hamlet to Lettuceville? __40 miles__
7. from Crunchy Town to Bunsberg? __20 miles__

Page 83

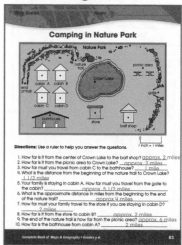

Camping in Nature Park

Nature Park

Scale: 1 inch = 1 mile

Directions: Use a ruler to help you answer the questions.

1. How far is it from the center of Crown Lake to the bait shop? __approx. 2 miles__
2. How far is it from the picnic area to Crown Lake? __approx. 2 miles__
3. How far must you travel from cabin C to the bathhouse? __1 mile__
4. What are the distance from the beginning of the nature trail to Crown Lake? __1 1/2 miles__
5. Your family is staying in cabin A. How far must you travel from the gate to the cabin? __approx. 5 1/2 miles__
6. What is the approximate distance in miles from the beginning to the end of the nature trail? __approx 4 miles__
7. How far must your family travel to the store if you are staying in cabin D? __2 miles__
8. How far is it from the store to cabin B? __approx. 2 miles__
9. The end of the nature trail is how far from the picnic area? __approx. 6 miles__
10. How far is the bathhouse from cabin A? __2 miles__

Page 84

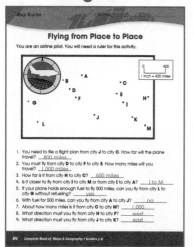

Flying from Place to Place

You are an airline pilot. You will need a ruler for this activity.

Scale: 1 inch = 400 miles

1. You need to file a flight plan from city J to city C. How far will the plane travel? __800 miles__
2. You must fly from city D to city F to city E. How many miles will you travel? __1,000 miles__
3. How far is it from city H to city C? __600 miles__
4. Is it closer to fly from city I to city M or from city I to city A? __I to M__
5. If your plane holds enough fuel to fly 500 miles, can you fly from city L to city G without refueling? __yes__
6. With fuel for 500 miles, can you fly from city A to city J? __no__
7. About how many miles is it from city C to city M? __1,000__
8. What direction must you fly from city H to city F? __west__
9. What direction must you fly from city J to city K? __east__

Page 85

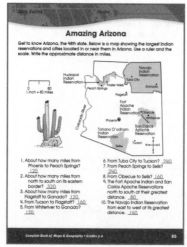

Amazing Arizona

Get to know Arizona, the 48th state. Below is a map showing the largest Indian reservations and cities located in or near them in Arizona. Use a ruler and the scale. Write the approximate distance in miles.

Scale: 1 inch = 80 miles

1. About how many miles from Phoenix to Peach Springs? __120__
2. About how many miles from north to south on its eastern border? __320__
3. About how many miles from Flagstaff to Ganado? __120__
4. From Tucson to Flagstaff? __160__
5. From Whiteriver to Ganado? __120__
6. From Tuba City to Tucson? __240__
7. From Peach Springs to Sells? __240__
8. From Cibecue to Sells? __160__
9. The Fort Apache Indian and San Carlos Apache Reservations north to south at their greatest distance. __80__
10. The Navajo Indian Reservation from east to west at its greatest distance. __140__

Page 86

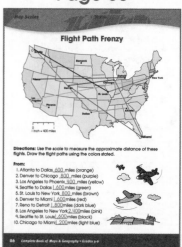

Flight Path Frenzy

Scale: 1 inch = 400 miles

Directions: Use the scale to measure the approximate distance of these flights. Draw the flight paths using the colors stated.

From:
1. Atlanta to Dallas __600__ miles (orange)
2. Denver to Chicago __800__ miles (purple)
3. Los Angeles to Phoenix __400__ miles (yellow)
4. Seattle to Dallas __1,600__ miles (green)
5. St. Louis to New York __800__ miles (brown)
6. Denver to Miami __1,800__ miles (red)
7. Reno to Detroit __1,800__ miles (dark blue)
8. Los Angeles to New York __2,400__ miles (pink)
9. Seattle to St. Louis __1,600__ miles (black)
10. Chicago to Miami __1,200__ miles (light blue)

Page 87

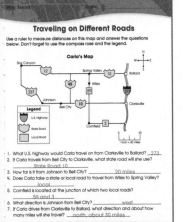

Traveling on Different Roads

Use a ruler to measure distances on this map and answer the questions below. Don't forget to use the compass rose and the legend.

Carla's Map

1. What U.S. highway would Carla travel on from Clarksville to Ballard? _273_
2. If Carla travels from Bell City to Clarksville, what state road will she use? State Road 10
3. How far is it from Johnson to Bell City? _20 miles_
4. Does Carla take a state or local road to travel from Wiles to Spring Valley? _local_
5. Comfeld is located at the junction of which two local roads? _59 and 3_
6. What direction is Johnson from Bell City? _west_
7. If Carla drives from Clarksville to Ballard, what direction and about how many miles will she travel? _north, about 30 miles_

Page 88

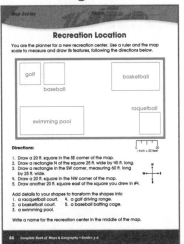

Recreation Location

You are the planner for a new recreation center. Use a ruler and the map scale to measure and draw its features, following the directions below.

golf   baseball   basketball   raquetball   swimming pool

Directions:
1. Draw a 20 ft. square in the SE corner of the map.
2. Draw a rectangle N of the square 25 ft. wide by 45 ft. long.
3. Draw a rectangle in the SW corner, measuring 60 ft. long by 25 ft. wide.
4. Draw a 20 ft. square in the NW corner of the map.
5. Draw another 20 ft. square east of the square you drew in #4.

Add details to your shapes to transform the shapes into
1. a racquetball court.   4. a golf driving range.
2. a basketball court.   5. a baseball batting cage.
3. a swimming pool.

Write a name for the recreation center in the middle of the map.

Page 89

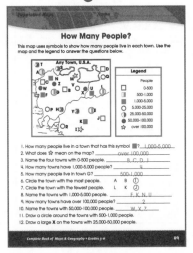

How Many People?

This map uses symbols to show how many people live in each town. Use the map and the legend to answer the questions below.

Any Town, U.S.A.

Legend — People: 0-500, 500-1,000, 1,000-5,000, 5,000-25,000, 25,000-50,000, 50,000-100,000, over 100,000

1. How many people live in a town that has this symbol? _1,000-5,000_
2. What does ☆ mean on the map? _over 100,000_
3. Name the four towns with 0-500 people. _B, C, D, J_
4. How many towns have 1,000-5,000 people? _4_
5. How many people live in town G? _500-1,000_
6. Circle the town with the most people. _A B ①_
7. Circle the town with the fewest people. _L K ⑦_
8. Name the towns with 1,000-5,000 people. _F, K, N, U_
9. How many towns have over 100,000 people? _2_
10. Name the towns with 50,000-100,000 people. _W, X, Z_
11. Draw a circle around the towns with 500-1,000 people.
12. Draw a large **X** on the towns with 25,000-50,000 people.

Page 90

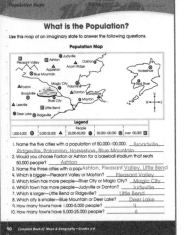

What is the Population?

Use this map of an imaginary state to answer the following questions.

Population Map

Legend — People: 1,000-5,000, 5,000-25,000, 25,000-50,000, 50,000-100,000, over 100,000

1. Name the five cities with a population of 50,000-100,000. _Broadville, Ridgeville, Palomino, Horseshoe, Blue Mountain_
2. Would you choose Foxton or Ashton for a baseball stadium that seats 50,000 people? _Ashton_
3. Name the three cities with a pop. _Ashton, Pleasant Valley, Little Bend_
4. Which is bigger—Pleasant Valley or Mayton? _Pleasant Valley_
5. Which town has more people—River City or Magic City? _Magic City_
6. Which town has more people—Judyville or Danton? _Judyville_
7. Which is larger—Little Bend or Ridgeville? _Little Bend_
8. Which city is smaller—Blue Mountain or Deer Lake? _Deer Lake_
9. How many towns have 1,000-5,000 people? _4_
10. How many towns have 5,000-25,000 people? _6_

Page 97

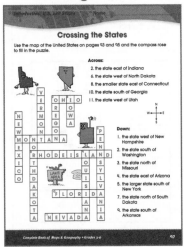

Crossing the States

Use the map of the United States on pages 93 and 95 and the compass rose to fill in the puzzle.

Across:
2. the state east of Indiana
6. the state west of North Dakota
8. the smaller state east of Connecticut
10. the state south of Georgia
11. the state west of Utah

Down:
1. the state west of New Hampshire
2. the state south of Washington
3. the state north of Missouri
4. the state east of Arizona
5. the larger state south of New York
7. the state north of South Dakota
9. the state south of Arkansas

Page 98

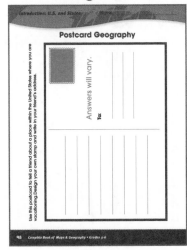

Postcard Geography

Answers will vary.

Use this postcard to tell a friend about a place within the United States where you are vacationing. Design your own stamp and write your friend's address.

Page 99

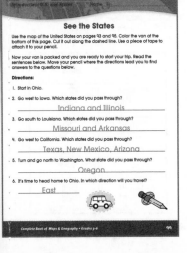

See the States

Use the map of the United States on pages 93 and 95. Color the van at the bottom of this page. Cut it out along the dashed line. Use a piece of tape to attach it to your pencil.

Now your van is packed and you are ready to start your trip. Read the sentences below. Move your pencil where the directions lead you to find answers to the questions below.

Directions:
1. Start in Ohio.
2. Go west to Iowa. Which states did you pass through? _Indiana and Illinois_
3. Go south to Louisiana. Which states did you pass through? _Missouri and Arkansas_
4. Go west to California. Which states did you pass through? _Texas, New Mexico, Arizona_
5. Turn and go north to Washington. What state did you pass through? _Oregon_
6. It's time to head home to Ohio. In which direction will you travel? _East_

Page 101

What a Vacation!

Key:
David's trip, Becky's trip, Adam's trip, Sheila's trip, home, National Baseball Hall of Fame and Museum, Fossil Butte National Monument, Dahlonega Gold Museum, Sea World, Grand Canyon, U.S. Space and Rocket Center, Grasshopper Glacier, Naismith Memorial Basketball Hall of Fame, Virginia City (old mining town)

1. Use a yellow crayon to trace David's route.
2. Use a blue crayon to trace Becky's route.
3. Use a red crayon to trace Adam's route.
4. Use a green crayon to trace Sheila's route.
5. Which person traveled the farthest west? _David_
6. Which person probably likes sports? _Adam_
7. Which person traveled the farthest south? _Becky_
8. Write the names of the places Sheila saw on her vacation. _Grass Hopper Glacier, Fossil Butte National Monument_
9. Where did Becky go in Florida? _Sea World_

Page 102

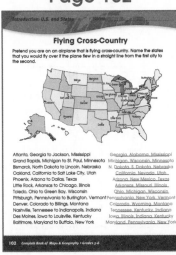

Flying Cross-Country

Pretend you are on an airplane that is flying cross-country. Name the states that you would fly over if the plane flew in a straight line from the first city to the second.

Atlanta, Georgia to Jackson, Mississippi — Georgia, Alabama, Mississippi
Grand Rapids, Michigan to St. Paul, Minnesota — Michigan, Wisconsin, Minnesota
Bismarck, North Dakota to Lincoln, Nebraska — N. Dakota, S. Dakota, Nebraska
Oakland, California to Salt Lake City, Utah — California, Nevada, Utah
Phoenix, Arizona to Dallas, Texas — Arizona, New Mexico, Texas
Little Rock, Arkansas to Chicago, Illinois — Arkansas, Missouri, Illinois
Toledo, Ohio to Green Bay, Wisconsin — Ohio, Michigan, Wisconsin
Pittsburgh, Pennsylvania to Burlington, Vermont — Pennsylvania, New York, Vermont
Denver, Colorado to Billings, Montana — Colorado, Wyoming, Montana
Nashville, Tennessee to Indianapolis, Indiana — Tennessee, Kentucky, Indiana
Des Moines, Iowa to Louisville, Kentucky — Iowa, Illinois, Indiana, Kentucky
Baltimore, Maryland to Buffalo, New York — Maryland, Pennsylvania, New York

Page 103

State Snatcher

The State Snatcher has stolen the abbreviations of some of the states. Write the missing abbreviations on the map. Use another U.S. map to help you.

Postal Abbreviations Chart

Alabama	AL	Indiana	IN	Nebraska	NE	South Carolina	SC
Alaska	AK	Iowa	IA	Nevada	NV	South Dakota	SD
Arizona	AZ	Kansas	KS	New Hampshire	NH	Tennessee	TN
Arkansas	AR	Kentucky	KY	New Jersey	NJ	Texas	TX
California	CA	Louisiana	LA	New Mexico	NM	Utah	UT
Colorado	CO	Maine	ME	New York	NY	Vermont	VT
Connecticut	CT	Maryland	MD	North Carolina	NC	Virginia	VA
Delaware	DE	Massachusetts	MA	North Dakota	ND	Washington	WA
Florida	FL	Michigan	MI	Ohio	OH	West Virginia	WV
Georgia	GA	Minnesota	MN	Oklahoma	OK	Wisconsin	WI
Hawaii	HI	Mississippi	MS	Oregon	OR	Wyoming	WY
Idaho	ID	Missouri	MO	Pennsylvania	PA		
Illinois	IL	Montana	MT	Rhode Island	RI		

Page 104

Super Cities

Write the name of each city in the blank by its number. Then, write each state's two-letter state abbreviation. Use another U.S. map to help you.

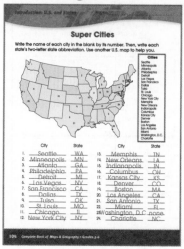

	City	State			City	State
1.	Seattle	WA	13.	Memphis	TN
2.	Minneapolis	MN	14.	New Orleans	LA
3.	Atlanta	GA	15.	Indianapolis	IN
4.	Philadelphia	PA	16.	Columbus	OH
5.	Detroit	MI	17.	Kansas City	KS
6.	Las Vegas	NV	18.	Denver	CO
7.	San Francisco	CA	19.	Boston	MA
8.	Dallas	TX	20.	Los Angeles	CA
9.	Tulsa	OK	21.	San Antonio	TX
10.	St. Louis	MO	22.	Miami	FL
11.	Chicago	IL	23.	Washington, D.C.	none
12.	New York City	NY	24.	Charlotte	NC

Page 105

Play Ball!

Page 106

Play Ball!

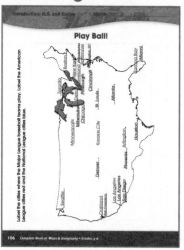

Page 107

Mystery States I

Can you identify these state shapes? Use a U.S. map to help you. Write the name of each state and its capital city ☆.

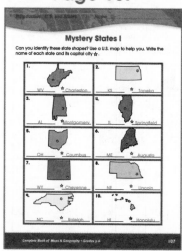

1. WV ☆ Charleston
2. KS ☆ Topeka
3. AL ☆ Montgomery
4. IL ☆ Springfield
5. OH ☆ Columbus
6. ME ☆ Augusta
7. WY ☆ Cheyenne
8. NE ☆ Lincoln
9. NC ☆ Raleigh
10. HI ☆ Honolulu

Page 108

Mystery States II

Can you identify these state shapes? Use a U.S. map to help you. Write the name of each state and its capital city ☆.

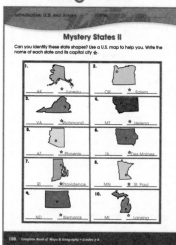

1. AK ☆ Juneau
2. OR ☆ Salem
3. VA ☆ Richmond
4. MT ☆ Helena
5. AZ ☆ Phoenix
6. IA ☆ Des Moines
7. RI ☆ Providence
8. MN ☆ St. Paul
9. ND ☆ Bismarck
10. MI ☆ Lansing

Page 109

Mystery States III

Can you identify these state shapes? Use a U.S. map to help you. Write the name of each state and its capital city ☆.

1. MA ☆ Boston
2. NV ☆ Carson City
3. SC ☆ Columbia
4. CT ☆ Hartford
5. AR ☆ Little Rock
6. GA ☆ Atlanta
7. PA ☆ Harrisburg
8. NY ☆ Albany
9. VT ☆ Montpelier
10. UT ☆ Salt Lake City

Page 110

Mystery States IV

Can you identify these state shapes? Use a U.S. map to help you. Write the name of each state and its capital city ☆.

1. TN ☆ Nashville
2. TX ☆ Austin
3. NH ☆ Concord
4. MO ☆ Jefferson City
5. NM ☆ Santa Fe
6. NJ ☆ Trenton
7. DE ☆ Dover
8. CO ☆ Denver
9. ID ☆ Boise
10. IN ☆ Indianapolis

Page 111

Mystery States V

Can you identify these state shapes? Use a U.S. map to help you. Write the name of each state and its capital city ☆.

1. CA ☆ Sacramento
2. KY ☆ Frankfort
3. MD ☆ Annapolis
4. LA ☆ Baton Rouge
5. OK ☆ Oklahoma City
6. FL ☆ Tallahassee
7. MS ☆ Jackson
8. WA ☆ Olympia
9. SD ☆ Pierre
10. WI ☆ Madison

Page 112

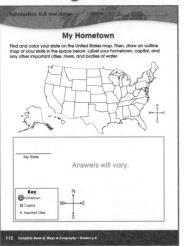

My Hometown

Find and color your state on the United States map. Then, draw an outline map of your state in the space below. Label your hometown, capital, and any other important cities, rivers, and bodies of water.

My State

Answers will vary.

Key
- Hometown
- ☆ Capital
- • Important Cities

Page 113

Near My State

Use a map of the United States to locate your state. Write the names of any bordering states, countries, or bodies of water on the chart below. Write each one in its correct location relative to your state.

Northwest	North	Northeast
West	**My State**	**East**
	Answers will vary.	
	Draw an outline of your state.	
Southwest	**South**	**Southeast**

Page 114

"We're Going Places" Mileage Chart

Let's take a trip around your state. On the left side of the chart, fill in the names of five cities in your state. The first one should be your hometown. Then, write the names of five additional cities or places to visit in your state across the top. Use a state highway map or other source to find the number of miles between each place. Complete the chart.

Places to Visit in My State

Cities in My State

My Hometown

Answers will vary.

Page 115

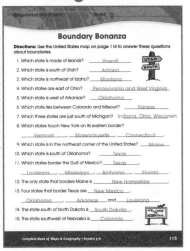

Boundary Bonanza

Directions: Use the United States map on page 116 to answer these questions about boundaries.

1. Which state is made of islands? **Hawaii**
2. Which state is south of Utah? **Arizona**
3. Which state is northeast of Idaho? **Montana**
4. Which states are east of Ohio? **Pennsylvania and West Virginia**
5. Which state is west of Arkansas? **Oklahoma**
6. Which state lies between Colorado and Missouri? **Kansas**
7. Which three states are just south of Michigan? **Indiana, Ohio, Wisconsin**
8. Which states touch New York on its eastern border?
   Vermont, **Massachusetts**, **Connecticut**
9. Which state is in the northeast corner of the United States? **Maine**
10. Which state is south of Oklahoma? **Texas**
11. Which states border the Gulf of Mexico? **Texas**, **Louisiana**, **Mississippi**, **Alabama**, **Florida**
12. The only state that borders Maine is **New Hampshire**
13. Four states that border Texas are **New Mexico**, **Oklahoma**, **Arkansas** and **Louisiana**
14. The state south of North Dakota is **South Dakota**
15. The state southwest of Nebraska is **Colorado**

Page 116

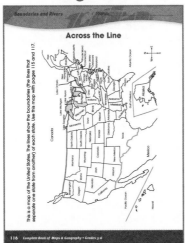

Across the Line

This is a map of the United States. The lines show the boundaries (the lines that separate one state from another) of each state. Use this map with pages 115 and 117.

Page 117

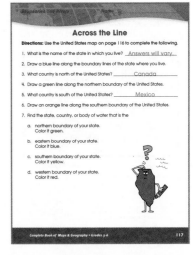

Across the Line

Directions: Use the United States map on page 116 to complete the following.

1. What is the name of the state in which you live? **Answers will vary.**
2. Draw a blue line along the boundary lines of the state where you live.
3. What country is north of the United States? **Canada**
4. Draw a green line along the northern boundary of the United States.
5. What country is south of the United States? **Mexico**
6. Draw an orange line along the southern boundary of the United States.
7. Find the state, country, or body of water that is the
   a. northern boundary of your state. Color it green.
   b. eastern boundary of your state. Color it blue.
   c. southern boundary of your state. Color it yellow.
   d. western boundary of your state. Color it red.

Page 118

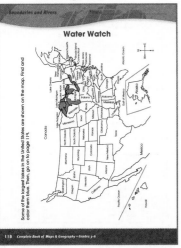

Water Watch

Some of the largest lakes in the United States are shown on the map. Find and color them blue. Then, go on to page 119.

Page 119

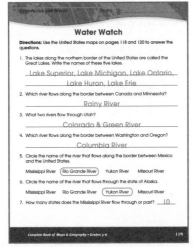

Water Watch

Directions: Use the United States maps on pages 118 and 120 to answer the questions.

1. The lakes along the northern border of the United States are called the Great Lakes. Write the names of these five lakes.
   Lake Superior, Lake Michigan, Lake Ontario, Lake Huron, Lake Erie
2. Which river flows along the border between Canada and Minnesota?
   Rainy River
3. What two rivers flow through Utah?
   Colorado and Green River
4. Which river flows along the border between Washington and Oregon?
   Columbia River
5. Circle the name of the river that flows along the border between Mexico and the United States.
   Mississippi River | (Rio Grande River) | Yukon River | Missouri River
6. Circle the name of the river that flows through the state of Alaska.
   Mississippi River | Rio Grande River | (Yukon River) | Missouri River
7. How many states does the Mississippi River flow through or past? **10**

Page 120

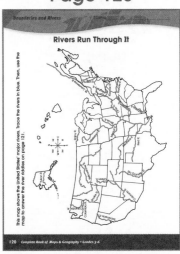

Rivers Run Through It

This map shows the United States' major rivers. Trace the rivers in blue. Then, use the map to answer the river riddles on page 121.

Page 121

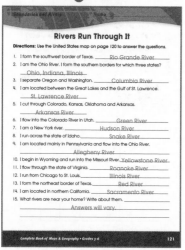

Rivers Run Through It

Directions: Use the United States map on page 120 to answer the questions.

1. I form the southwest border of Texas. _Rio Grande River_
2. I am the Ohio River. I form the southern borders for which three states? _Ohio, Indiana, Illinois_
3. I separate Oregon and Washington. _Columbia River_
4. I am located between the Great Lakes and the Gulf of St. Lawrence. _St. Lawrence River_
5. I cut through Colorado, Kansas, Oklahoma and Arkansas. _Arkansas River_
6. I flow into the Colorado River in Utah. _Green River_
7. I am a New York river. _Hudson River_
8. I run across the state of Idaho. _Snake River_
9. I am located mainly in Pennsylvania and flow into the Ohio River. _Allegheny River_
10. I begin in Wyoming and run into the Missouri River. _Yellowstone River_
11. I flow through the state of Virginia. _Roanoke River_
12. I run from Chicago to St. Louis. _Illinois River_
13. I form the northeast border of Texas. _Red River_
14. I am located in northern California. _Sacramento River_
15. What rivers are near your home? Write about them. _Answers will vary._

Page 122

River Boundaries

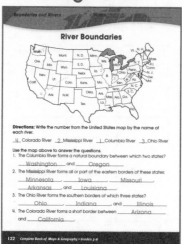

Directions: Write the number from the United States map by the name of each river.

_4_ Colorado River _2_ Mississippi River _1_ Columbia River _3_ Ohio River

Use the map above to answer the questions.
1. The Columbia River forms a natural boundary between which two states? _Washington_ and _Oregon_
2. The Mississippi River forms all or part of the eastern borders of these states: _Minnesota_, _Iowa_, _Missouri_, _Arkansas_, and _Louisiana_.
3. The Ohio River forms the southern borders of which three states? _Ohio_, _Indiana_, and _Illinois_
4. The Colorado River forms a short border between _Arizona_ and _California_.

Page 123

Up the Lazy River

"The steamboat is coming!" was a cry heard in the many small river towns in the 1800s. Steamboats carried people and packages along the waterways before the faster railroads were developed.

The shipping tags below tell where each package is beginning and ending its journey. Use a map, atlas, or the Internet to find the river on which the steamboat will be traveling. Some steamboats may have to travel on more than one river.

Directions: Write the name of the river route on each shipping tag.

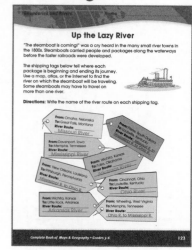

Page 124

Focusing on Four

Shown are four kinds of maps.

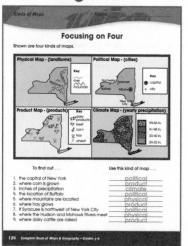

To find out . . .	Use this kind of map . . .
1. the capital of New York	political
2. where corn is grown	product
3. inches of precipitation	climate
4. the location of Buffalo	political
5. where mountains are located	physical
6. where hay grows	product
7. if Syracuse is northwest of New York City	political
8. where the Hudson and Mohawk Rivers meet	physical
9. where dairy cattle are raised	product

Page 126

United States Maps

Page 127

State Smart

Use this map of some of the states to answer the questions below.

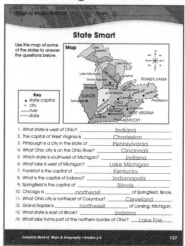

1. What state is west of Ohio? _Indiana_
2. The capital of West Virginia is _Charleston_
3. Pittsburgh is a city in the state of _Pennsylvania_
4. What Ohio city is on the Ohio River? _Cincinnati_
5. Which state is southwest of Michigan? _Indiana_
6. What lake is west of Michigan? _Lake Michigan_
7. Frankfort is the capital of _Kentucky_
8. What is the capital of Indiana? _Indianapolis_
9. Springfield is the capital of _Illinois_
10. Chicago is _northeast_ of Springfield, Illinois.
11. What Ohio city is northeast of Columbus? _Cleveland_
12. Grand Rapids is _northwest_ of Lansing, Michigan.
13. What state is east of Illinois? _Indiana_
14. What lake forms part of the northern border of Ohio? _Lake Erie_

Page 128

What is a Political Map?

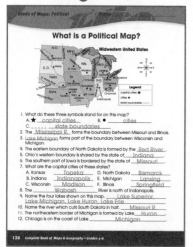

1. What do these three symbols stand for on this map?
   A. ★ _capital cities_ B. ● _cities_
   C. ▬ _state boundaries_
2. The _Mississippi R._ forms the boundary between Missouri and Illinois.
3. _Lake Michigan_ forms part of the boundary between Wisconsin and Michigan.
4. The eastern boundary of North Dakota is formed by the _Red River_.
5. Ohio's western boundary is shared by the state of _Indiana_.
6. The southern part of Iowa is bordered by the state of _Missouri_.
7. What are the capital cities of these states?
   A. Kansas _Topeka_ D. North Dakota _Bismarck_
   B. Indiana _Indianapolis_ E. Michigan _Lansing_
   C. Wisconsin _Madison_ F. Illinois _Springfield_
8. The _Wabash_ River is north of Indianapolis.
9. Name the four lakes shown on this map. _Lake Superior, Lake Michigan, Lake Huron, Lake Erie_
10. Name the river which cuts South Dakota in half. _Missouri R._
11. The northeastern border of Michigan is formed by Lake _Huron_.
12. Chicago is on the lake of Lake _Michigan_.

Page 129

Counties in Arizona

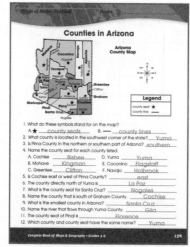

1. What do these symbols stand for on the map?
   A. ★ _county seats_ B. ▬ _county lines_
2. What county is located in the southwest corner of the state? _Yuma_
3. Is Pima County in the northern or southern part of Arizona? _southern_
4. Name the county seat for each county listed.
   A. Cochise _Bisbee_ D. Yuma _Yuma_
   B. Mohave _Kingman_ E. Coconino _Flagstaff_
   C. Greenlee _Clifton_ F. Navajo _Holbrook_
5. Is Cochise east or west of Pima County? _east_
6. The county directly north of Yuma is _La Paz_
7. What is the county seat for Santa Cruz? _Nogales_
8. Name the county that is south of Graham County. _Cochise_
9. What is the smallest county in Arizona? _Santa Cruz_
10. Name the river that flows through Yuma County. _Gila_
11. The county seat of Pinal is _Florence_
12. Which county and county seat have the same name? _Yuma_

Page 130

Natural Wonders

The earth's physical features are its natural formations. Match each formation with its definition by writing a number in each blank.

_8_ river 1. land rising high above the land around it
_4_ bay 2. land surrounded completely by water
_2_ island 3. piece of land surrounded by water on all but one side
_11_ gulf 4. inlet of a large body of water that extends into the land; smaller than a gulf
_1_ mountain 5. an opening in the earth's crust that spills lava, rock, and gases
_9_ plain 6. long inland body of water
_6_ lake 7. lowland between hills or mountains
_3_ peninsula 8. long, narrow body of water
_7_ valley 9. large area of flat grasslands
_5_ volcano 10. vast body of salt water
_10_ ocean 11. large area of a sea or ocean partially enclosed by land

Directions: Write each feature's number on the map.

Features Map

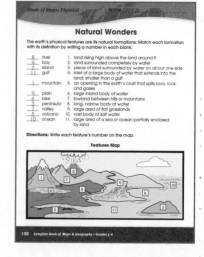

Page 131

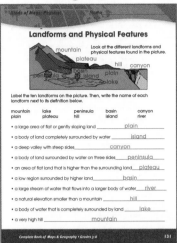

Landforms and Physical Features

Look at the different landforms and physical features found in the picture.

mountain, plateau, hill, canyon, peninsula, island, basin, plain, lake

Label the ten landforms on the picture. Then, write the name of each landform next to its definition below.

mountain   lake   peninsula   basin   canyon
plain   plateau   hill   island   river

- a large area of flat or gently sloping land ___plain___
- a body of land completely surrounded by water ___island___
- a deep valley with steep sides ___canyon___
- a body of land surrounded by water on three sides ___peninsula___
- an area of flat land that is higher than the surrounding land ___plateau___
- a low region surrounded by higher land ___basin___
- a large stream of water that flows into a larger body of water ___river___
- a natural elevation smaller than a mountain ___hill___
- a body of water that is completely surrounded by land ___lake___
- a very high hill ___mountain___

Page 132

Land Regions

Physical maps show natural features of the earth such as water, mountains, deserts, and high and low regions. Follow the directions to complete the map.

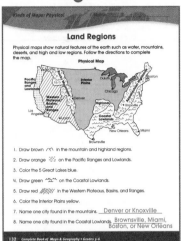

Physical Map

1. Draw brown ⌒ in the mountain and highland regions.
2. Draw orange ⠿ on the Pacific Ranges and Lowlands.
3. Color the 5 Great Lakes blue.
4. Draw green ⌒⌒ on the Coastal Lowlands.
5. Draw red ///// in the Western Plateaus, Basins, and Ranges.
6. Color the Interior Plains yellow.
7. Name one city found in the mountains. ___Denver or Knoxville___
8. Name one city found in the Coastal Lowlands. ___Brownsville, Miami, Boston, or New Orleans___

Page 133

Physical Features of the United States

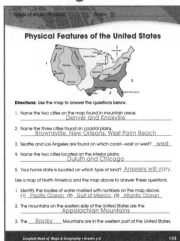

Directions: Use the map to answer the questions below.

1. Name the two cities on the map found in mountain areas. ___Denver and Knoxville___
2. Name the three cities found on coastal plains. ___Brownsville, New Orleans, West Palm Beach___
3. Seattle and Los Angeles are found on which coast—east or west? ___west___
4. Name the two cities located on the interior plains. ___Duluth and Chicago___
5. Your home state is located on which type of land? ___Answers will vary.___

Use a map of North America and the map above to answer these questions.

1. Identify the bodies of water marked with numbers on the map above.
   (1) ___Pacific Ocean___ (2) ___Gulf of Mexico___ (3) ___Atlantic Ocean___
2. The mountains on the eastern side of the United States are the ___Appalachian Mountains___
3. The ___Rocky___ Mountains are in the western part of the United States.

Page 135

Types of Land

Directions: Use this map of the United States and another map, atlas, or the Internet to answer the questions.

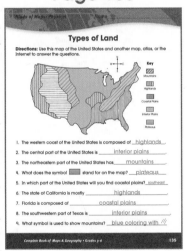

Key
Mountains
Highlands
Coastal Plains
Interior Plains
Plateau

1. The western coast of the United States is composed of ___highlands___.
2. The central part of the United States is ___interior plains___.
3. The northeastern part of the United States has ___mountains___.
4. What does the symbol ▦ stand for on the map? ___plateaus___
5. In which part of the United States will you find coastal plains? ___southeast___
6. The state of California is mostly ___highlands___.
7. Florida is composed of ___coastal plains___.
8. The southwestern part of Texas is ___interior plains___.
9. What symbol is used to show mountains? ___blue coloring with ///___

Page 136

Comparing Two States

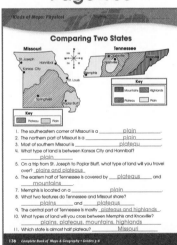

Key
Mountains   Highlands
Plateau   Plain

Key
Plateau   Plain

1. The southeastern corner of Missouri is a ___plain___.
2. The northern part of Missouri is a ___plain___.
3. Most of southern Missouri is ___plateau___.
4. What type of land is between Kansas City and Hannibal? ___plain___
5. On a trip from St. Joseph to Poplar Bluff, what type of land will you travel over? ___plains and plateaus___
6. The eastern half of Tennessee is covered by ___plateaus___ and ___mountains___.
7. Memphis is located on a ___plain___.
8. What two features do Tennessee and Missouri share? ___plains___ and ___plateaus___.
9. The central part of Tennessee is mostly ___plateaus and highlands___.
10. What types of land will you cross between Memphis and Knoxville? ___plains, plateaus, mountains, highlands___
11. Which state is almost half plateau? ___Missouri___

Page 137

Alaska and New York

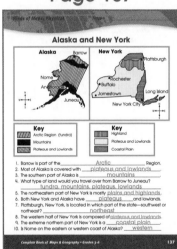

Key
Arctic Region (tundra)
Mountains
Plateaus and Lowlands

Key
Highland
Plateaus and Lowlands
Coastal Plain

1. Barrow is part of the ___Arctic___ Region.
2. Most of Alaska is covered with ___plateaus and lowlands___.
3. The southern part of Alaska is ___mountains___.
4. What type of land would you travel over from Barrow to Juneau? ___tundra, mountains, plateaus, lowlands___
5. The northeastern part of New York is mostly ___plains and highlands___.
6. Both New York and Alaska have ___plateaus___ and lowlands.
7. Plattsburgh, New York, is located in which part of the state—southwest or northeast? ___northeast___
8. The western half of New York is composed of ___plateaus and lowlands___.
9. The extreme northern part of New York is a ___coastal plain___.
10. Is Nome on the eastern or western coast of Alaska? ___western___

Page 138

Poetic Forms

Just as there are many kinds of landforms and physical features, there are also many forms of poetry. Use what you know about landforms and physical features to write a diamanté poem. Look at the sample below.

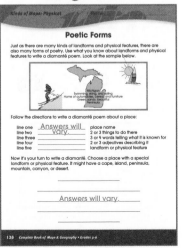

Follow the directions to write a diamanté poem about a place:

line one ___Answers will vary.___   place name
line two   2 or 3 things to do there
line three   3 or 4 words telling what it is known for
line four   2 or 3 adjectives describing it
line five   landform or physical feature

Now it's your turn to write a diamanté. Choose a place with a special landform or physical feature. It might have a cape, island, peninsula, mountain, canyon, or desert.

___Answers will vary.___

Page 139

Natural Wonders of the United States

Listed below are ten natural features found in the United States. Use an encyclopedia, atlas, or the Internet to complete the chart. Write the number of each feature on the U.S. Products and Natural Resources Map on page 140.

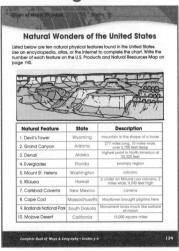

Natural Feature	State	Description
1. Devil's Tower	Wyoming	mountain in the shape of a tower
2. Grand Canyon	Arizona	277 miles long, 10 miles wide, over 5,700 feet deep
3. Denali	Alaska	highest point in North America at 20,320 feet
4. Everglades	Florida	swampy region
5. Mount St. Helens	Washington	volcano
6. Kilauea	Hawaii	a crater on Mauna Loa volcano, 2 miles wide, 4,040 feet high
7. Carlsbad Caverns	New Mexico	caverns
8. Cape Cod	Massachusetts	Mayflower brought pilgrims here
9. Badlands National Park	South Dakota	Monument looks much like surface of moon
10. Mojave Desert	California	15,000 square miles

Page 140

U.S. Products and Natural Resources

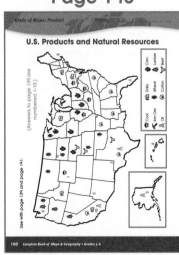

(Answers to page 139 are numbered 1-10.)

Use with page 139 and page 141.

Corn   Lumber   Beef
Dairy   Wheat   Cotton
Coal   Iron Ore

Page 141

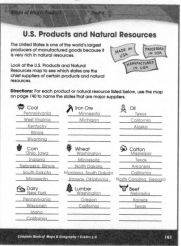

Kinds of Maps: Product — Name

U.S. Products and Natural Resources

The United States is one of the world's largest producers of manufactured goods because it is very rich in natural resources.

Look at the U.S. Products and Natural Resources map to see which states are the chief suppliers of certain products and natural resources.

Directions: For each product or natural resource listed below, use the map on page 140 to name the states that are major suppliers.

Coal
Pennsylvania
West Virginia
Kentucky
Illinois
Wyoming

Iron Ore
Minnesota
Michigan

Oil
Texas
California
Alaska

Corn
Ohio, Iowa
Indiana
Nebraska, Illinois
South Dakota
Minnesota

Wheat
Washington
Minnesota
North Dakota
Montana, South Dakota
Kansas, Oklahoma

Cotton
Mississippi
Texas
Arkansas
California
North Carolina, Georgia

Dairy
New York
Pennsylvania
Wisconsin
Idaho
California

Lumber
Washington
Oregon
California

Beef
Nebraska
Kansas
Texas

Complete Book of Maps & Geography • Grades 3-6   141

Page 142

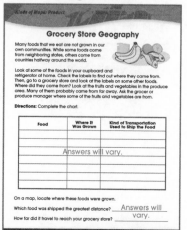

Kinds of Maps: Product — Name

Grocery Store Geography

Many foods that we eat are not grown in our own communities. While some foods come from neighboring states, others come from countries halfway around the world.

Look at some of the foods in your cupboard and refrigerator at home. Check the labels to find out where they came from. Then, go to a grocery store and look at the labels on some other foods. Where did they come from? Look at the fruits and vegetables in the produce area. Many of them probably came from far away. Ask the grocer or produce manager where some of the fruits and vegetables are from.

Directions: Complete the chart.

Food	Where It Was Grown	Kind of Transportation Used to Ship the Food
	Answers will vary.	

On a map, locate where these foods were grown.

Which food was shipped the greatest distance? Answers will vary.

How far did it travel to reach your grocery store?

142   *Complete Book of Maps & Geography • Grades 3-6*

Page 145

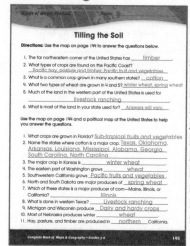

Kinds of Maps: Product — Name

Tilling the Soil

Directions: Use the map on page 144 to answer the questions below.

1. The far northeastern corner of the United States has ___timber___.
2. What types of crops are found on the Pacific Coast? Pacific hay, pasture and timber; Pacific fruit and vegetables
3. What is a common crop grown in many southern states? ___cotton___
4. What two types of wheat are grown in 4 and 57? winter wheat, spring wheat
5. Much of the land in the western part of the United States is used for livestock ranching
6. What is most of the land in your state used for? Answers will vary.

Use the map on page 144 and a political map of the United States to help you answer the questions.

1. What crops are grown in Florida? Sub-tropical fruits and vegetables
2. Name the states where cotton is a major crop. Texas, Oklahoma, Arkansas, Louisiana, Mississippi, Alabama, Georgia, South Carolina, North Carolina
3. The major crop in Kansas is ___winter wheat___
4. The eastern part of Washington grows ___wheat___
5. Southwestern California grows Pacific fruits and vegetables.
6. North and South Dakota are major producers of ___spring wheat___
7. Which of these states is a major producer of corn—Maine, Illinois, or California? ___Illinois___
8. What is done in western Texas? ___Livestock ranching___
9. Michigan and Wisconsin produce ___Dairy and hardy crops___
10. Most of Nebraska produces winter ___wheat___
11. Hay, pasture, and timber are produced in ___northern___ California.

Complete Book of Maps & Geography • Grades 3-6   145

Page 146

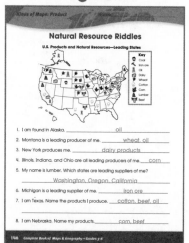

Kinds of Maps: Product — Name

Natural Resource Riddles

U.S. Products and Natural Resources—Leading States

Key: Coal, Iron ore, Dairy, Wheat, Cotton, Corn, Lumber, Beef

1. I am found in Alaska. ___oil___
2. Montana is a leading producer of me. ___wheat, oil___
3. New York produces me. ___dairy products___
4. Illinois, Indiana, and Ohio are all leading producers of me. ___corn___
5. My name is lumber. Which states are leading suppliers of me? Washington, Oregon, California
6. Michigan is a leading supplier of me. ___iron ore___
7. I am Texas. Name the products I produce. ___cotton, beef, oil___
8. I am Nebraska. Name my products. ___corn, beef___

146   *Complete Book of Maps & Geography • Grades 3-6*

Page 147

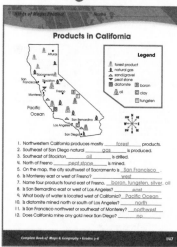

Kinds of Maps: Product — Name

Products in California

Legend: forest product, natural gas, sand/gravel, peat stone, diatomite, oil, boron, clay, tungsten

1. Northwestern California produces mostly ___forest___ products.
2. Southeast of San Diego natural ___gas___ is produced.
3. Southeast of Stockton ___oil___ is drilled.
4. North of Fresno ___peat stone___ is mined.
5. On the map, the city southwest of Sacramento is ___San Francisco___.
6. Is Monterey east or west of Fresno? ___west___
7. Name four products found east of Fresno. boron, tungsten, silver, oil
8. Is San Bernardino east or west of Los Angeles? ___east___
9. What body of water is located west of California? ___Pacific Ocean___
10. Is diatomite mined north or south of Los Angeles? ___north___
11. Is San Francisco northwest or southeast of Monterey? ___northwest___
12. Does California mine any gold near San Diego? ___no___

Complete Book of Maps & Geography • Grades 3-6   147

Page 148

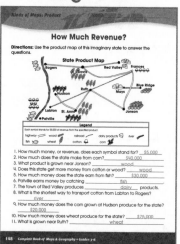

Kinds of Maps: Product — Name

How Much Revenue?

Directions: Use the product map of this imaginary state to answer the questions.

State Product Map

Each symbol stands for $5,000 of revenue from the specified product.

Legend: highway, wood, railroad, dairy products, river, corn, cotton, fish

1. How much money, or revenue, does each symbol stand for? ___$5,000___
2. How much does the state make from corn? ___$40,000___
3. What product is grown near Jonson? ___wood___
4. Does this state get more money from corn or wood? ___wood___
5. How much money does the state earn from fish? ___$30,000___
6. What does the symbol ■ stand for? ___fish___
7. The town of Red Valley produces ___dairy___ products.
8. What is the shortest way to transport cotton from Labton to Rogers? ___river___
9. How much money does the corn grown at Hudson produce for the state? ___$20,000___
10. How much money does wheat produce for the state? ___$75,000___
11. What is grown near Ruth? ___wheat___

148   *Complete Book of Maps & Geography • Grades 3-6*

Page 149

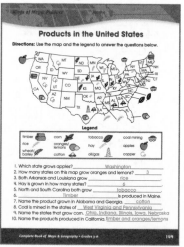

Kinds of Maps: Product — Name

Products in the United States

Directions: Use the map and the legend to answer the questions below.

Legend: timber, corn, tobacco, coal mining, rice, oranges/lemons, apples, wheat/barley, hay, oil/gas, copper

1. Which state grows apples? ___Washington___
2. How many states on this map grow oranges and lemons? ___3___
3. Both Arkansas and Louisiana grow ___rice___
4. Hay is grown in how many states? ___6___
5. North and South Carolina both grow ___tobacco___
6. ___Timber___ is produced in Maine.
7. Name the product grown in Alabama and Georgia. ___cotton___
8. Coal is mined in the states of ___West Virginia and Pennsylvania___
9. Name the states that grow corn. Ohio, Indiana, Illinois, Iowa, Nebraska
10. Name the products in California. timber and oranges/lemons

Complete Book of Maps & Geography • Grades 3-6   149

Page 150

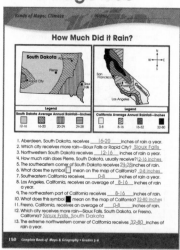

Kinds of Maps: Climate — Name

How Much Did it Rain?

South Dakota / **California**

Legend — South Dakota Average Annual Rainfall—Inches: 12-16, 16-20, 20-24, 24-28
Legend — California Average Annual Rainfall—Inches: 0-8, 8-16, 16-32, 32-80

1. Aberdeen, South Dakota, receives ___16-20___ inches of rain a year.
2. Which city receives more rain—Sioux Falls or Rapid City? ___Sioux Falls___
3. Northwestern South Dakota receives ___12-16___ inches of rain a year.
4. How much rain does Pierre, South Dakota, usually receive? ___12-16 inches___
5. The southeastern corner of South Dakota receives ___24-28___ inches of rain.
6. What does the symbol ☐ mean on the map of California? ___0-8 inches___
7. Southeastern California receives ___0-8___ inches of rain a year.
8. Los Angeles, California, receives on average of ___8-16___ inches of rain a year.
9. The northeastern part of California receives ___8-16___ inches of rain.
10. What does this symbol ■ mean on the map of California? ___32-80 inches___
11. Fresno, California, receives an average of ___0-8___ inches of rain.
12. Which city receives more rain—Sioux Falls or Fresno, or Fresno, California? ___Sioux Falls, South Dakota___
13. The extreme northwestern corner of California receives ___32-80___ inches of rain a year.

150   *Complete Book of Maps & Geography • Grades 3-6*

Page 151

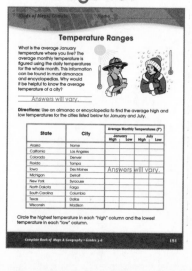

Kinds of Maps: Climate — Name

Temperature Ranges

What is the average January temperature where you live? The average monthly temperature is figured using the daily temperatures for the whole month. This information can be found in most almanacs and encyclopedias. Why would it be helpful to know the average temperature of a city? Answers will vary.

Directions: Use an almanac or encyclopedia to find the average high and low temperatures for the cities listed below for January and July.

State	City	January High	January Low	July High	July Low
Alaska	Nome				
California	Los Angeles				
Colorado	Denver				
Florida	Tampa		Answers will vary.		
Iowa	Des Moines				
Michigan	Detroit				
New York	Syracuse				
North Dakota	Fargo				
South Carolina	Columbia				
Texas	Dallas				
Wisconsin	Madison				

Circle the highest temperature in each "high" column and the lowest temperature in each "low" column.

Complete Book of Maps & Geography • Grades 3-6   151

Page 152

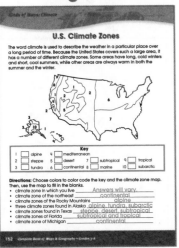

Page 155

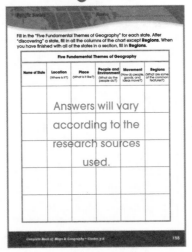

Page 157

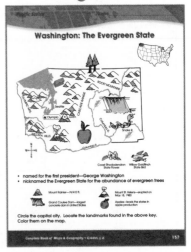

Page 158

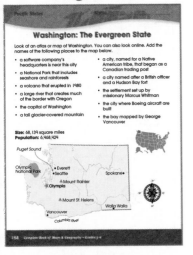

Page 159

Page 161

Page 162

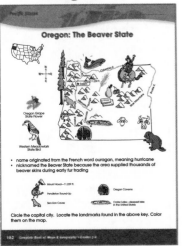

Page 163

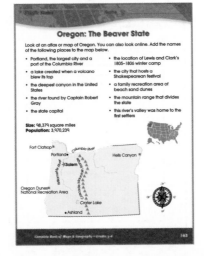

Page 165

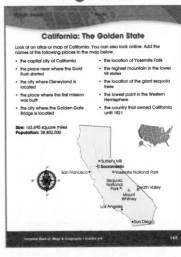

Page 166

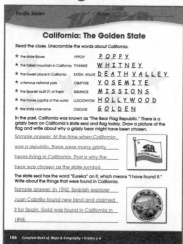

California: The Golden State

Read the clues. Unscramble the words about California.

★ the state flower — YPPOP — P O P P Y
★ the tallest mountain in California — TYHNWE — W H I T N E Y
★ the lowest place in California — EATDH AVLLVE — D E A T H V A L L E Y
★ a famous national park — OSMTYEE — Y O S E M I T E
★ the Spanish built 21 of them — SBMNICS — M I S S I O N S
★ the movie capital of the world — LLDOOHYOW — H O L L Y W O O D
★ the state nickname — OGDLNE — G O L D E N

In the past, California was known as "The Bear Flag Republic." There is a grizzly bear on California's state seal and flag today. Draw a picture of the flag and write about why a grizzly bear might have been chosen.

Sample answer: At the time when California
was a republic, there were many grizzly
bears living in California. That is why the
bear was chosen as the state symbol.

The state seal has the word "Eureka" on it, which means "I have found it." Write about the things that were found in California.

Sample answer: In 1542, Spanish explorer
Juan Cabrillo found new land and claimed
it for Spain. Gold was found in California in
1848.

Page 167

California: The Golden State

- named by early explorers, possibly referring to a treasure island in a Spanish story
- nicknamed the Golden State, possibly for its gold fields, its golden pastures, and its sunshine

Circle the capital city. Locate the landmarks found in the above key. Color them on the map.

Page 168

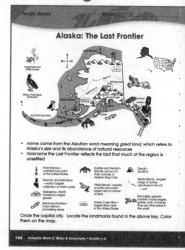

Alaska: The Last Frontier

- name came from the Aleutian word meaning *great land*, which refers to Alaska's size and its abundance of natural resources
- nickname the Last Frontier reflects the fact that much of the region is unsettled

Circle the capital city. Locate the landmarks found in the above key. Color them on the map.

Page 169

Alaska: The Last Frontier

Look at an atlas or map of Alaska. You can also look online. Add the names of the following places to the map below.

- a chain of islands crossing into the eastern hemisphere
- the highest mountain in North America
- a gold rush town and Alaska's second largest city
- the state capital where Chief Kowee first found gold
- a narrow waterway between Alaska and Russia, named for a Danish explorer
- the northern beginning of the Trans-Alaska Pipeline
- the northernmost point in the United States
- the Trans-Alaska Pipeline ends at Valdez and this large area of water
- the island first settled by Russians
- the city named after the man who purchased Alaska

Size: 665,384 square miles
Population: 736,732

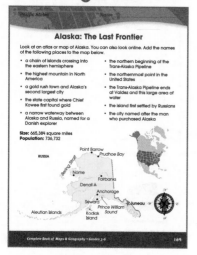

Page 170

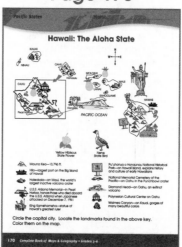

Hawaii: The Aloha State

Circle the capital city. Locate the landmarks found in the above key. Color them on the map.

Page 172

Hawaii: The Aloha State

Look at an atlas or map of Hawaii. You can also look online. Add the names of the following places to the map below.

- Honolulu, the capital city of the islands
- Hawaii, the "big island"
- the island of Maui
- the location of Volcanoes National Park
- the island where the Polynesian Cultural center is located
- Pearl Harbor
- the "Pineapple Island" of Lanai
- the "Friendly Island" of Molokai
- the "Forbidden Island" of Niihau

Size: 10,970 square miles
Population: 1,419,561

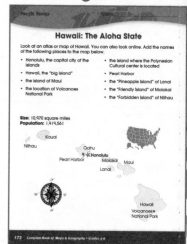

Page 174

The Mountain States

Fill in the "Five Fundamental Themes of Geography" for each state. After "discovering" a state, fill in all the columns of the chart except **Regions**. When you have finished with all of the states in a section, fill in **Regions**.

		Five Fundamental Themes of Geography			
Name of State	Location (Where is it?)	Place (What is it like?)	People and Environment (What do the people do?)	Movement (How do people, goods, and ideas move?)	Regions (What are some of the common features?)
		Answers will vary according to the research sources used.			

Page 175

The Mountain States

		Five Fundamental Themes of Geography			
Name of State	Location (Where is it?)	Place (What is it like?)	People and Environment (What do the people do?)	Movement (How do people, goods, and ideas move?)	Regions (What are some of the common features?)
		Answers will vary according to the research sources used.			

Page 176

Idaho: The Gem State

- name originated from the Shoshone Indian word *ee-dah-how*, which means *sun coming down the mountain* or *daybreak*
- nicknamed the Gem state for the gold, silver, and other minerals in the area that brought a mining boom

Circle the capital city. Locate the landmarks found in the above key. Color them on the map.

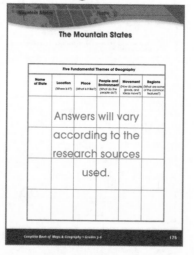

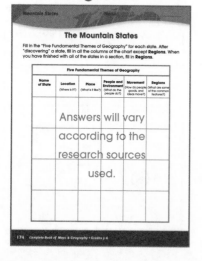

Page 177

Idaho: The Gem State

Look at an atlas or map of Idaho. You can also look online. Add the names of the following places to the map below.

- the city where Philo Farnsworth invented the television
- the oldest town in Idaho
- the capital of Idaho
- site of the first trading post in Idaho
- the site of the Bear River Massacre

- Lake Coeur d'Alene
- Craters of the Moon National Park
- The Birds of Prey Natural Area is on this river
- Borah Peak, Idaho's tallest mountain
- Hells Canyon National Park

Size: 83,569 square miles
Population: 1,634,464

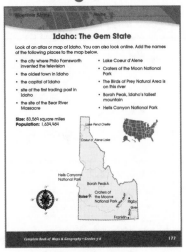

Page 178

Montana: The Treasure State

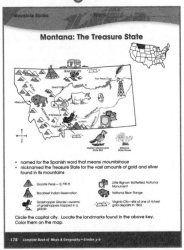

- named for the Spanish word that means *mountainous*
- nicknamed the Treasure State for the vast amounts of gold and silver found in its mountains

Granite Peak—12,799 ft.
Blackfeet Indian Reservation
Grasshopper Glacier—swarms of grasshoppers trapped in a glacier
Little Bighorn Battlefield National Monument
National Bison Range
Virginia City—site of one of richest gold deposits in 1863

Circle the capital city. Locate the landmarks found in the above key. Color them on the map.

Page 179

Montana: The Treasure State

Look at an atlas or map of Montana. You can also look online. Add the names of the following places to the map below.

- mountain range in the western part of the state
- the country to the north of the state
- the capital of Montana
- one of the biggest dams in the world
- the river where Lt. Col. Custer was defeated

- the National Park with year-round snow
- the city near the site of 1,000-year-old cave drawings
- the place near where Jeannette Rankin was born
- where silver was discovered
- the city where gold was discovered in a gulch

Size: 147,040 square miles
Population: 1,023,579

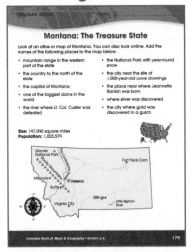

Page 180

Wyoming: The Equality State

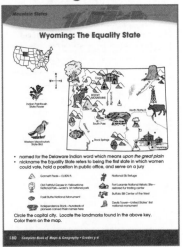

- named for the Delaware Indian word which means *upon the great plain*
- nickname the Equality State refers to being the first state in which women could vote, hold a position in public office, and serve on a jury

Gannett Peak—13,804 ft.
Old Faithful Geyser in Yellowstone National Park—world's 1st national park
Fossil Butte National Monument
Independence Rock—hundreds of pioneers carved their names here
National Elk Refuge
Fort Laramie National Historic Site—restored fur trading center
Buffalo Bill Center of the West
Devils Tower—United States' first national monument

Circle the capital city. Locate the landmarks found in the above key. Color them on the map.

Page 181

Wyoming: The Equality State

Look at an atlas or map of Wyoming. You can also look online. Add the names of the following places to the map below.

- this city is just east of central Wyoming
- the capital of Wyoming
- a city in northwest Wyoming
- this river passes through the Grand Teton National Park
- the first national park
- these beautiful mountains are in their own national park

- this river passes by Casper
- a city near Cheyenne
- this state is to the west and borders Montana
- this mountain range divides North America
- this state is to the east and borders Colorado
- the Continental Divide

Size: 97,813 square miles
Population: 584,153

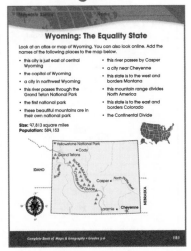

Page 182

Nevada: The Silver State

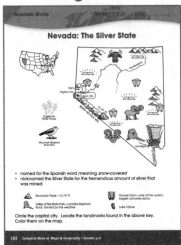

- named for the Spanish word meaning *snow-covered*
- nicknamed the Silver State for the tremendous amount of silver that was mined

Boundary Peak—13,147 ft.
Valley of Fire State Park—contains Elephant Rock, formed by the weather
Hoover Dam—one of the world's largest concrete dams
Lake Tahoe

Circle the capital city. Locate the landmarks found in the above key. Color them on the map.

Page 183

Nevada: The Silver State

Look at an atlas or map of Nevada. You can also look online. Add the names of the following places to the map below.

- the capital of Nevada
- a very large dam
- this town is Nevada spelled backward
- Waddie Mitchell was born here
- this is Nevada's tallest mountain
- this river forms a small part of Nevada's border with Arizona

- odds are you can find gamblers in this southern city
- this lake is near the Hoover Dam
- this state shares Nevada's eastern border
- this is the biggest mountain lake
- this desert is in southeastern Nevada

Size: 110,572 square miles
Population: 2,839,099

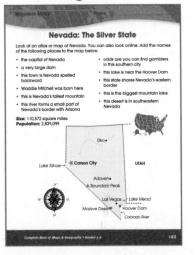

Page 184

Utah: The Beehive State

- named for the Ute Indians
- nicknamed the Beehive State because pioneers called the region *Deseret*—a Mormon term for *honeybee*

King's Peak—13,528 ft.
Hovenweep National Monument—housed Anasazi Indians about A.D. 1200–1300
International Speedway—cars race on flat salt beds
Promontory—first transcontinental railroad completed in 1869
Four Corners Monument—where Utah, Arizona, New Mexico, and Colorado meet
Bonneville Salt Flats
Arches National Park
Rainbow Bridge National Monument—one of the world's largest natural stone bridges

Circle the capital city. Locate the landmarks found in the above key. Color them on the map.

Page 185

Utah: The Beehive State

Look at an atlas or map of Utah. You can also look online. Add the names of the following places to the map below.

- Merlin Olsen is from here
- the other states making the "four corners"
- Utah's capital
- a freshwater lake
- where racecar records are set

- a town near Utah Lake
- many Western movies are filmed here
- you can float in this lake
- see dinosaur bones here

Size: 84,898 square miles
Population: 2,942,902

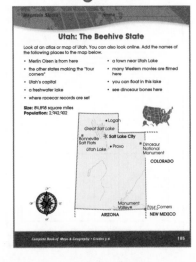

Page 186

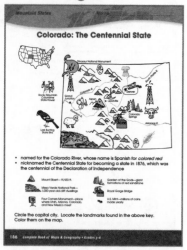

Page 187

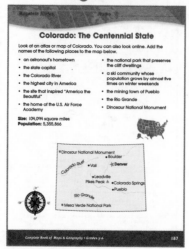

Page 188

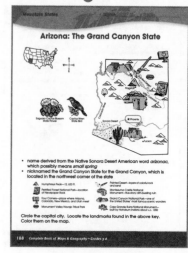

Page 189

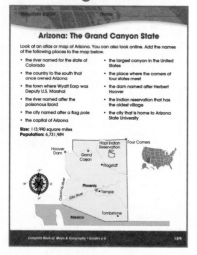

Page 190

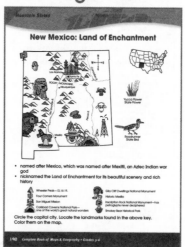

Page 191

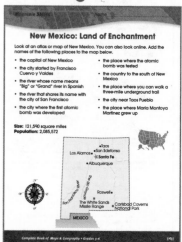

Page 193

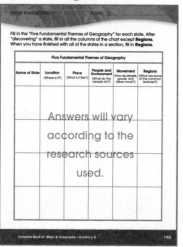

Page 194

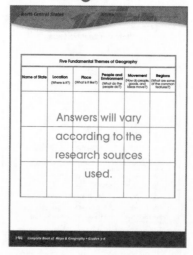

Page 195

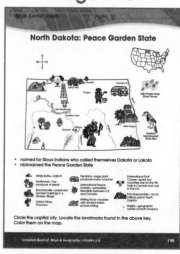

Page 196

North Dakota: Peace Garden State

Look at an atlas or map of North Dakota. You can also look online. Add the names of the following places to the map below.

- the capital
- the river that shares a name with a state
- the country to the north
- the city where Lewis and Clark built a fort
- the first European settlement
- the cities with the two United States Strategic Air Commands
- the National Park to honor Theodore Roosevelt
- the city near Writing Rock
- the town that hosts "Pioneer Days at Bonanzaville"
- the lake named for Lewis and Clark's guide
- the state to the south that was once part of the Dakota Territory

Size: 70,648 square miles
Population: 739,482

Page 197

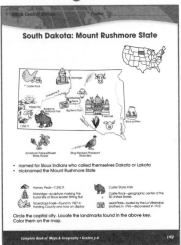

South Dakota: Mount Rushmore State

- named for Sioux Indians who called themselves Dakota or Lakota
- nicknamed the Mount Rushmore State

Circle the capital city. Locate the landmarks found in the above key. Color them on the map.

Page 198

South Dakota: Mount Rushmore State

Look at an atlas or map of South Dakota. You can also look online. Add the names of the following places to the map below.

- A part of Citibank headquarters is here
- two of the world's longest caves
- home of Allen Neuharth
- Yankton Reservation
- Badlands National Park
- the world's largest drugstore is here
- Devil's Gulch, a 20-foot wide canyon
- hometown of Hubert Humphrey
- South Dakota's capital
- Wounded Knee Creek
- Waubay Lake

Size: 77,116 square miles
Population: 853,175

Page 199

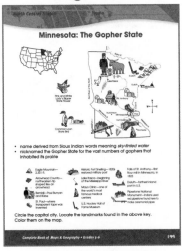

Minnesota: The Gopher State

- name derived from Sioux Indian words meaning *sky-tinted water*
- nicknamed the Gopher State for the vast numbers of gophers that inhabited its prairie

Circle the capital city. Locate the landmarks found in the above key. Color them on the map.

Page 200

Minnesota: The Gopher State

Look at an atlas or map of Minnesota. You can also look online. Add the names of the following places to the map below.

- Fort Snelling and the rivers that meet there
- the location of the Mayo Clinic
- the lake that borders northeastern Minnesota
- the city near St. Anthony's Falls
- the city where Bob Dylan was born
- the northernmost point of the lower 48 United States
- the city of Judy Garland's childhood home
- the capital of Minnesota
- the county to the north of Minnesota

Size: 86,935 square miles
Population: 5,457,173

Page 201

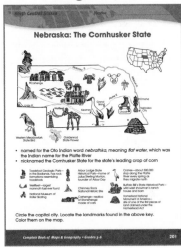

Nebraska: The Cornhusker State

- named for the Oto Indian word *nebrathka*, meaning *flat water*, which was the Indian name for the Platte River
- nicknamed the Cornhusker State for the state's leading crop of corn

Circle the capital city. Locate the landmarks found in the above key. Color them on the map.

Page 202

Nebraska: The Cornhusker State

Look at an atlas or map of Nebraska. You can also look online. Add the names of the following places to the map below.

- the North Platte river flows from this state
- Omaha is on this river
- this state is to the east of Nebraska
- the capital of Nebraska
- this state shares Nebraska's northern border
- this area makes up most of Nebraska
- this state cuts into southwest Nebraska
- Nebraska shares this area with Iowa
- this river passes by Grand Island and flows into the Missouri River
- this state is due south of Nebraska
- Malcolm X's birthplace

Size: 77,347 square miles
Population: 1,881,503

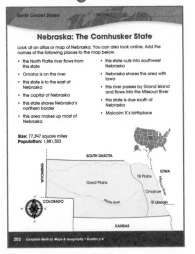

Page 203

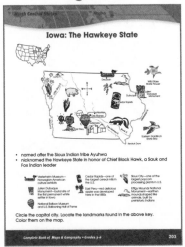

Iowa: The Hawkeye State

- named after the Sioux Indian tribe Ayuhwa
- nicknamed the Hawkeye State in honor of Chief Black Hawk, a Sauk and Fox Indian leader

Circle the capital city. Locate the landmarks found in the above key. Color them on the map.

Page 204

Iowa: The Hawkeye State

Look at an atlas or map of Iowa. You can also look online. Add the names of the following places to the map below.

- this city is known for making popcorn
- the capital of Iowa
- mined lead could be sent down this eastern river
- the state to the south of Iowa
- the river that shares the same name as the capital
- this town celebrates Capt. James T. Kirk's birthday each year
- a city where early settlers came to mine lead
- this river makes up Iowa's western border
- the state to the north of Iowa

Size: 56,273 square miles
Population: 3,107,126

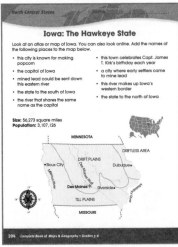

Page 205

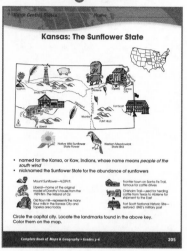

Kansas: The Sunflower State

- named for the Kansa, or Kaw, Indians, whose name means *people of the south wind*
- nicknamed the Sunflower State for the abundance of sunflowers

Circle the capital city. Locate the landmarks found in the above key. Color them on the map.

Page 206

Kansas: The Sunflower State

Look at an atlas or map of Kansas. You can also look online. Add the names of the following places to the map below.

- the state capital
- the city that has the same name as the state
- the river that separates Kansas and Missouri
- the place where salt was first produced
- the birthplace of Melissa Etheridge
- the states that border Kansas
- the birthplace of Amelia Earhart
- the city that was an important site in the Underground Railroad
- Location of Dwight D. Eisenhower Presidential Library and Museum
- the city that produces small aircraft

Size: 82,278 square miles
Population: 2,904,021

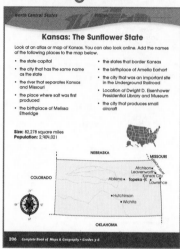

Page 207

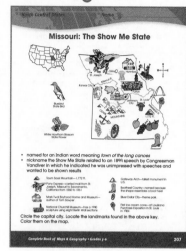

Missouri: The Show Me State

- named for an Indian word meaning *town of the long canoes*
- nickname the Show Me State related to an 1899 speech by Congressman Vandiver in which he indicated he was unimpressed with speeches and wanted to be shown results

Circle the capital city. Locate the landmarks found in the above key. Color them on the map.

Page 208

Missouri: The Show Me State

Look at an atlas or map of Missouri. You can also look online. Add the names of the following places to the map below.

- the lake where Bagnell Dam is located
- the capital of Missouri
- the mighty river on which many steamboats traveled
- the mountains in Missouri
- the place where the Pony Express started
- the city that has the same name as Kansas
- the river that borders Missouri on the west
- the states that border Missouri
- the location of the Harry S. Truman home and library
- the boyhood home of Mark Twain

Size: 69,707 square miles
Population: 6,063,589

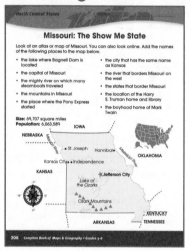

Page 210

Fill in the "Five Fundamental Themes of Geography" for each state. After "discovering" a state, fill in all the columns of the chart except **Regions**. When you have finished with all of the states in a section, fill in **Regions**.

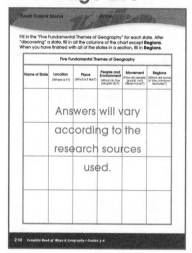

Five Fundamental Themes of Geography

Name of State	Location (Where is it?)	Place (What is it like?)	People and Environment (What do the people do?)	Movement (How do people, goods, and ideas move?)	Regions (What are some of the common features?)

Answers will vary according to the research sources used.

Page 211

Oklahoma: The Sooner State

- name derived from the Choctaw Indian words *okla*, meaning *people*, and *homma*, meaning *red*
- nicknamed the Sooner State for the settlers who arrived before the land was opened for settlement

Circle the capital city. Locate the landmarks found in the above key. Color them on the map.

Page 212

Oklahoma: The Sooner State

Look at an atlas or map of Oklahoma. You can also look online. Add the names of the following places to the map below.

- the states that border Oklahoma
- the river that separates Texas and Oklahoma
- three rivers that run through the state
- the capital of Oklahoma
- the area called the Panhandle
- Tulsa, the second largest city
- the location of the University of Oklahoma
- a city in the Panhandle
- a city north of Tulsa
- the location of Oklahoma State University

Size: 69,899 square miles
Population: 5,878,051

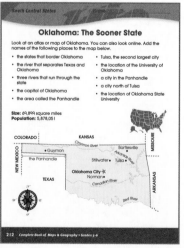

Page 213

Texas: The Lone Star State

- name comes from the Spanish pronunciation of the Indian word *tejas*, which means *allies or friends*
- nickname the Lone Star State comes from having only one star on its state

Circle the capital city. Locate the landmarks found in the above key. Color them on the map.

Page 214

Texas: The Lone Star State

Look at an atlas or map of Texas. You can also look online. Add the names of the following places to the map below.

- the city where the Alamo is located
- the city where the first two missions were built
- the location of the Texas Rangers Hall of Fame
- the capital of Texas
- the city where John F. Kennedy was assassinated
- the location of the Lyndon B. Johnson Space Center
- the country to the south
- the state to the north
- the Rio Grande River
- the Gulf of Mexico

Size: 268,597 square miles
Population: 26,956,958

Page 215

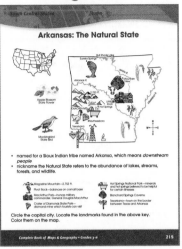

Page 216

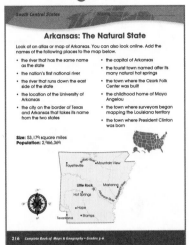

Page 217

Page 218

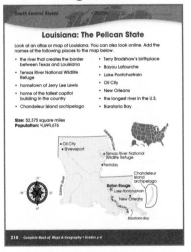

Page 220

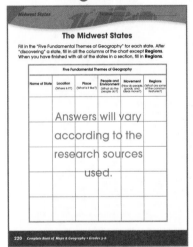

Page 221

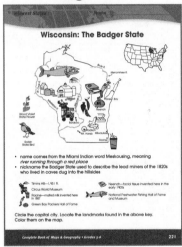

Page 222

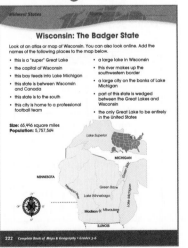

Page 223

Page 224

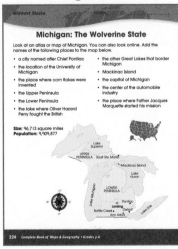

Page 225

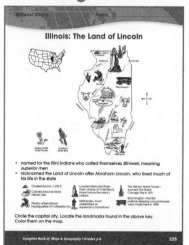

Illinois: The Land of Lincoln

- named for the Illini Indians who called themselves *Illiniwek*, meaning *superior men*
- nicknamed the Land of Lincoln after Abraham Lincoln, who lived much of his life in the state

Circle the capital city. Locate the landmarks found in the above key. Color them on the map.

Page 226

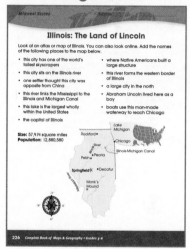

Illinois: The Land of Lincoln

Look at an atlas or map of Illinois. You can also look online. Add the names of the following places to the map below.

- this city has one of the world's tallest skyscrapers
- this city sits on the Illinois river
- one settler thought this city was opposite from China
- this river links the Mississippi to the Illinois and Michigan Canal
- this lake is the largest wholly within the United States
- the capital of Illinois
- where Native Americans built a large structure
- this river forms the western border of Illinois
- a large city in the north
- Abraham Lincoln lived here as a boy
- boats use this man-made waterway to reach Chicago

Size: 57,914 square miles
Population: 12,880,580

Page 227

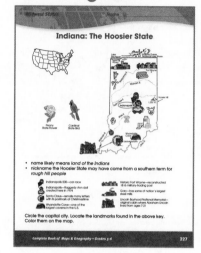

Indiana: The Hoosier State

- name likely means *land of the Indians*
- nickname the Hoosier State may have come from a southern term for *rough hill people*

Circle the capital city. Locate the landmarks found in the above key. Color them on the map.

Page 228

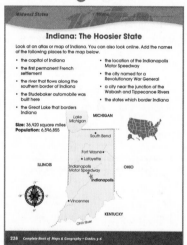

Indiana: The Hoosier State

Look at an atlas or map of Indiana. You can also look online. Add the names of the following places to the map below.

- the capital of Indiana
- the first permanent French settlement
- the river that flows along the southern border of Indiana
- the Studebaker automobile was built here
- the Great Lake that borders Indiana
- the location of the Indianapolis Motor Speedway
- the city named for a Revolutionary War General
- a city near the junction of the Wabash and Tippecanoe Rivers
- the states which border Indiana

Size: 36,420 square miles
Population: 6,596,855

Page 229

Ohio: The Buckeye State

- name derived from Iroquois Indian word meaning *great water*
- nicknamed the Buckeye State for its abundance of buckeye trees

Circle the capital city. Locate the landmarks found in the above key. Color them on the map.

Page 231

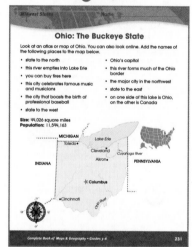

Ohio: The Buckeye State

Look at an atlas or map of Ohio. You can also look online. Add the names of the following places to the map below.

- state to the north
- this river empties into Lake Erie
- you can buy tires here
- this city celebrates famous music and musicians
- the city that boasts the birth of professional baseball
- state to the west
- Ohio's capital
- this river forms much of the Ohio border
- the major city in the northwest
- state to the east
- on one side of this lake is Ohio, on the other is Canada

Size: 44,026 square miles
Population: 11,594,163

Page 232

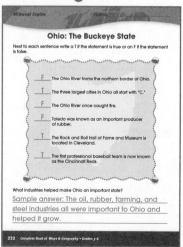

Ohio: The Buckeye State

Next to each sentence write a T if the statement is true or an F if the statement is false.

- F — The Ohio River forms the northern border of Ohio.
- T — The three largest cities in Ohio all start with "C."
- F — The Ohio River once caught fire.
- F — Toledo was known as an important producer of rubber.
- T — The Rock and Roll Hall of Fame and Museum is located in Cleveland.
- T — The first professional baseball team is now known as the Cincinnati Reds.

What industries helped make Ohio an important state?
Sample answer: The oil, rubber, farming, and steel industries all were important to Ohio and helped it grow.

Page 234

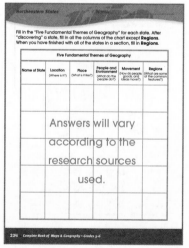

Fill in the "Five Fundamental Themes of Geography" for each state. After "discovering" a state, fill in all the columns of the chart except **Regions**. When you have finished with all of the states in a section, fill in **Regions**.

		Five Fundamental Themes of Geography			
Name of State	Location (Where is it?)	Place (What is it like?)	People and Environment (What do the people do?)	Movement (How do people, goods, and ideas move?)	Regions (What are some of the common features?)

Answers will vary according to the research sources used.

Page 235

Fill in the "Five Fundamental Themes of Geography" for each state. After "discovering" a state, fill in all the columns of the chart except **Regions**. When you have finished with all of the states in a section, fill in **Regions**.

		Five Fundamental Themes of Geography			
Name of State	Location (Where is it?)	Place (What is it like?)	People and Environment (What do the people do?)	Movement (How do people, goods, and ideas move?)	Regions (What are some of the common features?)

Answers will vary according to the research sources used.

Answer Key

Page 236

Maine: The Pine Tree State

- name believed to have originated from the English explorers who used the term *main* to refer to the mainland, as opposed to the islands
- nicknamed the Pine Tree State for the abundance of pine tree forests

Mount Katahdin—5,268 ft.

Matinicus Island—sanctuary for puffins and other seabirds

Satellite Earth Station—sends and receives orbiting satellites' signals

Sebago Lake—Camp Fire Girls originated here in 1910

West Quoddy Head Light—located on land that is the most easterly point of U.S.

Farmington—Earmuff Capital of the World, first earmuffs patented here in 1877

Portland Head Light—among the best known lighthouses in the U.S.

Circle the capital city. Locate the landmarks found in the above key. Color them on the map.

Page 237

Maine: The Pine Tree State

Look at an atlas or map of Maine. You can also look online. Add the names of the following places to the map below.

- the capital of Maine
- the place where many lobster boats dock
- the country that borders Maine
- the one state that borders Maine
- the site where the L.L. Bean Company is located
- the town where Stephen King lives
- the coastal town that was closest to one of the first Revolutionary War naval battles
- the name of the body of water off the southern coast of Maine
- Penobscot River
- the Longfellow Mountains

Size: 35,380 square miles
Population: 1,330,089

Page 238

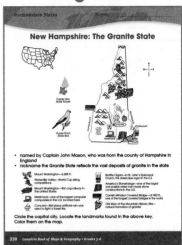

New Hampshire: The Granite State

- named by Captain John Mason, who was from the county of Hampshire in England
- nickname the Granite State reflects the vast deposits of granite in the state

Mount Washington—6,288 ft.

Waterville Valley—World Cup skiing competitions

Mount Washington—first cog railway in the United States

Merrimack—one of the largest computer companies in the U.S. located here

Concord—first place artificial rain was used to fight a forest fire

Brattle Organ—in St. John's Episcopal Church, the oldest pipe organ in the U.S.

America's Stonehenge—one of the largest and possible oldest man-made stone constructions in the U.S.

Cornish-Windsor Covered Bridge—at 460 ft., one of the longest covered bridges in the world

Old Man of the Mountain Historic Site—natural formation of granite

Circle the capital city. Locate the landmarks found in the above key. Color them on the map.

Page 239

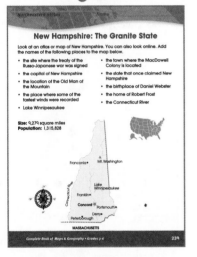

New Hampshire: The Granite State

Look at an atlas or map of New Hampshire. You can also look online. Add the names of the following places to the map below.

- the site where the treaty of the Russo-Japanese war was signed
- the capital of New Hampshire
- the location of the Old Man of the Mountain
- the place where some of the fastest winds were recorded
- Lake Winnipesaukee
- the town where the MacDowell Colony is located
- the state that once claimed New Hampshire
- the birthplace of Daniel Webster
- the home of Robert Frost
- the Connecticut River

Size: 9,279 square miles
Population: 1,315,828

Page 240

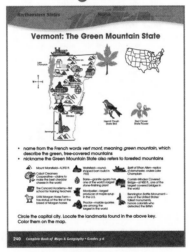

Vermont: The Green Mountain State

- name from the French words *vert mont*, meaning *green mountain*, which describe the green, tree-covered mountains
- nickname the Green Mountain State also refers to forested mountains

Mount Mansfield—4,393 ft.

Cabot Creamery Cooperative—claims to make the best cheddar cheese in the world

The Concord Academy—first school for training teachers

UVM Morgan Horse Farm—has statue of the first of the breed of Morgan horses

Wofstfield—round-shaped barn built in 1901

Barre—granite quarry has one of the world's largest stone-finishing plant

Montpelier—largest producer of maple syrup in the U.S.

Proctor—marble quarries are among the largest in the world

Spirit of Ethan Allen—replica of sternwheeler, cruises Lake Champlain

Cornish-Windsor Covered Bridge—at 460 ft., one of the largest covered bridges in the world

Bennington Battle Monument—one of the United States' tallest monuments, honors colonists who defeated the British

Circle the capital city. Locate the landmarks found in the above key. Color them on the map.

Page 241

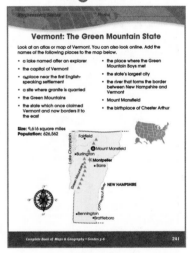

Vermont: The Green Mountain State

Look at an atlas or map of Vermont. You can also look online. Add the names of the following places to the map below.

- a lake named after an explorer
- the capital of Vermont
- a place near the first English-speaking settlement
- a site where granite is quarried
- the Green Mountains
- the state which once claimed Vermont and now borders it to the east
- the place where the Green Mountain Boys met
- the state's largest city
- the river that forms the border between New Hampshire and Vermont
- Mount Mansfield
- the birthplace of Chester Arthur

Size: 9,616 square miles
Population: 626,562

Page 242

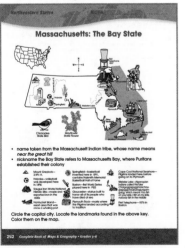

Massachusetts: The Bay State

- name taken from the Massachuset Indian tribe, whose name means *near the great hill*
- nickname the Bay State refers to Massachusetts Bay, where Puritans established their colony

Mount Greylock—3,491 ft.

Holyoke—volleyball was developed here

Saugus Iron Works National Historic Site—made and exported iron in the 1600s

Nantucket Island—resort area that was once a whaling base

Springfield—basketball invented here in 1891, contains Naismith Memorial Basketball Hall of Fame

Boston—first World Series played here in 1903

Gloucester—statue built to honor all of its people who have died at sea

Plymouth Rock—marks where the Pilgrims landed according to tradition

Cape Cod National Seashore—Pilgrims landed here before going on to Plymouth

Webster Lake—Algonquian Indians called this lake Chargoggagoggmanchauggagoggchaubunagungamaugg, which means has all the best fishing; no fight in the middle, nobody fish in the middle

First Telephone—1876 in Boston

Circle the capital city. Locate the landmarks found in the above key. Color them on the map.

Page 243

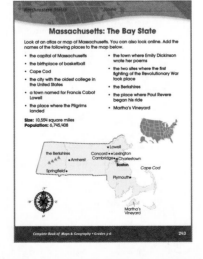

Massachusetts: The Bay State

Look at an atlas or map of Massachusetts. You can also look online. Add the names of the following places to the map below.

- the capital of Massachusetts
- the birthplace of basketball
- Cape Cod
- the city with the oldest college in the United States
- a town named for Francis Cabot Lowell
- the place where the Pilgrims landed
- the town where Emily Dickinson wrote her poems
- the two sites where the first fighting of the Revolutionary War took place
- the Berkshires
- the place where Paul Revere began his ride
- Martha's Vineyard

Size: 10,554 square miles
Population: 6,745,408

Page 244

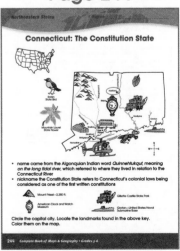

Connecticut: The Constitution State

- name came from the Algonquian Indian word *Quinnehtukqut*, meaning *on the long tidal river*, which referred to where they lived in relation to the Connecticut River
- nickname the Constitution State refers to Connecticut's colonial laws being considered as one of the first written constitutions

Mount Frissell—2,380 ft.

American Clock and Watch Museum

Gillette Castle State Park

Groton—United States Naval Submarine Base

Circle the capital city. Locate the landmarks found in the above key. Color them on the map.

Page 245

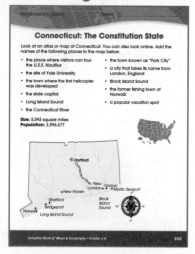

Page 246

Page 247

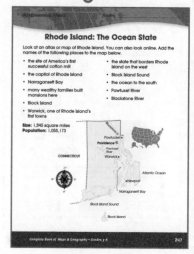

Page 248

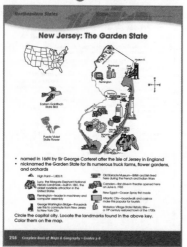

Page 249

Page 250

Page 251

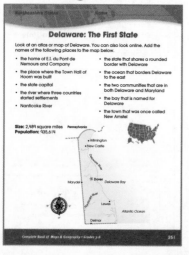

Page 252

Page 253

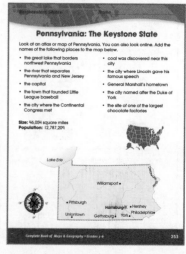

Page 255

New York: The Empire State

Read each clue. Use the code to find the answers.

1-A	5-E	9-I	13-X	17-X	21-U	25-Y
2-G	6-J	10-P	14-D	18-R	22-V	26-F
3-C	7-B	11-M	15-O	19-Z	23-W	
4-N	8-H	12-L	16-S	20-T	24-Q	

first name of New York's famous actor and director   W O O D Y

a river named for an explorer   H U D S O N

first name of first explorer   G I O V A N N I

used to be called Fort Orange   A L B A N Y

home of George Eastman   R O C H E S T E R

Unscramble the circled letters to write the name of the famous Iroquois leader.

H I A W A T H A

Pictures will vary.

The Statue of Liberty was the first thing many immigrants saw when they came to Ellis Island and entered New York Harbor. The Statue of Liberty stands for freedom.

If you built a new statue to welcome people to New York, what would it look like? Draw a picture of your statue and write about what it stands for.
Answers will vary. Children might draw a dollar bill, a dollar sign, a computer, a camera, etc. Children might write, "A dollar bill or dollar sign stands for a country with good jobs." "A computer stands for America's use of the Internet." "A camera stands for America's inventors." "A guitar stands for America's music."

Page 256

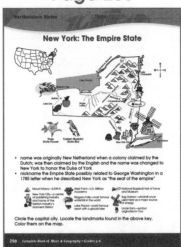

New York: The Empire State

- name was originally New Netherland when a colony claimed by the Dutch; was then claimed by the English and the name was changed to New York to honor the Duke of York
- nickname the Empire State possibly related to George Washington in a 1785 letter when he described New York as "the seat of the empire"

Circle the capital city. Locate the landmarks found in the above key. Color them on the map.

Page 258

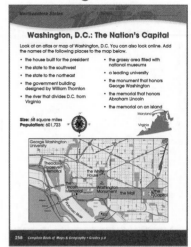

Washington, D.C.: The Nation's Capital

Look at an atlas or map of Washington, D.C. You can also look online. Add the names of the following places to the map below.

- the house built for the president
- the state to the southwest
- the state to the northeast
- the government building designed by William Thornton
- the river that divides D.C. from Virginia
- the grassy area filled with national museums
- a leading university
- the monument that honors George Washington
- the memorial that honors Abraham Lincoln
- the memorial on an island

Size: 68 square miles
Population: 601,723

Page 259

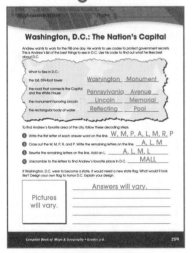

Washington, D.C.: The Nation's Capital

Andrew wants to work for the FBI one day. He wants to use codes to protect government secrets. This is Andrew's list of the best things to see in D.C. Use his code to find out what he likes best about D.C.

What to See in D.C.:

the tall, 554-foot tower   Washington   Monument

the road that connects the Capitol and the White House   Pennsylvania   Avenue

the monument honoring Lincoln   Lincoln   Memorial

the rectangular body of water   Reflecting   Pool

To find Andrew's favorite area of the city, follow these decoding steps.

① Write the first letter of each answer word on the line.   W, M, P, A, L, M, R, P

② Cross out the W, M, P, R, and P. Write the remaining letters on the line.   A, L, M

③ Rewrite the remaining letters on the line. Add an L.   A, L, M, L

④ Unscramble to the letters to find Andrew's favorite place in D.C.   MALL

If Washington, D.C., were to become a state, it would need a new state flag. What would it look like? Design your own flag to honor D.C. Explain your design.

Pictures will vary.

Answers will vary.

Page 261

Fill in the "Five Fundamental Themes of Geography" for each state. After "discovering" a state, fill in all the columns of the chart except Regions. When you have finished with all of the states in a section, fill in Regions.

	Five Fundamental Themes of Geography				
Name of State	Location (Where is it?)	Place (What is it like?)	People and Environment (How do people, goods, and ideas move?)	Movement (What do the people do?)	Regions (What are some of the common features?)
			Answers will vary according to the research sources used.		

Page 262

	Five Fundamental Themes of Geography				
Name of State	Location (Where is it?)	Place (What is it like?)	People and Environment (What do the people do?)	Movement (How do people, goods, and ideas move?)	Regions (What are some of the common features?)
			Answers will vary according to the research sources used.		

Page 263

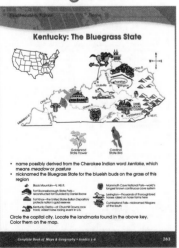

Kentucky: The Bluegrass State

- name possibly derived from the Cherokee Indian word *kentake*, which means *meadow* or *pasture*
- nicknamed the Bluegrass State for the bluish buds on the grass of this region

Circle the capital city. Locate the landmarks found in the above key. Color them on the map.

Page 264

Kentucky: The Bluegrass State

Look at an atlas or map of Kentucky. You can also look online. Add the names of the following places to the map below.

- the home of the Kentucky Derby
- the capital of Kentucky
- the location of the gold reserve
- the river which flows along the northern border of Kentucky
- the river which forms a part of the western boundary of Kentucky
- the longest cave in the world
- the home of the Corvette plant
- the seven states that border Kentucky

Size: 40,408 square miles
Population: 4,413,457

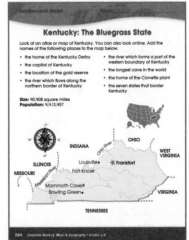

Page 265

West Virginia: The Mountain State

- named when northwestern counties separated from Virginia during the Civil War and sided with the North
- nicknamed the Mountain State for its rugged mountains, steep hills, and narrow valleys

Circle the capital city. Locate the landmarks found in the above key. Color them on the map.

Page 266

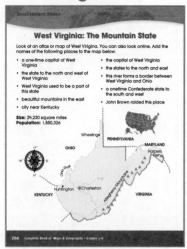

West Virginia: The Mountain State

Look at an atlas or map of West Virginia. You can also look online. Add the names of the following places to the map below.

- a one-time capital of West Virginia
- the state to the north and west of West Virginia
- West Virginia used to be a part of this state
- beautiful mountains in the east
- city near Kentucky

- the capital of West Virginia
- the states to the north and east
- this river forms a border between West Virginia and Ohio
- a onetime Confederate state to the south and west
- John Brown raided this place

Size: 24,230 square miles
Population: 1,850,326

Page 267

Maryland: The Old Line State

- named in 1632 for Henrietta Maria, the wife of England's King Charles I
- nicknamed the Old Line State in honor of the troops from Maryland who fought so bravely on the line during the Revolutionary War

Circle the capital city. Locate the landmarks found in the above key. Color them on the map.

Page 268

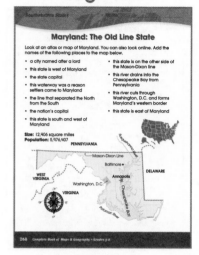

Maryland: The Old Line State

Look at an atlas or map of Maryland. You can also look online. Add the names of the following places to the map below.

- a city named after a lord
- this state is west of Maryland
- the state capital
- this waterway was a reason settlers came to Maryland
- the line that separated the North from the South
- the nation's capital
- this state is south and west of Maryland

- this state is on the other side of the Mason-Dixon line
- this river drains into the Chesapeake Bay from Pennsylvania
- this river cuts through Washington, D.C. and forms Maryland's western border
- this state is east of Maryland

Size: 12,406 square miles
Population: 5,976,407

Page 269

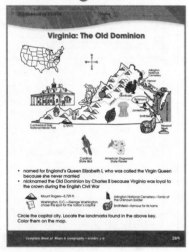

Virginia: The Old Dominion

- named for England's Queen Elizabeth I, who was called the Virgin Queen because she never married
- nicknamed the Old Dominion by Charles II because Virginia was loyal to the crown during the English Civil War

Circle the capital city. Locate the landmarks found in the above key. Color them on the map.

Page 270

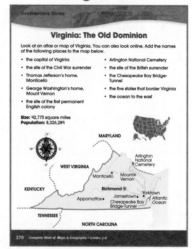

Virginia: The Old Dominion

Look at an atlas or map of Virginia. You can also look online. Add the names of the following places to the map below.

- the capital of Virginia
- the site of the Civil War surrender
- Thomas Jefferson's home, Monticello
- George Washington's home, Mount Vernon
- the site of the first permanent English colony

- Arlington National Cemetery
- the site of the British surrender
- the Chesapeake Bay Bridge-Tunnel
- the five states that border Virginia
- the ocean to the east

Size: 42,775 square miles
Population: 8,326,289

Page 271

Tennessee: The Volunteer State

- named for a Cherokee village, *Tanasie*
- nickname the Volunteer State refers to the large number of men who unhesitatingly volunteered for military service during the War of 1812 and the Mexican War

Circle the capital city. Locate the landmarks found in the above key. Color them on the map.

Page 272

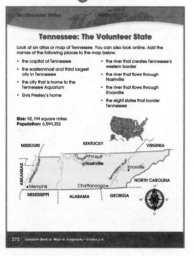

Tennessee: The Volunteer State

Look at an atlas or map of Tennessee. You can also look online. Add the names of the following places to the map below.

- the capital of Tennessee
- the easternmost and third largest city in Tennessee
- the city that is home to the Tennessee Aquarium
- Elvis Presley's home

- the river that creates Tennessee's western border
- the river that flows through Nashville
- the river that flows through Knoxville
- the eight states that border Tennessee

Size: 42,144 square miles
Population: 6,549,352

Page 273

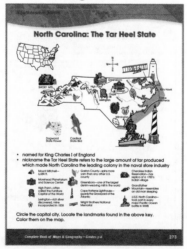

North Carolina: The Tar Heel State

- named for King Charles I of England
- nickname the Tar Heel State refers to the large amount of tar produced which made North Carolina the leading colony in the naval store industry

Circle the capital city. Locate the landmarks found in the above key. Color them on the map.

Page 274

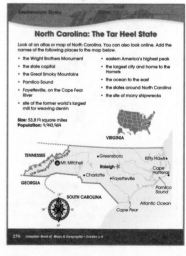

North Carolina: The Tar Heel State

Look at an atlas or map of North Carolina. You can also look online. Add the names of the following places to the map below.

- the Wright Brothers Monument
- the state capital
- the Great Smoky Mountains
- Pamlico Sound
- Fayetteville, on the Cape Fear River
- site of the former world's largest mill for weaving denim

- eastern America's highest peak
- the largest city and home to the Hornets
- the ocean to the east
- the states around North Carolina
- the site of many shipwrecks

Size: 53,819 square miles
Population: 9,943,964

Page 275

South Carolina: The Palmetto State

- named for King Charles I of England; "South" was added when the Carolinas separated
- nickname the Palmetto State may be the result of an incident during the Revolutionary War where soldiers fought from a palmetto log fort and smoke from a burning British ship resembled the state's palmetto tree

Circle the capital city. Locate the landmarks found in the above key. Color them on the map.

Page 276

South Carolina: The Palmetto State

Look at an atlas or map of South Carolina. You can also look online. Add the names of the following places to the map below.

- this is a popular seaside spot
- the ocean to the east of South Carolina
- this large city is in the northwestern part of the state
- an island near the southern border
- a big city on the ocean
- the capital of South Carolina
- a large lake between Columbia and Charleston
- historic shots were fired here
- the state south and west of South Carolina
- the state to the north

Size: 32,020 square miles
Population: 4,832,482 NORTH CAROLINA

Page 277

Mississippi: The Magnolia State

- name taken from two Indian words, *misi* and *sipi* meaning *big river* or *great water*
- nickname the Magnolia State refers to the many magnolia trees that grow in the state

Circle the capital city. Locate the landmarks found in the above key. Color them on the map.

Page 278

Mississippi: The Magnolia State

Look at an atlas or map of Mississippi. You can also look online. Add the names of the following places to the map below.

- this river is one of the most important in the whole country
- this state is south of Mississippi
- the capital of Mississippi
- the Mississippi flows into this body of water
- this connects two rivers
- this state is to the north
- an important battle was fought here
- go east to get to this state
- this city is named after the Native Americans who lived there
- this state is to the northwest of Mississippi

Size: 48,441 square miles
Population: 2,994,079

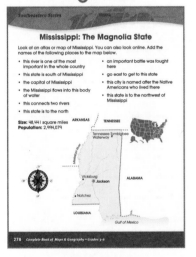

Page 279

Alabama: The Heart of Dixie

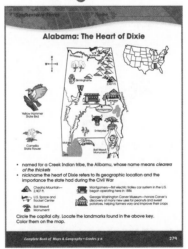

- named for a Creek Indian tribe, the Alibamu, whose name means *clearers of the thickets*
- nickname the heart of Dixie refers to its geographic location and the importance the state had during the Civil War

Circle the capital city. Locate the landmarks found in the above key. Color them on the map.

Page 280

Alabama: The Heart of Dixie

Look at an atlas or map of Alabama. You can also look online. Add the names of the following places to the map below.

- the capital of Alabama
- the site of the starting point of the 1960s civil rights protests
- the large body of water to the south of Alabama
- the city that shares the name of the Tuskegee Institute
- the city named after Andrew Jackson
- the river named after the state
- the cave where humans lived more than 10,000 years ago
- the site of NASA's largest flight center
- the first French settlement
- the town named after a Choctaw chief

Size: 52,420 square miles
Population: 4,849,377

Page 281

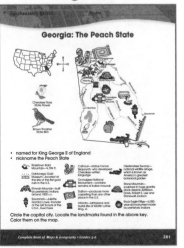

Georgia: The Peach State

- named for King George II of England
- nickname the Peach State

Circle the capital city. Locate the landmarks found in the above key. Color them on the map.

Page 282

Georgia: The Peach State

Look at an atlas or map of Georgia. You can also look online. Add the names of the following places to the map below.

- capital of Georgia
- The Girl Scouts were founded in this city
- you can swim in this ocean
- the state to the south of Georgia
- Georgia shares these mountains with South Carolina
- Georgia's eastern border is shared with this state
- the large city in central Georgia
- "Land of the Trembling Earth"
- a city on the border with Alabama
- you can see Confederate heroes here

Size: 59,425 square miles
Population: 10,097,343

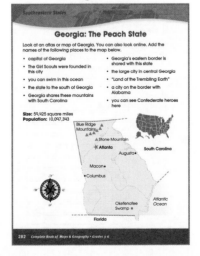

Page 283

Florida: The Sunshine State

- named from the Spanish word *florida*, meaning *flowery*, by Spanish explorer Juan Ponce de León
- nickname the Sunshine State for its warm and sunny climate

Circle the capital city. Locate the landmarks found in the above key. Color them on the map.

Page 284

Florida: The Sunshine State

Look at an atlas or map of Florida. You can also look online. Add the names of the following places to the map below.

- the ocean that borders Florida
- the space shuttle is launched from this spot
- this is Florida's largest lake
- the capital of Florida
- a long bridge links these islands
- the body of water Florida shares with Alabama

- Gloria Estefan was in a group with this city's name
- the first permanent Spanish settlement
- Mickey Mouse lives here
- this area is known for its alligators and crocodiles

Size: 65,757 square miles
Population: 19,893,297

Page 285

Abbreviate Those States!

When you mail something to someone, the state in the address is always abbreviated using two uppercase letters. See how many postal abbreviations you know!

AL Alabama	LA Louisiana	ND North Dakota
AK Alaska	ME Maine	OH Ohio
AZ Arizona	MD Maryland	OK Oklahoma
AR Arkansas	MA Massachusetts	OR Oregon
CA California	MI Michigan	PA Pennsylvania
CO Colorado	MN Minnesota	RI Rhode Island
CT Connecticut	MS Mississippi	SC South Carolina
DE Delaware	MO Missouri	SD South Dakota
FL Florida	MT Montana	TN Tennessee
GA Georgia	NE Nebraska	TX Texas
HI Hawaii	NV Nevada	UT Utah
ID Idaho	NH New Hampshire	VT Vermont
IL Illinois	NJ New Jersey	VA Virginia
IN Indiana	NM New Mexico	WA Washington
IA Iowa	NY New York	WV West Virginia
KS Kansas	NC North Carolina	WI Wisconsin
KY Kentucky		WY Wyoming

Page 288

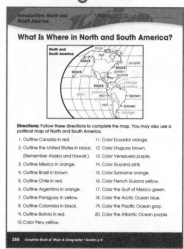

What Is Where in North and South America?

Directions: Follow these directions to complete the map. You may also use a political map of North and South America.

1. Outline Canada in red.
2. Outline the United States in black. (Remember Alaska and Hawaii.)
3. Outline Mexico in orange.
4. Outline Brazil in brown.
5. Outline Chile in red.
6. Outline Argentina in orange.
7. Outline Paraguay in yellow.
8. Outline Colombia in black.
9. Outline Bolivia in red.
10. Color Peru yellow.
11. Color Ecuador orange.
12. Color Uruguay brown.
13. Color Venezuela purple.
14. Color Guyana pink.
15. Color Suriname orange.
16. Color French Guiana yellow.
17. Color the Gulf of Mexico green.
18. Color the Arctic Ocean blue.
19. Color the Pacific Ocean gray.
20. Color the Atlantic Ocean purple.

Page 289

Neighboring Countries

Use a map of North America to locate your country. In the direction boxes, write the names of all the countries and/or bodies of water surrounding your country.

Northwest	North	Northeast
Pacific Ocean	Canada	Atlantic Ocean
West	**My Country**	**East**
Pacific Ocean	USA	Atlantic Ocean
	Draw an outline map of your country.	
Southwest	**South**	**Southeast**
Pacific Ocean	Mexico	Atlantic Ocean

Page 290

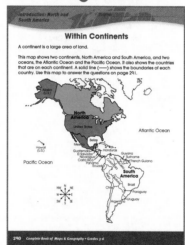

Within Continents

A continent is a large area of land.

This map shows two continents, North America and South America, and two oceans, the Atlantic Ocean and the Pacific Ocean. It also shows the countries that are on each continent. A solid line (———) shows the boundaries of each country. Use this map to answer the questions on page 291.

Page 291

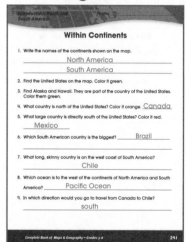

Within Continents

1. Write the names of the continents shown on the map.
   North America
   South America

2. Find the United States on the map. Color it green.

3. Find Alaska and Hawaii. They are part of the country of the United States. Color them green.

4. What country is north of the United States? Color it orange. Canada

5. What large country is directly south of the United States? Color it red.
   Mexico

6. Which South American country is the biggest? Brazil

7. What long, skinny country is on the west coast of South America?
   Chile

8. Which ocean is to the west of the continents of North America and South America? Pacific Ocean

9. In which direction would you go to travel from Canada to Chile?
   south

Page 293

Political Map of Canada

Use with page 292.

Page 294

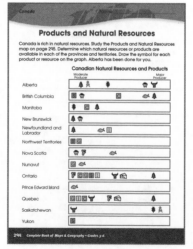

Products and Natural Resources

Canada is rich in natural resources. Study the Products and Natural Resources map on page 295. Determine which natural resources or products are available in each of the provinces and territories. Draw the symbol for each product or resource on the graph. Alberta has been done for you.

Canadian Natural Resources and Products

	Moderate Producer		Major Producer
Alberta			
British Columbia			
Manitoba			
New Brunswick			
Newfoundland and Labrador			
Northwest Territories			
Nova Scotia			
Nunavut			
Ontario			
Prince Edward Island			
Quebec			
Saskatchewan			
Yukon			

Page 296

Northern Neighbors

Write each province or territory name abbreviation by the correct number on the map.

1. British Columbia (B.C.)
2. Alberta (Alta.)
3. Saskatchewan (Sask.)
4. Manitoba (Man.)
5. Ontario (Ont.)
6. Quebec (Que.)
7. Newfoundland and Labrador (N.L.)
8. New Brunswick (N.B.)
9. Nova Scotia (N.S.)
10. Prince Edward Island (P.E.I.)
11. Northwest Territories (N.W.T.)
12. Yukon Territory (Y.T.)
13. Nunavut (Nvt.)

Answer the questions.

1. Which provinces are north of the Great Lakes? Ontario & Quebec
2. Which province contains the national capital? Ontario
3. What province is east of British Columbia? Alberta
4. What province is southeast of New Brunswick? Nova Scotia
5. Manitoba is east of Saskatchewan.

Page 298

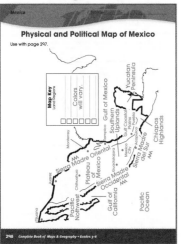

Page 301

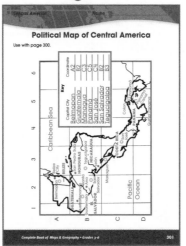

Page 303

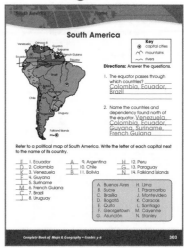

Page 304

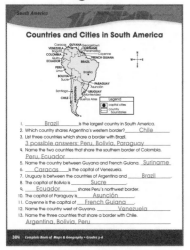

Page 305

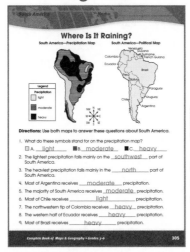

Page 306

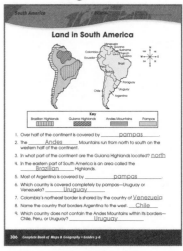

Page 308

Page 309

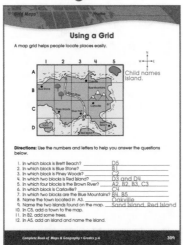

Page 310

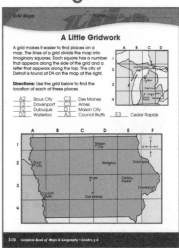

Page 311

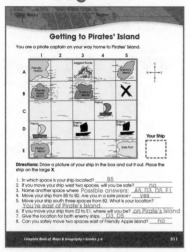

Getting to Pirates' Island

You are a pirate captain on your way home to Pirates' Island.

Directions: Draw a picture of your ship in the box and cut it out. Place the ship on the large **X**.

1. In which space is your ship located? __B5__
2. If you move your ship west two spaces, will you be safe? __no__
3. Name another space where __Possible answers: A5, D3, D5, E1__
4. Move your ship from B5 to B2. Are you in a safe place? __yes__
5. Move your ship south three spaces from B2. What is your location? __You're east of Pirates' Island.__
6. If you move your ship from E2 to E1, where will you be? __on Pirate's Island__
7. Give the location for both enemy ships. __D3, D5__
8. Can you safely move two spaces east of Friendly Apple Island? __no__

Page 312

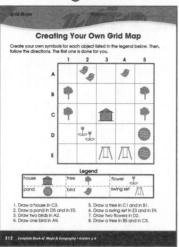

Creating Your Own Grid Map

Create your own symbols for each object listed in the legend below. Then, follow the directions. The first one is done for you.

Legend

| house | tree | flower |
| pond | bird | swing set |

1. Draw a house in C3.
2. Draw a pond in D5 and in E5.
3. Draw two birds in A2.
4. Draw one bird in A4.
5. Draw a tree in C1 and in B1.
6. Draw a swing set in E3 and in E4.
7. Draw two flowers in D2.
8. Draw a tree in B5 and in C5.

Page 313

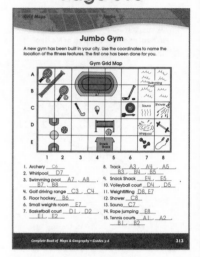

Jumbo Gym

A new gym has been built in your city. Use the coordinates to name the location of the fitness features. The first one has been done for you.

Gym Grid Map

1. Archery __C6__
2. Whirlpool __D7__
3. Swimming pool __A7, A8, B7, B8__
4. Golf driving range __C3, C4__
5. Floor hockey __B6__
6. Small weights room __E7__
7. Basketball court __D1, D2, E1, E2__
8. Track __A3, A4, A5__
9. Snack Shack __E4, E5__
10. Volleyball court __D4, D5__
11. Weightlifting __D8, E7__
12. Shower __C8__
13. Sauna __C7__
14. Rope jumping __E8__
15. Tennis courts __A1, A2, B1, B2__

Page 314

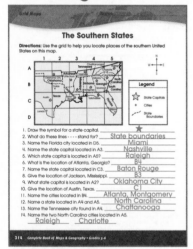

The Southern States

Directions: Use the grid to help you locate places of the southern United States on this map.

Legend
- ★ State Capitals
- • Cities
- ✦✦✦ State Boundaries

1. Draw the symbol for a state capital. ★
2. What do these lines - - - - stand for? __State boundaries__
3. Name the Florida city located in D6. __Miami__
4. Name the state capital located in A3. __Nashville__
5. Which state capital is located in A5? __Raleigh__
6. What is the location of Atlanta, Georgia? __B4__
7. Name the state capital located in C3. __Baton Rouge__
8. Give the location of Jackson, Mississippi. __B3__
9. What state capital is located in A2? __Oklahoma City__
10. Give the location of Austin, Texas. __C1__
11. Name the cities located in B4. __Atlanta, Montgomery__
12. Name a state located in A4 and A5. __North Carolina__
13. Name the Tennessee city found in A4. __Chattanooga__
14. Name the two North Carolina cities located in A5.
   __Raleigh__   __Charlotte__

Page 315

We're Going Places

Directions: Draw an outline map of your state on the grid below. Label places or cities that are familiar to you. List them at the bottom of the page using the number and letter coordinates.

Answers will vary.

| City or Place | Location | City or Place | Location |

Page 316

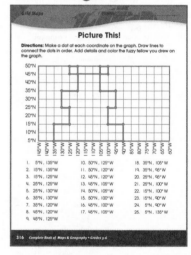

Picture This!

Directions: Make a dot at each coordinate on the graph. Draw lines to connect the dots in order. Add details and color the fuzzy fellow you drew on the graph.

1. 5°N, 135°W
2. 15°N, 135°W
3. 15°N, 125°W
4. 25°N, 130°W
5. 25°N, 130°W
6. 35°N, 130°W
7. 35°N, 120°W
8. 45°N, 120°W
9. 45°N, 125°W
10. 50°N, 125°W
11. 50°N, 95°W
12. 45°N, 120°W
13. 40°N, 105°W
14. 50°N, 105°W
15. 50°N, 100°W
16. 45°N, 100°W
17. 45°N, 105°W
18. 35°N, 105°W
19. 35°N, 95°W
20. 25°N, 95°W
21. 25°N, 100°W
22. 15°N, 100°W
23. 15°N, 90°W
24. 5°N, 90°W
25. 5°N, 135°W

Page 318

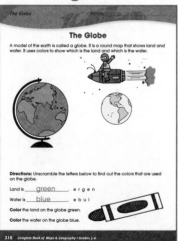

The Globe

A model of the earth is called a globe. It is a round map that shows land and water. It uses colors to show which is the land and which is the water.

Directions: Unscramble the letters below to find out the colors that are used on the globe.

Land is __green__ . e r g e n

Water is __blue__ . e b u l

Color the land on the globe green.

Color the water on the globe blue.

Page 320

It's a Round World

The picture of the globe on page 319 shows both halves of the world. It shows the large pieces of land called continents. There are seven continents. Find them on the globe.

Directions: Write the names of the seven continents.

1. __North America__
2. __South America__
3. __Europe__
4. __Africa__
5. __Asia__
6. __Australia__
7. __Antarctica__

There are four bodies of water called oceans. Find the oceans on the globe. Write the names of the four oceans.

1. __Atlantic__
2. __Pacific__
3. __Indian__
4. __Arctic__

Page 321

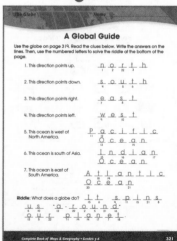

A Global Guide

Use the globe on page 319. Read the clues below. Write the answers on the lines. Then, use the numbered letters to solve the riddle at the bottom of the page.

1. This direction points up. __north__
2. This direction points down. __south__
3. This direction points right. __east__
4. This direction points left. __west__
5. This ocean is west of North America. __Pacific Ocean__
6. This ocean is south of Asia. __Indian Ocean__
7. This ocean is east of South America. __Atlantic Ocean__

Riddle: What does a globe do? __It spins around our planet.__

Page 322

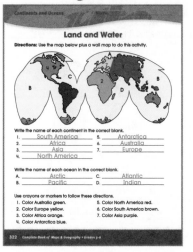

Land and Water

Directions: Use the map below plus a wall map to do this activity.

Write the name of each continent in the correct blank.
1. South America   5. Antarctica
2. Africa   6. Australia
3. Asia   7. Europe
4. North America

Write the name of each ocean in the correct blank.
A. Arctic   C. Atlantic
B. Pacific   D. Indian

Use crayons or markers to follow these directions.
1. Color Australia green.   5. Color North America red.
2. Color Europe yellow.   6. Color South America brown.
3. Color Africa orange.   7. Color Asia purple.
4. Color Antarctica blue.

Page 323

Color My World

Is it a city, state, country, continent, or body of water? Color each box according to the Color Key. Use an atlas for help.

Color Key
city—orange   state—green   country—yellow
water—blue   continent—purple

Atlantic Ocean	India	Colorado	Miami
Peru	Antarctica	Lake Michigan	Hawaii
New Orleans	Spain	Europe	Gulf of Mexico
Vermont	Phoenix	Japan	Paris
East China Sea	Egypt	Wyoming	Sweden
Africa	London	Hudson Bay	Connecticut
Greece	Minnesota	South America	Dallas
Oakland	Great Salt Lake	Argentina	Arctic Ocean
North America	Canada	Chicago	Arkansas
Lake Victoria	Iowa	Venezuela	Venezuela
Lima	Persian Gulf	Mexico	Moscow
Pacific Ocean	Maryland	Cincinnati	Brazil

Page 324

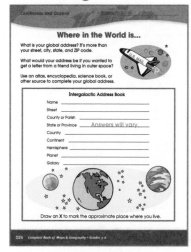

Where in the World is...

What is your global address? It's more than your street, city, state, and ZIP code.

What would your address be if you wanted to get a letter from a friend living in outer space?

Use an atlas, encyclopedia, science book, or other source to complete your global address.

Intergalactic Address Book

Name _____
Street _____
County or Parish _____
State or Province ___ Answers will vary. ___
Country _____
Continent _____
Hemisphere _____
Planet _____
Galaxy _____

Draw an **X** to mark the approximate place where you live.

Page 327

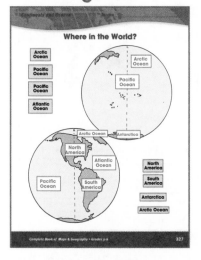

Where in the World?

Page 329

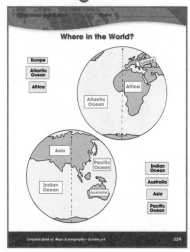

Where in the World?

Page 331

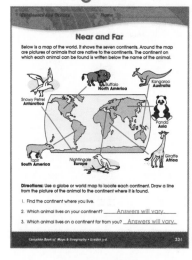

Near and Far

Below is a map of the world. It shows the seven continents. Around the map are pictures of animals that are native to the continents. The continent on which each animal can be found is written below the name of the animal.

Directions: Use a globe or world map to locate each continent. Draw a line from the picture of the animal to the continent where it is found.

1. Find the continent where you live.
2. Which animal lives on your continent? ___ Answers will vary. ___
3. Which animal lives on a continent far from you? ___ Answers will vary. ___

Page 332

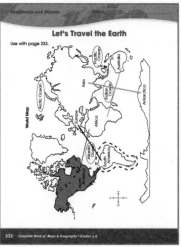

Let's Travel the Earth

Use with page 333.

Page 333

Let's Travel the Earth

Directions: Use the map on page 332 to answer the questions below. Circle the word that correctly completes each statement.

1. If you sail from North America to Antarctica, you will be on the . . .
   Arctic Ocean   (Atlantic Ocean)   Indian Ocean
2. If you fly east from Africa to Australia, you will fly over the . . .
   (Indian Ocean)   Pacific Ocean   Atlantic Ocean
3. To sail from Europe to South America, you will sail on the . . .
   Pacific Ocean   Arctic Ocean   (Atlantic Ocean)
4. To sail from North America to Europe, you will sail on the . . .
   Indian Ocean   (Atlantic Ocean)   Pacific Ocean
5. To travel from Europe to Asia, you must cross . . .
   the Pacific Ocean   the Indian Ocean   (land)

Fill in the blanks with the correct word.

1. The continent north of South America is ___ North America ___.
2. The ocean directly south of Asia is the ___ Indian Ocean ___.
3. The ocean directly north of Asia is the ___ Arctic Ocean ___.
4. The continent directly south of Europe is ___ Africa ___.
5. The continent directly south of Australia is ___ Antarctica ___.

Use a crayon or marker to follow these directions.

1. Draw a red line from North America to Africa.
2. Draw a green line from Asia to Antarctica.
3. Draw an orange line from Australia to Africa.
4. Draw a black line from Europe to South America.
5. Circle the names of all four oceans with blue.
6. Color North America green.
7. Draw a black dotted line (- - - - -) around South America.

Page 334

Hemispheres

The earth is a sphere. When the earth is cut in half horizontally along an imaginary line called the **equator**, the **Northern** and **Southern Hemispheres** of the earth are created.

Trace the equator in orange.

Label the two hemispheres shown on the globe.

Page 335

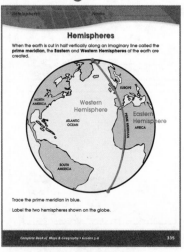

Page 336

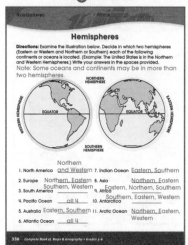

Page 337

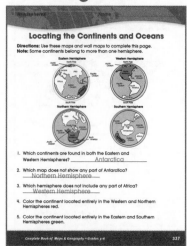

Page 338

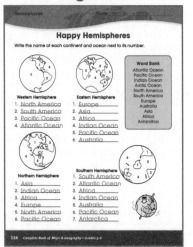

Page 339

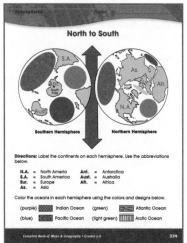

Page 340

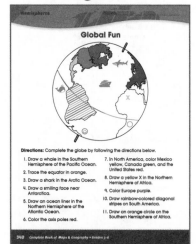

Page 341

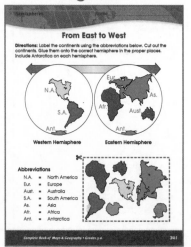

Page 343

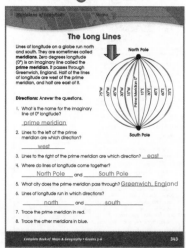

Page 344

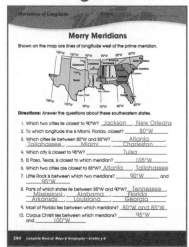

Answer Key

Page 345

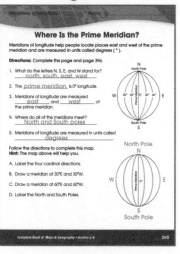

Where Is the Prime Meridian?

Meridians of longitude help people locate places east and west of the prime meridian and are measured in units called degrees (°).

Directions: Complete this page and page 346.

1. What do the letters N, S, E, and W stand for?
   north, south, east, west

2. The prime meridian is 0° longitude.

3. Meridians of longitude are measured
   east and west of
   the prime meridian.

4. Where do all of the meridians meet?
   North and South poles

5. Meridians of longitude are measured in units called
   degrees.

Follow the directions to complete this map.
Hint: The map above will help you.

A. Label the four cardinal directions.

B. Draw a meridian at 30°E and 30°W.

C. Draw a meridian at 60°E and 60°W.

D. Label the North and South Poles.

Page 346

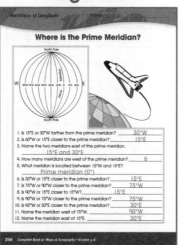

Where is the Prime Meridian?

1. Is 15°E or 30°W farther from the prime meridian? 30°W
2. Is 60°W or 15°E closer to the prime meridian? 15°E
3. Name the two meridians east of the prime meridian. 15°E and 30°E
4. How many meridians are west of the prime meridian? 6
5. What meridian is located between 15°W and 15°E? Prime meridian (0°)
6. Is 30°W or 15°E closer to the prime meridian? 15°E
7. Is 75°W or 90°W closer to 15°W? 75°W
8. Is 90°W or 15°E closer to 15°W? 15°E
9. Is 90°W or 75°W closer to the prime meridian? 75°W
10. Is 45°W or 30°E closer to the prime meridian? 30°E
11. Name the meridian west of 75°W. 90°W
12. Name the meridian east of 15°E. 30°E

Page 347

Lines of Longitude

Directions: Use the meridians shown on the globe to answer the questions.

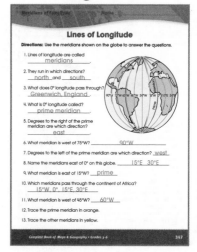

1. Lines of longitude are called meridians.
2. They run in which directions? north and south.
3. What does 0° longitude pass through? Greenwich, England.
4. What is 0° longitude called? prime meridian.
5. Degrees to the right of the prime meridian are which direction? east.
6. What meridian is west of 75°E? 90°W
7. Degrees to the left of the prime meridian are which direction? west
8. Name the meridians east of 0° on this globe. 15°E 30°E
9. What meridian is east of 15°W? prime
10. Which meridians pass through the continent of Africa? 15°E, 0°, 15°E, 30°E.
11. What meridian is west of 45°W? 60°W
12. Trace the prime meridian in orange.
13. Trace the other meridians in yellow.

Page 348

Locating Cities

This map shows part of the northeastern United States. All longitude meridians on this map are west.

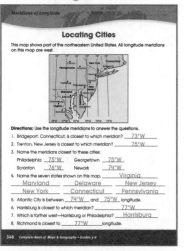

Directions: Use the longitude meridians to answer the questions.

1. Bridgeport, Connecticut, is closest to which meridian? 73°W
2. Trenton, New Jersey is closest to which meridian? 75°W
3. Name the meridians closest to these cities:
   Philadelphia 75°W Georgetown 75°W
   Scranton 76°W Newark 74°W
4. Name the seven states shown on this map. Virginia
   Maryland Delaware New Jersey
   New York Connecticut Pennsylvania
5. Atlantic City is between 74°W and 75°W.
6. Harrisburg is closest to which meridian? 77°W
7. Which is farther west—Harrisburg or Philadelphia? Harrisburg
8. Richmond is closest to 77°W longitude.

Page 349

North and South Dakota

Directions: Use this map to answer the questions. All longitude meridians are west.

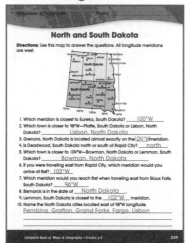

1. Which meridian is closest to Eureka, South Dakota? 100°W
2. Which town is closest to 98°W—Platte, South Dakota or Lisbon, North Dakota? Lisbon, North Dakota
3. Grenora, North Dakota is located almost exactly on the 104°W meridian.
4. Is Deadwood, South Dakota north or south of Rapid City? north
5. Which town is closer to 104°W—Bowman, North Dakota or Lemmon, South Dakota? Bowman, North Dakota
6. If you were traveling east from Rapid City, which meridian would you arrive at first? 102°W
7. Which meridian would you reach first when traveling east from Sioux Falls, South Dakota? 96°W
8. Bismarck is in the state of North Dakota.
9. Lemmon, South Dakota is closest to the 102°W meridian.
10. Name the North Dakota cities located east of 98°W longitude. Pembina, Grafton, Grand Forks, Fargo, Lisbon

Page 350

Lines of Longitude

The lines of longitude tell how far east or west of the prime meridian (0°) a point is.

All lines of longitude are measured from the prime meridian in degrees. Everything west of the prime meridian is labeled W for west, and everything east of the prime meridian is labeled E for east.

Directions: Use a globe or map to find the longitude for each city. Remember to indicate both the number of degrees and whether it is east or west of the prime meridian.

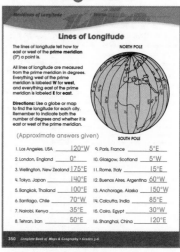

(Approximate answers given)

1. Los Angeles, USA 120°W
2. London, England 0°
3. Wellington, New Zealand 175°E
4. Tokyo, Japan 140°E
5. Bangkok, Thailand 100°E
6. Santiago, Chile 70°W
7. Nairobi, Kenya 35°E
8. Tehran, Iran 50°E
9. Paris, France 5°E
10. Glasgow, Scotland 5°W
11. Rome, Italy 15°E
12. Buenos Aires, Argentina 60°W
13. Anchorage, Alaska 150°W
14. Calcutta, India 85°E
15. Cairo, Egypt 30°W
16. Shanghai, China 120°E

Page 351

Locating Cities in Europe

Directions: Use this map to answer the questions. Pay particular attention to the location of the prime meridian.

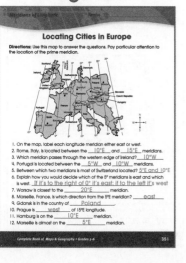

1. On the map, label each longitude meridian either east or west.
2. Rome, Italy, is located between the 10°E and 15°E meridians.
3. Which meridian passes through the western edge of Ireland? 10°W
4. Portugal is located between the 5°W and 10°W meridians.
5. Between which two meridians is most of Switzerland located? 5°E and 10°E
6. Explain how you would decide which of the 5° meridians is east and which is west. If it's to the right of 0° it's east; if to the left it's west
7. Warsaw is closest to the 20°E meridian.
8. Marseille, France, is which direction from the 5°E meridian? east
9. Gdansk is in the country of Poland.
10. Prague is west of 15°E longitude.
11. Hamburg is on the 10°E meridian.
12. Marseille is almost on the 5°E meridian.

Page 352

Lines of Latitude

Lines of latitude on a globe are called parallels. They run east and west. The equator is at 0° latitude. Use the map to answer the questions.

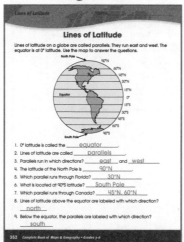

1. 0° latitude is called the equator.
2. Lines of latitude are called parallels.
3. Parallels run in which directions? east and west.
4. The latitude of the North Pole is 90°N.
5. Which parallel runs through Florida? 30°N
6. What is located at 90°S latitude? South Pole
7. Which parallel runs through Canada? 45°N, 60°N
8. Lines of latitude above the equator are labeled with which direction? north
9. Below the equator, the parallels are labeled with which direction? south

Page 353

Lateral Movement

Parallels measure the distance north or south from the equator. Zero degrees latitude (0°) is at the equator. Half of the parallels are north of the equator and half are south of it. The lines do not meet.

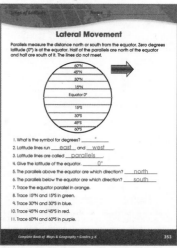

1. What is the symbol for degrees? °
2. Latitude lines run east and west.
3. Latitude lines are called parallels.
4. Give the latitude of the equator. 0°
5. The parallels above the equator are which direction? north
6. The parallels below the equator are which direction? south
7. Trace the equator parallel in orange.
8. Trace 15°N and 15°S in green.
9. Trace 30°N and 30°S in blue.
10. Trace 45°N and 45°S in red.
11. Trace 60°N and 60°S in purple.

Page 354

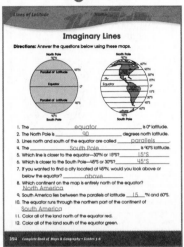

Imaginary Lines

Directions: Answer the questions below using these maps.

1. The _____equator_____ is 0° latitude.
2. The North Pole is _____90_____ degrees north latitude.
3. Lines north and south of the equator are called _____parallels_____.
4. The _____South Pole_____ is 90°S latitude.
5. Which line is closer to the equator—30°N or 15°S? _____15°S_____
6. Which is closer to the South Pole—45°S or 30°S? _____45°S_____
7. If you wanted to find a city located at 45°N, would you look above or below the equator? _____above_____
8. Which continent on the map is entirely north of the equator? _____North America_____
9. South America lies between the parallels of latitude _____15_____ °N and 60°S.
10. The equator runs through the northern part of the continent of _____South America_____.
11. Color all of the land north of the equator red.
12. Color all of the land south of the equator green.

Page 355

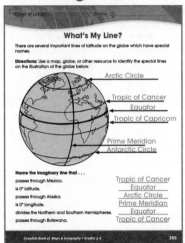

What's My Line?

There are several important lines of latitude on the globe which have special names.

Directions: Use a map, globe, or other resource to identify the special lines on the illustration of the globe below.

Arctic Circle
Tropic of Cancer
Equator
Tropic of Capricorn
Prime Meridian
Antarctic Circle

Name the imaginary line that . . .

passes through Mexico.	Tropic of Cancer
is 0° latitude.	Equator
passes through Alaska.	Arctic Circle
is 0° longitude.	Prime Meridian
divides the Northern and Southern Hemispheres.	Equator
passes through Botswana.	Tropic of Cancer

Page 356

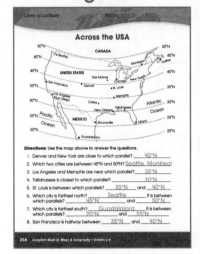

Across the USA

Directions: Use the map above to answer the questions.

1. Denver and New York are close to which parallel? _____40°N_____
2. Which two cities are between 45°N and 50°N? _____Seattle, Montreal_____
3. Los Angeles and Memphis are near which parallel? _____35°N_____
4. Tallahassee is closest to which parallel? _____30°N_____
5. St. Louis is between which parallels? _____35°N_____ and _____40°N_____
6. Which city is farthest north? _____Seattle_____ It is between which parallels? _____45°N_____ and _____50°N_____
7. Which city is farthest south? _____Guadalajara_____ It is between which parallels? _____20°N_____ and _____25°N_____
8. San Francisco is halfway between _____35°N_____ and _____40°N_____

Page 357

Latitude in North America

Directions: Use the map on page 356 to answer the questions.

1. Is Chicago closer to 40°N or 45°N? _____40°N_____
2. Name the three United States cities located between 25°N and 30°N. _____Brownsville, New Orleans, Miami_____
3. New York is closest to the _____40°N_____ parallel of latitude.
4. Name the eight United States cities located between 30°N and 40°N. _____San Francisco, San Diego, St. Louis, Dallas, Los Angeles, Denver, Memphis, Tallahassee_____
5. The _____Atlantic_____ Ocean is on the eastern side of the United States.
6. _____Mexico_____ is the country south of the United States.
7. Canada is the country _____north_____ of the United States.
8. On the west, the United States is bordered by the _____Pacific_____ Ocean.
9. Montreal is in the country of _____Canada_____.
10. Seattle is located closest to the _____50°N_____ parallel of latitude.
11. Des Moines is located between the _____30°N_____ parallel and the _____40°N_____ parallel.
12. Is Dallas north or south of the 30°N parallel of latitude? _____north_____
13. Name the four United States cities located between 40°N and 50°N. _____Seattle, Des Moines, Chicago, New York_____
14. Denver is closest to the _____40°N_____ parallel of latitude.
15. San Francisco is located south of _____40_____ °N.
16. Which parallel of latitude goes through Florida? _____30°N_____
17. Guadalajara is located in what country? _____Mexico_____

Page 358

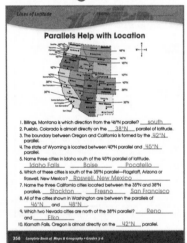

Parallels Help with Location

1. Billings, Montana is which direction from the 46°N parallel? _____south_____
2. Pueblo, Colorado is almost directly on the _____38°N_____ parallel of latitude.
3. The boundary between Oregon and California is formed by the _____42°N_____ parallel.
4. The state of Wyoming is located between 40°N parallel and _____45°N_____ parallel.
5. Name three cities in Idaho south of the 45°N parallel of latitude. _____Idaho Falls, Boise, Pocatello_____
6. Which of these cities is south of the 35°N parallel—Flagstaff, Arizona or Roswell, New Mexico? _____Roswell, New Mexico_____
7. Name the three California cities located between the 35°N and 38°N parallels. _____Stockton, Fresno, San Francisco_____
8. All of the cities shown in Washington are between the parallels of _____46°N_____ and _____48°N_____.
9. Which two Nevada cities are north of the 38°N parallel? _____Reno_____ and _____Elko_____
10. Klamath Falls, Oregon is almost directly on the _____42°N_____ parallel.

Page 359

Picture It!

Directions: Coordinates are sets of numbers that show where lines of latitude and longitude meet. Place a dot at each latitude / longitude coordinate on the graph. Draw lines to connect the dots in order.

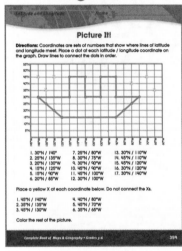

1. 30°N / 140°	7. 25°N / 80°W	13. 30°N / 110°W
2. 25°N / 135°W	8. 30°N / 75°W	14. 45°N / 110°W
3. 20°N / 130°W	9. 30°N / 90°W	15. 45°N / 120°W
4. 15°N / 125°W	10. 45°N / 90°W	16. 30°N / 140°W
5. 15°N / 90°W	11. 45°N / 100°W	17. 30°N / 140°W
6. 20°N / 85°W	12. 30°N / 100°W	

Place a yellow X at each coordinate below. Do not connect the Xs.

1. 45°N / 140°W	4. 40°N / 80°W
2. 35°N / 135°W	5. 45°N / 70°W
3. 45°N / 130°W	6. 35°N / 65°W

Color the rest of the picture.

Page 360

What Will They Be?

Directions: Place a dot at each of these latitude and longitude points on the graph.

1. 45°N / 105°W	9. 5°N / 105°W
2. 40°N / 110°W	10. 10°N / 100°W
3. 35°N / 115°W	11. 15°N / 95°W
4. 30°N / 120°W	12. 20°N / 90°W
5. 25°N / 125°W	13. 25°N / 85°W
6. 20°N / 120°W	14. 30°N / 90°W
7. 15°N / 115°W	15. 35°N / 95°W
8. 10°N / 110°W	16. 40°N / 100°W
	17. 45°N / 105°W

Draw lines to connect the dots in order. What have you drawn? _____diamond_____

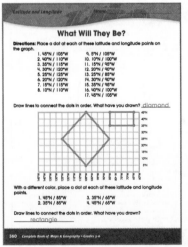

With a different color, place a dot at each of these latitude and longitude points.

1. 45°N / 85°W	3. 35°N / 65°W
2. 35°N / 85°W	4. 45°N / 65°W

Draw lines to connect the dots in order. What have you drawn? _____rectangle_____

Page 361

Using Lines to Draw a State

Directions: Place a dot on the grid for each point given. The first two have been done for you.

1. 38°N / 99°W	10. 31°N / 104°W	19. 28°N / 97 1/2°W
2. 38°N / 102°W	11. 30°N / 104°W	20. 29°N / 96 1/2°W
3. 36°N / 102°W	12. 26 1/2°N / 103°W	21. 30°N / 95°W
4. 32°N / 102°W	13. 30°N / 102°W	22. 31°N / 94°W
5. 34°N / 104°W	14. 30°N / 101°W	23. 33°N / 94°W
6. 34°N / 106°W	15. 29°N / 101°W	24. 35°N / 94°W
7. 32°N / 106°W	16. 28°N / 100°W	25. 35°N / 99°W
8. 32 1/2°N / 105°W	17. 27 1/2°N / 99°W	26. 35°N / 99°W
9. 32°N / 104 1/2°W	18. 26 1/2°N / 97 1/2°W	27. 37°N / 99°W

Draw a line to connect all of the dots in order. What state did you draw? _____Texas_____

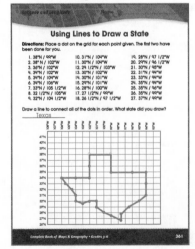

Page 362

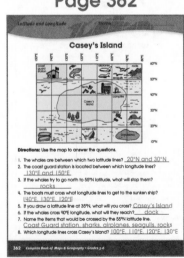

Casey's Island

Directions: Use the map to answer the questions.

1. The whales are between which two latitude lines? _____20°N and 30°N_____
2. The coast guard station is located between which longitude lines? _____130°E and 150°E_____
3. If the whales try to go north to 55°N latitude, what will stop them? _____rocks_____
4. The boats must cross what longitude lines to get to the sunken ship? _____140°E, 130°E, 120°E_____
5. If you draw a latitude line at 35°N, what will you cross? _____Casey's Island_____
6. If the whales cross 90°E longitude, what will they reach? _____dock_____
7. Name the items that would be crossed by the 55°N latitude line. _____Coast Guard station, sharks, airplanes, seagulls, rocks_____
8. Which longitude lines cross Casey's Island? _____100°E, 110°E, 120°E, 130°E_____

Page 363

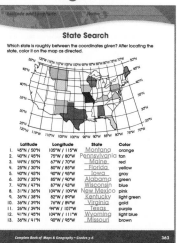

State Search

Which state is roughly between the coordinates given? After locating the state, color it on the map as directed.

	Latitude	Longitude	State	Color
1.	45°N / 50°N	105°W / 115°W	Montana	orange
2.	40°N / 45°N	75°W / 80°W	Pennsylvania	tan
3.	44°N / 50°N	67°W / 70°W	Maine	red
4.	25°N / 30°N	80°W / 85°W	Florida	yellow
5.	40°N / 45°N	90°W / 95°W	Iowa	gray
6.	30°N / 35°N	85°W / 90°W	Alabama	green
7.	43°N / 47°N	87°W / 93°W	Wisconsin	blue
8.	31°N / 36°N	104°W / 109°W	New Mexico	pink
9.	36°N / 38°N	82°W / 89°W	Kentucky	light green
10.	36°N / 39°N	76°W / 84°W	Virginia	gold
11.	26°N / 34°N	94°W / 107°W	Texas	purple
12.	41°N / 45°N	104°W / 111°W	Wyoming	light blue
13.	36°N / 41°N	90°W / 95°W	Missouri	brown

Complete Book of Maps & Geography • Grades 3-6   363

Page 364

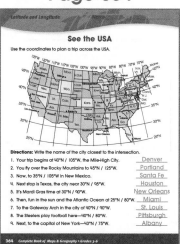

See the USA

Use the coordinates to plan a trip across the USA.

Directions: Write the name of the city closest to the intersection.

1. Your trip begins at 40°N / 105°W, the Mile-High City. — Denver
2. You fly over the Rocky Mountains to 45°N / 125°W. — Portland
3. Now, to 35°N / 105°W in New Mexico. — Santa Fe
4. Next stop is Texas, the city near 30°N / 95°W. — Houston
5. It's Mardi Gras time at 30°N / 90°W. — New Orleans
6. Then, fun in the sun and the Atlantic Ocean at 25°N / 80°W. — Miami
7. To the Gateway Arch in the city at 40°N / 90°W. — St. Louis
8. The Steelers play football here—40°N / 80°W. — Pittsburgh
9. Next, to the capital of New York—43°N / 75°W. — Albany

364   Complete Book of Maps & Geography • Grades 3-6

Page 365

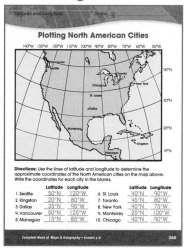

Plotting North American Cities

Directions: Use the lines of latitude and longitude to determine the approximate coordinates of the North American cities on the map above. Write the coordinates for each city in the blanks.

		Latitude	Longitude			Latitude	Longitude
1.	Seattle	50°N	120°W	6.	St. Louis	40°N	90°W
2.	Kingston	20°N	80°W	7.	Toronto	45°N	80°W
3.	Dallas	35°N	95°W	8.	New York	40°N	75°W
4.	Vancouver	50°N	125°W	9.	Monterrey	25°N	100°W
5.	Managua	15°N	85°W	10.	Chicago	40°N	90°W

Complete Book of Maps & Geography • Grades 3-6   365

Page 367

Four States

Use with page 366.

City	Coordinates
1. Salt Lake City, Utah	41°N / 112°W
2. Tucson, Arizona	32°N / 111°W
3. Santa Fe, New Mexico	36°N / 106°W
4. Oak Creek, Colorado	40°N / 107°W
5. Wilcox, Arizona	32°N / 110°W
6. Cripple Creek, Colorado	39°N / 105°W
7. Las Cruces, New Mexico	32°N / 107°W
8. Albuquerque, New Mexico	35°N / 107°W
9. Meeker, Colorado	40°N / 108°W
10. Saint George, Utah	37°N / 114°W

Coordinates	City
1. 33°N / 108°W	Glenwood, New Mexico
2. 41°N / 112°W	Salt Lake City
3. 39°N / 108°W	Delta or Rifle
4. 31°N / 111°W	Nogales
5. 37°N / 111°W	Mexican Hat
6. 40 1/2°N / 110°W	Roosevelt
7. 33 1/2°N / 107°W	Truth or Consequences
8. 39°N / 112 1/2°W	Fillmore
9. 35 1/2°N / 108 1/2°W	Gallup
10. 33°N / 111°W	Superior

Approximate Coordinates	State
32°N / 36°N and 110°W / 114°W	Arizona
36°N / 40°N and 110°W / 114°W	Utah
32°N / 36°N and 104°W / 108°W	New Mexico
36°N / 40°N and 104°W / 108°W	Colorado

Complete Book of Maps & Geography • Grades 3-6   367

Page 368

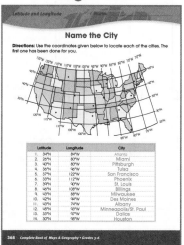

Name the City

Directions: Use the coordinates given below to locate each of the cities. The first one has been done for you.

	Latitude	Longitude	City
1.	34°N	84°W	Atlanta
2.	26°N	80°W	Miami
3.	40°N	80°W	Pittsburgh
4.	36°N	96°W	Tulsa
5.	37°N	122°W	San Francisco
6.	33°N	112°W	Phoenix
7.	39°N	90°W	St. Louis
8.	46°N	108°W	Billings
9.	43°N	88°W	Milwaukee
10.	42°N	94°W	Des Moines
11.	43°N	74°W	Albany
12.	45°N	93°W	Minneapolis/St. Paul
13.	33°N	97°W	Dallas
14.	30°N	95°W	Houston

368   Complete Book of Maps & Geography • Grades 3-6

Page 369

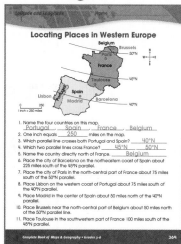

Locating Places in Western Europe

1. Name the four countries on this map.
   Portugal, Spain, France, Belgium
2. One inch equals 250 miles on the map.
3. Which parallel line crosses both Portugal and Spain? 40°N
4. Which two parallel lines cross France? 45°N 50°N
5. Name the country directly north of France. Belgium
6. Place the city of Barcelona on the northeastern coast of Spain about 225 miles south of the 45°N parallel.
7. Place the city of Paris in the north-central part of France about 75 miles south of the 50°N parallel.
8. Place Lisbon on the western coast of Portugal about 75 miles south of the 40°N parallel.
9. Place Madrid in the center of Spain about 50 miles north of the 40°N parallel.
10. Place Brussels near the north-central part of Belgium about 50 miles north of the 50°N parallel line.
11. Place Toulouse in the southwestern part of France 100 miles south of the 45°N parallel.

Complete Book of Maps & Geography • Grades 3-6   369

Page 371

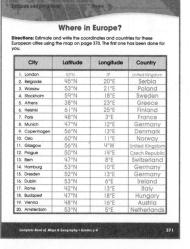

Where in Europe?

Directions: Estimate and write the coordinates and countries for these European cities using the map on page 370. The first one has been done for you.

	City	Latitude	Longitude	Country
1.	London	52°N	0°	United Kingdom
2.	Belgrade	45°N	20°E	Serbia
3.	Warsaw	53°N	21°E	Poland
4.	Stockholm	59°N	18°E	Sweden
5.	Athens	38°N	23°E	Greece
6.	Helsinki	61°N	25°E	Finland
7.	Paris	48°N	3°E	France
8.	Munich	47°N	12°E	Germany
9.	Copenhagen	56°N	13°E	Denmark
10.	Oslo	60°N	11°E	Norway
11.	Glasgow	56°N	4°W	United Kingdom
12.	Prague	50°N	14°E	Czech Republic
13.	Bern	47°N	8°E	Switzerland
14.	Hamburg	53°N	10°E	Germany
15.	Dresden	52°N	13°E	Germany
16.	Dublin	53°N	6°E	Ireland
17.	Rome	42°N	13°E	Italy
18.	Budapest	47°N	18°E	Hungary
19.	Vienna	48°N	16°E	Austria
20.	Amsterdam	53°N	5°E	Netherlands

Complete Book of Maps & Geography • Grades 3-6   371

Page 372

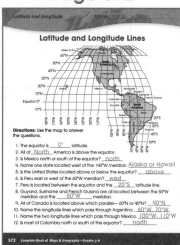

Latitude and Longitude Lines

Directions: Use the map to answer the questions.

1. The equator is 0° latitude.
2. All of North America is above the equator.
3. Is Mexico north or south of the equator? north
4. Name one state located west of the 140°W meridian. Alaska or Hawaii
5. Is the United States located above or below the equator? above
6. Is Peru east or west of the 60°W meridian? west
7. Peru is located between the equator and the 20°S latitude line.
8. Guyana, Suriname and French Guiana are all located between the 50°W meridian and the 60°W meridian.
9. All of Canada is located above which parallel— 60° or 40°N? 40°N
10. Name the longitude lines which pass through Argentina. 60°W, 70°W
11. Name the two longitude lines which pass through Mexico. 100°W, 110°W
12. Is most of Colombia north or south of the equator? north

372   Complete Book of Maps & Geography • Grades 3-6

Page 374

Do You Have The Time?

The earth spins on its axis in a west to east direction. This causes our day to begin with the sun rising in the east and setting in the west. Different areas of the United States can have different amounts of daylight at the same moment in time. For instance, when the sun is rising in New York, it is still dark in California.

A **time zone** is an area in which everyone has the same time. Every zone is one hour different from its neighbor. There are 24 time zones around the world. There are six time zones in the United States. The map above shows the four zones that cover the 48 contiguous, or touching, states.

When it is six o'clock in New York, what time is it in

Chicago 5 o'clock   Los Angeles? 3 o'clock   Denver? 4 o'clock

What is the name of the time zone in which you live? Answers will vary.

Name three other states in your time zone.
Answers will vary.

374   Complete Book of Maps & Geography • Grades 3-6

Page 376

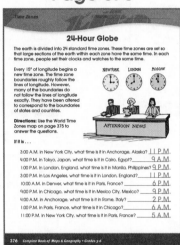

Time Zones   Name

24-Hour Globe

The earth is divided into 24 standard time zones. These time zones are set so that large sections of the earth within each zone have the same time. In each time zone, people set their clocks and watches to the same time.

Every 15° of longitude begins a new time zone. The time zone boundaries roughly follow the lines of longitude. However, many of the boundaries do not follow the lines of longitude exactly. They have been altered to correspond to the boundaries of states and countries.

NEW YORK   **LONDON**   **MOSCOW**

AFTERNOON NEWS

Directions: Use the World Time Zones map on page 375 to answer the questions.

If it is . . .

3:00 A.M. in New York City, what time is it in Anchorage, Alaska? **11 P.M.**
4:00 P.M. in Tokyo, Japan, what time is it in Cairo, Egypt? **9 A.M.**
1:00 P.M. in London, England, what time is it in Manila, Philippines? **9 P.M.**
3:00 P.M. in Los Angeles, what time is it in London, England? **11 P.M.**
10:00 A.M. in Denver, what time is it in Paris, France? **6 P.M.**
9:00 P.M. in Chicago, what time is it in Mexico City, Mexico? **9 P.M.**
4:00 A.M. in Anchorage, what time is it in Rome, Italy? **2 P.M.**
1:00 P.M. in Paris, France, what time is it in Chicago? **6 A.M.**
11:00 P.M. in New York City, what time is it in Paris, France? **5 A.M.**

376   *Complete Book of Maps & Geography • Grades 3-6*

Page 377

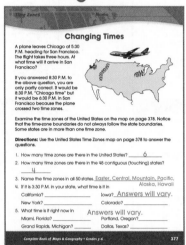

Time Zones   Name

Changing Times

A plane leaves Chicago at 5:30 P.M. heading for San Francisco. The flight takes three hours. At what time will it arrive in San Francisco?

If you answered 8:30 P.M. to the above question, you are only partly correct. It would be 8:30 P.M. "Chicago time" but it would be 6:30 P.M. in San Francisco because the plane crossed two time zones.

Examine the time zones of the United States on the map on page 378. Notice that the time-zone boundaries do not always follow the state boundaries. Some states are in more than one time zone.

Directions: Use the United States Time Zones map on page 378 to answer the questions.

1. How many time zones are there in the United States? **6**

2. How many time zones are there in the 48 contiguous (touching) states? **4**

3. Name the time zones in all 50 states. **Eastern, Central, Mountain, Pacific, Alaska, Hawaii**

4. If it is 3:30 P.M. in your state, what time is it in
   California? _____   Iowa? **Answers will vary.**
   New York? _____   Colorado? _____

5. What time is it right now in **Answers will vary.**
   Miami, Florida? _____   Portland, Oregon? _____
   Grand Rapids, Michigan? _____   Dallas, Texas? _____

Complete Book of Maps & Geography • Grades 3-6   377

Page 379

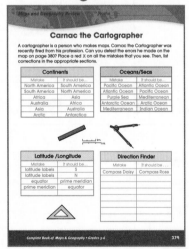

Maps and Geography Review   Name

Carnac the Cartographer

A cartographer is a person who makes maps. Carnac the Cartographer was recently fired from his profession. Can you detect the errors he made on the map on page 380? Place a red X on all the mistakes that you see. Then, list corrections in the appropriate sections.

Continents	
Mistake	It should be...
North America	South America
South America	North America
Africa	Asia
Australia	Africa
Asia	Australia
Arctic	Antarctica

Oceans/Seas	
Mistake	It should be...
Pacific Ocean	Atlantic Ocean
Atlantic Ocean	Pacific Ocean
Purple Sea	Mediterranean
Antarctic Ocean	Arctic Ocean
Mediterranean	Indian Ocean

Latitude /Longitude	
Mistake	It should be...
latitude labels	S
latitude labels	N
equator	prime meridian
prime meridian	equator

Direction Finder	
Mistake	It should be . . .
Compass Daisy	Compass Rose

Complete Book of Maps & Geography • Grades 3-6   379

Page 380

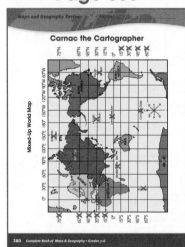

Maps and Geography Review   Name

Carnac the Cartographer

Mixed-Up World Map

380   *Complete Book of Maps & Geography • Grades 3-6*